Toxic Cultures

Genre Fiction and Film Companions

Series Editor: Simon Bacon

TOXIC

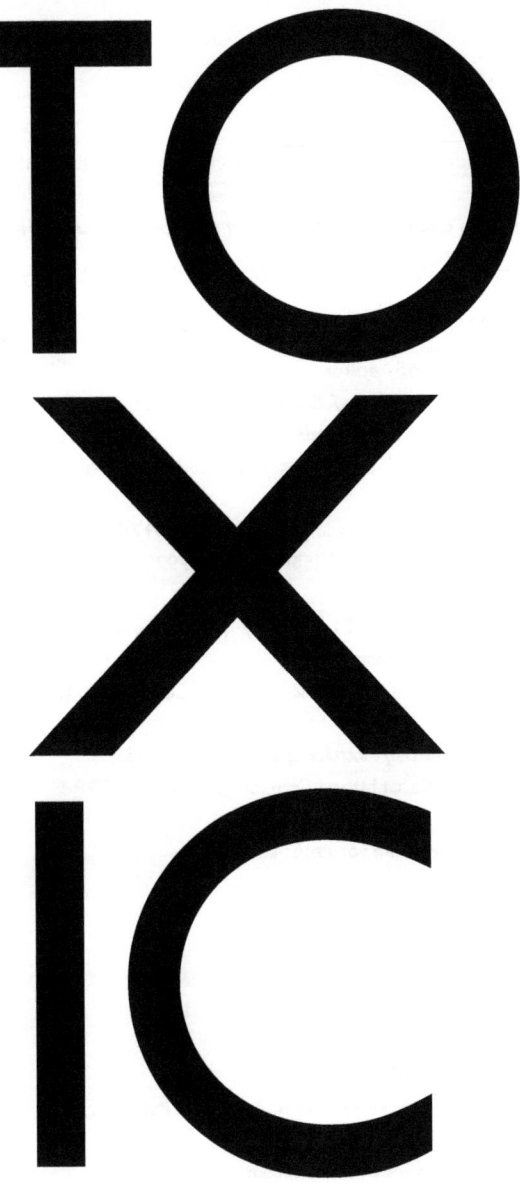

CULTURES

A Companion

Edited by Simon Bacon

PETER LANG
Oxford • Bern • Berlin • Bruxelles • New York • Wien

Bibliographic information published by Die Deutsche Nationalbibliothek. Die Deutsche Nationalbibliothek lists this publication in the Deutsche Nationalbibliografie; detailed bibliographic data is available on the Internet at http://dnb.d-nb.de.

A catalogue record for this book is available from the British Library.

Library of Congress Cataloging-in-Publication Data

Names: Bacon, Simon, 1965- editor.
Title: Toxic cultures : a companion / Simon Bacon, [editor]
Description: Oxford : New York : Peter Lang, 2022. | Series: Genre fiction and film companions, 2631-8725 ; vol. 8 | Includes bibliographical references and index.
Identifiers: LCCN 2021017993 (print) | LCCN 2021017994 (ebook) | ISBN 9781789979534 (paperback) | ISBN 9781789979541 (ebook) | ISBN 9781789979558 (epub)
Subjects: LCSH: Popular culture--21st century. | Mass media and culture. | Popular culture--Social aspects.
Classification: LCC HM621 .T689 2022 (print) | LCC HM621 (ebook) | DDC 302.23--dc23
LC record available at https://lccn.loc.gov/2021017993
LC ebook record available at https://lccn.loc.gov/2021017994

Cover design by Brian Melville for Peter Lang.

ISSN 2631-8725
ISBN 978-1-78997-953-4 (print)
ISBN 978-1-78997-954-1 (ePDF)
ISBN 978-1-78997-955-8 (ePUB)

© Peter Lang Group AG 2022
Published by Peter Lang Ltd, International Academic Publishers,
Oxford, United Kingdom
oxford@peterlang.com, www.peterlang.com

Simon Bacon has asserted his right under the Copyright, Designs and Patents Act, 1988, to be identified as Editor of this Work.

All rights reserved.
All parts of this publication are protected by copyright.
Any utilisation outside the strict limits of the copyright law, without the permission of the publisher, is forbidden and liable to prosecution. This applies in particular to reproductions, translations, microfilming, and storage and processing in electronic retrieval systems.

This publication has been peer reviewed.

Contents

Acknowledgements ix

Simon Bacon
Introduction 1

Patricia MacCormack
Prologue: From Toxic Humanity to Ahumanity 17

PART I Foundations

Carl Wilson
Bioshock, 2K Games (2007) – Toxicity and Contagion 27

Louis Bayman
Chernobyl, Craig Mazin (2019) – Toxic History 35

Kyle Moody
Succession, Jesse Armstrong (2018–present) – Toxic Ideology 45

Natalie Wilson
Get Out, Jordan Peele (2017) – Toxic Whiteness 53

Franziska E. Kohlt
The Coronavirus Act (2020), UK Government Communication (March 2020–present) – Toxic Language 63

Daniel Sheppard
Halloween, David Gordon Green (2018) – Toxic Nostalgia 71

PART II Sexuality and Gender

Cynthia Jones
Cinderella, Kenneth Branagh (2015) – Toxic Fairy Tales 81

Erin Giannini
Buffy the Vampire Slayer, Joss Whedon (1997–2003) – Toxic Masculinity 91

Paula Ashe
Pussyhat Movement (2017–Present) – Toxic Feminism 99

Callie Graham
Crazy Ex-Girlfriend, Rachel Bloom and Aline Brosh McKenna (2015–2019) – Toxic Relationships 107

Ildikó Limpár
Wayward Children Series, Seanan McGuire (2016–Present) – Toxic Parenting 119

PART III Popular Culture

Pembe Gözde Erdogan
Gelin Evi [Bride's House], Cem Semercioglu (2015–2019) – Toxic Television 131

Contents   vii

Mateusz Świetlicki
'Toxic', Britney Spears (2003) – Toxic Music   141

Cathleen Allyn Conway
Ghostbusters: Answer the Call, Paul Feig (2016) – Toxic Franchises and Misogyny   149

Debaditya Mukhopadhyay
Kabir Singh, Sandeep Reddy Vanga (2019) – Toxic Criticism   161

Bethan Jones
Star Wars Episodes VII–IX, Various (2015–2019) – Toxic Fandom and Racism   171

PART IV Society

Melody Blackmore
Paradise Hills, Alice Waddington (2019) – Toxic Positivity   183

Ken Monteith
'Sadfishing' (2019–Present) – Toxic Social Media   191

Jay Daniel Thompson
Troll Hunting, Ginger Gorman (2019) – Toxicity and Trolling   201

Madeline Muntersbjorn
'The Denialist Playbook', Sean Carroll (2020) – Toxic Denialism   209

Deborah G. Christie
'Title X Gag Rule' (2019–Present) – Toxic Censorship　　　217

PART V　Humanity

Martyn Colebrook
The City & the City, China Miéville (2009) – Toxic Cities　　　227

Phil Fitzsimmons and Edie Lanphar
Brimstone, Martin Koolhoven (2016) – Toxic Education　　　235

Blake I. Collier
Martyrs, Pascal Laugier (2008) – Toxic Fundamentalism　　　243

Tom Ue and Alexander Wills
Parasite, Bong Joon Ho (2019) – Toxic Economies　　　253

Rebecca Booth
The Last Winter, Larry Fessenden (2006) – Toxic Ecologies　　　261

Elana Gomel
Bird Box, Josh Malerman (2014) – Toxic Futures　　　269

Helen Gavin
Epilogue: Toxicity and Positivity　　　277

Bibliography　　　285

Notes on Contributors　　　321

Index　　　329

Acknowledgements

As always, a huge thank you to everyone that took part in this collection. For many reasons, it has been a torrid time during the production of this book and the fact that it has been completed is testament to the commitment and strength of all involved – so a huge well done to everyone.

Many thanks to the amazingly supportive online Horror and Gothic groups on Facebook (including the SCMS [Society of Cinema and Media Studies] Horror Studies Scholarly Interest Group; the Open Graves, Open Minds Project; Manchester Centre for Gothic Studies; the International Gothic Association; and Vampire Scholars) who always come up trumps when help, suggestions and contributors are needed – a true example of how social media can create a non-toxic environment and a network of support and encouragement. A big thank you to Laurel Plapp and the team at Peter Lang, who always help to make sure the finished book is the best it can possibly be. Most importantly, I want to thank my wife Kasia for her unending help, patience and support, without which none of this would be possible or worth doing. Also, our two not-so-little monsters, Seba and Majki, who always manage to provide some light relief and distraction no matter how stressful things get. And not forgetting the constant support (and *sernik Magdi*) of Mam i Tata Bronk.

Simon Bacon

Introduction

The word 'toxic' seems strangely common at the start of the twenty-first century. As an adjective, it is used to describe the negative side of a subject or category – toxic masculinity, toxic people, toxic relationships – and the list seems to be (unfortunately) continually growing. This is due in part to the increasing bipartisanship of politics across the globe, where the excesses of one side, often around a return to supposed 'traditional' values, are seen as a continuation and affirmation of systemic discrimination and labelled as toxic, and where these labels are themselves seen as exampling the toxicity of the opposing view, which further causes each side to double down on their original positions.[1] In some respects, the definition of toxic would seem to be emptied of any meaning, drained by its very ubiquity. However, its widespread usage can equally be seen to point to its importance in capturing the essence of an age in which extremes appear to be the norm and the dichotomies of religious, political and cultural differences are polarised by populism and an increasing loss of faith in neoliberal globalism. Indeed, as this companion will argue, 'toxic' truly captures the Geist of the 2010s and 2020s, expressing the many forms of negativity,

---

1   Much of this can be seen in the debates around historical statues: some see them as representing the glorious past and national values and identity, while others point out that these same figures also represent a time of colonialism, discrimination and slavery. The first group see the responses of the second as reactionary, politically correct and the work of the extreme liberal left. The second group see the continuation of the first group's values as out of touch, oppressive and the work of the far right. The first group then claim the far left wants to destroy all history and rewrite it. The second group claim that the far right wants to continue oppression and slavery. Each side becomes increasingly extreme and entrenched in their respective positions, with no possible chance of compromise or the creation of 'teachable' moments.

pollution and disillusion that typify the ongoing denial of ecological, environmental, ethnic, gender and sexual inequalities, state violence and even the notion of truth itself. In fact, to reflect this, the essays here purposely cover a wide range of topics, examples and perspectives to highlight how diverse and pervasive the idea of toxicity is – from computer games and novels to woollen hats, and from social media and television series to government language, to name but a few.[2]

The flourishing of toxicity in the twenty-first century was ushered in with much of Western culture preoccupied with conflict and the burgeoning war on terror. The Gulf War and other ongoing battles between Western colonial powers and regional religious extremists saw the new millennium begin with the attack on the Twin Towers in New York, followed by similar, if smaller-scale, events in Europe and the invasion of Iraq and Afghanistan. The effects of this on the popular consciousness, which exacerbated already existing divides in many nations involved, have often been described in psychoanalytic terms, seeing Western culture itself as becoming centred around and characterised by trauma. Unsurprisingly, many books published around that time confirmed the idea of a culture simultaneously experiencing shock, grief, anger and anxiety (Bracken 2002; Cvetkovich 2003; Kaplan 2005) over events that were often depicted as the beginning of a new era rather than the inevitable result of ongoing colonial interference. The resulting environment was itself unhealthy in many ways, not least in its creation of an emotionally hyper-charged atmosphere of imminent terror where violence, and indeed death, could happen at any moment – an impression that was encouraged via various governments in the West and especially in America through the creation of the Department of Homeland Security with its sweeping powers to investigate, apprehend and interrogate those suspected of being terrorists. This was often further encouraged through excessive television and media coverage of any suspected terror events that occurred, giving the impression that such events were happening continually and on a scale that threatened the

---

2   Language is of note here, as it is often the purposeful misuse of repurposing of language and certain words that fuels many toxic cultures. Obvious examples include the rhetoric of war or empire being regurgitated and repurposed for populist agendas or the wilful misuse of the language of compromise – freedom of speech or 'there's bad people on both sides' – to excuse abusive or toxic behaviours.

very fabric of Western society. In many ways, this environment of imminent terror provided the perfect impetus for a rise in nationalism and aggression towards those seen as outsiders, in particular those identified as coming from the Middle East – a situation exacerbated by the official attribution of violent attacks, with only those undertaken by non-whites on the white population of a country (mainly in Europe, Australasia and North America) being labelled as 'terrorist attacks'.[3]

This new age of trauma itself then changed to incorporate the language of the more direct trauma experienced by Western troops sent to the Middle East and with little support or understanding when they returned home, so post-traumatic stress disorder (PTSD) equally became a way to describe a culture trying to come to terms with the violence enacted in its name (Hinton and Good 2015). In a conflict where there was never going to be a sense of victory, only the re-establishment of an uneasy peace, the soldiers returning could never unreservedly be greeted as heroes, only put to one side in the hope they might vanish back into the home population. Though even this was not an entirely safe option, and popular television series such as *Homeland* (Ganza and Gordon, 2011–20) expressed the fear over veterans being 'turned' by their experiences in the alien world of the Middle East – much of the language around ISIS, for instance, spoke of them as being a barbaric cult that groomed and brainwashed people, and who were not from the modern world but from the Middle Ages; US troops going there literally went to an otherworldly place that would inherently change them, even infect them in some way. In this way, the soldiers coming home brought something of the alien land with them, framing them as outsiders in their own home. Of note here is the use of psychoanalysis, which is very much grounded in the study of the individual, being applied to a wider group or culture. While individual identity can seem to be as complex and contradictory as a national one, unthinkingly equating the two can be problematic in fully understanding the complexities at play in both categories. In some ways, it is the disparities between categories such as

---

3   A clear example of this is seen in the attacks which happened in London. One where a lone attacker, citing Allah as his God, killed a policeman was quickly designated as a terror attack, and a later one in which a white man who belonged to a far-right organisation drove a van into a crowd leaving a mosque was only belatedly given the same attribution.

national identity and individual experience that have produced and consolidated certain kinds of behaviours and practices which have gone on to create what has since been called 'toxic' – not least in the way that populist politics have made individual, and often disparate, experiences seem as though they are the result of one singular cause. Here the uniqueness of individual experience and the kinds of focused understanding and reparation it requires are purposely sublimated and 'screened'[4] by easy solutions.

The word 'toxic' emerged in the late seventeenth century from the Latin *toxicum*, meaning poison, and the Greek *toxikon*, translated as 'arrow poison' (*toxon* meaning 'bow/arrow'). Poisonous very much describes how it has been largely used: toxic waste, toxic fluids and toxic gases are just a few examples. It was not until the 1980s that it was used to describe an aspect of masculinity as, with the rise of feminism and the seeming disempowerment of men, male-centred self-help groups identified certain aspects of masculine behaviours enforced by society that were deemed harmful and negative, such as violence, competitiveness, independence and the suppression of emotions (Salter 2019). It was later that the term was picked up by academics in the social sciences to begin describing how traditional male attributes had toxic, or poisonous, effects not only on masculinity but on all aspects of gender politics and wider society. This has possibly been seen most demonstrably in the #MeToo movement, which has done much to uncover the ubiquity of male sexual misconduct, revealing it to not be just a 'few bad apples' but far more systemic in its occurrence and acceptance. The toxic environments in certain industries – such as entertainment, film and music – have been brought into sharp focus and, while there has been some success in redressing the imbalances of the almost inherently exploitative nature of the industries themselves, it is far from establishing the kinds of equality needed.

The move from noun to adjective begins to describe the changing nature of toxicity and its importance in describing culture in the twenty-first century. In being attributed to aspects of masculinity, toxic does not just describe the negative side of certain behaviours, but also their contagious nature and how this lets the behaviours spread and infect all areas of contact, such as

4   Sigmund Freud described how we often cover or obscure uneasy or unacceptable memories from our past with 'screen memories' rather than doing the 'work' of integrating them into our conscious mind to create a more holistic self-image. See Reed (2014).

relationships, parenting, the workplace, society and beyond. Much of this (what we might call) 'rhizomatic toxicity' equally informs the environment around ethnicity and racism, which, not unlike the #MeToo movement, has been brought into clearer view with Black Lives Matter, which rose to prominence after the death of George Floyd as he was taken into police custody in Minneapolis in 2020 – the movement itself started in 2013 after the killing of Trayvon Martin by George Zimmerman, later acquitted of murder. As with #MeToo, much has been done to highlight certain fields of high public visibility, such as sports, where racial abuse has heretofore been largely accepted or ignored. While there have been some gains, the systemic nature of racism in government-funded bodies such as the police force still goes unchecked, not coherently and consistently investigated and, where necessary, prosecuted. Here again the idea of a toxic environment created through systemic racism and/or sexism is often deflected by applying the 'bad apple' idea; yet the ubiquity and frequency of occurrences suggest that if it is not the system itself that is at fault, then such toxic events are amazingly contagious, infecting the 'body' of said establishment without any restraint.

In this sense, it is not surprising that the rise in the usage of toxic is mirrored by a similar ubiquity of ideas around contagion and disease with recent global and regional pandemics such as the SARS outbreak in 2003, the swine flu (H1N1 virus) outbreak in 2009–10, the Ebola outbreak in 2014–16 and, of course, the current COVID-19 pandemic, which have all, in part, been associated with the toxic atmosphere of twenty-first-century life – continued over-exploitation of planetary resources, urban overcrowding, global travel and crushing poverty in many areas of the world (though in a curious inversion, the effects of the coronavirus on global and local travel has often had positive effects on the environment). This will be discussed further, but the contagious nature of toxicity is worth keeping in mind throughout this collection, not just in the way that environments created around toxic masculinity, for instance, encourage those that enter them to copy such behaviours as being normal in some way. Those who are 'infected' then carry the behaviours into other environments. Of equal note is that toxic behaviour can then create an opposite though equally toxic reaction, not unlike when antibodies stop attacking the disease and attack the body itself. In this sense, extreme feminism, which is not necessarily opposite to toxic masculinity but is often seen as antithetical to it, arguably also discriminates against non-binary gender positions. This does not solve the issues caused by toxic masculinity, but rather exacerbates the overall toxicity of the environment itself.

The term 'toxic' is often used to describe aspects of people, groups and actions that do not comply to the tenets of neoliberal globalism, such as gender and minority equality and universal ethnic inclusion. Yet it is often the turn towards what is seen as the failure of those endeavours that has seen a rise of xenophobia, homophobia, racism and national isolationism, which has subsequently caused a rise in the usage of 'toxic' within media and academic discourse. This reactionary turn has seen something of a backwards-looking moment, looking to what is labelled as traditionalism and a 'time before' and constituting what might be termed 'toxic nostalgia', a nostalgia that accentuates and often promotes ideological viewpoints that are excessively heteronormative, patriarchal and nationalistic – such toxic nostalgia can be seen to have energised the populist movements behind Brexit and Trump's Make America Great *Again* campaign (my emphasis). By its very nature, of course, nostalgia is an idealised vision of the past, often to justify the mores of the present day. Here, though, history is recreated or certain aspects of it are exaggerated to influence future actions and decisions. Toxic nostalgia at best promotes delusion, but it can be used to manipulate and mislead those less likely to question the motivations of others who employ it in their vision of 'what the people want'.

Somewhat paradoxically, while much contemporary cultural toxicity can be described as an inability to divest ourselves from an outdated or unwanted past, alongside this is an equal incapacity to cope with the future, particularly in terms of smart technology and social media. Much of twenty-first-century culture, even more so during the recent pandemic, has become increasingly dependent upon smartphones and similar devices that have changed the nature of how we interact with our environment and each other – though even such seemingly positive online environments can be divisive on a larger scale and termed 'toxic economies' as not everyone can afford the technologies. This can be on individual, societal or even global levels. For example, some students may not be able to undertake online courses as they lack devices or Wi-Fi connection; people who do not have a phone are unable to receive pandemic updates or make payments by phone; and there are even countries where, due to insufficient infrastructure and investment, such systems are largely unavailable.[5] However, while the internet provides an invaluable means to cope with global pandemics and the rigors of isolation and quarantine, it is also a terrain that is still insufficiently regulated in many areas. Not just in terms of freedom of speech and the kinds of material being disseminated, but in relation to the collection and use of information, by whom and for what ends – although the inevitable monetising of the online environment rather dictates the answers to many such issues in relation to social media and sales/advertising platforms. Our capacity to understand and fully comprehend the full consequences of this are continually being shown to be insufficient with the effects of such non-comprehension being highlighted in recent national referendums and elections where voter opinion has been shown to be greatly influenced by the dissemination of biased information or outright lies to discredit candidates, parties, or the decisions involved. Consequently, with the increasing influence of media, pop-culture and the leisure industries upon our lives the possibilities for not only propagating the kinds of toxic behaviours/ideologies mentioned before but toxifying the very technologies themselves – largely through the denial or non-recognition of this being able to happen, – constructs a framework of toxicity that individuals and society are unable to negotiate successfully. Arguably, the most obvious example of many of the kinds of toxicity mentioned above have been utilised in the highly contentious and bipartisan 2020 presidential elections in the United States.

President Trump, himself a highly divisive figure, has continually decried the veracity of truth, science and the media while promoting the primacy of emotions and feelings on judging any given situation – an obvious swapping of balance and reason with volatility and incoherence. Indeed, part of his ongoing strategy is to deny what might be termed 'traditional' forms of toxicity (racism, sexism, homophobia, and environmental damage and climate change) to intensify the divide between those that feel they benefit, financially or personally, from such opinions and those that find the denial

---

5   A striking example of this was seen in the United States with eligibility for government subsidies to small businesses and also individuals required to complete online registration and/or possess business or personal bank accounts. This saw the poor and disenfranchised becoming even more so, either because of their inability to afford certain technological devices or due to their justified distrust of corporate institutions.

of such obvious contraventions of human and ecological rights unacceptable. This antagonism is then fuelled by the creation, promotion and distribution of conspiracy theories, fake news and obvious lies, and through channels that would normally disavow such inherently divisive and toxic material, that is, from the office of the President of America. The toxic nature of this is possibly seen most obviously and tragically in relation to the COVID-19 pandemic which has been shifted from a national health dilemma into one about one's political affiliations so that to prove one's freedom, one must deny the toxicity of the disease while simultaneously opening oneself up to its obvious toxic effects. A course of action which has seen the infection and death rates from the coronavirus in America spiral out of control. This is further exacerbated by ongoing disagreements over the results of the election where the President denies the reports from his own national security agencies and Department of Justice that the voting was not interfered with and that his opponent won. An ongoing focus on this by government departments and supporters of the President rather than on health precautions has exacerbated the situation as well as destabilising belief in the efficacy of vaccinations that might prevent the disease itself. In many senses then this has created an environment where truth and science are viewed as toxic, and what is dangerous, unhealthy and, indeed, toxic is seen as the right thing to do.

As seen above, the notion of what constitutes a toxic environment or a toxic culture can be seen to share very similar characteristics around ideas of discrimination, exploitation and often violence. Yet these too can engender problematic or simplistic responses that can equally create toxic environments or see others double-down on their own discriminatory behaviours. Such a scenario is seen in what has been termed 'cancel culture'. This can be seen to centre around social media and its use as an advertising and promotional tool for businesses, influencers, celebrities, politicians, etc. Individuals and companies gather followers or those that actively avoid them due to opinions or products they post online and has been a feature of such platforms for many years. However, this was brought into sharp focus by the well-known author J. K. Rowling, a globally renowned figure and revered by many. While she has largely positioned herself as a supporter of many minority causes and individual rights, she expressed an opinion that was largely viewed as being anti-transgender – a community that previously supported Rowling and her work. Rowling, rather than apologising for her 'toxic' remarks, doubled down on them, understandably causing a stronger backlash from those who were disappointed and subsequently boycotted her work. Seemingly surprised at the backlash she experienced for voicing such views, Rowling, along with some other well-known individuals, protested this as cancel culture and an attack on freedom of speech, rather than people exercising their individual and collective rights to not buy goods from or support someone whose views they do not agree with. Unsurprisingly then the level of toxicity and partisan division has been increased further by the ones who originally felt attacked now configuring cancel culture as an attack by the extreme left on freedom and any possibility of compromise.[6]

Consequently, much about the current culture wars fuels the toxicity of many situations and environments, and this can then seem to deepen divides rather than create ways to detoxify. This often has the effect of multiplying the amount of toxic categories there are, rather than simplifying them, making the subject increasingly complex and oftentimes contradictory. The *Toxic Cultures* companion then provides a timely and original examination of the subject as well as a road map of sorts to guide us through the minefield that toxicity appears to continually engender. To do this, the companion will further show how and why toxic cultures have become central to the cultural experience of the twenty-first century, informing all areas of popular culture and society. In doing so, *Toxic Cultures* will identify seminal categories where 'toxic' has been applied, using examples from films, television series, games and literature, but will also pinpoint less well known areas, revealing the ubiquity in contemporary times. The collection will provide a valuable introduction to those new to the subject while also intimating further areas of research for those more familiar with it.

---

6 This is caused entirely by the privileged classes, including Rowling, wanting to say what they like without any recriminations, which has nothing to do with freedom of speech.

Categories of Toxicity

The companion consists of twenty-seven short, original essays that all take a particular aspect of twenty-first-century toxicity as their focus, using a single text/film/game/idea as a lens to look at the wider implications of the topic. These essays are then grouped into five parts which, after a prologue on the inherent toxicity of the early twenty-first century, respectively consider central tenets of toxicity, sexuality and relationships, popular culture, societal constructs and more global concerns. The book ends with a more positive note in the Afterword on the ways in which toxicity might be combated or positivised. The essays here use a wide variety of examples to describe many different types of toxicity as seen in video games, films, television series, social media, real-world events and movements, philosophy and psychology, and so provide multiple perspectives and ways in which one might view and understand how toxic cultures are created, sustained and sometimes diffused. It should also be noted that many of these topics intersect and impinge on each other in many and varied ways so that, in some respects, the essays here and their categorisations could just as easily be changed and grouped into other configurations. I would argue though that this is more revealing of an underlying spirit, or Geist, behind them and the interconnectedness of life in the twenty-first century.

Patricia MacCormack opens the conversation with a prologue looking at the toxicity of the Anthropocene and the inherently toxic nature of humanity in the twenty-first century. Looking at films such as *Salò, or the 120 Days of Sodom* (Pasolini, 1975), *The Toxic Avenger* (Herz and Kaufman, 1984), *Earthlings* (Monson, 2005) and *Dominion* (Delforce, 2018), MacCormack describes how humans are the greatest single threat to life on the Earth and that the future is not so much a post-human one but a detoxified ahuman one. After this, Part I, 'Foundations', looks more closely at forms of toxicity that can be seen to underpin much of what follows. The first essay by Carl Wilson looks at the game *Bioshock* (2007) and its portrayal of 'toxicity and contagion'. In many ways, it is a representation of toxic processes outside of ideological imperatives, yet creates a something of a fundamental road map of the frameworks and pathways of burgeoning cultures of toxicity. Louis Bayman then applies some of the processes described in the first essay but in relation to 'toxic history' using the television series *Chernobyl* (Mazin, 2019) to show how the toxicity of the past bleeds and radiates into the present. History then becomes something of a toxic environment sustained by poor moral, ethical and political judgements enacting something of an ongoing 'spill' that refuses to be 'cleaned up'. Such histories then play into and are utilised by 'toxic ideology', as examined by Kyle Moody, who uses the series *Succession* (Armstrong, 2018–present) to reveal the toxic nature of twenty-first-century business and leadership practices. Within this is the patriarchal correlation of the head of the family with that of the business empire and/or nation, and the 'word' of the father being an ideological contagion that infects all its 'children'. Closely connected to this and the very particular characteristics of contemporary capitalism and power structures is 'toxic whiteness' which Natalie Wilson examines through the film *Get Out* (Peele, 2017). Wilson uses the film to show how systems that purport to encourage ethnic equality often continue the racial toxicity of the past, encouraging the continuance of exploitation and literal slavery and disavowing the acknowledgment that black lives matter. For Wilson, much of what is at issue is the use and control of language, and this is followed by Franziska E. Kohlt's close look at 'toxic language'. Kohlt specifically looks at the narratives created around the COVID-19 pandemic by the government in the United Kingdom and its unthinking use of the language of war in the 'battle' against the contagion, which actually not only complicates the situation but makes it even more dangerous. Daniel Sheppard ends Part I with a look at *Halloween* (Green, 2018) to discuss 'toxic nostalgia', which, not unrelated to the previous essay, looks at the dangers of unthinkingly using narratives from the past. Sheppard discusses the kind of nostalgia that cites the past without considering the effects of the change in historical context on the messaging being conveyed, often seeing its meaning becoming something that the original was specifically against.

Part II then moves on to what are arguably the most well known aspects of toxicity culture, 'Sexuality and Gender'. This begins with Cynthia Jones focusing on 'toxic fairy tales', often the bedrock of ongoing sexual and gender stereotypes, as seen through the story of Cinderella and specifically the live-action Disney version by Kenneth Branagh from 2015. After this is probably the most obvious category, 'toxic masculinity', and Erin Giannini looks at this through *Buffy the Vampire Slayer* or, more specifically, the male nerds in the show, who presciently prefigure the rise of incels and aggressive, abusive misogyny. This is not as straightforward as it seems and Giannini untangles some of the many strands of abuse and privilege that lead to such toxic manifestations. Next Paula Ashe considers 'toxic feminism', or rather the toxic elements within it, which are in many ways typified by the pussyhat movement, which, while promoting women's issues, does not recognise its inherent bias against those who are not white. This moves on to Callie Graham and 'toxic relationships' as seen through the recent television series *Crazy Ex-Girlfriend* (Rachel Bloom and Aline Brosh McKenna, 2015–19). The show is a knowing look at common tropes of the romcom genre which have established and promoted toxic behaviours such as stalking and gaslighting as acceptable in the pursuit of 'true' love. Appropriately Part II closes with a discussion of 'toxic parenting' where Ildikó Limpár looks at the Wayward Children series by Seanan McGuire (2016–present) and the often-never-ending trauma of childhood. Here parental abuse is often centred around non-heteronormative children who are denied support, love and encouragement due to their perceived otherness and/or monstrosity.

The third part, 'Popular Culture', more explicitly focuses on the world of entertainment and information that fills ever-increasing amounts of our time in the twenty-first century, especially evident during the pandemic, and which in many ways has evolved our engagement with and dependence on many forms of entertainment across many kinds of devices. It begins with Pembe Gözde Erdogan looking at 'toxic television' and the Turkish series *Gelin Evi* [Bride's House] to examine the frequently toxic messaging of reality television. This long-running series brings together brides to judge each other on their preparations for the wedding, possible gifts and decorations, and even the state of their homes, to not only belittle each other but to reinforce the roles of women within an already patriarchal society. Following this, Mateusz Świetlicki considers 'toxic music' and the song 'Toxic' by Britney Spears to discuss the toxic nature of the entertainment industry in general and the music industry in particular in relation to women and the exploitation of its younger 'stars'. As with most of the other examples, many kinds of denigration and exploitation from other areas of toxicity, misogyny, mental health and class come together to create an intensely toxic environment that can trap even the famous within them. In her look at 'toxic franchises and misogyny' Cathleen Allyn Conway broadens the focus to the way entertainment franchises can produce a toxic, negative environment around certain iterations of a popular, already established world. The example here is the remaking of the original *Ghostbusters* film with an all-female lead, which quickly produced vitriol and abuse from the diehard, largely male fan base that often brought in misogynist and racist language in their attacks. Debaditya Mukhopadhyay, in his examination of 'toxic criticism', further considers the environment created around films and franchises. This is not about when reviews about a film are negative, but the ways they are used to promote and encourage toxic elements from the movie itself and subsequently encourage such actions in the audience and even society. This speaks of a wider systemic toxicity, both with the film industry and the nation itself, that has a particular agenda to represent and affirm via popular culture. Bethan Jones rounds out this section with a more focused examination of 'toxic fandom and racism', revealing the downside of fan agency and identification within a franchise. Looking at some of the more recent iterations of the *Star Wars* franchise, Jones studies how imaginary pairings (shipping) of characters within the films leads to the trolling and abuse of actors who do not comply with the vision of certain groups of fans, often with racist biases.

Part IV, 'Society', considers how toxicity influences institutions and areas of public access that are generally purported to be free of such biases within the wider population. Melody Blackmore discusses 'toxic positivity', the promotion of positive emotions and the active denial of negative feelings. Using the film *Paradise Hills* (Waddington, 2019), which is something of a nod to *The Stepford Wives* (Forbes, 1975), Blackmore describes the dangers of a form of positivity that elides all emotional and psychological pain and inevitably dehumanises those consumed in the process. This is followed by the related topic of 'toxic social media', with Ken Monteith discussing the phenomenon of sadfishing. This is a largely online emotional tool/positioning specifically designed to illicit sympathy from the viewing audience. While seemingly an innocuous means of getting attention (advertising), it not only complicates and obfuscates the calls of those truly in need of help and sympathy but also becomes a means of grooming and abusing the innocent and unwary. Next is a look at 'toxicity and trolling' by Jay Daniel Thompson, who discusses the widespread phenomenon of online trolling, where certain users go out of their way to antagonise, denigrate and verbally abuse other users. The toxic nature and effects of this are well known, but Thompson looks more closely at the motivations of the trolls themselves and the environment around them, which can often exacerbate the situation and the subsequent levels of harm caused to those targeted. Madeline Muntersbjorn then considers an equally prominent and timely phenomenon of the twenty-first century, 'toxic denialism'. Focusing on narratives around the COVID-19 pandemic and their co-option by political parties in the United States, Muntersbjorn details how the 'playbook' of denialism is being utilised to deadly effect in the American presidential elections, creating a toxicity that is as contagious as the disease itself. The last essay in Part IV, by Deborah G. Christie, looks at the all-pervading nature of toxic media and the misuse of facts and misinformation in an age of extreme political partisanship, in this case in relation to the Title X gag rule (2019–present) brought into effect by the Trump administration.

Part V, 'Humanity', is more expansive in terms of its relation to fundamental aspects of life and development in the twenty-first-century global environment. This part starts with Martyn Colebrook's examination of 'toxic cities'. Colebrook looks closely at China Miéville's novel *The City & the City* and how it uncovers the toxic nature of city life and the social and economic divisions that are hidden with its architecture and spaces. This is followed by Phil Fitzsimmons and Edie Lanphar's focus on the film *Brimstone* (Koolhoven, 2016) to discuss 'toxic education'. Here the conversation focuses on the foundations of education and how the toxicity formed at points of origin resonates down the years as a kind of traumatic echo that can never be excised from the system. Next, in his look at 'toxic fundamentalism', based on examination of the film *Martyrs* (Laugier, 2008), Blake I. Collier continues the idea of knowledge and our quest to understand the world around us. Yet, as with toxic denialism, this can be seen to take darker, more toxic directions that are not founded on verifiable facts or reason but on increasingly emotive decisions and purposefully deceitful pronouncements for personal or political gains. After this, Tom Ue and Alexander Wills examine 'toxic economies' and the unequal distribution of wealth and power through a consideration of the film *Parasite* (Bong, 2019). As the narrative unfolds, it reveals the interconnectedness of society from the poorest to the wealthiest but also the toxicity of a system that only allows for one iteration of inclusion and belonging. Then, to look more closely at 'toxic ecologies', which equally affect the shape and indeed future of the world, Rebecca Booth analyses the film *The Last Winter* (Fessenden, 2006). In the anthropocenic mode, the environment is shown to react to both the physical (plundering of resources) and ideological (capitalist) impact of humanity to produce monstrous reactions to save itself. The last essay in this part examines 'toxic futures'. Elana Gomel uses the novel *Bird Box* (Malerman 2014) to discuss dystopian outcomes of the excesses of contemporary society and the breakdown of human relations with the environment around them. More so, Gomel notes the purposeful lack of vision of humanity when imagining the future, literally 'seeing' it a journey into darkness.

While much of what has gone before intimates a point of no return for humanity and that in the early twenty-first century the levels of toxicity in everyday life have reached a tipping point from which there is no return, the volume ends with a therapeutic afterword offering a different perspective on where we are. Helen Gavin, in her epilogue, titled 'Toxicity and Positivity', talks to many of the topics discussed with regard to toxic environments and how even psychology itself can be turned towards what might be termed the 'dark side'. However, as Gavin notes, maybe the best antidote to such toxicity is humanity itself or, rather, in being humane and remembering what makes us the same rather than pinpointing and emphasising differences.

This companion, then, as well as providing an overview of how toxic terrains take form and grow, also offers something of a guide to how areas of toxicity often overlap and/or inform other ones. Importantly, it also highlights how many types of toxicity come about in reaction to other ones and that toxicity is, in many senses, a reactionary environment – one where people are directed to find a threat where there is none and differences where there are not any. This does not mean that acceptance or even a measure of compromise will suddenly detoxify the world. There are many truly horrifying toxic areas of exploitation, discrimination and brutality in the world that require affirmative and even aggressive actions to resolve – continued human slavery being an obvious example. However, at a time in our history when many actively seek to divide communities and vilify others for their own financial and political gain, this companion provides a timely and important intervention into the conversations occurring about where we might be heading and whether we can make that considerably less dystopian than it currently promises to be.

Patricia MacCormack

Prologue
From Toxic Humanity to Ahumanity

There is a tendency in us humans (both the overinvested and the reluctant – all of us 'we', none of us liking it or belonging) to parasite. We parasite from the others of the Earth. Our anthropo-supremacism calls it deserved spoils or, more insipidly, symbiosis and sustainability. We love to take. When we contemplate toxicity as poison, we can include also the poisons we ourselves take, that make us human – our refusal to leave the other be, to stop consuming and taking, tilling and pillaging. Cinema has developed genres around the reluctance to give and to leave be, especially horror cinema. Two genres spring to mind. Zombie and porn films develop manias of consumption devoid of mutual affect while also attesting to a fascination with self-destruction based around degeneration of mutuality itself. Zombies are scary because we know they are us in fast forward (even slow zombies). They are rotting bags of degenerating flesh squeezing every last bit of life from whatever they can even while denying the fact they are dead. Porn which holds the promise of transgression is only ever transgressive when showing affective reciprocity. This is unmarketable. The bodies have to be voraciously taking; the other must be an object of consumption. Always monodirectional. Good (in every sense) porn is rare because bad porn is a zombie film where phallo-oracularity plays the zombie. Both the fucker and the zombie show humanity for what it is – a mindless repetition of human impulses no longer masquerading behind the hypocritical niceties that use words like sustainability, consensual exploitation or ethical capitalism. Both genres are proof we are already dead inside our endless repetition cycles, where the terror of difference, of singularity of affect, is frightening, while human habit is a somnambulistic nepenthe we call freedom. Two films come to my mind when thinking of the toxicity of the expelled and returned poisonous Anthropocene. Pasolini's *Salò* (1975) has its three central circles: the circle of manias, the circle of shit and the circle of violence. Entranced by the zombie-like, decidedly anthropocentric perversion of a commitment to human supremacy so extreme that even the abject becomes elevated to greatness (make shit great again!), Pasolini offers Sade's conversion of transgression to man-made signification, encompassing all excess so that nothing escapes. Ultimately, everything belongs to the first circle, everything becomes a man-made mania; give a human anything and they will at once convert it to their own use and meaning while making it devoid of any materiality, singular affective expression or reality.

Pasolini's critique, in his own words, is a combination of capitalism's fascist '"repository of every vulgarity, and of the hatred for reality" [...] "Genocide is this adaptation to the power of Italian consumerism"' (in Chiesi 2011)

Figure 1. Scene from *Salò, or the 120 Days of Sodom* (Pasolini, 1975).

(see Figure 1). An abject understanding of shit both borders death and induces us to expel in order to live:

> These body fluids, this defilement, this shit are what life withstands, hardly and with difficulty, on the part of death. There, I am at the border of my condition as a living being. My body extricates itself, as being alive, from that border. [...] If dung signifies the other side of the border, the place where I am not and which permits me to be, the corpse, the most sickening of wastes, is a border that has encroached upon everything. (Kristeva 1982: 3)

When all is shit to the anthropocentric eye, borders no longer exist. The children's bodies of *Salò* are shit, meaning is shit, even any delight at novel transgression is shit. Because the only true mania for humans is power, which at once encroaches upon everything while remaining an absolute emptiness. This is the fascism of the everyday, what Foucault would call a bringing together of contemporary fascisms within us all – political revolutionary bureaucrats, consumerist desirers, anthropo-analysts; 'the fascism in us all, in our heads and in our everyday behaviour, the fascism that causes us to love power, to desire the very thing that dominates and exploits us' (Foucault 1983: xiii). Kristeva's 'powers of horror' are positively delicious in comparison because at least they are real. They are the shit that threatens to cross species and make plagues; they are the shit that contaminates water; they are the shit that is a complex ecosystem of bacterial life far more complex than we can as yet imagine, an effulgent cosmos of flora within a banal smear. The multiplicitous, various trajectory, metonymically and metaphorically contextual incarnations of shit may sometimes lead to death but are not in themselves toxic, because they are never an always or an already. Fascism's toxicity is the always already reducing single power of power itself (in the sense of *pouvoir*, rather than affective capacity to act, *puissance*), so distanced from the entirely singular affects of anything that it is watched, like *Salò*'s torture, through anthropocentric binoculars, incapable of actual encounter. The affects of the anthropocentrism are, however, very real indeed. The distance between this act of emptying realities in service of anthropocentric power and those affected is what Scarry describes as the immeasurable infinite distance between the torturer and the tortured, because physical affects such as pain have 'no referential context. It is not *of* or *for* anything. It is precisely because it takes no object that it, more than any other phenomenon, resists objectification in language' (Scarry 1987: 5; italics

Figure 2. Image from *Earthlings* (Monson, 2005).

in the original). The torturer, wilful or not (most anthropocentric violence is for consumption of the world, not necessarily aggression towards it), sees the world as for himself, the tortured has no access to the language of the dominant anyway, they are the different.

Beautiful perversions, unique desires are expelled as abject when the human embraces only the world as their world, for themselves, enslaving themselves to their servitude. White supremacy does not mobilise the white working class, but it does have affects of violence upon other lives. Toxic masculinity does not give men more of anything, but it does show men the world is not just for them. Heteronormativity allows us to pass, but it Oedipalises our every relationship, so that our breeding destroys the Earth because equality means reproduction at any cost. Ecology maintains the 'humans first' argument and is named terrorist when it goes over from humans first to Earth first, in spite of the former being toxic and the latter materially ethical. For the abject, neither object nor subject, there is still a space, a place, it cannot disappear. For the anthropocentric, there is no place for the other, the waste goes to the 'developing' world, the refugee goes to a detention centre, the slaughterhouse is invisible. Ask any horror afficionado (not snuff fanboys, but visceral cinephiles) what

Figure 3. Scene from *Dominion* (Delforce, 2018).

the worst horror film of all time is and they will not say *Salò* or *A Serbian Film* (Spasojevic, 2010) or *Irreversible* (Noé, 2002), but *Earthlings* (Monson, 2005) and *Dominion* (Delforce, 2018). (Yes, the former are not documentary footage, while the latter are; however, documentary footage of genocide of humans is considered censorable, while that banal everyday genocide of the latter two films is simply unwatchable because it is unconsumable or quite literally, unpalatable.)

Even films hypnotised by despair, many of which include real animal death as surrogate to human death as some kind of badge of edgelordness (its own special kind of toxicity), such as *Faces of Death* (Schwartz, 1978) or *Men Behind the Sun* (Tun Fei Mou, 1988), still utilise narrative or other anthropocentric tropes to alleviate their relentlessness. The second film which comes to my mind when thinking toxicity is *The Toxic Avenger* (Herz and Kaufman, 1984). Perhaps showing my generation, toxic came, instead of its attachment to human dominance (masculinity, whiteness, heterosexuality, wealth) from its poisonous origins. The Toxic Avenger was the hero of the abject because in many ways he repudiated the health club, man-child, privileged jocks, a less contrived version of *Salò*'s salon members with identical impulses.

Figure 4. Melvin, *The Toxic Avenger* (Herz and Kaufman, 1984).

Melvin is denigrated down the anthropocentric chain of dominance – wearing a tutu and kissing a sheep before being set on fire and drowned in toxic waste while his tormentors, already versed in the distance between torturer and tortured, see this devolved hierarchy as quintessential to both identity and pleasure. Melvin becomes the 'monster hero' in the film, performed at a crossroads of anthropocentric toxicity: the expelled other who is never really gone because out of sight does not mean out of the real, and the effects of the expelled when it comes back, in this case both the expelled nerd and the expelled toxic waste. While the social wrongs he rights persistently problematically insinuate racism in crime (gangs are Mexican but their leader is the mayor, a white man in power), the victims represent the perception of devolution of the dominant – a blind woman and her dog, child rape victims. The combination of the two expelled elements of failed-macho-low-wage-worker-nerd and toxic spillage create a dynamic superforce which, conceptually at least, shows what can happen when instead of trying to be included in the anthropocentric fascist impulses of 'counting within', we remain expelled and join forces. The Toxic Avenger incarnates what Deleuze and Guattari call 'unnatural participations', interkingdom becomings, refusing incorporation into human signifying systems. Unnatural nuptials create sorcerers, giving 'the incredible feeling of an unknown nature – *affect*. For the affect is not a personal feeling, nor is it a characteristic; it is the effectuation of a power of a pack that throws itself into upheaval and makes it reel' (Deleuze and Guattari 1987: 240; emphasis in the original). Melvin is not poisoned; the waste is no longer waste nor even toxic. Both are becoming together in a collective because of their unlikeness – symbiosis forms a third creature where neither is master. We who love monsters, we who are monsters, have always known this third way, repudiating the toxic limitations of binary anthropocentrism that makes us choose between only two, and as if the non-dominant side of the gender or race or sexuality or ability limitation is elucidated as simply failure and thus servant of the majoritarian. The toxicity of incels shows what happens when those who fall on the privileged side of binaries still fail. The toxicity of working-class white people voting Tory, voting for Brexit, the women who voted for Trump – these show that the toxin can poison any victim willing to drink the Kool-Aid rhetoric of the dominant. The only inoculation against anthropocentric toxicity is a repudiation of anthropocentrism, what I have elsewhere termed the 'ahuman'. We cannot *not* be human, not entirely. We cannot forget the past, whether we were complicit or even alive or not. Ethical accountability involves acknowledging the past in order to identify novel trajectories which allow escape from anthropocentric toxic tendencies. This is why toxic anthropocentrics decry 'cancel culture'. Cancel culture does not ruin everyone's fun; it does not censor or ban. It is simply the de-territorialising of saturated patterns of anthropocentric dominance based on a single model, a toxic model that normalises rape, genocide, prejudice, towards all people, species. Cancel culture only cancels toxic privilege. It could be renamed 'proliferation culture' or 'flourish culture' – the poison is removed and the multiple unthought worlds thrive simultaneously. As a simple example, instead of the toxicity of the same white men being reprinted over and over, we are seeing an increase in publishing 'lost' writing by women, by non-white authors, by working-class writers, by queer writers, from the last three centuries, being printed for the first time since first runs; and it is delicious. Toxicity is the chemo non-therapy of the same white straight dude being printed by six publishers, thrivings are reading for the first time in our lifetime authors of difference. Becomings are only reading authors who do not confirm our own identities. Ahumanism is encountering without understanding, but still manifesting affects of curiosity and compassion, where destruction of the (anthropocentric) self is a goal on the way to otherworldly becomings and life lived with and for the other as a tiny part of a myriad incomprehensible ecology. The 'a' of ahumanism is unapologetically swiped from Guattari's call for asignifying asemiotic regimes. These shatter those modes of enunciation in service to systems of desire which re-establish the anthropocentric obedience to mastery and the desire for power without specific quality or content – found in Church, State, Family, and what we would now call 'media' – technology, capital and enslavement to the cult of the self. Guattari critiques the perceived separation of desire from politics. All signifying regimes are based on desire, which does not differentiate between power and pleasure, erotics and politics, subjectivity and self, ethics and aesthetics. Regarding issues of representations, where our society focuses on the object over the signifying style, Guattari states:

> Nothing essential leads to the subjugation of the child, the woman, or the homosexual. In a word it is not centred on dominant significations and values: it participates in open a-signifying semiotics, available for better or worse. Nothing depends here on destiny, but on collective arrangements in action [...] the real repression of cinema is not centred on erotic images; it aims above all at imposing a respect for dominant representations and models used by the power to control and channel the desire of the masses. In every production, in every sequence, in every frame, a choice is made between a conservative economy of desire and a revolutionary breakthrough. [...] In the last resort, what will be determined by the political and aesthetic plane is not the words and content of ideas, but essentially a-signifying messages that escape dominant semiologies. (Deleuze and Guattari 1987: 153–4)

Toxicity comes from repeat, unifying semiologies which turn storytelling into poison, where desire is for dominance, and all content falls away, is made abject cadaver (cadre/to fall), in service of the empty exchange of signs that all signify increase of that power. This is a peculiarly anthropocentric impulse, and itself transcends individual subjective classifications of race, gender, sexuality, ability. Ahuman experiments in becoming forsake 'counting' as human as an indicator of equality or success, because counting belongs to the anthropocentric narrative of power semiology.

Part I

Foundations

Carl Wilson

Bioshock, 2K Games (2007)

For blood to be considered toxic, one may understand this to mean that the fluid that runs through the body, largely comprised of plasma and water, possesses at least one of two features: it may contain properties that are dangerous to the preservation of the self or it may be deemed hazardous to other individuals. Although comparable, toxic blood should be considered in a different strain to how viral blood is depicted within fiction. As a lifelike organism that spreads to other hosts in order to survive through propagation and replication, the viral outbreak is the fuel of zombie stories or cataclysmic end-of-the-world narratives; whereas, for blood to become toxic, it has to be introduced through external agency. For the purposes of inciting dramatic events in her novels, Agatha Christie's 'preferred method of homicide was poison' (Acocella 2013), making her method of dispatchment analogous in effect to the fantasy scenarios that magically befall Disney's panoply of sleeping princesses. Toxic blood can also be used as a sustained plot device and as a means of swiftly concluding events. For example, the acid blood of the predatory Xenomorph species from the *Alien* series of movies (e.g. Scott, 1979) is not a threat to the creature itself but poses a continual problem to anyone who encounters it, in the same way that Superman kills Dracula by accident in an issue of the *Superman* comic, as 'Superman is a living solar battery', so 'Dracula took a big bite out of the sun and it wasn't pretty' (Loeb and Johns 2002: 21).

Video games differ from other types of media in that they give the player agency to operate within the diegesis, with an emphasis on heightened interactivity as well as immersion (see Stobbart 2019). A novel or film will continue to a structured finish; in video games, players are frequently tasked with the handling of events to propel and sustain the narrative, often to avoid the abrupt consequences of defeat. Within this framework, the avatar being poisoned can also be considered a standard status effect, which can be permanent or temporary, and it may buff (help) or debuff (hinder) the player through an alteration of the underlying statistics that govern the capabilities of the hero. In *Bloodstained: Ritual of the Night* (2019), the protagonist can become infected by Poison Toads, which drains the player's health over a period of time; but as a consumable item obtained through slaying the same monsters, poison can be used by the player to enhance offensive magic attacks such as Toxic Storm.

The terms used here are indebted to the role-playing game (RPG) community that pre-exists their usage within video games. Released in 1975 for the University of Illinois' PLATO (Programmed Logic for Automated Teaching Operations) system, *dnd* is a game that consciously borrows many of the elements from the tabletop game *Dungeons & Dragons* (1974). *Avatar* (1979), also made for the PLATO system, was subsequently influenced by *dnd*, but 'added some firsts of its own', including that '[m]onsters could perform special attacks (like poison or paralysis)' (Moss 2016). RPGs emphasise choice and decision-making in handling events; yet, while a special attack from a digital bestiary can function as a variation to generate novel encounters and emergent solutions, it can also have further significance beyond gameplay mechanics or the unfolding of events within the story. Massive multiplayer online RPG *World of Warcraft* (2004) presents one such example. In 2005 an enemy character's debuff spell, Corrupted Blood, spread from avatar to avatar, going on to affect millions of players worldwide. Researchers have since found that the 'high rates of mortality and, much more importantly, the social chaos that comes from a large-scale outbreak of deadly disease' within the game also 'raised the possibility for valuable scientific content to be gained from this unintentional game error' with potential applications for the real world (Lofgren and Fefferman 2007: 625).

Where *Warcraft* is notable for an error of game coding, *BioShock* (2007) is a useful case study in purposeful design. *BioShock* is an RPG in the first-person shooter mould, in which the art-deco-ornamented underwater city of Rapture has collapsed into ruin after an implosive civil war among its people. With central themes that encompass 'individual agency versus external manipulation; and individual effort versus the collective enterprises of society', toxic blood is a mechanism through which these tensions are explored (Wilson 2017: 14).

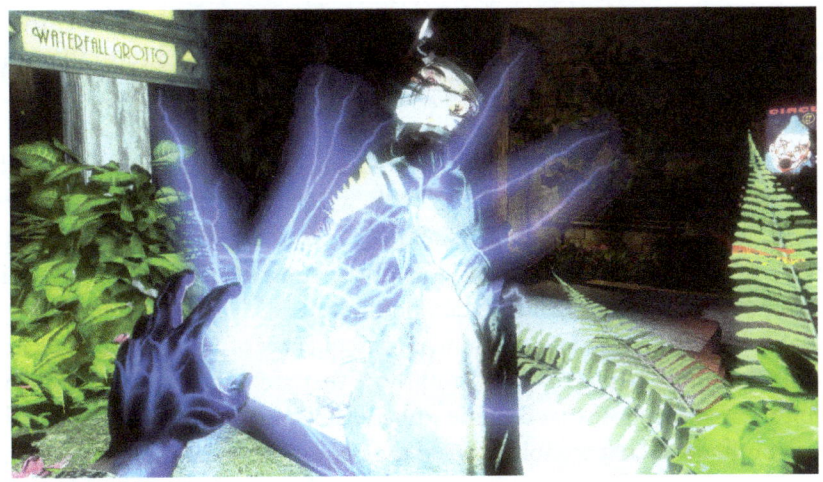

Figure 5. Frying tonight with the Electro Bolt Plasmid in *BioShock* (Levine, 2007).

Within the fiction of *BioShock*, the 1950s world of Rapture was founded by Andrew Ryan following an objectivist philosophy analogous to the works of Ayn Rand (see Courcier, El Kanafi and Lucas 2017). Separated from the cultures perceived as inferior on the surface, Rapture is a city where, its creator declares, 'the artist would not fear the censor, where the scientist would not be bound by petty morality, where the great would not be constrained by the small' (see Figure 5). A fundamental aspect of this rise-to-the-top edict, which soon becomes a fatal flaw, is that those who hold power are unrestrained and all others are in ceaseless rivalry. One consequence of this unfettered experimentalism and social competition is the discovery and rampant addiction to a Sea Slug secretion called ADAM. Shared within an in-game audio log by the discoverer of the drug, Brigid Tenenbaum, ADAM 'acts like a benign cancer, destroying native cells and replacing them with unstable stem versions. While this very instability is what gives it its amazing properties, it is also what causes the cosmetic and mental damage.' Within Rapture, ADAM is harvested and refined into an addictive serum called a Plasmid. Described within in-game advertisements as 'Evolution in a Bottle!', these Plasmids are the saleable products that, when injected directly into the bloodstream, confer specific properties on the user. The use of Plasmids by civilians may make them objectively better at sport or, more subjectively, attractive; it can also allow the user to propel a swarm of aggressive insects out of their hands. The effects of Plasmids are permanent. The general populace also had access to passive and interchangeable Plasmids in the form of Gene Tonics, endowing them with fleeting powers such as rapid hair growth, weight loss or a resistance to the effects of fire. However, as Tenenbaum goes on to explain: 'You need more and more ADAM just to keep back the tide. From a medical standpoint, this is catastrophic. From a business standpoint, well … .'

BioShock presents three prominent consequences of ADAM use that form a volatile, circular pattern of control: those that are in power are able to exploit the masses; those that become addicted become physically and mentally disfigured; those that are able to wield the Plasmids can use them as weapons to gain power. Crucially, while this logic can be applied to the archetypal hierarchy of enemies encountered, it can also be applied to the protagonist, who likewise consumes Plasmids throughout the course of the game. *BioShock* uses narrative cues to explore how this dynamic came to be sustained and internally validated within the diegesis. One of the early boss encounters is with Doctor J. S. Steinman, who designates himself as surgery's answer to the art world's Picasso, able to use Plasmids to craft his unwitting subjects into grotesque, abstract forms. Another meeting takes place with Sander Cohen, a pre-eminent artist and popular musician of his period, who asks the player to photograph the corpses of disfigured former disciples for a mixed-media installation. An additional figure of significance is Doctor Yi Suchong, who, before he was murdered, strode the line between science and artistic endeavours, having used his Free Clinic to carry out his own experiments, enthralled by the questionable idiom that 'ADAM is a canvas of genetic modification … but Plasmids are the paint'. 'Toxicity' is a term that can be applied to the bonds of society, and *BioShock* demonstrates how, through the ADAM-abused guise of science and the arts being conjoined in simpatico, the pursuit of the self can run contrary to any outward claims of aiding civilisation. While Rapture features eugenic analysis and genetic modification laboratories, the fear of being tainted by some form of invading and destabilising toxic corruption ultimately comes from within, a theme that is best represented by the final boss, Frank Fontaine, the master manipulator within the diegesis and also eventually the greatest ADAM addict, as visually corrupted as he is morally unrestrained.

The obsession with advancement through toxic blood experimentation has resulted in a society of Splicers (the term being borrowed from genetic research). Colin Fix, Senior Character Concept Artist on *BioShock 2* (2010), explains: 'The spliced characters were Norman Rockwell American ideal characters, but totally distorted' (qtd in Thomas 2010: 14). In *BioShock*, the ideal has long since faded, as Splicers in substantial numbers have wiped out the rest of Rapture, leaving the ADAM-thirsty rabble behind to compete with each other. By the time that the player encounters them in their post-fall state, the Splicers are disfigured, covered in cancerous growths and polyps, and are 'spliced so heavily and fast that their very flesh would grow around their [tattered] clothing' (Thomas 2010: 28). The Splicers also exhibit extraordinary powers, all of which aid in their sole motivation to violently acquire additional Plasmids directly from the bloodstreams of other human beings. Over the course of the game, the player encounters various types of Splicer, yet, while these enemy variants are novel twists on genre conventions with the addition of their collectively tragic backstories, they are also significant in how they hunt non-player characters called Little Sisters. In the *BioShock* universe, Little Sisters are orphan children that have been mentally and physically conditioned to generate ADAM, in part through being implanted with Sea Slugs, but also eventually to harvest ADAM from the corpses of those lost to the violent consequences of addiction. To aid in their protection from exploitation, the Little Sisters are symbiotically connected through Pavlovian conditioning and pheromone sprays with their hulking protectors, Big Daddies, although this does not fully halt the thirsty endeavours of Rapture's inhabitants.

There are points within the game where Splicers attempt to attack a Little Sister, and there are moments where a Little Sister is alone with their Big Daddy. At these junctures, the protagonist can choose to interject and intervene in either dynamic. In a game where choice is foregrounded as an arbitrary illusion of conditioning or as a demonstration of the needs of the individual set against the demands of the social field, should the player find themselves alone with a Little Sister, an unescapable binary decision is offered: press a button on the gaming peripheral to Harvest or press a button to Rescue. The effects of consuming ADAM in the form of Plasmids and tonics are consistently shown to be degenerative, yet, for the player to succeed in their lethal objectives, these same provisions are provided, and their use is encouraged.

Figure 6. Pick your plasmid in the opening scenes of *BioShock* (Levine, 2007).

Figure 7. Harvesting Little Sisters in *BioShock* (Levine, 2007).

In a reflexive acknowledgement that the player is just as tied to conditioning as the protagonist within the diegesis, acquiring new powers through the ingestion of drugs continues to be a rewarding standard video game trope, as is the receipt of currency through defeating enemies. In *BioShock*, the player can collect ADAM, which in turn can be used to purchase extra health, energy or Plasmid powers. The powers that can be accrued are greatly beneficial to the player (a shock ability can fry large groups of enemies should they all stand in water, or one can freeze the hoards to then shatter them on impact). The stark choice between exsanguinating the Little Sisters or liberating them also feeds into the mechanics of the game, but it does so in a way that directly encourages the player to interrogate their own sense of ethics within the diegesis through the same reward economy available to the Rapturites (see Ante-Contreras 2018). Should the player follow the example set by others in Rapture and harvest the girls, they receive 160 units of ADAM and a visual indication of the negative effects on the child; should the player rescue them, they receive the smaller amount of only 80 units, although, as the girls escape through vents to safety, the player is later rewarded with a 200-unit gift for every third girl saved. While a player may wish to make their game easier through an increased acquisition of empowering resources, there are narrative consequences, as the ending of the game shifts drastically depending on the decisions that are made at the transactional point of commodified toxic consumption. With all the girls rescued, the protagonist escapes Rapture, upon which they all become a happy family unit; with any or all of the girls harvested, the protagonist takes over the city and acquires nuclear weaponry, ready for surface warfare. Once more, the way in which individuals are treated inflects the direction of a wider social design, with toxic blood being the fulcrum on which this dynamic rests.

Video games such as *The Elder Scrolls V: Skyrim* (2011), *Dark Souls* (2011) and *Tomb Raider* (2013) feature poison arrows within the combat arsenal of the protagonist with no direct consequence to the player's own well-being. In titles such as *Death Stranding* (2019), where the protagonist's blood is the only effective countermeasure against the spectral hordes, and is weaponised as such, or in *Vampire the Masquerade: Bloodlines 2* (2021) where the Tremer clan of vampires engage in the practice of blood thaumaturgy (blood magic), there is a greater risk/reward dynamic where overuse can directly lead to a depleted health bar or can violate the cultural rules that govern the protagonists.

Figure 8. There is no safe way to contain the contagious blood in *BioShock* (Levine, 2007).

Within *BioShock*, there is an entire offensive ecosystem built around the effects of corrupted blood, which condones macabre and inventive usage but also incorporates a broader thematic concern that both condemns and punishes a society capable of using the same tools to encourage competition (see Ledder 2015). Subsequent titles in the series, *BioShock 2* and *BioShock Infinite* (2013), feature narrative endings where the lives of the protagonists catch up with them, leading to a final act of ablution, self-reflection and sacrifice. *BioShock* does not force nor feature such a definitive conclusion, offering instead a further redemptive path. The collective trauma of toxic blood need not be definitive of the culture in which it is created, provided that measures are made by the individual to move beyond their social conditioning in taking action. However, in being a game where agency is firmly in the hands of the player, *BioShock* kindly requires the player to take the first step.

Louis Bayman

Chernobyl, Craig Mazin (2019)

> The populace
> Sees God's great wrath and waits for death.
> All is destroyed: bread and abode.
> And how to live? (Pushkin 1833)

The five-part HBO and Sky Atlantic miniseries *Chernobyl* retells the events surrounding the explosion of a nuclear reactor on 26 April 1986 in the Ukrainian republic of the Soviet Union. It does so as a gripping dramatic statement about the human capacity for science, ingenuity, heroic sacrifice and the search for truth. At the same time, it provides a spectacular example of the catastrophic consequences of irrationality, human fallibility and collectively induced delusion. Both aspects draw their force from the wider meanings our culture accords to history. In this article, I will offer an understanding of toxicity that starts from the physical contamination produced by the accident but ends by describing the corrosive effects of a faulty social structure. *Chernobyl* offers an acute demonstration that any increase in our stock of technological ambition incurs a consequent increase in the costs of malfunction, and thus a warning that the path of history does not lead inevitably to improvement, but also, potentially, to extermination.

The Horror of History

History is responsible for the dramatic power of *Chernobyl*, not only in its pleasures of meticulous period recreation. The series demonstrates that all knowledge is historical, that wisdom is a product of experience and so is unavailable to those fate charges with being the protagonists of events. But rather than placing the audience in a comfortable position, this makes every calm rationalisation by the characters and each attempt to deny that the worst has happened a source of terror. An audience already aware of the magnitude of the disaster watches firefighters go to the blaze inadequately protected and the authorities undertake their fatal, futile decision to seal off the nearby city of Pripyat. Classically, belated knowledge is the province of the tragic hero, who realises the truth once it is too late to do anything about it. *Chernobyl*'s status as known historical event makes its retelling closer to horror (see Bayman 2019). There is no purifying tragic catharsis, but simply the abandonment of the reactor and town to the overgrowth of nature in the contaminated area of the exclusion zone, covering a total of 2,600 kilometres.

The scale of the damage is felt not in the sudden violence of the explosion so much as the gradual unfolding of its effects. The blast is shown in the distant background through the domestic apartment window of a pregnant young woman, Lyudmilla Ignatenko (Jessie Buckley), who does not notice it until the sound waves arrive several seconds later. Such delays are a significant part of the series' poetic grace. But the lags are also what separate toxicity from mere damage. It is only by the central episode of the five, named 'Open

Figure 9. Toxic history.
Source: *Chernobyl* (Mazin, 2019).

Wide, O Earth' (a phrase taken from Eastern Orthodox funeral rites), that Ignatenko's firefighter husband finally succumbs to an agonising two weeks of radiation sickness; it is at the end of the penultimate episode that Ignatenko delivers her baby, its father dead, the foetus stillborn.

The series has an expressive power that is often akin to a mosaic, for its elements must be pieced together bit by bit. While this conveys the slow tempo of toxic damage, it gives the drama the effect of a historical – or as it becomes in the final episode, a courtroom – investigation, as the viewpoint it produces is retrospective. The morning after the blast, a group of schoolchildren run laughing in the springtime sun, but the camera does not follow them, instead tracking backwards to a point behind them where a bird drops, dishevelled, onto its back, its talons curling in on themselves. The backwards movement indicates how we are to read events, as it also imbues historical recreation with a sense of mourning. The opening scene takes place on the night of 26 April 1988, as Valery Legasov (Jared Harris), the scientist who helped lead the effort to stop a meltdown, prepares suicide. It then cuts to the moment before the blast, 'two years and one minute earlier'. The intertitle positions the explosion as the countdown to his eventual death, and that of the world to which he belongs. It is a grim anniversary in the memorialising society of the USSR – where monuments, plaques, tributes and commemorations fix a common purpose in place through the constant presence of the past.

The series biologizes history, by which I mean that its protagonists share their fate with the wider social structure of which they are part. Legasov informs his co-protagonist Boris Shcherbina (Stellan Skarsgård) that their time at the reactor means they will die within five years; unbeknownst to anyone at the time, this would be the eventual lifespan of the Soviet Union itself, which was dissolved in 1991. The correlation the series establishes between historical and individual death recalls the medieval notion of the body politic, and the idea that society is itself an organism, for country and citizen share a common sickness. But *Chernobyl* also biologizes history another way. On the night of the blast, an executive committee of town and plant managers is called to order by an ageing operative banging his walking stick on the ground, who reminds them of the plant's official name, the Vladimir I Lenin Nuclear Power Station, then states how proud Lenin would be of their decision to seal the town. The senescence of the elderly official is emblematic of a gerontocracy that cloaks its decrepitude in the symbols of the bygone revolutionary dynamism of their youth.

Dynamics of Historical Progress

As is the norm with period dramas, *Chernobyl* has faced controversy over its historical accuracy. Russian TV has reportedly commissioned its own, patriotic response to the series' negative portrayal of the USSR (Roth 2019). Meanwhile, Masha Gessen, in the pages of *The New Yorker* (2019), has criticised *Chernobyl* for the improbability of its Hollywoodised courtroom dramatics. Between didactic simplification, Stalinist distortion and Americanised heroics, we might almost forget the series' own plea from Legasov's diaries that the health of any society depends upon its ability to distinguish truth from lies.

To the critic, if not to the historian, the imaginative aspects of dramatic licence are of equal interest to the accuracy. *Chernobyl* suggests the perhaps perennial attraction to disaster on a colossal scale, as it also testifies to the continued interest in the lost world of Eastern European communism. But it does not employ the so-called *Ostalgie* of affectionate nostalgia demonstrated towards Communist East Germany, exemplified in *Good Bye Lenin!* (Wolfgang Becker, 2003). Rather, the series affirms Chernobyl's status as a byword for the interdependence of political and physical health, one that maintains a contemporary currency, judging by the recent CNN headline 'In Belarus, Covid-19 Is a Modern-day Chernobyl' (Shkliarov 2020). Chernobyl has come to mean much more than simply a geographical location, signifying, like Watergate or Waterloo, an era-defining shift in political power. The closing titles repeat Mikhail Gorbachev's claim from his biography that Chernobyl was 'perhaps the true cause of the end of the Soviet Union'. While this is surely writerly simplification, Chernobyl's sudden, cataclysmic exposure of systemic malfunctions shows the importance of dramatic events in making multiple, long-term processes of history comprehensible. As an encapsulation of epochal change, Chernobyl is to the collapse of Soviet communism what Julius Caesar crossing the Rubicon was to Rome, or what Martin Luther nailing his *Ninety-Five Theses* on the church door was to the Reformation.

Yet *Chernobyl* differs in kind to these other dramatic ruptures. It contains no history-making Julius Caesar or Martin Luther, with Gorbachev having only a bit part to facilitate other people's attempts to mitigate the disaster. In this, it represents more than just a shift from one historical period to another; rather, it suggests a fundamental change in our understanding of history itself. Marxism drew upon the optimism of an age for which the historic past was proof of the possibility of progress. Such wider optimism had become definitional of history, with the conservative author Thomas Carlyle describing 'Universal History' as 'the history of what man has accomplished in this world' (Carlyle [1840] 2008) and the idealist philosopher Friedrich Schelling claiming '[w]hat is not progressive is no object of history' (qtd in Berger and Conrad 2015: 9). The view of history as a narrative progressing beyond the horizon of the present towards a better future is distinct from the pre-modern idea of *historia magistra vitae*, which values the past as a series of lessons on how to live in the present. The progressive view, while claiming to have discovered the objective laws of historical motion, contained also a moral purpose, since for Marx 'history is the judge, its executioner – the proletarian' ([1856] 1969: 500) while revolutionary leader Leon Trotsky welcomed the Russian revolution as the 'revenge of history'.

Confidence in the logic of development has always been somewhat undercut by recognition of the role of accident in history, as put by Enlightenment thinker Blaise Pascal (1669) when he asked whether the shape of Cleopatra's nose 'changed the face of the world' by inspiring Mark Antony to follow Cleopatra when her troops retreated in the Battle of Actium. The rise of the nineteenth-century historical novel occurred in part to explore this tension between logical development and uncontrollable accident. Italian patriotic novelist Alessandro Manzoni dramatised the outbreak of plague in 1630 in Milan in *The Betrothed* as an opportunity to condemn the poor governance of the city (Manzoni [1827] 2013). But the novel ends with the city emerging from plague and the protagonists returning to the natural goodness of the rural landscape. The enormous success of *The Last Days of Pompeii* by Edward Bulwer-Lytton ([1834] 2008), a Whig in the British parliament, told the story of the cataclysmic eruption of Vesuvius in AD 79 – what Madame de Staël called 'death's abrupt invasion' – as a lesson on the decadence of pagan civilisation and its eventual replacement with Christendom. Pushkin was inspired by the flood of the river Neva in 1824 to write his historical narrative poem 'The Bronze Horseman' (1833), about Peter the Great's construction of St Petersburg against the odds posed by a hostile nature.

Like the historical novel, *Chernobyl* uses the particularity of the singular event to illustrate the general social structure: the exposure of the reactor core exposes the fatal flaws of the systems that created it, of both the RBMK (*reaktor bolshoy moshchnosty kanalny*) reactor design and the wider system of Soviet mismanagement and lies. But this exposure produces only sickness and decline, without the regeneration that is the conclusion of the historical narratives listed above. *Chernobyl* dramatises less the dynamics of historical progress than those of historical regress. Causes are preceded by their effects in a narrative made up of delayed responses, flawed thinking and futile deeds. The plant managers see graphite on the ground, the telltale sign that the reactor has exploded, but deny its visible presence even at the cost of their own health. Repeatedly, female characters recognise the truth in *Chernobyl*, being less invested in social position than the men, as embodied in Ulana Khomyuk, played by Emily Watson, a composite character intended to represent the scientific community in general. But ultimately it is fatal harm that teaches what ideology obscures. Things seep out of the body in *Chernobyl*: blood leaks from open wounds, vomit interrupts speech and burns leave blisters on the skin. Radiation produces 'flesh-witnesses', a description Yuval Harari gives to solders whose privileged contact with the truth is gained, like the eyewitness, through direct physical encounter (2008: 7). Unlike Harari's battlefield narratives, the truth brings no transformation, merely decay. Science eventually reveals what political expediency denies in *Chernobyl*; but sacrifice comes first, and justice does not catch up at all.

Sacred and Unclean

In recapturing this moment from the 1980s, *Chernobyl* recalls the sci-fi of the 1950s, the spy film of the 1960s, the disaster movie of the 1970s, all within the category of the quality HBO drama prevalent since the 1990s. And yet

Figure 10. The danger to come.
Source: *Chernobyl* (Mazin, 2019).

the principle mood despite the retro is one of dread, a mood which involves an unwilling anticipation of what is to come. Taking a break outside of the courtroom in the final episode, Shcherbina tells Legasov that it is built on land that hosted pogroms, Stalin's forced removals and Nazi invasion, although despite all the death 'no one ever thinks it's going to happen to them', before coughing blood into his handkerchief and remarking 'and here we are'. The explosion of the reactor and consequent implosion of the Soviet Union itself provide a full stop to the calamities of twentieth-century history, but rather than a new future of human advancement, the series seems to herald a post-truth present of bitter cynicism about politics and species-threatening environmental degradation.

Chernobyl acts as a reminder of the petty pretensions of human vanity in the face of the unleashed energies of the universe, by employing what anthropologist Mary Douglas has termed 'natural symbols', where bodily metaphors – in this case sickness and terminal decay – enable an understanding of the social and political order (Douglas 2013). Pollution and dirt, hygiene and cleanliness, establish the boundaries of any social order, according to Douglas (1966), because they elaborate visions of what upholds or threatens any given society's internal structure. The toxicity of radiation poisoning breaks down boundaries in *Chernobyl*, fatally undoing the structures that are necessary for life – those of the provision of energy, political organisation, the natural ecosystem and the human body. This breakdown has its own spectacular attraction. The twisted metal and scattered debris around the core bespeak the destructive grandeur of an apocalyptic sublime that is likened several times to the surface of the moon, while the natural glow of the fire and billowing plumes of smoke contain a vital energy against the sickly dullness of the general colour scheme.

Marx describes communism as a historical inevitability because it was the only logical way that the struggle between worker and bourgeoisie could achieve progress. But the toxic history of *Chernobyl* ends up in a different temporal register that is not one of progress at all. Mary Douglas also writes of the proximity across cultures of concepts of the sacred to those of pollution, which both denote that which is set aside from the social order (Douglas 1966). In its final sequence, the industrial, groaning sounds of Hildur Guðnadóttir's celebrated soundtrack give way to a choral piece, a liturgical chant called 'Memory Eternal'. The 60-metre-tall concrete covering which finally buried the reactor and its hundreds of tonnes of radioactive materials is commonly referred to as the 'sarcophagus'. The word 'Chernobyl' means a form of wormwood, a

Figure 11. The destructive sublime.
Source: *Chernobyl* (Mazin, 2019).

coincidence which prompted US president Ronald Reagan, among others, to believe the explosion was prophesied in the Book of Revelation (Plohy 2018: 75). Certain events, it seems, require a temporality outside the bounds of history that only religious reference can provide. Not for nothing is Svetlana Alexievich's classic eyewitness account of the disaster titled *Chernobyl Prayer: A Chronicle of the Future* (2016).

To 'come clean' is an interesting metaphor for the moral toxicity associated with lies. But toxicity in *Chernobyl* goes beyond simply depicting past political crimes to offer a warning for our common future. Living while conscious of the imminence of death is the experience of the terminally ill. *Chernobyl* shows that not only individuals but also whole societies can be in terminal decline, whether conscious of it or not. Its ecological premises imply, further, the impending danger of an extinction that threatens not merely one form of society, but human life itself.

Kyle Moody

Succession, Jesse Armstrong (2018–present)

Toxic Ideology

This study looks at the television series *Succession* (2018–present) and illustrates the toxic ideologies, in this case characterised by toxic masculinity, that patriarch Logan Roy (Brian Cox) transfers onto the show's multiple 'protagonists' – his children. Since *Succession* is famously based on the family of modern media mogul Rupert Murdoch (Davis n.d.), it takes its inspiration from a public figure and his progeny. This chapter will explore how Logan's personality – formulated through abuse, self-loathing, bitter competition and a flagrant representation of right-wing media moguls including Murdoch and former American president Donald Trump – is a toxic influence on the Roy family, and how this extremist conservatism, rooted in misogyny and abuse, impacts the children's various personalities.

Succession filters Murdoch's sensibilities and public image into the Roys, a fictional family that is obsessed with the question of which adult child will take over the family media company started by Logan. There are similarities to how former president Trump turned control of his Trump Organization over to his adult sons, Donald Trump Jr and Eric Trump. In the show, Logan Roy holds sway over his children much like he does his business, steamrolling his way through the process and creating incalculable damage through his actions, which are then reflected in his offspring. *Succession* teaches its viewers how such toxicity is carried on by family members learning from their father. The narrative backdrop of the programme (a familial fight for corporate takeover) illustrates that the presence of Logan Roy has created a poison among his family that persists throughout his world, along with the paternal self-hatred that is outwardly directed at the adult children.

Toxic Ideology

Toxicity in this case refers to the overall corruption of the family unit through the ideology espoused by Logan Roy, often through the characteristics of toxic masculinity. Here, I am defining toxic masculinity as linked to hegemonic masculinity, where domination and power are associated with performative gender displays (Boise 2019: 147; Harrington 2020). Since Logan identifies – quite explicitly at times – that he is a man, and a certain type of man at that, toxic masculinity is the root point of discussion for this comparison. *Succession* is a show about choice, or the possible lack thereof for its protagonists. The Roy children are consumed by their father's petty grievances and familial tensions and end up re-enacting and recreating his bellicose animosity during the show.

In January 2019, the American Psychological Association (APA) released updated guidelines for working with those who identify as men and boys and specifically how to address 'traditional masculinity' displayed by its adherents (Boise 2019: 147). The APA defines traditional masculinity as 'marked by stoicism, competitiveness, dominance and aggression [which] is, on the whole, harmful' (Boise 2019: 147). Those who practice it often exhibit a series of gendered attitudes, manifest more frequently in behaviours by those who identify as men. The APA suggests that these 'traditional' behaviours are actively damaging to multiple parties, both those on the receiving end of this toxicity (violence; transphobic, misogynistic, homophobic or racist bullying; sexual assault or harassment) *and* the people who themselves subscribe to such gendered constructs (excessive drinking, physical injuries from fighting, use of steroids, body dysmorphia, drug-taking, inability to express emotions; Boise 2019: 147). Though the term has been used since the mid-1980s, the idea of toxic masculinity emerged during the rise of the #MeToo movement, coinciding with the growing popularity of Murdoch's Fox News channel on American cable television and the increasing visibility of the Trump presidency in the United States (2017–21; Boise 2019).

That *Succession* made its debut during the presidency of Donald J. Trump is no small coincidence. The show is the story of an overbearing conservative figurehead and his weak-willed offspring, and the parallels drawn between the show and the real-world dramatics of the 45th president go deeper. Much has been written about Trump and toxic masculinity during his presidency (see Dignam and Rohlinger 2019; Pizarro-Sirera 2020; Salter 2019; Sexton 2016).

The Roys are styled as fictional media representations of the Trump family, and these stylisations illustrate the depth and breadth of the real Donald Trump's toxicity as well as that of the Roy children. Whether it is Connor's (Alan Ruck) penchant for yelling at his employees, Kendall's (Jeremy Strong) cut-throat business acumen and ability to cut down other people, Roman's (Kieran Culkan) braggadocious nature emblematic of male sexual prowess (on the surface) or Siobhan's (called Shiv by her family and peers; Sarah Snook) keen analytical mind and desire for power and respect, the children are different elements of Logan Roy, himself modelled after Murdoch and Trump. Indeed, the Roy children embody these traits even as they extend from Logan's toxic masculinity, itself drawn from real-world analogues in media moguls and presidents.

Connor Roy, Logan's eldest progeny, is a unique element of toxicity. He does not have a stake in his father's media conglomerate, but he does enact toxicity through his hospitality management enterprise by frequently cutting down his employees during events, reflective of toxic masculine hospitality business owners in real life. He later pursues a career in politics to no avail, which was meant to be indicative of the Trump campaign's focus on promoting an outsider to politics while admitting that he was not prepared for the rigours of political life.

Kendall is the most emblematic representation of his father's toxicity brought to life. His ultimate diminishment at his father's hands is commenced in the series premiere when Logan tells him that he will not be stepping down as CEO of Waystar Royco – the media conglomerate owned by the Roys – which was what Kendall had expected. The entire first season follows Kendall as he tries to usurp his father, culminating in an almost-successful coup that is derailed at his sister Shiv's wedding overseas. After informing Logan that he has enough votes to throw him out of the CEO position, Kendall ingests several drugs and leaves with a valet, who proceeds to crash their car into a lake near the town. Kendall leaves and trudges back to the wedding, seemingly having escaped with no one the wiser, only to find that Logan knows about his manslaughter and will avoid telling the police in exchange for his capitulation on the vote. A broken Kendall acquiesces, setting the stage for becoming his father's lackey throughout season two, until it ends with his public betrayal of Logan.

The toxicity changes him completely. Kendall becomes more like Logan each episode, from vicious firings of employees to the misogynist language that he uses when former workers spit in his face. This is again meant to reflect Donald Trump's relationship with his own son, Donald Trump Jr. And Kendall's transformation into a sicker version of Logan also results in the loss of his own personality, a vacuum of soul that evinces itself through his relapse into drug use and the continued lies to himself as he becomes ever more entangled with his father's various crimes and scandals.

If Kendall becomes a mirror version of Logan that shatters by the second season finale, his brother Roman is already a toxic caricature of his father's brusque masculinity at the series outset. A braggadocious exemplar of sexually avaricious humour, in reality Roman is unable to perform with his lovers. He covets power and respect while covering up his needs via a constant stream of insults. He constantly mocks his fellow siblings and needles his father, which resulted in him being slapped backstage at a major media event (judging by Kendall's reaction, the audience can assume it is not the first time this has occurred), but he lacks the respect of his family, which drives him to act in even

Figure 12. Kendall Roy offers his father a salute and an original rap song in celebration of Logan's fiftieth anniversary of running Waystar Royco.

Source: *Succession*; created by Jesse Armstrong (HBO 2018–present).

Succession, Jesse Armstrong (2018–present)

more unscrupulous ways. Furthermore, his sexually toxic relationships and inability to perform makes him a social representation of falsehoods, with his sadomasochistic relationship with trusted family executive Gerri (J. Smith-Cameron) illustrative of his problems.

If Kendall becomes fiercer and more dogmatic throughout the series, we see Shiv grow from a self-centred individual to one whose relationships are charged with a focus on family. Even as she tries to hide her affair with a fellow presidential campaign worker and former lover by telling new husband Tom Wambsgans (Matthew Macfadyen) that they need to try having an open marriage – a declaration she makes on their wedding night outside of the ceremony – she still wants to have a path forward with him. Her desire to have it all comes from the toxicity of Logan, whose obsession with family unity conflicts with his unapologetic desires. Shiv becomes a more sympathetic representation of Murdoch's progeny, and it is impossible to avoid comparisons with Ivanka Trump and her continued integration with her father's expanding political world.

Figure 13. The Roy family – from left to right: Kendall (Jeremy Strong), Roman (Kieran Culkin), Logan (Brian Cox), Siobhan/Shiv (Sarah Snook) and Connor (Alan Ruck).

Source: *Succession*; created by Jesse Armstrong (HBO 2018–present).

The drama turns on the shifting relationships of the Roy children and patriarch, always winding through new developments with a focus on personal success at the expense of relationships between characters. No matter who comes into the world of the Roys, they are always eventually ejected from their orbit. The only ones that can survive this world eventually become toxic. Kendall's various paramours never last, because they see the goodness in him, and that goodness is ultimately crushed by his father's need to be the overriding element in his life. Roman is broken by his father's overbearing nature, a rejection of the cries for attention that propel Roman through his insouciance. Shiv and Tom will survive as a unit because Tom knows how to be as ruthless as his father-in-law. Logan's new spouse, Marcia (Hiam Abbass), maintains power over Logan by remaining a fearsome adversary who is unafraid to tear down Logan's biological children. Connor eventually shuts out his partner and all good sense during his beleaguered presidential campaign, emphasising divisive political rhetoric that ultimately staggers his playwright girlfriend's (Justine Lupe) theatrical piece. None of it matters for their narrative drive to succession and power.

Furthermore, the presence of strong theatre actors such as Brian Cox, Jeremy Strong and Cherry Jones (in the role of Nan Pierce) illustrates the link between the Shakespearean bona fides of the cast and the show's roots in Shakespearean tragedy (Wald 2020). The link between *King Lear* and *Succession* is accentuated when examined through the return of the predecessor, stymieing the ascension of the progeny into the role of paternal figurehead. The succession dynamic is itself a cause for concern. All of the children are fundamentally millionaires, set for life in a world where nothing is guaranteed. But it's never enough. The toxicity driving the Roy family propels a death match for control, seeking absolution for any problems through absolute power. It is a lie; one the Roy children can clearly see but prize too much anyway. They do not know anything else.

But perhaps they can learn. The end of *Succession*'s second season may herald a way forward. The conclusion of the season, 'This Is Not For Tears' (Season 2, Episode 10), finds Roy progeny Kendall at a press conference, appearing to choose to take the blame for multiple scandals within the organisation and be fired from the company. This seemingly selfless act would prove that

Succession, Jesse Armstrong (2018–present)

Waystar Royco is serious about changing its act after other news outlets scoop a massive cover-up concerning major crimes aboard the company's cruise ships.

Midway through the press conference, the plot twists, and Kendall tells the reporters that his story was a pre-planned bit. He explicitly places blame on Logan for the crimes and tells reporters that he will be presenting documents (held by show favourite Cousin Greg; Nicholas Braun) showing his father's involvement. He then strides off-screen, leaving his younger siblings agog at the television and his father seemingly smiling as the show cuts to black (see Figure 14).

This series of events – while shocking in the parlance of 'peak TV' (a term referring to the glut of high-quality television programming available across platforms) – is indicative of Kendall taking back his life from the toxicity of his family, and in particular the toxic masculinity of its patriarch. Over the course of two seasons, we the audience have witnessed his descent into the hardscrabble techniques of business and cut-throat management over media companies within his family's employ. It represents a potential rejection of his father's toxic male ideology and a possible end for Logan's control over the company.

Succession is a show marked by toxicity, illustrating how a vacuum of love inhales all that surround it. It represents a place where toxic masculinity has

Figure 14. The second season finale where Logan offers a whisper of a smile after watching Kendall sell him out on TV.

Source: *Succession*; created by Jesse Armstrong (HBO 2018–present).

negatively impacted nearly every character within the world of the show and how the need for success becomes an all-consuming zero-sum game that none of the characters win. The work done by producer Adam McKay and creator Jesse Armstrong illustrates how a world that could exist within a parody of itself instead belies a sad truth of toxic black holes and scam artists selling a simulacrum of love. Here, accomplishment is coded as love, and a lack of it is derided as loneliness, but only within the diegetic world of the characters. All the audience can see is a vortex of loss and pain, one that is succoured by the need to triumph at the expense of others. That is *Succession*, a comedy drama that is a mirror of our own chase. It gives the audience a look at the world that we cannot enter, only to question why we are gazing in the first place. It purposefully shows us how a chase for love in a world where one can 'have it all' illustrates how the dynamics of the rich and the famous are symbolic of the pursuit of Icarus. In the end, all the Roys fly too close to the sun, never realising they already lived in the clouds.

Natalie Wilson

Get Out, Jordan Peele (2017)

With white supremacy as its primary pollutant and systemic racism as its result, white toxicity – like toxins generally – causes lasting damage to human bodies. In Jordan Peele's *Get Out*, this toxicity disproportionately harms black bodies, much as it does in the real world. A cogent response to the anti-black racism poisoning American culture, the film charts the story of a young black photographer, Chris Washington (Daniel Kaluuya), who is targeted by a modern-day enslavement enterprise headed by a wealthy white family, the Armitages. The daughter of the family, Rose Armitage (Allison Williams), in the guise of sweet white girlfriend, lures Chris to her family's estate. Once there, Chris is hypnotised against his will (see Figure 15) and auctioned off to the highest bidder at the Armitages' annual garden party. Once 'won' his body will undergo the surgical procedure at the heart of the Armitage family business – a Stepford-esque implantation of white brains into black bodies.

Positioning present realities such as racial profiling, colour-blind racism and police brutality in conversation with enslavement, slave patrols and lynching, the film lasers in on the racialised trauma that has been heaped upon black bodies for over 400 years in the land mass now known as the United States. Many of these and other consequences of white supremacy target – and live in – the body, a factor explored at length by Resmaa Menakem in his 2007 book *My Grandmother's Hands*. Insisting that racial conflict in America cannot be solved if we do not root racism out of our bodies, Menakem's work characterises racism as a toxin baked into our flesh and blood. Racism, he argues, is 'in the air we breathe, the water we drink, and the culture we share' – it is, in other words, a pervasive toxin (2017: xvii, xix).

Figure 15. Chris under hypnosis.
Source: *Get Out*; directed by Jordan Peele (Universal Pictures, 2017).

Toxins are anything that causes damage to the body. *Toxicity* refers to how toxic – or poisonous – something is and, by extension, how much harm it causes. White toxicity, as I conceive it, is similar to the 'somatic trauma' Menakem's work explores. This toxic whiteness, like most toxins, can be difficult to detect and even harder to eradicate. Ta-Nehisi Coates, in his National Book Award-winning *Between the World and Me*, also explores the impact of toxic racism on the black body. 'Racism is a visceral experience', Coates writes near the start of his memoir; it 'dislodges brains, blocks airways, rips muscle, extracts organs, cracks bones, breaks teeth' (2015: 10). Like Menakem, Coates focuses on the trauma done to black individuals and communities across history. 'In America', he writes, 'it is traditional to destroy the black body – it is heritage' (2015: 104).

In the current US landscape, this heritage plays out at a rate of approximately 1,000 black bodies killed by police each year. It plays out in the school-to-prison pipeline where black students are disciplined for 'unruly' hair. It plays out via the criminalisation of the black community and their vastly disproportionate incarceration.[1] It plays out in police violence directed at the black body. *Get Out* reads as a fitting response to such realities in the years surrounding its release. *Get Out* premiered shortly after Donald Trump took office and was in the works before Trayvon Martin's killing, before tear gas was released

---

1   Black males, as documented in *13th* (DuVernay 2015), make up 40.2 per cent of the prison population but only 6.5 per cent of the US population on the whole.

on citizens in Ferguson as they protested Michael Brown's killing, before the birth of the Black Lives Matter movement. According to Peele, it began to percolate in his brain as Barak Obama and Hillary Clinton were battling it out for the presidency. Though Obama's win was read as proof America had entered a post-racial era, as representing 'national atonement for the original sin of slavery and the stain of segregation', in actuality, as described by Nick Bryant (2017) of BBC News, Obama's win led – not unpredictably – to a white supremacist backlash. After Obama's election, hate groups welcomed a surge of new members, something David Duke, former leader of the Ku Klux Klan, predicted, citing Obama as an important 'visual aid' for fuelling white nationalism.[2] Some years later, Duke proudly announced his support for Obama's successor, declaring he and his followers aimed to 'fulfill the promises of Donald Trump' and 'take our country back' (qtd in Manchester 2017). Not long after this, Unite the Right events in Charlottesville, Virginia, led to violent clashes between white nationalists and counterprotestors. Though white supremacists had beaten and injured counterprotestors, killing one woman and injuring at least twenty others, Trump refused to denounce them, instead indicating they were 'very fine people' (see Drobnic 2019).

Peele's movie does not include outspoken racists of Duke's or Trump's ilk, but it does respond to these twenty-first-century manifestations of white toxicity. An unsettling tale of an upper-class white family of purported Obama-voting liberals, the Armitages, the film provides an incisive takedown of 'post-racial' America. The 'very fine people' at its centre are the founders of the Order of the Coagula, an organisation that offers its members prolonged life via 'transmutation', a surgical procedure which transplants the brain of a white person into a black person's skull. After the parasitic operation is complete, the black victim is no longer able to control their body; instead, they are ruled by an inner 'white master'. The justification for this toxic infiltration, that 'black is in fashion', as a character from *Get Out* puts it, accords with the historical commodification, dehumanisation and monetising of black lives – of blacks as not human, but thing. According to Menakem, this supposition, that

2   For a discussion of the rise in hate group membership surrounding Obama's election, see the 2008 Associated Press article 'White Supremacists See Hope in Obama Win'. For Obama as 'visual aid', see 'How White Supremacy Morphed Into White "Victimization"' by Clarence Page (2017).

blacks are not quite human, 'lives in our bodies' and results in not only white supremacy, but white *body* supremacy (Brach 2020). For the Armitages and their ilk, white body supremacy has led them to believe they deserve to live forever. Dean Armitage (Bradley Whitford), current patriarch of the Order of the Coagula, speaks to this belief near the close of the film as he describes the founding rational of the order to Chris. 'We are divine', he explains. 'We are the gods trapped in cocoons.' Whites, by his way of thinking, are *more* than human, are divine, and thus deserve to rule, to conquer, to achieve immortality. Blacks, in contrast, are viewed as not fully human, their bodies expendable and their lives unimportant. These suppositions are foundational for the Order of the Coagula, an enterprise whose very survival depends on the desecration of black bodies.

Such desecration is witnessed in the opening moments of the film. In the scene, a black man, Andre Hayworth (LaKeith Stanfield), is walking down a suburban street trying to find a specific address. 'Got me out in this creepy, confusing-ass suburb '… I feel like a sore thumb out here,' he mutters into his cell phone. 'It's like a fucking hedge maze out here', he grumbles. A car pulls up. Aware his black body is 'inappropriate' in the 'manicured' white space, he gives himself a pep talk of sorts: 'Not today. Not me.' Alas, his number is up. A driver wearing a medieval helmet emerges from the vehicle and attacks him. He is dragged to the car and forced into the trunk, treated as if a mere carcass (see Figure 16). The song playing from the car's radio, 'Run Rabbit Run', equates Andre to a hunted rabbit. More obliquely, the song hints that Andre is akin to a slave on the run, connotations of which are hidden in the ancestry of the song – 'Run Rabbit Run' is a descendent of the folk song 'Run, Ni**er Run'. The original song, about a runaway slave trying to avoid capture, transforms into one about a farmer hunting a rabbit in the 1939 hit.

In the film's main narrative, Chris will play the primary 'running rabbit', one initially ensnared by Rose and then hunted by her murderous family, comprised of her father, Dean, a neurosurgeon, her mother, Missy (Catherine Keener), a psychiatrist, and her brother, Jeremy (Caleb Landry Jones), the masked hunter that abducts Andre in the opening scene. In the first scene of the film proper, Rose arrives at Chris' apartment as he is preparing for their trip to meet her parents. He asks if they know he is black, adding 'I don't want to

Figure 16. In the opening scene of *Get Out*, Andre Hayworth is abducted by Jeremy Armitage.

Source: *Get Out*; directed by Jordan Peele (Universal Pictures, 2017).

get chased off the lawn with a shotgun'. She insists her parents are not racist. If they were, she assures him, 'I wouldn't be bringing you home to them'. Yet, the fact they are racist is the very reason she takes him home – to serve up his black body to her white supremacist family. Chris, like the mounted deer head later witnessed in the Armitage basement, is meant to become a bodily trophy for her family's Coagula enterprise, a factor that furthers the lynching motifs scattered throughout the film, one in which Chris is the 'black buck' hunted and tortured by the Armitage mob (see Ryan-Bryant 2020).

Overturning the black buck trope, one historically used to 'justify' lynching, *Get Out* emphasises Chris' innocence. Symbolically aligned with the deer Rose hits on the drive out to her parents, Chris is more Bambi than buck. Like Bambi, Chris' mother is killed – not by a hunter, but as a result of a hit-and-run. The deer Rose strikes with her car thus hints at the danger Chris is in while also echoing his mother's demise. Soon, Rose's father will further such symbolic linkages in a speech tinged with genocidal glee: 'I'm telling you I do not like the deer', he complains. 'I'm sick of it. They're taking over. They're like rats. They're destroying the ecosystem. If I see a dead deer on the side of the road, I think to myself that's a start.' In the trajectory of the film up to this point, blacks have been equated to rabbits, deer and rats. Later, Jeremy will suggest Chris is a beast. Yet, in a reversal of the notion blacks are akin to expendable vermin, the Armitages and their white friends are the true scourge – ones cast as 'super predators' unable to tolerate not being at the top of the food chain, so to speak. As much is made clear when Dean takes Chris on a tour of the home and points out a photo of Jesse Owens, referencing the image as documenting '[m]y dad's claim to fame'.

Dean goes on to relate how his father Roman lost out to Owens at the 1936 Olympics. Dean adds that Hitler 'with all his perfect Aryan race bullshit' was watching when '[t]his black dude comes along and proves him wrong in front of the entire whole world'. His father, he quips, 'almost got over it'. This short snippet hints at the motivation behind the Order of Coagula, one based in a refusal to concede a black body could ever 'best' a white one. Interpreting the black body as a threat to white supremacy (and, in this specific case, Olympic victory), Roman Armitage sets in motion an agenda to control the black body from within. This agenda is in keeping with what scholar Wallace Best (2014) refers to as a fear 'deeply ingrained in our national psyche' – that of the black body in motion. Contending that all a black body needs do to become a threat is *move*, Best reads this historically sedimented fear in relation to the preponderance of murders of innocent members of the black community by police. This 'recent reign of terror on black bodies', as Best calls it, takes a metaphorical turn in Peele's film. Rather than being killed, black individuals are rendered virtual zombies, enslaved from within by white minds.[3] Rather than being immobilised via incarceration, they are imprisoned in 'the sunken place', an empty void that will become their permanent residence once they have been 'coagulated'.

A physical manifestation of white toxicity, the sunken place in Peele's film is reminiscent of what Coates names 'the essential below', or the positioning of blacks 'beneath, and beyond, the umbrella of rights' (2015: 106, 115). Significantly, black victims of the Order of the Coagula end up in the sunken place due to manipulation and control carried out by whites – first via hypnosis, then via the transmutation surgery that implants a white brain in their skull. The sunken place and its founding ethos thus literalises Menakem's contention that 'the most dangerous place for a black person is in the mind of the white collective' (qtd in Brach 2020). The toxic whiteness of this collective

---

3   For a reading of *Get Out* through the lens of the Haitian zombie, see Wilson (2020).

Get Out, Jordan Peele (2017)

Figure 17. Chris strapped to a chair in the Armitage basement.
Source: *Get Out*; directed by Jordan Peele (Universal Pictures, 2017).

imagination acts as a neurological parasite within the film, one seeking to build white supremacy from the inside out. An imperialist, colonialist infiltration of individual black bodies, the eugenically informed procedure will not destroy the victim – instead, 'white masters' will be implanted into black bodies in such a way that leaves the black person's body alive and their consciousness intact. As explained to Chris by Jim Hudson (Stephen Root), the winning bidder for his body, 'you won't be gone, not completely ... you'll be able to see and hear what your body is doing, but your existence will be as a passenger'.

To prevent such colonisation of his body, Chris, once trapped in the Armitage basement, plugs his ears with cotton to prevent further hypnosis. When Jeremy arrives to transport him to the in-house operating room, Chris hits him over the head with a croquet ball. He then pulls the mounted stag head from the wall and impales Dean before ascending to the main floor of the house. As Missy lunges for the teacup she used to hypnotise him, Chris smashes it. This teacup, itself a trinket of imperialism, evokes the slave-era practice of summoning 'house slaves' in a similar manner while the cotton Chris uses to plug his ears suggests what Coates names 'the prime product rendered by our stolen bodies' (2015: 101). To add to the symbolism evoking slavery, imperialism and white privilege, we have the croquet ball, an item from a leisure game of the white and wealthy, and the mounted stag head, a hunting trophy suggestive of the white imperialist hunter. Turning the tables by using these physical manifestations of toxic whiteness against his captors, Chris, in effect, escapes from the master's house by repurposing the master's tools.

In the closing scenes, as Chris drives from the house in Jeremy's car, the 'Run Rabbit Run' song plays from the car radio, an auditory circling back to the opening scene and its construction of the black body as prey. Adorned in the hunting jodhpurs favoured by big-game hunters, Rose emerges from the house and gives chase with a rifle. Alas, her last-ditch effort to destroy the black body she has been hunting from the film's start is interrupted by the blaring sirens and flashing lights of an approaching vehicle. Donning the guise of white damsel in distress, she calls out: 'Help me, help me.'

In the alternate ending, the one that did not make it into theatres, white police officers emerge from the car and bark 'show me your hands' as they move towards Chris, guns at the ready.[4] Some months later, Rod (Lil Rel Howery), Chris' best friend, visits him in prison, encouraging him to review what happened at the Armitages, presumably in hopes of proving Chris' innocence. Chris shuts down this sentiment saying, 'I stopped it', indicating that ridding the world of the Armitages was enough. In the closing seconds of this alternate ending, we witness Chris walking back to his cell flanked by a white guard. Several barred, white gates slam closed behind him. White toxicity, in this conclusion, lands him in the real world's sunken place – prison. In the other ending, the one that made it into theatres, it is not white law enforcement that arrives on the scene, but Rod in his Transportation Security Administration (TSA) vehicle. Chris still puts his hands in the air, believing the police have arrived, but Rod emerges instead, quipping 'I told you not to go into that house'. As they drive away, Chris asks how he found him. 'I'm TS motherfucking A', Rod replies, 'We handle shit. That's what we do. Consider this situation ... fucking handled.'

Put a different way, Rod sorted it out. 'Sort' comes from the French word *triage*. In English, 'triage' has come to mean the sorting of bodily injury or illness into degrees of urgency. The Armitages, their name containing all the letters of 'triage', injure black bodies to 'sort out' declining, ageing white bodies. Armed with the weapons of whiteness, they triage black bodies to

---

4   Chris puts his arms in the air to signal his compliance in both versions of the ending, something evoking the 'hands up, don't shoot' rallying cry against police brutality that spread across the United States following the 2014 shooting of Michael Brown.

their in-house surgical suite. But Chris refuses to be sorted. Rewriting the fate, the Armitages have scripted for him (one metaphorically evoked when Missy stabs him with a letter opener), Chris escapes from their toxic basement. In the film's final cut, which hit screens less than a week after Trump took office, the real monster – the racism that lives in the white supremacist mind and spreads toxic waste throughout the United States – gets *sorted* by two black men.[5] Chris does not end up inside the prison-industrial complex, one Peele deems the 'the dark hole we throw black people in' (qtd in Lopez 2017). Instead, Chris becomes a testament to the truism currently sounding the death knell of white toxicity – 'BLACK LIVES MATTER'.

---

5   Of note, in several interviews, as in Shaw-King (2017), Peele references racism as the real monster.

Franziska E. Kohlt

The Coronavirus Act (2020), UK Government Communication (March 2020–present)

Toxic Language

As the flurry of the COVID-19 pandemic in 2020 stirred up minds struggling to conceptualise the nature and impact of the novel coronavirus, it had already begun solidifying and settling into discernible and distinct linguistic forms on printed pages. Among them, the genre comprised of letters to editors, columns, blogs penned by medical staff decrying their political leaders' language of public health crisis as 'warfare'. Particularly pronounced in some anglophone and francophone cultures, leaders consistently referred to the 'battle' against the novel coronavirus, their governments as 'war cabinets', healthcare institutions as front lines, and the deaths of health workers as 'sacrifice'. On the flip side, health and other 'key' workers felt ignored, silenced or even, when they spoke up against such language, 'abused' and portrayed as 'villains' (Wise 2020; Asbury and Kim 2020: 2).

Their opposition to such language was far from being only a private sentiment, of discomfort or distaste, but was, more significantly, in line with both a long-established scholarly emphasis on the inefficacy and indeed danger of martial metaphors in science, medicine and healthcare – responding to an equally established culture of their use that has concluded they are 'ironic, unfortunate and unnecessary' (Nie et al. 2016: 3).

Moreover, such recent evocations of warfare in public health crisis, at times unnoticed but at other times employed deliberately, replicate narrative patterns employed deliberately to polarise social discourses. These have become commonplace over the past decades in nutrition or climate change debates – as commonplace as their being referred to as 'toxic' in their effects. This chapter will shine a light on how words or narratives act to destabilise, to corrode, to disable functioning, or even healing power, of these discourses – at the cost of human health – and how they thus act virtually like a social poison, irrespective of whether used unconsciously or deliberately. It will illustrate why reflection and adjustment of rhetoric in health contexts is thus not a matter of preference, but of ethics, and why it yet can appear as socially undesirable.

Toxic Narratives

Narratives hold 'useful', essential functions in medical settings. They help to deal with an 'altered situation', thus mending 'disruption' caused by illness (Gabe et al. 2004: 83). They can answer the 'why?' and 'what can be done now?' in ways medicine and its model may find difficult, and are thus capable of creating healing which medicine itself may not (yet) be. Greenhalgh and Hurwitz even state they are 'intrinsically therapeutic' (1999: 49). This holds true in the framing of individual illness, population health or global health threats.

Narratives are a powerful tool in any general setting, but not in all cases healing – especially not automatically. Even when they appear to be, they may hold the potential to cause greater harm in the longer term. Thus, narratives share the properties of substances which, employed in one way, can bring healing, but if misapplied, used without consideration or without considering short-term relief over long-term damage, in the wrong places or circumstances, or in too great a dosage, cause damage, and often in a creeping, not immediately apparent way. To examine in what circumstance and under which conditions a narrative becomes toxic, some attention must first be directed to the mechanics of narrative.

Narratives, as Friedmann observes, 'do not happen, they are made' (2019: 10). Phelan establishes that narratives are a 'purposeful communicative act'. They are '*consciously* constructed towards a *distinct* and *intended* effect' 'to engage and influence' their audiences' cognition, emotions and values (2007: 203, my emphasis). While Phelan's and Friedmann's definitions suggest narrative as a fully conscious act of communication, our 'conceptual system[s]' are fundamentally shaped by narrative and metaphor in ways we are often unconscious of: we adapt them 'readily and familiarly' and yet we often 'do not see *them*, we see *through* them' (Lakoff and Johnson [1980] 2003;

Curtis 1994: 434). We *rarely consciously* utilise narratives to makes sense of a situation in our own minds. As a result, when we adapt narratives to which we have ourselves been exposed in our own explanations, we even more rarely question them as we use them.

Lakoff and Johnson look at the example of how the metaphor of warfare shapes the language of discussion, debate and argument in the English language to the degree that we come to perform these actions as if they *were* warfare. Phrases such as 'your claims are *indefensible*', 'he *attacked* every weak point in my argument', 'his criticisms were right *on target*', 'he *shot down* all of my arguments' come to mean that an argument *can be* won or lost (Lakoff and Johnson [1980] 2003: 4). They invite their readers to imagine a culture in which argument is understood as dance, as balanced and aesthetically pleasing, and note how the act of arguing itself becomes unrecognisable as argument to the anglophone observer who has come to recognise this process as warfare, yet is, most of the time, unconscious of it. Unnoticed and unconsciously perpetuated, narratives are thus often wielded not as a conscious, but an unconscious, act of communication, *possibly* geared towards an intended effect, but in either case causing the effects of the narrative employed – whether intended or not. This is complicated further when narratives known to direct thought and action in damaging directions are employed deliberately under the guise of the intent to heal. Those using damaging narratives without ill intent could become conflated with those of the former category.

Damaging narratives could, especially in health contexts, have a significant and direct impact on morbidity and mortality – in individual and population health settings alike. The following section will offer strategies for reflection and tools for identifying potential narrative sources of harm.

Toxic Narratives in Health Settings

That Lakoff and Johnson chose the theme of warfare to illustrate the persuasion of words as their opening example is poignant. The metaphor of 'war' has seemingly become the most intuitive framing to denote any sort of conflict, contradiction, disagreement, change or indeed any noticeable action upon a status quo. News headlines and politicians evoke war against nature, against cancer, poverty or terror with such regularity, audiences run a risk of becoming desensitised to the gravity the word implies.

In this vein, it is also persistent – and notorious – as a narrative framing in health and welfare settings. Countless studies have examined its use in relation to cancer (Segal 2012; Hansen 2018) or HIV (Nie et al. 2016), with the rhetoric of personal 'battle' and pharmaceutical 'warfare'. Segal laments it imposes a 'tyranny of genre' in which patients must perform as 'heroes' (Segal 2012: 298, 293). Peryakoil adds that a phrase such as ' "fighting a valiant battle with cancer" creates an artificial win-lose dichotomy thereby obligating the soldier/patient to fight to the end' (2008: 842). A dangerous transformation occurs. Narrative that could be 'intrinsically healing' becomes the opposite. By means of language, the act of 'refuting harmful treatment options' – those not beneficial to healing, their rejection therefore *desirable* from a medical point of view – is turned into 'the equivalent of a cowardly retreat from the battlefield' – something socially and morally *un*desirable (Peryakoil 2008: 842).

Once dominant, an inappropriate narrative that has become attached to a medical context can, even without the narrative intervention of an individual, pre-emptively mislead those under pressure to act in unproductive, or even reckless ways. Pressure increased through rhetoric of heroism may lead the patient to 'sit it out' and 'be tough', whereas seeking help would have been advantageous for well-being or even treatment outcomes. What may be medically desirable is suddenly socially stigmatised, retreat is cowardice, death is defeat or even failure. This narrative transformation, a truly changed understanding of reality, which is now seen *through* a narrative, opens up space for lamenting apparent lack of action, preparedness, willpower or optimism – even when it is uncertain whether these would have changed the outcome of disease or certain that they would not have.

Good science or medical communication, especially in risk scenarios, aims for the prevention of morbidity and mortality (Rogers and Pearce 2013: 66). The measure of an appropriate metaphor is, therefore, determined by the word itself: to 'transfer meaning' as closely as possible, to support and reinforce clear medical advice and its aims. A metaphor or narrative used in a health situation should therefore sustain or amplify the transfer of meaning, not hinder, skew, obscure or even invert it. Martial narratives in medical settings are thus ironic, as 'medicine's primary goals has always been to save lives and to treat injuries caused by acts of collective violence' (Nie et al. 2016: 3). They risk becoming that very collective violence – yet more stealthily so: true 'toxic narratives', words which, initially or not, 'aggressively oppose expertise' and 'vilify marginalised groups', such as in an individual health setting, can subtly, and cumulatively, shift perceptions of reality in such a direction (Boswell 2015: 315).

As this brief consideration of individual illness shows, narrative framing can actively influence and potentially undermine therapeutic and curative measures; this illuminates the ways in which this applies on the scale of communication to wider society. Just as a toxin spreads beyond the body, and thus into its environment, narratives become perpetuated by 'mass media and popular science' without scrutiny of their 'moral', and indeed ethical, implications (Nie et al. 2016: 4). Their ready and often unreflected adoption in personal vocabulary makes them a public health risk. Dan Kahan aptly refers to this as 'polluted science communication environment[s]': a verbal act of poisoning akin to anthropocentric environmental pollution, affecting health and wellbeing in unexpected and indirect ways (2017: 421). It is crucial, therefore, to generate sensitivity to the points of the bifurcation of intention and effect of narrative, through which words denoting the virtuous come to be, from a medical perspective, harmful. The final section will examine a recent example.

The 'War Against COVID-19' in the United Kingdom

The framing of management of the COVID-19 pandemic as warfare was top-down and consistent, and it intensified with increased mortality (Kohlt 2020). From the beginning, it was, above all, government representatives who 'declare[d] war on coronavirus' (Smith 2020), but newspapers framed their coverage around the same kind of cultural cues. When the Prime Minister said he hoped to 'allow a more significant return to normality from November at the earliest – possibly in time for Christmas' (BBC News 2020), headlines echoed it'll be 'over by Christmas', recalling a slogan made popular in the historiography of World War I (e.g. Peck 2020; Hyde 2020), even though that was not the original wording.

It was not only words that were used in this way; rituals from war remembrance were consciously mimicked to frame the response to COVID-19 and the deaths resulting from it. When the health secretary responded to the deaths of health workers, he did so through linguistic formulae and customs ordinarily reserved for the UK's Remembrance Day: 'This morning, at 11 o'clock, we paused to remember the 85 NHS colleagues and 19 social care colleagues who have lost their lives with coronavirus. [...] They are the nation's fallen heroes. And we will remember them' (Hancock 2020). Health service fundraisers with military themes dominated consistently and received the widest coverage on national media, sustaining the warfare framing as the dominant narrative response. These included the veteran Captain Tom, whose sponsored walks led to a knighthood, a book contract and a film contract, and a military-style flypast by a Spitfire and a Hurricane over his home.

Alec Ryrie (2020) highlights how the warfare framing, particularly evoking phrases and events from World War II, such as the 'Blitz spirit', served as 'sacred story' and provided the moral compass for perceived desirable behaviours in response to the pandemic. As the term 'sacred' implies, the use of religious terminologies and narratives, describing the virus as 'devilish' and 'evil', amplified the imperative of that moral compass (Johnson 2020e). Such phrasings conflate military and moral virtues in a similar manner as outlined for individual health scenarios, yet equally have no currency in a public health setting, as has been most vocally expressed by its professionals. In the United Kingdom, a health worker wrote 'the NHS isn't staffed by heroes'. 'I'm not in the army and we aren't engaged in military combat. [...] I really don't need [...] people clapping. [...] I don't even (whisper it) need Colonel Tom' (Anonymous 2020). 'You cannot sing "Rule Britannia" to a virus', another concluded (Okwonga 2020). And yet another acknowledged the 'eloquent and moving' nature of military ritual, but pleaded: 'forget medals and flypasts', as the 'increasingly bombastic proposals for honouring our "sacrifice" are beginning to feel more burdensome than uplifting' (Clarke 2020). They wanted their concerns to be heard, but instead felt marginalised and silenced. Teachers expressing concerns about their safety even saw themselves and their profession vilified (Asbury and Kim 2020: 2) – the markers of toxic narratives outlined by Boswell (2015: 315).

The widespread framing of the pandemic *as* warfare led to an understanding of it in these terms, and to behaviours *as if* indeed engaged in war. And it is in the juxtaposition of the perceived advantages of such rhetoric with their consequences that the analogy of narratives as toxic becomes most apparent. War rhetoric is perceived as morale-boosting, mood-lifting and reassuring. Yet Wessely and Daniels note that considerable evidence suggests it 'does not work'; instead, it 'offers transient false comfort that rapidly fades', 'rarely ameliorate[s] distress, but might do the opposite' and 'elicit fear' – *especially* in health settings (2020). It can galvanise populations into action, which can bring psychological reward of collective endeavour and shared identity. However, this can be actively life-threatening when it endorses 'bringing the nation together' in the 'Blitz spirit' of 'defiant' group activity while scientific advice dictates 'social distancing'. This is, equally, not unexpected: warfare narratives in health settings have repeatedly been shown to 'negatively control the problem-solving that was originally intended', or even create additional problems (Hansen 2018: 225–6).

In the inebriated cumulative power of toxic narratives, control – over actions or damages once released into a system – is, like that of their analogous counterpart, elusive. Thus, this chapter proposes treating words with the same caution as potentially toxic substances, complementing Greenhalgh, Hurwitz, Gabe and others who have called for the study of narrative to be included in medical training and on population level. Just as awareness of the mechanics and dangers of toxic substances ensures population health, so too can awareness of toxic narratives.

Daniel Sheppard

Halloween, David Gordon Green (2018)

'Slasher films are uniquely violent against women', or so male critics warned at their popularisation in the early 1980s (Linz and Donnerstein 1994: 246). 'Get back in your place', Gene Siskel claimed, was the ideologically intertwined message in these films – 'a primordial response' to the women's movement of the 1970s ('Women in Danger', Season 5, Episode 4 of *Sneak Previews*). Even in theorising backlash post-feminism, Susan Faludi identifies a critic who 'proposes that feminists produced the rise in slasher movies' (Faludi 2006: 3). Here, early teen slasher films are mischaracterised as the cultural artifice of a 'new traditionalism' where feminist ideology is violently denounced, reminiscent of a past where 'traditional values were (supposedly) popular' (Projansky 2001: 72).

Interrogating such claims of violent anti-feminism, Carol J. Clover published 'Her Body, Himself: Gender in the Slasher Film' in 1987, a shortened and revised version of which later appeared in *Men, Women, and Chain Saws: Gender in the Modern Horror Film* (Clover 1992). Where male criticism had previously ostracised the female figure as lone victim, Clover sought to problematise such a reductive conclusion, using her voice to accredit the role of the surviving female protagonist. Here, Clover conceptualised the 'Final Girl' to methodically reconfigure the relationship between teen slasher, female representation and critical discourse. By drawing critical attention to the Final Girl, Clover opened a space to consider multifarious issues of characterisation and identification, using her work to scrutinise the assumption that early teen slasher films adopt a sustainably sadistic male gaze that invites 'audience identification not with the victim but with the killer' (Ebert 1981: 55).

For this particular purpose, Clover wrote 'Her Body, Himself' to conceptualise a shifting male gaze, theorising early teen slasher in sadomasochistic terms. Yet this familiar narrative is a simplified one within horror studies, failing to acknowledge how Clover's contributions belong to a school of thought that situates itself not in horror studies but, rather, feminist film studies, which weaponised psychoanalysis as part of its political project in the 1980s. Clover's school of thought does not simply problematise the sadistic-voyeuristic masculine gaze of Laura Mulvey's 1975 article 'Visual Pleasure and Narrative Cinema', but equally the masochistic feminine gaze that immerses itself in passivity (see Doane 1987). Indeed, Clover's work is in dialogue with other feminist film theorists who collectively sought to develop theories of sadomasochistic spectatorship. Here, feminist film theorists worked to demonstrate the oscillation between sadistic and masochistic subject positions, achieved through the spectator's bisexual identification with both male and female characters, in order to dismantle the inherent misogyny that has historically defined psychoanalytic paradigms as fixed: male/female, masculine/feminine, sadism/masochism, active/passive, etc. While much of this feminist film theory has been appropriated by horror studies as a disciplinary field – Barbara Creed (1993), Carol J. Clover (1992) and Linda Williams (1984, 1991), most notably – the theory itself rigidly defines horror as a fantasy genre, employed as a vehicle to radically reinterpret Freud's accounts of masochistic fantasy, gendered subjectivity and misrecognition (see Cowie 1984). Although such feminist film theory often brings male spectatorship to the forefront, this radical reinterpretation brings into question the cinematographic apparatus' ability to fix spectators in the oppressive structures of sexual difference, liberating the 'masochistic' female spectator and the 'sadistic' male spectator in its reversal: the cinematographic apparatus invites the gendered spectator to fantasise and identify with multiple, shifting subject positions.

Just as Clover's thesis has been canonised within horror studies, the psychoanalytic specificity of her contribution to feminist film studies has been written out of discourse, bringing into question Clover's emphasis on sadomasochistic male spectatorship. This has influenced a body of criticism of Clover's work by focusing on female spectatorship, dismissing feminist film studies' psychoanalytic tradition, in order to negotiate the feminist potentialities of characterisation and identification (see Paszkiewicz and Rusnak 2020). This, however, has been at the cost of overestimating the feminism of the teen slasher, exemplified by this chapter's consideration of Blumhouse's *Halloween* (Green, 2018). While *Halloween* appears to lack a reflexive edge, this chapter examines the film's conscious appropriation of Clover's theoretical framework, suturing a masculinised subject position into the filmic body. Yet, in its appropriation of Clover's identificatory framework, *Halloween* appears misguided by the bisexual oscillation between male and female characters that defines the sado*masochism* of Clover's teen slasher film. This chapter, accordingly, argues that *Halloween* actively embodies a toxic nostalgia for the essentialist sadism of the early teen slasher, implicating the feminist film theory that proceeded to define the subgenre by digressing from the masochistic subject positions detailed by Clover. Toxic nostalgia, in this sense, describes *Halloween*'s desire to become the object of false memory by attempting to (re)masculinise the teen slasher film and its violence in a way that early critical discourse denounces. By attempting to (re)masculinise the teen slasher and its violence, *Halloween* denounces the masochism of teen slasher and, thus, its ability to be gendered as a feminine cultural product.

According to Clover, straight teenage boys are 'the slasher film's implied audience, the object of its address' (1992: 23). Within this narrative, they are not offered a sustainable point of male identification. Their most sustainable point of identification, instead, in accordance with the narrative's trajectory, comes in the Final Girl. On the premise that the Final Girl comes out triumphant, critics frequently interpret Clover's theorisation as 'supposedly progressive' (Williams 2015: 198). Klaus Rieser exemplifies this, stating that contrary to Clover's progressive claims, 'the slasher film nonetheless remains deeply implicated in patriarchal ideology' (Rieser 2001: 375). Yet Clover says it herself: 'To applaud the Final Girl as a feminist development [...] is, in light of her figurative meaning, a particularly grotesque expression of wishful thinking' (1992: 53). In accordance with the narrative's trajectory, Clover merely theorises that the Final Girl is the straight teenager's *final* point of identification. As she attempts to demonstrate, identification in the slasher film is not sustainable – 'neither fixed nor entirely passive' (Williams 1991: 8) – signifying that those critics who have engaged with the Final Girl have not acknowledged the intricate identificatory trajectory that Clover sets out.

By Clover's account, for the majority of the slasher film, the killer provides an identificatory model for male audiences, albeit an unsustainable one. It is precisely because of this that the killer remains mostly 'unseen or barely glimpsed'. Indeed, identification is implicated once the killer's physicality is finally detailed, as male audiences are unable to 'elicit immediate or conscious empathy' (Clover 1992: 44). The killer's presence is instead signified in a series of 'point of view' shots, situating male audiences in the eye of the beholder. Should this paralleling of characteristic and identificatory maleness not be clearer, Clover equates the killer's phallic weaponry to the penis, constituting 'personal extensions of the body' (1992: 32). As in the classical Hollywood cinema that Laura Mulvey interrogates, the killer 'articulates the look and creates the action', providing 'a main controlling figure with whom the spectator can identify' (Mulvey 1975: 12–13).

As Clover's straight audiences share an identificatory gaze with the killer, it is clear as to why he claims his male victims in a fashion that 'is nearly always swift', either from a distance, in dim light or off-screen without a glimpse (1992: 35). If, in the slasher film, 'violence and sex are not concomitants but alternatives' (Clover 1992: 29), audiences are not offered the gratuitous spectacle of male death because 'the male figure cannot bear the burden of sexual objectification' (Mulvey 1975: 12). Read in allegorical terms, as a man penetrates another with his weapon, male audiences are spared the homoerotic spectacle of penetrative gay sex. Yet when the spectacle of male penetration is shown, which is more often than Clover is prepared to acknowledge, critics often subvert this logic of homoeroticism to one that is heteronormative. Here, the spectacle of male penetration is read as a feminisation of the body – a symbolic castration that leaves the male body resembling woman's bleeding wound (see Creed 1993).

If the spectacle of male death is informed by misogynistic logic, this logic is made overt when audiences witness the spectacle of female death, said to literalise woman's symbolic meaning. Long before her death, however, Mulvey identifies that woman remains 'subjected to her image as bearer of the bleeding wound' by arousing castration anxiety in male audiences (Mulvey 1975: 7). First, then, male audiences must adopt a fetishistic gaze to objectify woman and disarm the threat of castration. This is precisely why Clover recognises the female victim as 'first and foremost a sexual transgressor' (1992: 33). Indeed, her primary function in coital scenes is to pose nude and arouse male youth, inviting male audiences to deny her sexual transgression through objectification. Once objectified, male audiences can then safely gaze upon her with a sadistic voyeurism, 'asserting control and subjecting the guilty person through punishment' (Mulvey 1975: 14). Far from being a merciful subgenre, the female victim is slashed to death by the killer – and, by extension, the identifying male spectator – who imposes the image of the bleeding wound upon her, mapping onto her body the very symbolism she tries to transgress.

Here, Clover is keen to assert that the female victim is punished through a misogynistic lens, 'filmed at closer range, in more graphic detail, and at greater length' (1992: 35). While she acknowledges the empathetic possibilities of this misogynistic lens, positing that death needs to be seen in order to be felt, her insistence on a heteronormative viewpoint implicates any positive reading of this: 'It may be through the female body that the body of the audience is sensationalised, but the sensation is an entirely male affair', making the violation of the body 'imaginable, for males, only in nightmare' (Clover 1992: 52–3). Using the female body to experience the 'nightmare' of penetration, male audiences are invited to 'experience forbidden desires and disavow them on the grounds that the visible actor is, after all, a girl' (Clover 1992: 18). The female victim serves as a 'heterosexual deflection', averting a homoerotic scenario through gender displacement as male audiences are made penetrable only in their sensationalised mimicking of the female body (Clover 1992: 52). The sadism that underlies identification with the killer, then, is theorised to unsustainably coincide with a masochistic identificatory process with his female victims, conceptualising a fluid sadomasochistic framework.

Situating Clover's fluid identificatory framework in Blumhouse's *Halloween*, the film actively disrupts this oscillation between sadistic and masochistic subject positions, disavowing the masochistic aesthetic that she theorises. *Halloween* specifically achieves this through its aversion of the 'I-camera' that John Carpenter's *Halloween* (1978) so famously popularised. According to Clover, the I-camera is characteristic of early teen slasher's low production values, in which 'one cannot help wondering how and why critics have taken it so seriously' (Clover 1992: 191). Here, the I-camera's artifice makes itself known through a dizzying unsteadiness, creating a failed gaze 'that more or less successfully passes itself off as *the* gaze' (Clover 1992: 211, emphasis added). Kaja Silverman spells out what this gaze fundamentally indicates, observing how 'the fascination of the sadistic point of view is merely that it provides the best vantage point from which to watch the masochistic story unfold' (Silverman 1980: 5).

Blumhouse's *Halloween* evidences a certain sophistication in its conscious disavowal of the I-camera, all too knowing that it is indicative of a failed gaze. Clover bespeaks her reservations over Hollywood's mainstream appropriation of the low-budget early teen slasher, and *Halloween*'s sophistication, with great precision, illustrates why (see Clover 1992: 231–6). If Carpenter's *Halloween* successfully feigns the gaze to cover over its investment in masochism, Blumhouse's *Halloween* successfully turns a feigned gaze into *the* gaze, demonstrating a mastery of the narrative and announcing its sadistic inclination. While it might seem progressive that male and female victims are presented in equal balance, *Halloween*'s disavowal of the masochistic aesthetic – a failed gaze – makes its investment in sadistic violence inherently clear. As *Halloween* continues to direct violence against women, both its aesthetic and ideological function shift, rendering the contemporary teen slasher a less redemptive source of critical enquiry for feminism.

Among an array of female victims, Clover recognises the Final Girl as exceptional, 'the distressed female most likely to linger in memory' (Clover 1992: 35). Once again, the spectatorial body is sensationalised through the female victim, only here, without her subsequent death, as scenes of agonising torture register the Final Girl as a masochistic identificatory model. Here, empathy allows male audiences to feel emasculating expressions of emotion. However, because this is 'registered as a "feminine" experience', the Final Girl's gender invites male audiences to deny the phenomenon as emasculating (Clover 1992: 61). Spectating male bodies are invited to consider themselves emotionally depleted only in their sensationalised mimicking of the female body, for 'crying, cowering, screaming, fainting, trembling, begging for mercy belong to the female' (Clover 1992: 51). With this, Clover recognises the Final Girl and the female victim as a collective – their 'femaleness' equally serves as 'the artifact of heterosexual deflection' – suggesting a critical double standard when, respectively, one is glorified and the other tainted (Clover 1992: 52).

Indirectly, Clover herself has questioned this double standard, aiming to rectify by addressing it. Writing in retrospect, she observes how 'in wider discourse, the sketch version more or less hijacked not only the character of the Final Girl but the chapter in which she figures' (Clover 2015: x). Clover's so-called 'sketch version' of the Final Girl might very well constitute this oft-cited excerpt:

> The Final Girl is boyish, in a word. Just as the killer is not fully masculine, she is not fully feminine – not, in any case, feminine in the ways of her friends. Her smartness, gravity, competence in mechanical and other practical matters, and sexual reluctance set her apart from the other girls and ally her, ironically, with the very boys she fears or rejects, not to speak of the killer himself. Lest we miss the point, it is spelled out in her name: Stevie, Marti, Terry, Laurie, Stretch, Will, Joey, Max. (Clover 1992: 40)

With an emphasis on her smartness, gravity and competence in practical matters – let alone her sexual reluctance, which is read as a symptom of these qualities – critics regard Clover's sketch of the Final Girl with a feminist sensibility, dismissing the male audiences' supposed identification with the killer, not to speak of the victims before her. In this light, the Final Girl is female, offering an emancipatory point of identification for female audiences, but also masculinised, offering a non-emasculating point of identification for male audiences. What is not taken into account, then, is how Clover's sentiments are setting up her main argument about the Final Girl, hence defining her in relation to what the other girls are not.

Just as the Final Girl is exempt from death, she is the one to look at the killer, bringing him into the audience's vision. Where male audiences once saw from his perspective, here they adopt the Final Girl's point of view, bearing witness to the killer's grotesque look. With this look, the killer is dismissed as an identificatory model, unable to elicit immediate or conscious empathy. It is here, then, that male audiences are said to switch their identificatory core, transcending the killer in favour of the Final Girl. Where audiences once identified with her 'feminine' impulses, it is here that 'she stops screaming, faces the killer, and reaches for the knife', phallicised by the weaponry once held by the killer (Clover 1992: 48). At the moment of her phallicism, the Final Girl becomes the final core identificatory model for male audiences. If, before, the 'feminisation' of male audiences died along with the victim – resuming the killer's sadistic gaze, shifting back and forth – here, the 'feminisation' of male audiences dies at the moment of the Final Girl's 'masculinisation', reforming their position as gendered subjects in heteropatriarchal relations. Like Mulvey's male protagonist, Clover's Final Girl is as 'a male surrogate' – 'female not despite the maleness of the audience, but precisely because of it. The discourse is wholly masculine', inviting the male spectator to 'use her as a vehicle for his own sadomasochistic fantasies' (Clover 1992: 53).

Blumhouse's *Halloween* makes its conscious engagement with Carol J. Clover known when Allyson (Andi Matichak) and her boyfriend, Cameron (Dylan Arnold), announce that they are dressing up as Bonnie and Clyde for Halloween. As the wholly predictable nuance of their costume sees Cameron dressed as Bonnie and Allyson dressed as Clyde, it is no coincidence that Allyson enters immediate danger only after the fact of her trans-sex costume change. Where Clover describes the Final Girl as a vehicle for the male spectator's sadomasochistic fantasies, *Halloween* only seems engaged in the masculine sadism of Allyson's transformation, never leaning into an aesthetic of so-called 'feminine masochism' (Clover 1992: 215). Indeed, *Halloween* rehearses an identificatory trajectory that appropriates the fluidity of Clover's sadomasochistic framework, like so many other teen slasher films, in favour of a linear identificatory shift between the killer and the Final Girl, paralleled along the lines of masculine sadism. This is precisely why *Halloween* ends with Allyson holding the phallus, bloodied with the remnants of sadistic violence.

Part II

Sexuality and Gender

Cynthia Jones

Cinderella, Kenneth Branagh (2015)

'Toxic' was the Oxford Word of the Year for 2018, citing it as the most used descriptor for current topics in 2018 – 'used in array of contexts, both in its literal and more metaphorical senses' (Oxford Languages n.d.). Three years later, the term 'toxic' continues to nuance subjects such as workplace culture, relationships, masculinity, femininity and, in this particular case, *toxic* fairy tales.

The term 'toxic' comes from the Greek *toxikòn phármakon*, meaning 'bow poison' or 'poison used on arrows'; dropping the *phármakon* in late Latin, the term became *toxicus*. The metonymic process from *toxikòn phármakon* to *toxicus* emphasises the symbolic aggressivity and action of the arrow rather than the poisonous substance in which it was dipped. The adjectival form, toxic, and the noun, toxin, refer to something – a substance or a chemical – that is harmful to the health of a living being, either by causing death or severe debilitation. Within the scientific community, one often differentiates poison from toxin by specifying that a toxin is a poisonous substance that is produced in a living organism (Science Learning Hub n.d.). Although a substance may be toxic, whether or not it causes death depends on the amount of toxins present. Therefore, toxicity can be read as more of a spectrum: the more toxins present, the greater the degree of toxicity and its harmful effects. By the same token, if we understand toxic as an adverse product produced by/within a living body, then it is possible to extend the meaning of this term to reference cultural products and/or practices formed within the body of a society that are harmful to its community. For this reason, 'toxic fairy tales' will be defined as the perpetuation of systems, structures and ideals that are indeed harmful to the health of the society that created them.

The importance of fairy tales on child development, and its influence on culture and societal constructions have been noted by a multitude of scholars

(Bruno Bettelheim, Alan Dundes, Marina Warner, Maria Tatar, Jack Zipes, etc.). Therefore, it is not surprising that there is a proliferation of fairy-tale adaptations within modern culture; these narratives are deeply ingrained within the cultural psyche and continue to play a role in affirming or reaffirming cultural values. The unique pervasiveness of the fairy tale also serves as a launch pad for fractured fairy tale or revised fairy tale that offer new societal values. While there has been much study devoted to fairy tale with a twist, the present study is concerned with the continued presence of traditional fairy-tale narratives and their impact on contemporary society. Walter Benjamin notes the instructional role of the fairy tale, 'which to this day is the first tutor of children because it was the first tutor of mankind. [...] Whenever good counsel was at a premium, the fairy tale had it, and where the need was greatest, its aid was nearest' (Benjamin [1936] 2006: 373–4). Furthermore, Linda T. Parsons observes the traces of these formative narratives within mass media culture, attesting that 'we are *surrounded* be the vestiges of fairy tales from the marketing of Disney products to the perpetuation of romance ideology, the binary positioning of women and men, and women's and girls' obsession to manifest socially defined beauty' (2004: 135). Fairy tales, although not exclusively responsible, play a large part in solidifying and disseminating cultural norms and ideals. The question that arises is what if these narratives could be considered *toxic*, in the sense that they preserve structures that promote harmful behaviour and/ or negatively affect the mental and social health of members within a society? How can we identify and understand this toxicity? And where do we see the 'vestiges' of these toxic tropes in modern representations of fairy tales?

In order to narrow the scope and examine more closely toxicity in fairy tales and its effect on society, this study will concentrate on one narrative in particular: Cinderella. Considering that there are over 700 documented versions of this tale ranging across the globe, it is one of the most well known fairy-tale narratives – and universal, in the sense that this fairy-tale trope spans across many different cultures (Parsons 2004: 143). Furthermore, Bruno Bettelheim, in his foundational work *The Uses of Enchantment: The Meaning and Importance of Fairy Tales* (1975), remarks that not only was Cinderella a prominent fairy tale, it is 'probably also the best-liked'.[1] While Bettelheim's

---

1   In a study entitled 'The Pervasiveness and Persistence of the Feminine Beauty Ideal in Children's Fairy Tales', the authors Lori Baker-Sperry and Liz Grauerholz found that

approach to the fairy tale is steeped in psychoanalysis, this study will draw upon cultural and sociological theories to discuss its toxic nature within contemporary social structures, specifically within Western culture. The corpus for this analysis will include the source text, 'Cinderella, or The Little Glass Slipper' ([1697] 1889) by Charles Perrault,[2] along with contemporary film versions that are inspired by this narrative: the 1950 animated film by Disney titled *Cinderella* and the 2015 live-action film of the same title. A close reading of Perrault's text will shed light on the toxic ideals that permeate the aforementioned contemporary versions. Then this study will discuss how these toxic notions permeate contemporary versions of the fairy tale. Lastly, this exploration of toxicity within the 'Cinderella' narrative will look at an example of how the toxic structure of women-bullying-women created within the fairy tale is represented in other contemporary films.

Charles Perrault (1628–1703) is credited as being the original author of 'Cinderella' (though many oral versions existed); he penned the work in his collection of fairy tales, *Les contes de ma mère l'oie* (1697). He used these tales to reflect, criticise and comment on courtly life under the rule of Louis XIV (King of France). There are strong themes that dictate the proper conduct of women in the court – and the many ways that these women could also be mis-led. Perrault's version of Cinderella entails the iconic pumpkin carriage with six mice for horses, six lizards for footmen, and a rat as a coachman, all of which find their way into the 1950 Disney animated film *Cinderella*. His tale unfolds as the story of a young girl 'of unparalleled goodness and sweetness of temper' (64) whose father remarried after the death of her mother. The stepmother grew jealous of the little girl and could no longer bear her

---

out of 168 Grimm's tales analysed, 'the most frequently reproduced tale is *Cinderella*, for which 332 reproductions were recorded' (Baker-Sperry and Grauerholz 2003: 720).

2   Another well-known version is 'Cinderella' by Jacob and Wilhelm Grimm (1812, revised 1819). This version is particularly interesting due to the violent corporeal punishment the sisters receive for their cruel acts towards Cinderella. In order to squeeze their foot into the slipper, each sister cuts off a part of her foot. However, they are found to have lied, and the shoe is returned to the rightful owner. At the end of the narrative, the sisters' eyes are pecked out by Cinderella's birds as penalty for their rotten behaviour. While this text is indeed iconic and nearly equally as famous as Perrault's version, the 1950 film *Cinderella* by Disney, which subsequently has become the 'new' reference source for the Cinderella narrative, is based on Perrault's text.

presence because her good qualities 'made her own daughters appear the more odious' (64). Cinderella was demoted to servant status, all the while retaining her kind (beautiful) disposition. Then, one day, the prince announces that all will be invited to his ball. Cinderella laments her sullied state, but her fairy godmother rescues her with a dress and entourage befitting of a princess. At the ball, she wins the heart of the prince through her beauty, and even extends kindness to her sisters despite their inability to recognise her. On the second day of the ball, she nearly misses the clock's warning of midnight, and in her haste, she leaves behind one of her glass slippers. The prince insists that he will marry the girl whose foot fits the glass slipper. Thus, much to everyone's surprise, when the ashen-faced Cinderella easily slips on the shoe, the fairy godmother restores her rightful rank and adorns her in a beautiful gown. Rather than punish her sisters, Cinderella opts to invite them to the palace and matches them with lords of the court.

At the end of each tale, Perrault would highlight the lesson to be learned, the moral, through a little poem – in the event that the narrative itself was not clear enough. In fact, at the end of 'Cinderella', he offers two morals, one highlighting the feminine ideal and the other coyly pointing out the divine role in one's social station. In the first lesson, he states:

> Beauty in a woman is a rare treasure that will always be admired. Graciousness, however, is priceless and of even greater value. This is what Cinderella's godmother gave to her when she taught her to behave like a queen. Young women, in the winning of a heart, graciousness is more important than a beautiful hairdo. It is a true gift of the fairies. Without it nothing is possible; with it, one can do anything. (71)

At first glance, Perrault implies that gentility and politeness are greater qualities than superficial beauty. However, Cinderella's beauty is tied to her graciousness (which is bestowed upon her by the divine – a fairy godmother); the two are inextricably linked, rendering beauty into an ethical ideal. Heather Widdows outlines the ways in which beauty is linked to goodness and, conversely, ugliness with evil. Observing that 'for Plato […] it is the love of beauty that sets us on the moral path towards goodness and moral virtue', she highlights the equation that 'the outside must match the inside: the beast must become a beautiful prince […]; the evil stepmother must be punished […] for trying to compete with, or steal beauty from, the young' (Widdows

2018: 17). Therefore, for Perrault, the superficiality of the right hairdo and clothes cannot compete with the true ethical ideal of graciousness, which in this case can only be awarded through divine intervention. This emphasis on graciousness as a 'true gift of the fairies' also offers Perrault's commentary on the importance and rigidity of social class and birth rank, which is again echoed in the second moral:[3]

> Without doubt it is a great advantage to have intelligence, courage, good breeding, and common sense. These, and similar talents come only from heaven, and it is good to have them. However, even these may fail to bring you success, without the blessing of a godfather or a godmother. (71)

Here, Perrault, in a tongue-in-cheek manner, reminds his courtly audience that birth and rank can only get one so far without the favour of someone else above them. In this case, it is possible that he is referencing Louis XIV, who is appointed through divine right. Therefore, even the highest-ranking noble will not succeed without the esteem of the king. Furthermore, as it pertains to women, only submissiveness and the complete lack of agency will receive the ultimate reward: marriage to the prince.

Parsons, in her analysis of Perrault's 'Cinderella', points out the heroine's missing voice: 'messages about women and submissiveness, dependence, and beauty are embedded in this version of the tale' (144). Rather than exert any autonomy over her situation, Cinderella is the passive heroine: the story happens *to* her. She meekly accepts the workload thrust upon her, rather than bringing it up to her father – who is still alive. When her sisters leave for the ball, she only follows them with her eyes, making no attempt of her own to attend

---

3   In Laura Diaz de Arce's master's thesis, entitled *Diamonds and Ash: Class and Social Mobility in Seventeenth Century Cinderella* (2016), she analyses the common trope that upward social mobility is prohibited and that the elite must maintain and/or regain their status. Moreover, she argues that the seventeenth-century Cinderella is not a story of social mobility through marriage, but rather a narrative of being reinstated or regaining one's nobility – which can only come from the divine (one is born noble). While Diaz de Arce's study focuses solely on the seventeenth century, Jane Yolen had also previously noted the noble birth of Cinderella in 'America's Cinderella' (1988), stating that 'Cinderella is *not* a story of rags to riches, but rather riches recovered; *not* poor girl into princess but rather rich girl (or princess) rescued from improper or wicked enslavement' (306).

the ball. 'This Cinderella cannot speak for herself, she cannot act on her own behalf, and she cannot function autonomously: yet she is rewarded' (Parsons 2004: 144). It is this Cinderella that inspired Disney's 1950 animated version.

Drawing largely from Perrault's narrative, Disney revamped and reshaped Cinderella to reflect – and further institutionalise – male-dominated ideals of feminine beauty. Cinderella's noble status is downplayed in order to express favoured American qualities of social mobility through hard work and proper conduct. The role and agency of the stepmother is increased, as the father is erased from the narrative. However, Cinderella herself remains mild, meek, gracious, and above-all, submissive. It is this version of Cinderella that will become the 'new' traditional tale. Kodi Maier, in her study 'Princess Brides and Dream Weddings: Investigating the Gendered Narrative of Disney's Fairy Tale Weddings', maintains that 'when Disney translates a fairy tale from more "traditional" or "original" versions [...] Disney's version of that fairy tale is then canonised within the American psyche' (2019: 183). It is this version that will shape and condition young viewers.

As previously mentioned through Bruno Bettelheim, the fairy tale plays an important role in the development of the young child. However, these tales become toxic when they promote antiquated ideals that further oppress women. 'Children's fairy tales, which emphasize such things as women's passivity and beauty, are indeed gendered scripts and serve to legitimize and support the dominant gender system' (Baker-Sperry and Grauerholz 2003: 711). Disney's Cinderella maintains all of the passivity found in Perrault's heroine. When her father dies, she is shuffled up to the attic, where she happily remains – befriending the mice and birds who eventually make her a gown so that she may attend the ball. Furthermore, she meekly stands by as her sisters tear off parts of her gown, leaving it tattered and torn. Her fairy godmother appears and magically solves Cinderella's problems, without any intervention on her own account. She is meek, submissive and beautiful and, thus, without any of her own agency, rewarded the prince.

In addition to cementing the passive female ideal into Western society's psyche, this also brings up a toxic paradox of the feminine beauty ideal that Baker-Sperry and Grauerholz identify as 'those women who seek to gain power through their attractiveness are often those who are most dependent on men's resources' (2003: 712). In this instance, resources are rare; there is only one

Cinderella, Kenneth Branagh (2015)

Figure 18. Cinderella passively stands by as her sisters strip her of her ball gown and necklace.
Source: *Cinderella*; directed by Wilfred Jackson, Hamilton Luske and Clyde Geronimi (Disney, 1950).

prince, and, therefore, the women turn on each other as they vie for sparse resources. In an article entitled 'Why do Women Bully Each Other at Work?', Olga Khazan refers to psychologist Joyce Benenson's theories about female-to-female aggression, noting 'that women undermine one another because they have always had to compete for mates and for resources' (Khazan 2017). While these theories are considered quite controversial within the academic community, they do offer some insight about the scarcity of resources among women in a male-dominated system.

In the more recent Disney live-action film adaptation, *Cinderella* (2015), directed by Kenneth Branagh, cruelty among the sisters plays an even more prominent role in the depiction of the female characters. The two sisters (Holliday Grainger and Sophie McShera) at times gang up on Ella (Lily James) and in other instances turn on each other in the fight for social mobility and scarce resources. The narrator states that these sisters 'could be every bit as ugly within as they were fair without'. This is of course in contrast to Ella, who still upholds the feminine ideal of graciousness and beauty. By keeping her promise to her dying mother, she has vowed to 'have courage, and be kind'. Although for a majority of the film, 'have courage' seems to imply having the bravery to accept the lot that has been handed to her rather than the daring to defy the 'Queen Bee', her stepmother (Cate Blanchette).

In the scene, shown also in the animated version, where Cinderella floats down the grand staircase outfitted in her mother's old dress (see Figure 19), the stepmother's attack on Ella is even more frightening. Just moments before, she asserts that 'no one in the kingdom will outshine her daughters'; then she catches a glimpse of the fair Cinderella. This mother of two transitions into full attack mode and gangs up on the demure girl, flanked by her two daughters close behind. Threatened by the very presence of the feminine ideal, the stepmother (and her daughters) strive to maintain their agency (see Figure 20). Unable to bear the presence of Cinderella in anything but rags, they tear her dress apart. Her stepmother defends her actions, exclaiming 'I will not have anyone associate my daughters with you. It will ruin their prospects to be seen arriving with a ragged servant girl, because that is what you are and that is what you will always be' (Disney 2015).

This strife for agency is often seen in real-life situations like school and workplace women-bullying-women. In a study on women-bullying-women, researchers found that the

> *oppressed group* behavior can result in horizontal violence, aggressive behavior by oppressed group members towards others of the same group. As few women rise in masculine

Figure 19. The Queen Bee defends her agency.
Source: *Cinderella*; directed by Kenneth Branagh (Disney 2015).

Cinderella, Kenneth Branagh (2015)

Figure 20. The Queen Bee flanked by her subordinates.
Source: *Mean Girls*; directed by Mark Waters (Paramount Pictures 2004).

hierarchies, they will [...] 'almost always during the initial stages of the struggle [...] lend themselves to become oppressors or "sub-oppressors"'. (Lutgen-Sandvik et al. 2012: 65, citing Friere)

Essentially, all three sisters belong to the same *oppressed group*, which necessitates the need to reduce competition. This toxic type of female aggression can also be seen in the 2004 hit film *Mean Girls*. While stretching the Cinderella trope, this film highlights the ever-present male-dominated feminine ideal that is upheld by a clique called the 'plastics'. In order for the new girl, Cady (Lindsay Lohan), to gain power and agency, she must engage in the same toxic behaviour as exhibited by the 'mean girls'. In this dystopic Cinderella, where the goal is to become popular and get the boy, the protagonist, rather than maintain the passive and submissive 'graciousness' that would, according to Perrault, enhance her own physical beauty, competes for her own agency in a system that is already designed to pit women against each other by adhering to prescribed gender roles.

Moreover, according to the study by Lutgen-Sandvik et al., 'when women use bullying as a way of interacting with other women, they become complicit in reproducing systems that oppress women, further marginalizing themselves and other females' (2012: 70). In order to break free of this particular paradigm, 'Cinderella' will need to look past the present obstacles set up by her stepmother and stepsisters and challenge the patriarchal system that has set them out against each other in the first place.

In conclusion, through this incredibly brief exploration of the toxic fairy tale and its permeation in popular culture, this study has explored the source text ('Cinderella, or The Little Glass Slipper' [1697] 1889), that subsequently inspired the 1950 Disney animated adaptation, which further necessitated the 2015 live-action version. Through these narratives, it is possible to see the development of a toxic culture saturated by the male-dominated feminine ideal that does not allow the female protagonist any agency of her own. While there have been feminist revisions and rewritings of the Cinderella narrative, the 1950 and 2015 Disney versions are still the most widely known versions of the seventeenth-century tale. However, now that we are aware of the toxic structures that continue to influence contemporary society, an exploration of how to negate and revise the toxic ideals reinforced by this text may be in order.

Erin Giannini

Buffy the Vampire Slayer, Joss Whedon (1997–2003)

Toxic Masculinity

In 1984's *Revenge of the Nerds*, a campus comedy focused on the trials and tribulations of a group of outcasts and geeks, the 'nerds' in question go on the offensive when confronted with the fraternity jocks (the Alpha Betas) who torment them – that is, the 'revenge' suggested in the title. This revenge, however, seems primarily to be directed at the jocks' sister sorority: they install hidden cameras in their bedrooms and showers of sorority members and watch the footage constantly, later distributing naked pictures gleaned from their live feed. The film never suggests this is not justified; both the jocks' behaviour and the women's rejection of them vindicate these actions. When Alpha Beta president Stan (Ted McGinley) discovers said pictures – one of which is a close-up of his girlfriend Betty's (Julia Montgomery) vagina – he is horrified. Not for her sake, but for his: 'That's my pie!' is his only response. While Stan and the rest of the appropriately named 'Alpha' Betas are positioned as the antagonists, the behaviour of the nerds is presented as justified; they have been put down and rejected, and therefore they are entitled to whatever actions they take. As William Bradley writes: 'It's true that the nerds stand up to their bullies and empower themselves, but they are only able to do so by victimizing women whose chief crimes are snootiness and bad taste in boyfriends'[1] (Bradley 2015). This is

---

1   While it is easy to dismiss the film's blatant misogyny as a product of the times, *Real Genius* (Coolidge, 1985), released a year later, also features nerds/geeks as their main characters who use their intelligence for revenge; however, in this instance, the nerds are working against the military-industrial complex they realise is using their skills for nefarious ends, rather than jocks or women who reject them. As Emmet Asher-Perrin

the same logic that powers the 'incel' (involuntary celibacy) movement, embodied by Elliot Rodger, who followed up his manifesto on women's 'snootiness' and 'bad taste in boyfriends' with a deadly killing spree.

Because of the common representation of 'nerds' or 'geeks' as being bullied, the toxic elements of their behaviour are too often overlooked. Anastasia Salter and Bridgett Blodgett's *Toxic Geek Masculinity in Media* remains one of the only full-length studies of a culture that includes Gamergate, fandom trolling (e.g. a segment of *Star Wars* fans hounding Kelly Marie Tran off social media; Zimmerman 2018) and the aforementioned incel movement. As Eleanor Lockhart writes: 'The #GamerGate movement combines nerd persecution and nerd supremacy', in which they position themselves as '[n]ot just morally righteous victims or genius rulers of the world in waiting' but 'empowered to defend themselves as well as retaliate against those who threaten their interests' (2015: 139). Jonathan McIntosh, who created the 'Buffy vs Edward' mash-up to expose the *Twilight* franchise's toxic elements (McIntosh 2009), also created two separate long-form videos about *The Big Bang Theory* for his Pop Culture Detective YouTube channel, addressing both its 'complicity of geek masculinity' (McIntosh 2017b) and the 'adorkable misogyny' (McIntosh 2017a) it embodied. That is, the 'typical gatekeeper learned incorrect and toxic belief systems that instilled in them a fragile victimhood for being a nerd' (Jardel 2017) and thus justified in their actions towards others, including 'harassing, entitled, sexist behavior' (McIntosh 2017a). C. J. Pascoe suggests that fan culture offers camaraderie to those who embody geek or 'cerebral' masculinity, yet because they fail to conform to traditional masculine definitions, they 'transfer their failure onto people deemed culturally inferior to themselves' and feel threatened by the 'increasing equality and visibility for women and queer people' in what they had considered their safe (or sacred) spaces (Tourjée 2016).

Thus, in this essay I will examine one of the earliest texts to flag up the toxic nature of masculine geek culture: *Buffy the Vampire Slayer*. Airing in 2001–02, the sixth season of the series positioned its antagonists not as the

---

suggests, the film is 'not about proving their superiority over another group, but instead about taking back control over what they created' and portrays women as 'real, unique individuals with different preferences' rather than merely adjuncts to the male characters (Asher-Perrin 2015).

usual vampires or demons bent on either world domination or taking down Buffy (Sarah Michelle Gellar) as slayer, but as a group of intelligent young people who had experienced significant bullying as children and teens: three young men already known to Buffy and one she considered to be her best friend. For all four, their combined sense of injustice and entitlement offered an early mirror – and warning – of the (now realised) potential for toxicity within these communities.

'You Bunch of Little Boys, Playing at Being Men!' The Trio

Introduced in the fourth episode of the sixth season, the Trio,[2] comprised of Warren Meers (Adam Busch), Jonathan Levinson (Danny Strong) and Andrew Wells (Tom Lenk), initially conform to the stereotypical 'geek' seen in popular media. They live and plot in Warren's mom's basement, decorated with assorted action figures, computers and a large-screen TV. Both Warren and Jonathan were already known to both the audience and Buffy. Warren's first appearance occurs in the previous season: he builds a robot girlfriend that goes rogue and searches for him after he callously abandons her ('I Was Made to Love You', Season 5, Episode 15). Jonathan appears in numerous episodes of the previous seasons – first as a potential victim ('Inca Mummy Girl', Season 2, Episode 4) or a punchline ('The Wish', Season 3, Episode 9), then spotlighted in two episodes from the third and fourth seasons. In 'Earshot' (Season 3, Episode 18), Buffy discovers him in the school attic with a gun and tries to convince him that he is not alone in his pain: 'The beautiful ones, the popular ones, the guys that pick on you. ... If you could hear what they were

2   It should be noted that another character, Spike (James Marsters), turned into a vampire in Victorian England, would have easily fitted into the 'geek' stereotype when he was the human William Pratt. He was mercilessly teased for his bad poetry, and the woman he wrote it for, Cecily (Kali Rocha), rejected him harshly ('Fool for Love', Season 5, Episode 7). As a human, however, he merely destroyed his work, rather than attacking Cecily. While Spike displays toxic behaviour throughout the series, space does not allow for a deeper analysis.

feeling. The loneliness, the confusion. ... It's deafening.' In season four, he attempts to take a shortcut to feeling better about himself by casting a spell that makes him a paragon and reduces everyone else to fans and supporters ('Superstar', Season 4, Episode 17). Buffy again attempts to get through to him: 'you can't keep trying to make everything work out with some big gesture' ('Superstar').

Unfortunately, neither of these moments penetrate for long. What Warren, Jonathan and Andrew share, besides a sense of victimisation, is a disinclination to making an effort to improve their social or financial circumstances. Rather than translating their considerable intelligence in programming and engineering into either study or work, they opt to invent objects such as the freeze ray (to steal a diamond; 'Smashed', Season 6, Episode 9) or summon demons (as distraction while they rob a bank to fund their endeavours; 'Flooded', Season 6, Episode 4). Narratively and visually, there is a cartoon aspect to their supposed villainy, recalling 1960s-era *Batman* episodes (or perhaps *Scooby-Doo*) rather than the demons and hell gods Buffy faced in previous seasons; when first introduced, they even attempt 'evil laughs' ('Flooded'). This is underscored when Buffy and her friends attempt to research what are, to them, random occurrences: a frozen security guard, thefts and targeted attacks on Buffy. As her friend Anya (Emma Caulfield) puts it, 'we're not going to find this thing because it does not exist. There's no such thing as a frost monster that eats diamonds' ('Smashed').

These early escapades are easily dismissed as silly, and yet there is a persistent dark undercurrent to the Trio's behaviour, particularly that of Warren. Having identified Buffy as the primary person blocking the Trio's ability to 'take over Sunnydale', Warren not only points a demon in her direction ('Flooded') but also shows a callous disregard for the potentially fatal consequences of their actions towards her (a series of 'tests' that put her in danger ['Life Serial', Season 6, Episode 5] or hitting her with an invisibility ray that will eventually kill her ['Gone', Season 6, Episode 11]). It is with 'Dead Things' (Season 6, Episode 13), however, that Warren becomes the villain he aspires to be, with Andrew and Jonathan complicit. In this episode, having developed the 'cerebral dampener', a device to hypnotise people, Warren immediately puts it to use on his ex-girlfriend Katrina (Amelinda Embry). Drawing a parallel to Rohypnol – colloquially known as 'roofies' or the 'date rape drug' – the dampener takes away Katrina's ability to refuse Warren. Saying he is willing to 'share' her once he is done, Warren takes her to his bedroom and orders her to her knees, only for the effects to wear off. When she rightly accuses him of attempted rape, he kills her, then attempts to frame Buffy for the crime.

That this particular crime occurs between formerly intimate partners is significant. As Buffy's friend Willow (Alyson Hannigan) says to him later: 'You never felt you had the power with her. Not until you killed her. ... You get off on it' ('Villains', Season 6, Episode 20). While there is less of the conventional 'gatekeeping' with the Trio – they are less concerned about women encroaching on their interests or fandom than being unable to deal with women at all – they nonetheless share the toxic features of the bullied nerds in *Revenge*: for them, women are objects and prizes rather than individuals. The consequence is 'a frightening look into the entitled, misogynistic rhetoric that rose to the surface during the Gamergate culture wars of 2014 and has seemingly infiltrated everything since' (Robinson 2017). This entitlement culminates in Warren's attempted shooting of Buffy (in her own backyard) near the end of the season, shouting 'You think you can just do that to me?' before firing another shot that hits an upstairs window and kills Willow's girlfriend, Tara Maclay (Amber Benson; 'Seeing Red', Season 6, Episode 19). That he views his behaviour as justified merely because Buffy prevented him from doing what he wanted (which was illegal) further underscores Warren's combined sense of injustice and entitlement that makes him one of the series' most significant antagonists.

The Fine Line Between Justice and Vengeance: Willow

Viewers' first introduction to Willow, in the pilot episode ('Welcome to the Hellmouth', Season 1, Episode 1), sees her being mocked by high school queen bee Cordelia (Charisma Carpenter), a scene that suggests a long pattern of similar behaviour towards the intelligent, shy young woman, later confirmed to have happened throughout junior high and high school ('Two to Go', Season 6, Episode 21). Because Willow represents one of the main characters throughout *Buffy*'s seven seasons, it is easier to sympathise with actions she carries out that, particularly in the sixth season, run surprisingly parallel to Warren's. However, having Willow exhibit behaviour similar to Warren's suggests that the toxicity of certain aspects of geek culture transcends gender, insofar as it can be appropriated by either men or women, although the way that it plays out in the series has Willow taking on masculine linguistic signifiers in her quest for vengeance (e.g. 'I'm just getting a wood for the violence' or referring to herself as 'side man'; 'Two to Go'). Beyond her final, dark turn after Tara's death, in which she (literally) flays Warren alive and then targets Jonathan and Andrew, Willow engages in several questionable behaviours, including using magic to control people's behaviour ('Smashed') and casting a spell that makes Tara 'forget' they had a fight ('All the Way', Season 6, Episode 6). Unlike the Trio, whose interpersonal dynamics are self-reinforcing of their own worst instincts, Willow is continually called to account. Tara breaks up with her after discovering the memory spell, telling her directly that her actions constituted a violation ('Tabula Rasa', Season 6, Episode 8), and her friends make numerous attempts to help her, even after she crosses numerous ethical and legal lines.

The other element of Willow's character that recalls Warren is that in her quest to enact her own revenge on the remaining members of the Trio, she targets Buffy, as Warren does – that is, as an obstacle to be overcome. Like the Trio, she believes her own victimisation is enough justification to victimise others. Positioning Willow, whose character has at this point been developed over six seasons, as part of the toxic culture Warren, Jonathan and Andrew embody allows *Buffy* to suggest the important elements leading to such behaviours – lack of accountability, self-negation ('loser' is how Willow describes herself) and the absence of a healthy, supportive, diverse community – are enormously challenging to overcome.

Conclusion

On 10 February 2021, *Buffy* and *Angel* actress Charisma Carpenter confirmed what had been hinted about her departure from *Angel*'s fourth season; it was caused by a pattern of abusive and toxic behaviour on the part of *Buffy* creator

Joss Whedon, a self-proclaimed feminist who has been lauded by fans as a geek god.³ Carpenter – who came forward out of support for Ray Fisher's earlier accusations regarding Whedon's behaviour on the *Justice League* set (Vary 2020) – detailed not only the disparaging remarks Whedon directed at her, but also more egregious actions, such as demanding she chose between staying on the show or continuing her pregnancy (Vary 2021). Later details by both actors and writers on Whedon's series suggested a mix of cutting remarks, gatekeeping and favouritism predominated within his late 1990s/early 2000s series; *Firefly* writer Jose Molina indicated that '[m]aking female writers cry' during a notes session was fun for Whedon (Vary and Wagmeister 2021).

Given that environment, it is perhaps not surprising that Marti Noxon, who took over showrunner duties for *Buffy*'s sixth season, created villains who embodied toxic geek stereotypes. Writing on the twentieth anniversary of *Buffy*'s debut, Joanna Robinson suggests that the sixth season, reviled by many when it originally aired, was perhaps the timeliest of the series, with its focus on 'female anger, sexual aggression, self-destruction, and frustrated masculinity' (Robinson 2017). While it is easy to see the misogyny in portrayals of more conventional aggressive behaviour (fighting, physical abuse), situating these same views within geek culture, which is often embodied by men who appear less 'masculine', suggests it is a defect in thinking, a product of social isolation and more culturally widespread than is acknowledged, even within a series so prescient in elucidating its dangers and created by one who embodied them.

3   Indeed, Amy Pascale's 2014 biography of Whedon is actually titled *Joss Whedon: Geek King of the Universe*.

Paula Ashe

Pussyhat Movement (2017–Present)

Toxic feminism is an approach to feminism that is exclusive, reactionary and significantly shaped by racism, white supremacy and white privilege. The phrase itself is a contemporary one, most often described in the United States by its more confrontational characterisation as white or 'mainstream' feminism. 'White feminism' is a somewhat pejorative (yet accurate) term that addresses the collusion between patriarchy and racism. While the phrase 'toxic feminism' may be somewhat new, the ideology itself is not.

In the United States, three eras of feminist movement are roughly demarcated as the first wave of the late nineteenth and early twentieth centuries, the second wave from the sixties to the nineties and the third wave from the nineties to (perhaps arguably) the present day. Each wave clustered around specific issues born of the sociocultural and sociopolitical milieu of each era.

The first wave focused on women's suffrage, as the transition from agrarian demands to industrial expectations meant massive shifts in class composition and the division of household labour. Patriarchal norms limited citizenship rights (ownership of property, voting and political representation, marriage annulment and child custody and support) to white, landowning men, leaving women with few options. For Black women and women of Colour, the stakes were even higher and the risks more severe. Enslaved women faced the horrors of white supremacy alongside the misogyny and sexism that undergirded the chattel slavery system. For example, as Deborah K. King writes in 'Multiple Jeopardy, Multiple Consciousness: The Context of a Black Feminist Ideology', Black women's 'institutionalized exploitation as the concubines, mistresses, and sexual slaves of white males distinguished our experience from that of white females' sexual oppression because it could only have existed in relation to racist and classist forms of domination' (1988: 47).

The second wave of US feminism developed amid the sociocultural tumult of the time, coalescing around 'identity politics' and most concisely described by the popular feminist slogan, 'the personal is the political'. The civil rights movement, the women's movement, the gay rights movement and movements for liberation by various racial and ethnic groups, combined with the protests against the Vietnam War, created a zeitgeist of simultaneous cultural critique and individual introspection. As Kroløkke and Sørensen state,

> radical second-wave feminism cannot ... be discussed separately from other movements of the 1960s and 1970s. In fact, it grew out of leftist movements in postwar Western societies, among them the student protests, the anti–Vietnam War movement, the lesbian and gay movements, and, in the United States, the civil rights and Black power movements. (2006: 8)

Betty Friedan's *The Feminine Mystique*, published in 1963, exposed the pathological dissatisfaction felt by middle-class, educated, married, white women in regard to their circumscribed lives as wives and homemakers. Several years later, a group of queer Black women activists known as the Combahee River Collective crafted a revolutionary declaration outlining the multiple oppressions that marginalised queer Black women faced while also acknowledging the racism that influenced the wider (white) feminist movement. They stated that '[e]liminating racism in the white women's movement is by definition work for white women to do, but we will continue to speak to and demand accountability on this issue' (Combahee River Collective 1977). For example, the first wave of feminism in the United States was primarily concerned with the right for women to vote, but as social and political mores changed after the Civil War, white supremacy became the rhetorical linchpin around which white women's right to vote was secured.

In 1848, the Seneca Falls Convention met with the express purpose of establishing a political and social revolution to secure women's voting rights. Attendees included Elizabeth Cady Stanton, Mary M'Clintock, and Lucretia Mott, who were among the organisers, and Frederick Douglass. Initially, the suffrage movement was closely aligned with other progressive movements of the era. Quakers, abolitionists, temperance reformers, workers' rights activists, and others, all contributed to the cause. The racial solidarity between Northern white women suffragettes and anti-slavery Black abolitionists was a major catalyst for political change that almost secured both women's suffrage and the right for freed Blacks to vote.

However, as ShaRonda Knott-Dawson describes:

> After the Civil War, the Northern coalition between Black folks and White women was strong. With the win and a majority in the House and Senate, they quickly went to work on changing government policies to allow new participants. However, when the 13th, 14th and 15th Amendments were passed, White women were left behind. (Knott-Dawson 2019)

Those three amendments to the Constitution, known as the Civil War amendments, guaranteed citizenship and freedom to the formerly enslaved and extended voting rights to Black men. White women suffragettes felt like this decision (one that was entirely out of the hands of those it most intimately impacted) was a betrayal, and, as a result, they began courting Southern white women in their cause. Southern white women were deeply invested in racism and white supremacy. The antebellum era saw Southern whites stripped of their social and economic superiority, and they retaliated against the dissolution of slavery and the Confederacy by terrorising Black Americans in almost every way possible. While Blacks were legally allowed to vote, Southern states enacted laws that logistically prevented them from doing so. Poll taxes, literacy tests and other obstacles ensured political supremacy by whites in terms of voting and civic engagement.

This history of disenfranchisement by Black people on behalf of women's suffrage is one of the origins of toxic feminism. While suffragettes did not call themselves 'feminists', their methods and results were distinctly 'feminist' in that they were concerned with the agency of (white) women and the dismantling of political patriarchy. While the second wave of the feminist movement found more collaboration and coalition-building between Black and white feminists (the iconic 1971 black-and-white photograph of Gloria Steinem and Dorothy Pitman Hughes with fists upraised in the Black Power salute is a clear example of this), tensions remained between the two groups. White feminists saw racism and white supremacy as secondary issues, while Black feminists recognised the interconnected nature of both forms of marginalisation. The presence of racism and white supremacy as part of the feminist movement persisted throughout the third wave, though many efforts were made to acknowledge and reconcile this history. Third wave feminism came of age in the nineties, grappling with the fall of the Berlin Wall and end of the Cold War, the deployment of the World Wide Web as a new method of interpersonal communication and political agitation, and the globalisation wrought by late-stage capitalism. As Kroløkke and Sørensen write, 'postcolonial, third-wave feminism is concerned with establishing a new critical global perspective and creating alliances between Black, diasporic, and subaltern feminism' (2006: 19).

The third wave crested through the new millennium and saw enormous media backlashes against feminism. This dynamic was perhaps no better represented in the United States than in the polarising figure of Hillary Clinton. Initially as First Lady to Bill Clinton, then as secretary of state in the Obama Administration and finally as opposition to Donald Trump in the 2016 presidential election. Clinton emblematised the political agency women had gained over the course of fifty years, but also the fraught and feared nature of that agency. Clinton also represented the collusions between racism and US political power when, in 1996, while stumping for then President Bill Clinton's 1994 Violent Crime Control and Law Enforcement Act, she indirectly described Black youths as 'superpredators' (Graves 2016). Hillary Clinton lost the election to Donald Trump (though she did win the popular vote amidst a maelstrom of controversy and foreign election interference). Which brings us to the twenty-first century. A worldwide gathering of three million people in protest of Trump's ascendancy to the highest seat of US political power marked the first day of the Republican incumbent's single presidential term. The Women's March was held on 21 January 2017, and while it started in the US capitol of Washington DC, it was mirrored in protests held on every continent, in every major city across the globe. The protesters gathered explicitly to oppose the election of Donald Trump and his policies, which seemed poised to dismantle the numerous civil rights gains enacted by previous administrations.

As described and documented in many media outlets, the unifying symbol of the march was the pink 'pussyhat' (see Figure 21). According to the Pussyhat Project:

> Little Knittery owner Kat Coyle designed a simple and brilliant pattern that would allow people of all knitting levels to be part of the project. The name Pussyhat™ was chosen in part as a protest against vulgar comments Donald Trump made about the freedom he felt

to grab women's genitals, to de-stigmatize the word 'pussy' and transform it into one of empowerment, and to highlight the design of the hat's 'pussycat ears'. Leveraging social media and the close-knit nature of the global knitting community, word was spread, and the fuse was lit. (The Pussyhat Project n.d.)

The popularity of the pussyhat was initially met with enthusiasm and solidarity. Online and in real life, people exchanged instructions and materials to make them. However, for Black women, women of Colour, and trans*women, the pussyhat was just another representation of white feminist performativity. It became a commodified symbol of 'wokeness', all the while failing to acknowledge the oft-cited statistic that 52 per cent of American white women who voted in 2016 did so for Trump. In the 2020 presidential election, this number increased to 54 per cent. As Wendy Kozol states in 'White Privilege and the Pink Pussy Hat', 'gender advocacy needs to reckon with, rather than ignore or deny, the racism that has been built into the fabric of feminist movements' (2017).

Figure 21. Example of a pussyhat from the Women's March in Washington, DC.

Source: Thirty Two, 21 January 2017. In the Public Domain @<https://commons.wikimedia.org/wiki/File:Women%27s_March_on_Washington_-_pussyhat_0456.jpg>.

Yet, the Women's March met with its own controversy in 2018 when Women's March, Inc co-founder Carmen Perez was accused of attacking Women's March leadership using anti-Semitic language and co-founder Tamika Mallory expressed support for noted anti-Semite and Nation of Islam leader Louis Farrakhan. Much of the furore stems from a 2018 investigation by Leah McSweeney and Jacob Siegel for *Tablet* magazine titled 'Is the Women's March Melting Down?' The lengthy examination describes the origins of the Women's March, including the conglomeration of activists, grassroots organisers, noted public intellectuals and media personalities who participated in and/or publicised the events. According to McSweeney and Siegel,

> Perez and Mallory allegedly first asserted that Jewish people bore a special collective responsibility as exploiters of black and brown people – and even, according to a close second-hand source, claimed that Jews were proven to have been leaders of the American slave trade. (2018)

An article for *Vox* by Anna North also mentions that in addition to the verbal abuse allegations, Mallory attended a Nation of Islam event in which Farrakhan expressed anti-Semitic and homophobic ideals (North 2018). She even posted clips of Farrakhan's speech to her Instagram account. In light of the criticism, both women responded by denying the allegations, and the Women's March organisation (which was made up of several state chapters and an organising national body) dissolved, with some leaders continuing their work in an organisation called March On.

The dalliance between the Women's March organisers and Louis Farrakhan rightfully caused concern. Not only does such support seem in direct opposition to the tenets espoused by the Women's March and its participants, but it also raises suspicions surrounding the 'progressive' aims of the movement. For example, in 'The Perversity of Intersectionality', the director of publications for the American Jewish Committee, Lawrence Grossman, writes:

> If proponents of intersectionality like Tamika Mallory and the Women's March can't denounce [Farrakhan's] malign idiocy, and instead feel the need to include the [Nation of Islam] within their circle of 'marginalized' groups, they assuredly can deserve no place in our democratic and pluralistic society. (Grossman 2018)

Farrakhan's bigoted language is undoubtedly dangerous and worthy of significant censure. However, Grossman's interpretation of intersectionality as indicative of anti-Semitic prejudice is a gross mischaracterisation and misunderstanding of the theory. The title alone indicates Grossman's bias against the idea, while his analysis illustrates a paucity of even cursory engagement with the term. For example, Grossman describes intersectionality as a 'recent state-of-the art term', when the concept actually has roots reaching to the 1970s when Black legal scholars began examining the connections between white supremacy and the continued injustices experienced by Black people in the United States (Grossman 2018).

Intersectionality as an articulated concept was first conceived of by legal scholar Kimberlé Crenshaw. It is firmly rooted in the controversial framework of critical race theory, which posits that the US legal system (law enforcement, courts and corrections) is – as an institution – just as susceptible to bias, discrimination and racism as individuals are. Because individuals working as judges, attorneys, law clerks, police officers, police chiefs, etc., can hold white supremacist ideals, those ideals are deployed throughout the systems of lawmaking, law enforcement and corrections. In the 1991 article 'Mapping the Margins: Intersectionality, Identity Politics, and Violence Against Women of Color', Crenshaw examines the legal pitfalls working against Black women within the US juridical system. As the legal system was established and shaped by patriarchal and white supremacist notions of justice, fairness and equality, Black women are doubly vulnerable to the realities of sexual and domestic violence – and the significant lack of repercussions for perpetrators of both. Crenshaw writes: 'Because of [Black women's] intersectional identity as both women *and* of color within discourses that are shaped to respond to one or the other, women of color are marginalized within both' (1991: 1244). While intersectionality started with and continues to centre Black women and women of Colour, the theory is about recognising the systems of privilege and oppression that almost everyone, including Jewish people and those of Jewish descent, experiences within a hegemonic society.

As Kavita Rai writes in the article 'Women's March Controversy Illuminates Why We Need Intersectionality':

> Ignorance can still exist in the feminist movement, and it often does. Until we start having productive conversations that are meant to support each other's intellectual journeys

rather than attack them, our movement will inherently regress. I want us to realize that the need for intersectionality transcends beyond the 'white man privilege' complex. We must all look at the biases we hold and push ourselves to make our activism more intersectional. (Rai 2019)

This 'feminism of ignorance' is exemplified by the methods and motives of toxic white feminism. Toxic white feminism is the very opposite of intersectionality in that it wishes to accord revolutionary freedom to women without considering the intractability of white supremacy, transphobia,[1] poverty, labour exploitation and other social ills that contribute to the continued oppression of women. It is a poisonous approach to the liberation of women (and, subsequently, everyone who experiences sex/gender-based oppression) because it functions not to liberate, but to recreate the hierarchies of white supremacy and patriarchy with white women at its peak.

As an exemplar of a movement, the pussyhat originated (ostensibly) from a desire to show solidarity between women for the purposes of political action and social change. However, as with all semantic messaging, there is the intended meaning to consider and the meaning that is received. Both interpretations are valid, but within a sociopolitical standpoint there is a place for inclusive and responsive overlap. It is easy to dismiss criticisms of the pussyhat as 'reaching' or navel-gazing, but the clear the corollaries between feminism espoused by those whose power was solidified via racism and those whose agency is grounded in resistance are tightly woven knots worth untangling.

---

[1] Trans-Exclusive Radical Feminists (TERFS) are biological essentialists and (sometimes) separatist feminists who do not believe that trans women are 'women' and see them instead as predatory men attempting to invade cis women spaces (i.e. bathrooms, domestic violence shelters, etc.). While the transmisogyny is evident (TERFs rarely express similar concerns regarding trans men), the term 'TERF' is contested, as some consider it a slur and instead use the term 'gender critical feminist'. This is particularly true in the UK where 'gender critical feminism' has gained notable traction among some public figures, such as author J.K. Rowling.

Callie Graham

Crazy Ex-Girlfriend, Rachel Bloom and Aline Brosh McKenna (2015–2019)

Crazy Ex-Girlfriend (*CEXGF*) is a musical romantic comedy series portraying the trials and tribulations of the dramatic Rebecca Bunch (Rachel Bloom) in her quest for love. Rebecca searches for love with Josh (Vincent Rodriguez III). And Greg (Santino Fontana). And Nathaniel (Scott Michael Foster). Rebecca is bright, bubbly and eccentric, but also moody, calculating and manipulative with a propensity for developing toxic relationships. Moreover, *CEXGF* mirrors how many toxic relationships develop: it starts as cute and funny but turns dark and toxic. The story unfolds with show tunes, love-facilitating antics and much hilarity while addressing complexities of relationships. This chapter explores depictions of toxic relationship behaviours in *CEXGF*, specifically outlining problems with romanticising love (leading to stalking and love bombing) and aversive behaviour (gaslighting and intermittent reinforcement).

Toxic Relationships

Although little formal research exists on toxic relationships, the popular press mentions emotional abuse, manipulation, addiction, co-dependency and having a partner with a Cluster B personality disorder (i.e. antisocial, borderline, histrionic or narcissistic) as characteristic of these relationships. In essence, toxic relationships are characterised by repeated aversive behaviour, resulting in negative personal and relational outcomes. Often, people in toxic relationships note extraordinary highs and agonising lows, making leaving toxic relationships challenging, akin to addiction withdrawal (see Redcay and Simonetti 2018). Importantly, a personality disorder is not a prerequisite for toxic relationships – the destructive dynamics of the *relationship* create toxicity, not necessarily the individuals (Motz 2014). Even when it is one partner that predominantly engages in the toxic behaviour, responses to that behaviour are part of the pattern of toxicity. Such is the case in *CEXGF*.

In season three, Rebecca is diagnosed with borderline personality disorder (BPD). People with BPD have maladaptive cognitive, emotional and behavioural patterns (APA 2013) and often exhibit attention-seeking behaviour, hot-and-cold behaviour, low self-esteem, emotional outbursts, and self-centredness, just as Rebecca does. Although tempting to solely blame people like Rebecca, who have personality disorders (or who exhibit associated behaviours), for relational havoc, toxic relationships are 'a lot more nuanced than that' ('Josh Just Happens to Live Here', Season 1, Episode 1). Reactions to toxicity influences behavioural patterns, for better or worse.

These nuanced behavioural patterns are evident in *CEXGF*. Many of Rebecca's relational partners enable her (e.g. Paula [Donna Lynne Champlin] tracks Josh's social network through GPS technology), and the 'success' (e.g. Josh sees Rebecca behind his girlfriend's back), mutuality (e.g. Greg and Rebecca play hot-and-cold) and encouragement (e.g. Nathaniel calls her obsessive behaviour 'flattering') of her maladaptive behaviours reinforce and sustain toxicity. Yet other people recognise and discourage her toxic behaviours. After initially befriending Rebecca as a case study for her abnormal psychology class, Heather (Vella Lovell) develops a friendship with Rebecca that is built on candour. Conversely, Josh's friend, 'White Josh' (David Hull), despite being enmeshed in her social network, opts out of interacting with Rebecca. These relationships (or lack thereof) demonstrate the key role interaction dynamics play in toxic relationships.

Romanticising 'The Power of Love'

In toxic relationships, negative behaviours reflecting obsession and control are often justified, excused or tolerated because of the perception they stem from love. The person engaging in toxic behaviours views them as necessary for obtaining and maintaining love, and sometimes the target excuses toxic behaviour because their partner 'loves them so much'. This romanticising often appears at the start of a soon-to-be toxic relationship when a pursuer idealises a partner and does whatever necessary to develop the relationship, including stalking, manipulation and love bombing.

Romanticising and Idealising

In the pilot of *CEXGF*, Rebecca's irrational decisions stem from romanticising love and idealising Josh. She is on the verge of a coveted promotion at her New York City law firm when she breaks down, pondering a butter campaign that asks, 'When was the last time you were truly happy?' The camera pans to – no, can it be – Josh Chan! Her first love from high school summer theatre camp! The last time she was truly happy! During their chance encounter, Josh mentions he is moving back to West Covina, California, where people are 'happy'. Naturally, Rebecca takes the butter campaign to heart and abandons New York City in pursuit of 'happiness' (and Josh).

Rebecca's romanticising continues in West Covina. Through a poppy musical number, she idealises how extraordinary life is in the mundane town where she will certainly (in her mind) be happy. The first show tune, 'West Covina', conveys how Rebecca sees her life: through grandiose musical theatre (see Figure 22). The pilot episode conveys to the audience that love-fuelled actions are exempt from the label 'crazy'. Rebecca's twisted ideology that love conquers – and justifies – all, in combination with her imaginative reality, propels Rebecca to engage in toxic behaviours throughout *CEXGF*.

At some level, of course, Rebecca knows it is ... unusual ... to leave her prestigious job and move across the country for a summer fling from high school, so she fabricates a story explaining her move: she received a 'generous offer' from a West Covina law firm. However, Paula, a legal assistant at the firm, senses Rebecca's deception and discovers the truth behind her move. Paula confronts Rebecca, who adamantly denies the truth:

> Here's what happened: I was in New York, I ran into Josh, he made me feel warm inside like glitter was exploding inside me, then I moved here. I did not move here because of Josh because that would be crazy and I am not crazy. ('Josh Just Happens to Live Here!' 2015)

Figure 22. Rebecca Bunch romanticises West Covina, California, after moving across the country to pursue love.

Source: *Crazy Ex-Girlfriend*; created by Rachel Bloom and Aline Brosh McKenna (The CW; 2015).

Digesting her own words, Rebecca spirals into hysterics, asserting she IS crazy. Surprisingly, Paula tells Rebecca she is brave, not crazy, to pursue love. Paula vows to help Rebecca win Josh's heart and promptly asks if Rebecca would like to drive by Josh's residence. Their friendship is born, with stalking 'in the name of love' at its foundation. Importantly, Paula's reaction is consistent with romanticising love, and in that context, perhaps her reaction is not so surprising after all.

Manipulation and Stalking

Moving to West Covina is the first of many steps Rebecca takes to secure Josh's love. She covertly pursues him by inserting herself into his life using manipulation and stalking. Stalking involves a pattern of unwanted pursuit, harassment or intrusion into another person's life that is considered threatening (Spitzberg et al. 2010), and it can occur in situations of unrequited love, like in *Fatal Attraction* (Lyne, 1987). In *CEXGF*, Rebecca uses strategies such as befriending Josh's girlfriend, Valencia (Gabrielle Ruiz; 'Josh's Girlfriend is Really Cool!', Season 1, Episode 2), and inviting herself to 'beach day' ('I'm Going to the Beach with Josh and His Friends', Season 1, Episode 9) to insert herself into Josh's life. And while Josh and Valencia are fighting, Rebecca plays a supportive role by expressing her admiration for Josh, praising his accomplishments, helping him acquire his dream job, and giving him a heartfelt note from their youth. Moreover, courtesy of Paula's co-stalking, Rebecca joins the Chan family Thanksgiving ('My First Thanksgiving with Josh', Season 1, Episode 6) and prepares a traditional Filipino dish, *dinuguan*, to impress the Chans. Rebecca even pursues a class action lawsuit with Josh as lead plaintiff. Overwhelmed by her genius (and large breasts), Josh kisses Rebecca at the conclusion of the case ('Josh and I Go to Los Angeles', Season 1, Episode 13). Her obsessive, manipulative efforts seem to be paying off.

This obsessive chase – where someone does everything they can to be with the person they want – is a common narrative in popular culture. In fact, the literature on obsessive relational intrusion suggests these cultural scripts help people rationalise this type of behaviour (Cupach and Spitzberg 2004). Many films and shows, such as *Say Anything* (Cameron Crowe, 1989), conclude with the underdog prevailing and winning over the love of their life after putting in substantial effort. Obsessive relational intrusion also includes 'hyper-intimacy' (i.e. making exaggerated claims of affection; Spitzberg et al. 2014), another strategy Rebecca commonly uses with love interests. Interestingly, in *CEXGF*, Rebecca's manipulative behaviour would not initially be considered obsessive relational intrusion, because Josh welcomes her actions; only later when Josh realises it is part of her manipulative campaign is it reassessed as such.

Importantly, romanticising love makes toxic behaviours seem more acceptable. Studies indicate television consumption increases audience acceptance of controlling behaviours as expressions of love (Aubrey et al. 2013). Viewing romcoms endorses both dysfunctional relationship beliefs (Johnson and Holme 2009) and stalking as an acceptable form of pursuit (Lippman 2015). Unfortunately, shows with toxic ideas about love target young adults, who are still forming attitudes about relationships and love (see Eggermont 2004 and Pardun et al. 2005). For example, viewers watching the supernatural drama *The Vampire Diaries* (Plec and Williamson, 2009–17) and its spin-off series *The Originals* (Plec, 2013–18) are entranced by vampires 'learning to love', and romanticise toxic behaviours (e.g. stalking and manipulation) as love and passion. Conflating toxic behaviours with love also occurs with viewers of the psychological thriller *You* (Berlanti and Gamble, 2018–present). *You* follows the seemingly innocuous Joe Goldberg (Penn Badgley), who believes 'you have to do anything for love' ('A Fresh Start', Season 2, Episode 1), and fans fawn over his fierce 'protection' of those he loves (Dodson 2019). Many stories in popular culture romanticise love as elusive, with the goal of 'happily ever after' justifying the means to achieve it. In this tradition, romcom *CEXGF* follows Rebecca's unrelenting pursuit of love, and fans adore the unfolding of her tale through 'crazy' antics and musical theatre.

Love Bombing and Subsequent Behaviour

If relationships started as toxic, they would likely never develop. Instead, in the beginning, toxic relationships are often fuelled by intense feelings and expressions of attraction and love, as well as hyper-intimacy. Love bombing is part of the first stage of a tumultuous relationship cycle – idealisation, devaluation and discarding – present in some toxic relationships (Howard 2019). As previously mentioned, part of idealisation involves romanticising love and seeing love with an idealised person as the answer to present and future happiness. Love bombing occurs when a person is showered with intense love and affection, as well as excessive praise and admiration, during the initial stages of a relationship while being idealised as the 'perfect partner'.

However, idealisation is typically short-lived. Once the affections of the desired person are secured, devaluation often begins. Now, in place of praise and affection, the previously 'perfect partner' suddenly becomes the target of harsh criticism. Reality sets in, and initial high expectations are not sustainable. The third stage of this toxic cycle is discarding (relational termination), which involves a slew of aversive behaviours, including gaslighting, lying and exploitative actions (Howard 2019). Occasionally a fourth stage, hoovering, occurs when the person tries to suck their former partner back into a relationship. These stages are not always linear – there are swings between idealising and devaluing and discarding and then idealising and hoovering back into the relationship. As described later in this chapter, the back-and-forth between intense positivity (idealisation) and extreme negativity (devaluing and discarding) can lead to patterns of intermittent reinforcement that keep people in toxic relationships.

Aversive Behaviour

Throughout *CEXGF*, Rebecca engages in the aforementioned tumultuous cycle, predominantly with Josh. She (and her partners) also exhibit many behaviours common during each of the devaluing and discarding stages, including gaslighting and intermittent reinforcement.

Gaslighting

In toxic relationships, gaslighting is often a defence mechanism used to confuse one's partner and create an altered sense of reality, thus providing a context for the continuation of a toxic relationship. Gaslighting is a psychological manipulation technique aimed at making the target question the legitimacy of their own thoughts, feelings and reality (Lay 2019). The term comes from the play *Gas Light* (Patrick Hamilton, 1938), where the husband dims the gas lights and acts like nothing has changed, making his wife question her reality and sanity.

A memorable gaslighting moment in *CEXGF* occurs when Josh learns the truth behind Rebecca's move to West Covina. Just as Rebecca's new romantic target, Greg, gets intoxicated and rejects Rebecca out of fear of being 'second place' to Josh, Valencia ends her relationship with Josh. Moments after the break-up, Josh approaches the abandoned, emotionally raw Rebecca, and they spend the evening together in sexual bliss. Remarkably, her stalking and manipulation appear successful ... until Rebecca confesses she moved to West Covina for him ('Paula Needs to Get Over Josh', Season 1, Episode 18; see Figure 23).

Figure 23. Rebecca and Josh after Rebecca reveals she left her life in New York City for him.

Source: *Crazy Ex-Girlfriend*; created by Rachel Bloom and Aline Brosh McKenna (The CW: 2016).

Josh asks Rebecca what she meant when she said that 'our love story can finally begin'. Then, the gaslighting commences. Rebecca realises she needs to control Josh's interpretation of events so he does not see her as manipulative and, well, crazy. To alter this reality, Rebecca turns his own question back on him:

> Okay, so let's recap the events of tonight. So, you show up at Jayma's wedding looking all Danny Zuko in a leather jacket that literally came out of space, clutching my old camp letter to your heart, saying you can't stop thinking about me. The more I think about this, actually, I get more uncomfortable. So, let's just stop talking about it, okay? Like, 'cause we've had sex once, and you're talking about love and I just think we need to pump the brakes. Actually, can you take me home? God, I'm so cold. ('Where is Josh's Friend?': Season 2, Episode 1)

Confused by her logic and rapid change of tone, Josh apologises, and Rebecca says she will forget about all the 'crazy stuff' he said because of how he 'did [her] so good back there' – classic gaslighting. Josh should, rightfully, feel uncomfortable after Rebecca's revelation, yet somehow, she flips the reality of her pursuit back on to him.

Rebecca frequently gaslights people to protect her relationships from falling apart; she deeply fears abandonment. This is common for people with BPD, who not only gaslight, but sometimes sabotage their relationships so they can leave on their own terms rather than be left by a partner (hence, devalue and discard; Kotton 2017). Fortunately for Rebecca, her gaslighting momentarily keeps Josh around – he even moves in with her, and they begin an intense, sexual relationship. However, Josh abruptly ends their relationship after Rebecca announces 'their' pregnancy, runs to the bathroom, emerges stating she is not pregnant, and suggests period sex ('All Signs Point to Josh … or Is It Josh's Friend?', Season 2, Episode 3). Josh, shocked and panicked, gaslights Rebecca, asserting they were never a couple, and leaves. At this point, viewers may believe Josh is finally through with Rebecca, but no – he goes back to her later after she brings him soup while he is sick (and dating someone else). Both Josh and Rebecca appear to have fallen into a pattern of responding to the rewards present within a larger pattern of intermittent reinforcement.

Intermittent Reinforcement

Intermittent reinforcement occurs when rewards are given inconsistently and infrequently against a backdrop of hurtful or neglectful behaviour, thereby creating a powerful desire to please and be rewarded (Dutton and Painter 1993; Walker 2009). In *CEXGF*, intermittent reinforcement is evident in Rebecca's relationships with men. It first becomes apparent with Greg, who is immediately drawn to Rebecca, saying, 'You're pretty, and you're smart, and you're ignoring me, so you're obviously my type' ('Josh Just Happens to Live Here', 2015). Throughout *CEXGF*, Rebecca and Greg unintentionally engage in reciprocal intermittent reinforcement. After Rebecca leaves their first date with another man ('I'm Going on a Date with Josh's Friend', Season 1, Episode 4), Rebecca and Greg develop mutual hostility. Yet, their hostility is peppered with tender moments, and attraction grows. Unfortunately, Greg's alcoholism leads Rebecca to refocus on Josh. Nevertheless, the strength of intermittent reinforcement continues to draw Rebecca and Greg to one another. Greg, in the song 'It was a Shit Show' ('When Will Josh and his Friend Leave Me Alone?', Season 2, Episode 4), explains the toxicity of their relationship:

> Dysfunction is our Lingua Franca
> We can't unscrew each other's friends
> We're Jerry Springer, not Casablanca
> There's 'hard to get', then there's neglect
> To say it's fate, you'd have to be a bit slow
> Not to be crass,
> But this sucked ass
> This was a shitshow [...]
> I won't forget, I won't regret
> This beautiful, heart-stopping
> Breathtaking life-changing [shitshow]!

Importantly, Greg makes the healthy decision to leave the relationship because of the agonising lows, while acknowledging the extraordinary highs that make leaving toxic relationships exceedingly difficult.

Nathaniel, one of Rebecca's other love interests, uses negging, a toxic behaviour designed to backhandedly compliment while simultaneously undermining someone's confidence, leading them to seek the manipulator's approval. Negging is a powerful tool that contributes to intermittent reinforcement: it simultaneously rewards and punishes someone, mirroring the overall pattern of positive and negative behaviour that leads people to crave reinforcement from the very person who hurt them. This behaviour is predominantly used by men, as seen in *Community* (Harmon, 2009–15), *You're the Worst* (Falk, 2014–19) and *Kingsman: The Secret Service* (Vaughn, 2015). In the song 'Let's Have Intercourse' ('Josh Is the Man of My Dreams, Right?', Season 2, Episode 11), Nathaniel negs Rebecca, opening with:

> Unfortunately, I want to have sex with you
> I don't know what happened
> Maybe you lost some weight

Between his negging and their underlying attraction, Rebecca kisses Nathaniel. Instead of telling Josh (who she is engaged to at that point), she moves their wedding forward from two years to two weeks.

Predictably, Josh abandons Rebecca on their wedding day, prompting Rebecca to turn into a 'woman scorned' who then successfully launches a smear campaign against Josh (discarding) before he has a chance to speak the truth. However, following her smear campaign, Rebecca experiences a major depressive episode and intentionally overdoses on prescription medication. Her suicide attempt is a turning point: she seeks help to manage her mental health, overcome maladaptive behaviours and take responsibility for her actions. Here is where *CEXGF* differs from 'traditional' romcoms: it acknowledges toxicity.

Acknowledging Toxicity

Trying to navigate the 'real world' while working through her newly diagnosed BPD in therapy proves difficult: Rebecca starts dating Nathaniel and catches herself repeating toxic behaviours, like stealing his shirt to smell his scent and stalking his father to help mend their father–son relationship. Nathaniel assures her it is 'flattering' and excuses her behaviour, consistent with romanticising love. While singing 'Nothing is Ever Anyone's Fault' ('Nathaniel Is Irrelevant', Season 3, Episode 13), Nathaniel blames toxic behaviours on childhood trauma, with them – as adults – bearing no responsibility for their actions. Though many toxic behaviours do emerge from foundational relationship experiences, people are responsible for how their behaviours impact others. As such, Rebecca ends their romantic relationship to focus on therapy ... though they continue a sexual relationship while Nathaniel dates another woman (therapy is an ongoing process). Interestingly, the development of the plot, in some ways, captures how people in toxic relationships feel. Initially, fans are charmed by Rebecca's optimistic attitude and quirky behaviour, but her behaviour becomes increasingly toxic, to the point that fans need a reason to still like her. The diagnosis of BPD helps Rebecca regain some of her likability as she struggles to cope with her borderline tendencies. In toxic relationships, people are also often drawn to their partner's charisma and (projected) confidence, but as they get to know each other better, the real unfiltered versions of themselves emerge.

Conclusion

Rebecca continues to focus on changing her toxic behaviours and thought processes. After making immense progress, her therapist encourages Rebecca to mindfully begin dating. Conveniently, former partners – Josh, Greg and Nathaniel – compete for her affections (intermittent reinforcement is a powerful force). Ultimately, Rebecca chooses herself, focusing on her own healing. Her antics, previously veiled by comedy, are addressed as disturbing and reprehensible, and she explicitly apologises to those she hurt. With BPD, Rebecca will always struggle with impulsivity and emotion regulation, but she can develop coping mechanisms to ameliorate her toxic behaviours. Importantly, many shows and movies, such as *10 Things I Hate about You* (Junger, 1999), *Love Actually* (Curtis, 2003) and *Twilight* (Hardwicke, 2008), glamorise stalking and manipulation without addressing its toxicity. Eventually, *CEXGF* does what other shows do not: it condemns toxic relationship behaviours obscured by the pursuit of love and shows how the central character is learning to better understand herself and her toxic behaviours.

Ildikó Limpár

Wayward Children Series, Seanan McGuire (2016–Present)

Toxic Parenting

Abusive parents are well-known denizens of stories intended for a young audience. Fairy tales, originally targeting an adult readership but then softened to suit children's needs, abound in the presentation of toxic parents (often transformed into step-parents to ease the anxiety coming from the reading) who are ready to harm or even kill their children; the evil Witch Queen in 'Snow White', the wicked stepmother in 'Hansel and Gretel' or the foster mother in 'Rapunzel' are but the best known examples.[1] In the past few decades, contemporary young adult fiction has developed a strong tendency of highlighting conflicts coming from problematic parenting (Just 2010). Physical, sexual and emotional abuse and child neglect[2] are problems that have found a way into youth literature, and the literature of the fantastic is no exception to this tendency. We may encounter parents with health issues abusing their child: in Paolo Bacigalupi's 2010 young adult dystopia, *Ship Breaker*, an alcohol- and drug-addicted father threatens the protagonist; in Theodora Goss's *The Extraordinary Adventures of the Athena Club* trilogy (2017–19), mad scientist fathers with a god complex experiment on their daughters. But fantastic fiction has deep roots in fairy

---

1   Ansam Yaroub (2014) lists twenty-one Brothers Grimm fairy tales and categorises them according to the type of abuse they include.
2   Based on the Child Abuse Prevention and Treatment Act (2003), 'the term 'child abuse and neglect' means, at a minimum, any recent act or failure to act on the part of a parent or caretaker, which results in death, serious physical or emotional harm, sexual abuse or exploitation, or an act or failure to act which presents an imminent risk of serious harm' (Clark et al. 2007: xii).

tales; accordingly, it utilises archetypes to a great extent and cherishes the hero narrative. In especially heroic fantasy, child abuse is often linked with a fear of that child's potential: the child hero or heroine often emerges from an oppressive, violent environment, just as Harry Potter rises from the toxic environment that the Dursleys provide (Rowling, 1997) or as Tara in the *Buffy the Vampire Slayer* television show (Whedon, 1997–2003) comes from a family that invents the myth of the demon girl to ensure patriarchal control over the family's magically talented women. These examples of parental abuse reflect fear of what the child may be capable of and/or hate that helps to shape the protagonist–antagonist conflict according to the rules of the heroic narrative.

This is the tradition that Seanan McGuire consistently subverts in her ongoing Wayward Children series. McGuire focuses on children who have their own hero narratives unfolding in an otherworld, but who, nevertheless, do not seem to have the potential that parents (or anyone else) may fear; in fact, one of the most important problems with them is that their parents think they fail to live up to their potential. Additionally, not only do these children appear as failures, who mostly generate more pity than fear, but they are also children who are not loved unconditionally, and this is a manner of toxic parenting that leaves permanent scars on these young people's lives.

The lack of unconditional love, as McGuire presents it in this series of novellas, comes from a toxic culture that the parents adhere to. These parents are so embedded in the culture they live in that they fail to embrace and support their child when (s)he turns out to be 'deviant' from the norm or the parental expectations rooted in what is considered normative. The concept behind McGuire's series is that such parental failure is so abusive that it ultimately pushes the children into rejecting the home and the world they live in. They find temporary (or, occasionally, permanent) refuge in an otherworld that becomes accessible via a door that only takes shape for those who may find a home on the other side because that world somehow resonates with their needs. These other worlds are not necessarily happy worlds, but they provide space where the children may be themselves. As a result, every one of these 'wayward' children identifies her otherworld as her home and finds her return to her native world a devastating experience.

The appearance of the portal door is always the result of toxic parenting that fails to accept children as they are, and McGuire explores the wide range of parental failures that are tightly linked with social expectations. Living in a world where '[t]he medical gaze plays a crucial role in invalidating bodies that do not conform to the norm' (Loja et al. 2013: 191), parents see their children with non-normative body types as people needing correction. This happens to Nadya (see Figure 24), born as a 'special needs' child, whose adoptive parents give her a prothesis to make her 'complete', thereby confirming that they see the girl as incomplete. In response to this parental failure, Nadya finds her ultimate home in Belyyreka, whose inhabitants see her lack of hand 'as an opportunity for her to craft a tool, a weapon, an extension of her own' (McGuire 2018: 173).

The medical gaze turns Cora into an othered bodied subject, too: she is seen as the ugly, 'fat' girl, embodying an unhealthy life, which is unforgivable in an ableist society where a damaging health cult distorts people's understanding

Figure 24. Nadya in Belyyreka – drawing by Csenge Limpár.

Source: reproduced with the permission of the artist.

about what is healthy. Yet Cora subverts all the stereotypes about society's concept about fat people: she is very athletic, flexible, a successful member of her swimming team, her extra weight coming not from diet issues but from 'her metabolism and her genes, neither of which she could control' (McGuire 2018: 118). Still, even her family expects her to be 'cured of all the things that made her who she [is]' (McGuire 2018: 93–4), and Cora's only motivation in her native world becomes finding her way back to her otherworld, where she can be herself. In both cases, toxic parenting springs from the parents' – and thus society's – toxic mentality that excludes and generates anxiety in people with corporeal otherness. The happy subject with a body extending potential – via a natural element, water – stands for inclusion that is not possible in the world of reality.

Most of the problems foregrounded in the Wayward Children series are clearly identified by the parents as psychological issues. Here belongs Christopher, whose unusual attitude to death stems from his early encounter with cancer. He sees his human existence as a threat to living comfortably with the knowledge that everyone is heading for a skeletal end, and thus he cherishes the idea of a life where death is not a prerequisite of that final skeletal condition. Instead of getting parental support, he is sent to Eleanor West's Home for Wayward Children, just like the other children, to be cured from his fixation on a possible romance with the Skeleton Girl (that his parents think must be a girl with anorexia). Rejected as a sick child, Christopher is determined to find his otherworld, where skeletal is not equivalent to sick and lethal.

Some of the parents see mental sickness in their children's inability to conform to society's expected gender norms. Both the transgender Kade and the asexual Nancy are sent to Eleanor West's Home for Wayward Children, just until they know better and are willing to embrace their femininity and the gender role that comes with it. They are sent to the home, which provides psychiatric help to children, hoping that the institute will 'fix' them and turn them average, meeting the societal norm about women.

The two (so far) most detailed adventures to the magical other worlds also reflect intensely on harmful gender stereotypes adopted by parents. Lundy's recurrent visits to the Goblin Market in the 1960s, recounted in *In an Absent Dream* (McGuire 2019), and Jack and Jill's repeated trips to the Moors in our present, narrated in three novellas of the series,[3] testify to the horrors that may come from a complete misuse of parental authority by focusing more on meeting societal expectations than on loving one's child and allowing her to unleash her full potential in the world she was born into.

McGuire builds up gradually the reasons that push Lundy to an other world. First, she presents an authoritative father and a passive mother as the primary motives for Lundy's isolation. It is parental neglect that sets things in motion: the mother is aware of Lundy's problem, but her tasks, which come from the gender role she needs to perform, occupy and exhaust her so much that she cannot help her daughter; at the same time, the father is simply ignorant of his own role in creating a suffocating atmosphere around his children, as a school principal who scares away her children's friends.

Lundy does not get fair treatment from her parents, so she is invited to a fantastic world where the controlling force is fairness. As everyone is expected to give fair value for everything – including any goods, service, information or promise – Lundy becomes trained in fairness, so the unfair nature of her birth world will be more and more painful to her after she returns. Her isolation now is doubled by her father's conscious attempt at transforming her into a proper lady, according to the social expectations of the age; and when she does not get fair treatment in math class just because her sex is not expected to be good at science, she feels compelled to leave again this unfair, humiliating environment.

In the Goblin Market, being unfair results in monsterisation: it gradually turns every unfair person into a human–bird hybrid[4] – a bird, in the end, if the person proves uncapable of paying off her debt. While to the not so observant

---

3   The second instalment in the series, *Down Among the Sticks and Bones* (2017), narrates the events of the twins' first adventure in the Moors, which ends with their fleeing from the other world. The immediate consequence of these events is narrated in the first volume of the series, *Every Heart a Doorway* (2016), which takes place in our world and ends with the girls' return to their otherworld. The fifth novella of the series, *Come Tumbling Down* (2020), returns to the girls' adventures and allows us to see the final upshot of their story in the Moors.

4   On hybridity as a determining feature of monsters, see, for instance, Carroll (1987: 50) and Cohen (1996: 6).

Figure 25. Lundy with her first feathers – drawing by Csenge Limpár.
Source: reproduced with the permission of the artist.

eye, the first feathers growing at the nape pass as decoration in the hair, they also reveal that unfairness is monstrous, even if it does not appear so to others.

While the Goblin Market is fair and turns the unfair into monsters, in contrast, in our unjust world it is the one who receives unfair treatment who is monsterised, otherised. Lundy's tragedy is that she tries to be fair both to herself and to her sister, who apparently needs her in such an unfair world; but Lundy's conflicting desires lead to her attempt at evading the law of her otherworld. The Goblin Market, therefore, doubly punishes Lundy for her trespass: it expels her from the market, and it leaves her with eternal hybridity: a maturing consciousness trapped in a child's body, ageing backward. Lundy is left in her birth world as a marked Other, whose body signals the very desire that brought about her own downfall: her wish to stay under the age of 18 to be able to visit her sister and be there for her, and her wish to have the market as her permanent home, which is possible only for children above 18. This conflict of interest comes from her loyalty towards her sister, but one must also see that her sense of responsibility is the result of the unjust world that drove her to the Goblin Market. As girls receive a great deal less fair treatment in Lundy's birth world than boys do, and Lundy's parents do not support her sister from the injustice of the world, Lundy tries to perform the impossible and steal time for herself – or, rather, for her sister.

If Lundy's fate is tragic, then Jack and Jill's story is monstrously cruel, and the root of the twin girls' tragic trajectory, again, is to be found in the parental attitude. The parents have a mistaken concept about perfect life: they are shaped by the consumer society they live in, and they measure the value of their life based on what they own. Their perspective is basically quantitative, and thus they value their children just as they value other goods in their lives. Having identical twins is a problem that they sort out by assigning them diverging 'content'; that is, different genders – they force their girls into two distinct stereotypical gender roles, to have richer content with which to decorate their life on display. Their harmful parenting reflects toxic consumerism as well as society's enforced toxic normativity of gender roles, and it results in a loveless parent–child relationship that prevents the twins from experiencing emotional safety. Without a rich emotional environment, the girls develop their potentials to become monsters – and, not surprisingly, they come to be invited to a world where monsters – a vampire and a Frankensteinian scientist – rule and shape the foundlings into monsters.

The girls' choice of foster parents is determined by their forced gender roles: they each desire the role that they were denied; moreover, their former gender performance influences the way they are able to analyse a situation and see into the depth of a matter. Jack (short for Jacqueline), who was assigned the passive role of the doll, is more perceptive and immediately senses that the vampire is the more dangerous monster, so she finds home at the mad scientist's windmill; Jill (short for Jillian), formerly performing the active role of the boy, never had time to contemplate on phenomena and thus only sees the surface luxury and beauty in what the vampire offers. She is ready to give up everything to get what she mistakenly equates with love and ends up as a monster – a psychopath who murders to win the vampire's love.

The vampire specifically embodies the consumerism in which the damaging parenting is rooted: the vampire is a metaphor of consumption, the monster whose existence relies on and is inseparable from consuming. To bite is to consume – the vampiric fangs, therefore, suggest the lethal threat on the

Figure 26. Jill receives her choker from her Master – drawing by Csenge Limpár.
Source: reproduced with the permission of the artist.

victim, the harm the revenant poses on one's life. The choker, the vampire's welcoming gift to Jill, hides the future site of penetration on Jill's neck, but at the same time marks the harm to come via consuming the human body (see Figure 26).[5] The vampire of the Moors is an apt expression of the monstrous nature of the parents, revealing that their extreme attachment to the consumerist world literally sucks out the life force from their daughters, cutting away their humanity and allowing them to be turned into monsters.

McGuire's Wayward Children series explicitly highlights the correlation between an unhappy, anxious childhood and toxic parenting that feeds on a culture's harmful ideologies about normativity concerning body, gender or mental state. The fact that the series' wayward children either find a home in another world or live a miserable life, forever longing for their magical refuge, heavily criticises the parental attitude that enforces normativity on the child who fails to conform to the norm and thus becomes othered with the active

[5] On the vampiric bite as the metaphoric expression of sexual penetration, see Limpár (2018: 284).

help of her parents. These stories claim that children may suffer harm to the extent that they will never be able to fit into this world: as their other worlds may be read as fantastic spaces linked to the characters' mental landscapes, these children are presented as anchored to their fantasies. Their escape into a space of imagination may provide temporary relief, but not a way back to integration, unless they receive fairer treatment from their families and society.

Part III

Popular Culture

Pembe Gözde Erdogan

Gelin Evi [Bride's House], Cem Semercioglu (2015–2019)

On 4 February 2019, around 840,000 people, mostly women, were casually spending their afternoon watching Fatma (age 30), a teacher from Mersin, Turkey, being reprimanded for her choices as a new bride by four other new brides on Show TV's reality competition show *Gelin Evi* [Bride's House] (henceforth *GE*; Cem Semerčioglu, 2015–19) – which will be analysed here as a toxic television format that perpetuates the gender ideologies that are detrimental to lives of women in Turkey. Due to financial problems, Fatma had to wait for seven years to get married to her sweetheart; hence her house was decorated on a sensible budget. During her episode, however, the other brides were unabashedly catty and incomprehensively harsh. Fatma's home was 'not at all like a new bride's house', her furniture too old, 'as if she took her mom's furniture and just varnished them'. Her house was 'lacking', as well as her trousseau, an essential category of items at a new bride's home. Fatma was raised as one of seven siblings by a single mother who never had the time or the budget to prepare delicate traditional wedding trinkets for her children. Throughout the episode, Fatma was also castigated for the lack of variety in her spread. Her family were unable to help, and she had time constraints due to her job as a full-time teacher. At one point, Fatma is forced to explain the lack of carpet in her kitchen as an attempt to prevent unnecessary housework. How could she 'try to avoid cleaning'? Was not cleanliness one of the best attributes of a new bride? (Episode 670).

This public verbal lashing masquerading as a reality competition episode was not a one-time fare. Fatma later joined her fellow brides in equally harsh critiques of other brides during the rest of that week, as required by the

Figure 27. Criticising the new bride's 'spread'.
Source: *Gelin Evi* [Bride's House]; created by Cem Semerčioglu (Show TV, 2015–2019).

format, aired between 2015 and 2019 in Turkey. How are we to make sense of the toxic behaviour these young women display towards one another? What is the rationale behind the insults these women gladly subject themselves to? Some of today's feminist scholars might be tempted to call this toxic femininity. However, a deeper glance at the sociopolitical circumstances that surround the production of *GE* would demonstrate that we would be at fault to locate the hurtful essence of this television text within individual femininities.

Popularised by the environmentalist movement, toxicity as metaphor within public discourse is rapidly gaining popularity in the twenty-first century and can be found in our workplaces, relationships and families. Toxic is the quintessential 'cultural code word for the irritants and pollutants that disrupt our lived experience' (Risam 2015). The toxic discourse is recognised to have 'iconographic power' (Buell 1998: 644) and has been applied to the analysis of rigid and regressive gender roles that hurt people's lives (Gilmore 2018). Used in this manner by feminist scholars, 'toxic' takes the place of earlier labels such as 'patriarchal', 'hegemonic' and 'normative'. On the other hand, toxic discourse has also been shown to be a powerful weapon of trashing among opposing groups and within the communities.¹ Indeed, McCann (2020) expresses her reluctance in using toxicity as a metaphor in relation to gender, because it depends on the toxic versus healthy binary, flattening any theorisation of hierarchy in gender studies.

Widening the lens of the toxic metaphor means basing it in a culture- and time-specific framework. Situating the metaphor in the social, cultural and political realities of 2010s Turkey, I propose that *GE* perfectly exemplifies 'toxic television'. In my analysis, toxicity has less to do with hurtful televised representations and more to do with the toxic effects of rigid formats of hegemonic television texts, particularly in societies where a mixture of neoliberalism and neoconservatism threatens lives of women.

Television as a cultural medium is no stranger to accusations of toxicity, mainly due to the potential effects on children of its frank display of violence, sexual content and coarse language (Bozell 1999; Chidley 1996). Within the television industry, reality TV has long been treated as the most harmful genre and regarded as 'trash', embodying narcissism, exhibitionism and voyeurism (Rushdie 2001). Reality TV has caused moral panic and outrage in different countries, generating complaints to regulatory bodies (see Lavie 2019 on Israel). It is also seen as anti-feminist or post-feminist in its representations of women (Pozner 2010; Douglas 2004).

Turkey saw a proliferation of reality TV formats in the 1990s after the entertainment industry gained a mass dimension through deregulation and privatisation practices. Most reality formats were taken from Western countries and shaped by local values, creating truly hybrid forms (Kilicbay 2005). As in most cultures, reality TV in Turkey has always been a paradoxical field, extremely popular among the viewing public (even when seen as 'guilty pleasure' TV) but also criticised as mind-numbing and toxic by critics/scholars from both conservative and liberal backgrounds.² Since the early 2000s, women's daytime reality programming has been a highly contested battleground. The

---

1   See Risam (2015) on how the label is used online to target women of colour feminists.
2   While a show like *Biri Bizi Gozetliyor* [Big Brother] (Zickler, 2001–03) can be condemned by Islamist scholars for depicting cohabiting youth engaging in sexual behaviour out of wedlock, a show like *Esra Erol ile Evlen Benimle* (a marriage show) can be criticised by feminist scholars for its perpetuation of rigid gender roles within Turkish society.

two categories of programme under the spotlight are marriage shows (where people meet in studio to find viable spouses) and women's talk shows (which aim to address the problems women face in their lives). These shows have generated thousands of petitions to the Radio and Television Supreme Council (RTÜK) and the parliament on the grounds that they violate the sanctity of private life, deteriorate Turkish family structure and cause a rise in cases of domestic violence. As a result of these complaints from conservative circles, these shows were banned on two occasions, causing them to evolve and change format. On the other side of the political spectrum, feminist cultural studies and media scholars have targeted these shows for legitimising oppressive gender ideology, perpetuating the sexual and economic dominance of men over women, victimising women and creating an atmosphere of fear. They claim that these shows fall short on the opportunity to make the personal political and, instead, commodify women's problems with sensationalist tabloid journalism (Kaya 2013; Cavdar 2019).

In such a charged atmosphere, where most daytime reality TV is seen as toxic, Show TV's *GE* appears to be innocent given its domestic format. In *GE* every week, five new brides visit each other's houses, competing and scoring each other (points are crocheted onto circular fabric boards). At the end of the week, the bride with the most points wins five gold bracelets and five gold coins.[3] Introductory segments prioritise age, occupation, length of time married and hobbies (that usually revolve around feminine activities and housework). The segments in each episode include gift giving, outfit critiques, a house tour (evaluation of house decoration, orderliness and cleanliness), a critique of the 'spread' (the food, the dining set, the tablecloth, the utensils) and the trousseau. The women watch and assess every intimate detail of the bride's wedding journey through videos and photos, and the bride is also assessed on her levels of subservience and hosting skills.

In an era when most Turkish women's daytime programming face charges of toxicity, why is *GE* not seen as toxic? I believe that the show is seen by most as a representation of the superficial fights of a group of brides over domestic affairs. Hence, *GE* does not threaten the hegemonic order since it does not render visible the underlying gender ideology. Furthermore, the brides in the

---

[3] Gold is the most prestigious gift to be presented at a Turkish wedding.

Figure 28. The display and assessment of the bridal trousseau.
Source: *Gelin Evi* [Bride's House]; created by Cem Semercioglu (Show TV, 2015–2019).

show are never left free to bond over the problems and issues in their private lives. I claim that *GE* is toxic television not because it is reality TV or because it shows women fighting, but because it serves as a neoliberal and neoconservative control mechanism. Within the framework of toxicity as metaphor, especially with regards to reality TV, I propose a reverse logic. Entertainment goes hand in hand with sensationalism and dramatisation, so reality TV cannot be expected to act like a social guardian, representing an idealised version of the society it reflects. On the contrary, no matter how sensationalist, the best reality TV is the one that can outrage both sides of the political spectrum. Seen in this light, reality TV, at its best (and worst), has the chance to show contemporary ideologies at work in any given society (Bignell 2005). It can be a key cultural site where contemporary anxieties and politics are negotiated.[4] The toxicity of a show like *GE* is hidden in its rigid format and the political background it renders invisible. My approach focuses on the 'poisonous' aspect

---

4 See Edwards (2013) on how reality TV works in relation to anxieties over family in the American context.

of toxicity, which can be hidden from sight just as toxic waste can be 'ingested, inhaled, or absorbed by the skin' (Aldag 2014).

In order to reveal the toxic ideology that *GE* perpetuates, we need to look at the ideological factory it is produced in and the palpable effects of that ideology on women in Turkey. Despite current legislation, cases of violence against women in Turkey are rising at unprecedented levels: 474 women were murdered in 2019, and the news of murders, beatings, mutilations and harassment increases every day (McKernan 2020). Kandiyoti talks about a 'chasm between the letter of the law and its implementation' when it comes to violence against women, implicating state officials and judges in its perpetuation. Offenders continuously get 'good behaviour reductions' in crimes triggered by 'perceived female disobedience and insubordination' (2016: 109). Violence against women is dealt within a moral economy of gratitude where women are seen as 'appreciative subjects of their benevolent protectors' rather than human beings with intrinsic rights (Babul 2015: 117). This is seen alongside a considerable gender inequality gap: according to the 2020 Global Gender Gap Index, Turkey ranks low at 130 of 153 countries (WEF 2020). The gender pay gap increased in Turkey between 2006 and 2017, and only 38 per cent of women participated in the labour force in 2018 (G20 2019). Yet, the instances of violence against women are seen by government officials as individual cases rather than a structural issue, and their link to the greater gender ideology promoted in the country is never established (GREVIO 2018).

How did a modern and secular nation like Turkey, that once vied for a place in the European Union regress to this extent in terms of gender equality? The answer lies in the systematic policies and discourses produced by the current Justice and Development Party (AKP) government since 2007. After the party's second election win, systematic changes were made to its strategy under the rubric of a 'New Turkey', 'a new, more abstractly defined discursive and operational space' (Burul and Eslen-Ziya 2018: 179). Many media outlets were acquired to serve as party propaganda machines, and the state officials started to produce a neoliberal, neoconservative, patriarchal discourse that required women to be responsible mothers and wives. This reflected the neoliberal 'shift from state-provided institutional care to familial care' (Yazici 2012: 104), the concept of strong family used as a discursive justification for the dismantling of state welfare. This is accompanied by a pronatalist discourse perpetuated by state officials, revolving around appropriate gender roles for women, their reproductive duties and their importance as the guardian of the family.[5] This mix of neoliberal, neoconservative and biopolitical agendas has been dubbed the 'politics of the intimate', where neoconservative disciplinary power works to regulate women's bodies through restrictions on behaviour and appearance and through comments on their reproductive choices, abortion rights and sexual orientation (Acar and Altunok 2013).[6]

Kandiyoti claims that the politics of gender is 'intrinsic rather than incidental' to the ruling ideology in Turkey (2016: 105). Turkish media, monopolised by a few business groups closely linked to the government, has played a significant role in disseminating this gender ideology (Burul & Eslen-Ziya 2018). At this point, a seemingly innocent media text like *GE* gains insidious dimensions in a geography where the very lives of women depend on their buy-in to an ideology that seeks to imprison them to the private sphere. *GE* can thus be seen as a perfect example of an Althusserian state apparatus, blending neoliberal and neoconservative ideologies with traditional wedding traditions in trying to promote the importance of the domestic sphere. This exemplifies the need for higher levels of coercion and ideological reproduction in Turkey to ensure patriarchy secures its place.[7]

GE is mostly a demonstration of rampant materialism and a discourse of spending. The format enforces an empty discourse of critique and taste on the brides. All the new brides are extremely harsh, and they relish every opportunity to put their peers down. A carpet can be criticised by one bride for being too light in colour and small and simultaneously criticised by another for being too dark and big. This meaningless critique normalises the larger materialistic and neoliberal positioning of women through an ideology of consumption within the domestic sphere. The brides ask the price of every single item in the house and of the wedding, and the amount then appears on the screen next to the item (see Figure 29). In one episode, twenty-two separate items were priced, including home decorations, appliances and wedding

---

5   See Korkut and Eslen-Ziya (2016) on how the political discourse circulated for public deliberation in Turkey generates the discursive governance of population politics.
6   See Cindoglu and Unal (2017) for a comprehensive analysis of biopolitics and gender ideology in Turkey.
7   Kandiyoti calls this 'masculinist restoration' (2016: 110).

Figure 29. Bridal house as consumerist heaven – price tags for domestic items.
Source: *Gelin Evi* [Bride's House]; created by Cem Semerčioglu (Show TV, 2015–2019).

expenses (Episode 256). The show focuses on more contemporary wedding practices firmly based on consumerism and show of status via spending. The grooms are expected to spend time and money on the 'proposal', offering romantic gifts and gestures. The couple needs to document the myriad of different ceremonies that are expected to initiate their marriage: the betrothal, the henna night, the bachelor(ette) party, the engagement and the wedding. As such, being an appropriate new bride requires that one is of a certain class.

The prevention of authentic expression and reflection on meaningful experience is neoliberal and toxic in itself, with scripted dialogues overriding any potential for valuable cultural insight or negotiation. In one episode, one bride tries to justify her opening of the kitchen cupboards to look for dust by saying, 'this is required by the format, we need to do this' (Episode 6). In another episode, someone off camera apparently nudges one of the brides and reminds her to ask the price of the curtains (Episode 51). In yet another, when the conversation among the brides naturally drifts into the dangerous territory of domestic problems (lack of help with the housework, lack of communication and the women's emotional frustration in these situations), one abruptly jumps in to cut the conversation off by asking the price of a chandelier (Episode 101). In this way, within *GE*'s format, harsh surveillance prevails over any form of normal human exchange.

It has been suggested by numerous scholars that reality TV is the perfect neoliberal TV form in its promotion of individualism and consumerism and its selling of surveillance as something to be desired (see Andrejevic 2004; Couldry 2008; Redden 2018). In this vein, *GE* is a platform where young brides in Turkey willingly submit themselves to intense scrutiny and surveillance of their proper roles within the domestic sphere. As mothers-in-law, fathers and grooms chip in via interviews and comment on the performances of new brides, and a male narrator describes their houses to the audience, their peers act as the enforcers of this strict neoliberal–neoconservative ideology. Thus, *GE* insidiously reproduces the ideology that women are happily trapped within their marriages, families and perfect houses for eternity.

Mateusz Świetlicki

'Toxic', Britney Spears (2003)

Toxicity can metaphorically refer to a lifestyle or an individual/systemic behaviour that is damaging on several levels. In such understanding, misogyny, sexism, racism, child exploitation can all be read as toxic. A good example of a poisonous environment combining numerous destructive systemic behaviours is show business. The industry itself can be read as toxic, especially considering the history of abuse of child and amateur performers. From Jackie Coogan, whose exploitation by his parents led to the introduction of the California Child Actor's Bill in 1939, through the sexual exploitation of the iconic Shirley Temple (Brolley 2018), to the breakdowns of more contemporary stars like Amanda Bynes, gifted young celebrities have been exposed as the victims of toxic behaviour. As Ruth Cigman notes in her analysis of the concept of giftedness, some children are 'no more than a product of pushy parenting, having been trained to perform in certain ways'; she calls them 'trophy-children' (2006: 196). Young celebrities, both trained and gifted, are subjected to the high expectations of their parents *and* constant media scrutiny. While this situation can be damaging, its victims are often unaware of it. After all, similar to poisonous substances, this type of toxicity also comes with temporary 'highs' – fame, wealth and glamour. It is like a glittering fantasy.

This essay aims to briefly examine the case of singer Britney Spears, who is known for the hit song 'Toxic' (2004b). Based on her example, I attempt to show the toxic ways in which young, gifted performers are treated in the American music business. Spears has been the source of several inspiring analyses, yet the toxic elements of growing up talented (and the consequences of being labelled 'gifted') have not been examined. Writing about Spears' marriage and divorce to Kevin Federline, her alleged lousy parenting and the notorious breakdown in 2007, Kimberly Bachechi (2015) analyses how the media deconstructed Spears' 'all-American girl' image, making her appear as a 'white trash' bad mother. In her thought-provoking examination of media attitudes to Spears' Southern background, Jennifer Musial notes that Spears' 'unkempt appearance and lack of etiquette marked not only her failure as a New Southern Belle, but also her failure as a neoliberal subject and working-class female celebrity' (2019: 86). While Musial and Bachechi focus on Spears' troubled young adulthood, they overlook the toxicity she has been surrounded by from childhood. Being a talented child, Spears started performing at the age of 3 and has been working ever since (Spears and Craker 2008: 56). It is worth noting that in her analysis of gifted children, Joan Freeman observes 'that the children whose parents had identified them as gifted had emotional problems far more frequently than identically gifted but unlabelled children' (2010: 10). After winning local talent shows, at the age of 8 Spears became a student at the Professional Performing Arts School in New York. Appearing in several commercials and performing in the off-Broadway musical *Ruthless!* and the TV series *Star Search*, Spears worked hard before being cast in *The All New Mickey Mouse Club* in 1993 alongside future boyfriend Justin Timberlake (Spears and Craker 2008: 56).

In 1997, at the age of 15, Spears recorded her first demo tape. Soon, and after singing Whitney Houston's 'I Have Nothing' at a casting for Jive Records, she signed a lucrative record deal. The success of Spears, a gifted teenage performer, came with costs. She was asked to change her singing technique completely. As musicologists Stan Hawkins and John Richardson observe, young Spears had 'a powerful, timbrally rounded voice that bears all the hallmarks of voice training for the theatre and concert hall: voice production characterized by a low laryngeal position and controlled breathing' (2007: 615). Spears' natural voice was shaped by producer Eric Foster White to sound the way we know it now, characterised by 'whiny vowel sounds, guttural groans, and lingering liquid phonemes [that] signify both immaturity and eroticism' (Hawkins and Richardson 2007: 615). Consequently, Spears evolved from a powerful young vocalist to a performer frequently criticised by the media for lip-synching yet praised for her dancing skills. Such evolution is undeniably connected to the influence the artificial vocal effects have had on her natural, and significantly lower, voice.

'Toxic', Britney Spears (2003)

Spears' voice was not the only thing the 15-year-old had to change to succeed. Raised in the Southern town of Kentwood, Louisiana, Spears wanted to record a more adult, contemporary type of music. The label pushed for a pop-dance sound. Even since the release of her debut number-one single and its parent album, Spears has been the target of constant media scrutiny and criticism connected to her voice, music and image. After all, as Freeman notes: 'No matter how high your potential when you are born, the big barriers of poverty and social disapproval can wreak havoc in your life' (2010: 10). Being still a minor, Spears was repeatedly slut-shamed by the media and called a bad role model (Schick 2014). On the fifth season of *MADtv*, her first single was notoriously parodied by Nicole Sullivan as 'Lick My Baby Back Behind'. On the one hand, she was mocked for being a virgin. On the other hand, the 1999 cover of *Rolling Stone* showing Spears lying on her bed wearing an open top and a bra while hugging a teletubby provoked the American Family Association to call it 'a disturbing mix of childhood innocence and adult sexuality' and asked 'God-loving Americans to boycott stores selling Britney's albums' (Blandford 2002: 36). Despite recording a few successful albums (and having writing credits on numerous songs), the singer was called a manufactured product and for years had to prove her credibility as an artist.

Unlike many of Spears' previous singles, 'Toxic', the second single released off her fourth studio album, *In The Zone* (2003a), was both a commercial *and* a critical success. It was named the third-best song of 2004 by Pitchfork (n.d.) and won Spears her only Grammy Award in 2005. After the limited American success of the Madonna collaboration 'Me Against the Music' (2003b), which went to number two in the United Kingdom but stalled at thirty-five in the United States, it was not Spears' label's first single choice. Jive wanted to release the more urban-sounding '(I Got That) Boom Boom' (featuring Ying Yang Twins) or 'Outrageous' (written by R. Kelly). Still, the singer insisted on releasing the dance-pop-oriented 'Toxic'. It is Spears' favourite song from her catalogue, as she has claimed on several occasions. The single went on to become her third top-ten single in the United States and the fourth number one (and first of two consecutive number ones) in the United Kingdom. As of November 2020, with daily streams of more than 421,748, 'Toxic' (2004) remains Spears' most popular track on Spotify. The official music video directed by Joseph Kahn (with Spears' original concept; see Spears 2009a) is the second-most-viewed content on Spears' YouTube (477 million views), after her iconic 1998 single '... Baby One More Time', which *Rolling Stone* (2020) recently named the greatest debut single of all time. With the growth of social media, Spears' 'Toxic' has become a staple of popular culture. References to the song have appeared on memes and T-shirts (e.g. 'The only Toxic that we allow in 2019 is Toxic by Britney Spears' or 'No more toxic friendships – only Toxic by Britney Spears') and even on protest signs (e.g. Greta Thunberg's 'No more toxic air/no more toxic waste/only Toxic by Britney Spears' sign or the 'PiS you are Toxic'[1] slogans on cardboard Spears silhouettes used in Poland in 2020).

Spears was starting to play a more active role in her career at the time of 'Toxic's release. She fought to release it as a single. She also came up with the official music video's symbolical plot in which she plays four different secret agent characters, inspired by female characters such as ones from James Bond movies, *Blade Runner*, *The Seven Year Itch* and the TV series *Alias* and *Dark Angel* (Hawkins and Richardson 2007). Analysing the video, Hawkins and Richardson argue that in 'Toxic', 'the question of who is the "real" Spears really starts surfacing. Femme fatale, dirty teenager, bible-promoting virgin? Spears has begun pushing her career forward by the antics of queering, reinvention, and reconstruction' (2007: 620). Spears recreated her idea twice. The anime music video for 'Break the Ice' (2008a), the third single off *Blackout* (2007a), is based on the characters of 'Toxic', and the video for her comeback single, 'Womanizer' (2008d), off *Circus* (2008b), is a direct sequel. The latter was released when Spears lost all agency over her career *and* private life.

Spears was 'pushing her career forward' even during her notorious breakdown in 2007. Despite her publicised personal struggles and media backlash after shaving her head and attacking a paparazzo's SUV with an umbrella, she released (and executively produced) *Blackout*, an album that became a major influence on the pop scene in subsequent years. 'Gimme More' (2007b), the lead single starting with the iconic lyric 'It's Britney, bitch', became the singer's highest-charting single since '... Baby One More Time', while 'Piece of Me' (2008c), the follow-up, won three MTV Video Music Awards in 2008. *Blackout* is her only record appearing in the Rock & Roll Hall of Fame's music library

---

1   PiS is the acronym for the right-wing Polish political party Prawo i Sprawiedliwość [Law and Justice Party], which is currently in power.

and *Rolling Stone*'s 500 Greatest Albums of All Time list. It was also the last project before Spears' conservatorship.

It comes as no surprise that after the conservatorship, Spears' team wanted her to recreate 'Toxic' in the 'Womanizer' video (see Spears 2009b; 'Womanizer' became her second number-one single in the United States). As Hawkins and Richards note, the 'characters in *Toxic* are what McAdams calls "agentic" meaning that they exhibit heightened agentic characteristics, being "aggressive, ambitious, assertive, autonomous, clever, courageous, daring, dominant"' (2007: 614). While the video for 'Womanizer' (2009b) follows similar agentic 'imagoes', at the time of its release, Spears' control over her career had become limited.

In the eyes of the general public, Spears' notorious breakdown following her divorce from Kevin Federline and the loss of custody of their children is a thing of the past. Since then, Spears has released four albums and numerous hugely successful singles, embarked on four world tours, performed 250 concerts during her *Britney: Piece of Me* Las Vegas residency from 2013 to 2017, was a judge on *The X Factor* (Cowell, 2011–13) in 2012 and guest-starred on *How I Met Your Mother* (in 'Ten Sessions' and 'Everything Must Go') in 2008. After all, the saying 'if Britney survived 2007, you can survive today' is a staple of mugs, T-shirts and postcards.

That is why the #FreeBritney movement, established in 2019, at first seemed so puzzling, as most casual fans were not aware of the conservatorship that Spears, as a young adult, was put under in 2008. While the hashtag was initially used by BreatheHeavy, the movement was started by comedians Tess Barker and Barbara Gray, hosts of the *Britney's Gram* podcast. In 2019, Spears was supposed to begin *Domination*, her second Las Vegas residency, but it was surprisingly cancelled because of the singer's alleged 'distress over her father's health', which let her take some 'me time' in a mental health treatment facility (Weatherby 2019). Barker and Gray were informed that the show was cancelled by Jamie Spears, the singer's father, as punishment after she stopped taking her medications and wanted to reclaim some control over her personal life. Contrary to the information provided by Spears' team, the singer was put in a facility against her will in mid-January of 2019 – not mid-April (Kaufman 2020). Barker and Gray's podcast went viral and, consequently, fans and the media began scrutinising the conservatorship that Spears was put under before the release of 'Womanizer'. While Jamie Spears reportedly called it a 'joke' and a 'conspiracy theory', #FreeBritney received support from the singer's mother, Lynne Spears, and Spears' ex-husband Jason Alexander, as well as celebrities like Cher, Alexandria Ocasio-Cortez, Miley Cyrus and David LaChapelle. The latter claims that while filming the video for the 2016 'Make Me', Spears had only one wish – to appear in a cage (Spanos 2020).

The type of conservatorship Spears has been under since 2008 *is* like a cage. Usually, such arrangements are reserved for older adults who have dementia, individuals who have to be fed and bathed. Consequently, the singer has no control over her career – a surprise considering the twelve years of constant work, generating millions of dollars. Spears has no agency over her personal life either, as she cannot make medical decisions, is not allowed to get married (or become pregnant), or to drive a car or make calls without permission (Rosenberg 2021). In 2008 it was Jamie Spears who was named by the court as being suitable to become his older daughter's conservator and controller of her finances, as he 'is the only person Britney is afraid of, so she will not disobey him' (Reinstein 2008). This seems surprising as in her 2008 memoir, Lynne Spears, who divorced Jamie in 2002, writes about her ex-husband's history of alcoholism and abusive behaviour. Recently, she described the relationship between Jamie and Britney as 'toxic' (Associated Press 2020).

The details regarding the conservatorship have remained concealed. As her attorney Samuel D. Ingham III said in September 2020, 'Britney herself is vehemently opposed to this effort by her father to keep her legal struggle hidden away in the closet as a family secret' (qtd in TMZ 2020). Talking about Jamie's reaction to #FreeBritney, Ingham highlights Jamie's 'aggressive use of the sealing procedure over the years to minimize the amount of meaningful information made available to the public' (qtd in TMZ 2020). With the #FreeBritney movement, the general public started questioning the validity of Jamie's claims and the court's 2008 decision. How is it possible that Spears, who, as her father alleges, has dementia and is disabled, has managed to work so hard for the last twelve years? Why, instead of the constant criticism, did the media not question the objectification of teenage Spears? What does Spears' situation say about the toxic way the media talk about mental health – in this case of a young mother who gave birth to two children in eighteen months and was stripped of her parental rights? As Lisa of the *Eat, Pray, Britney* podcast notes, at the time of Spears' infamous breakdown, '[w]e weren't thinking critically about the messages behind the media reporting, the misogyny and classism at time' (qtd in Kaufman 2020). Moreover, Spears' mental health has been mocked not only by the media but also by fellow celebrities, including Shawn Mendes, Katy Perry, Eminem, Wendy Williams, Kathy Griffin, Blake Shelton, and others.

The case of Spears can lead to a more extensive discussion on the multidimensional toxicity young performers face in show business. To paraphrase the lyrics of 'Toxic', it comes without warning. Since the beginning of her career, the singer's agency has been either limited or denied. Despite starting as a gifted child singer, her credibility as a vocalist was soon undermined. Moreover, she has never fully regained her dancing skills after injuring her knee on the video set for 'Outrageous' (2004a). Spears has been objectified and dehumanised by the media and treated as a product supposed to bring profit. Even in 2020, while having no control over her estate and life, she is endorsing a new perfume, amusingly called Glitter Fantasy. After all, even toxicity can glitter.[2]

---

[2] During the time of final production of this book, Britney's position has drastically changed, with the thirteen years of her conservatorship coming to an end on 13 November 2021. How this plays out in terms of her ongoing relationship with the media and the music industry, and whether its previous toxicity will be lessened in any way, is yet to be seen.

Cathleen Allyn Conway

Ghostbusters: Answer the Call, Paul Feig (2016)

Introduction: 'You Have Been Bullied Your Entire Life. Now You Will Be the Bully'

The all-female reimagining of the original *Ghostbusters* story, *Ghostbusters: Answer the Call*, simultaneously anticipated, endured and suffered from toxic backlash because its fandom did not want to see – nor see a need for – a story about smart, middle-aged women responding to or usurping toxic environments.

The story of Dr Erin Gilbert (Kristen Wiig), Dr Abby Yates (Melissa McCarthy), Dr Jillian Holtzmann (Kate McKinnon) and Patty Tolan (Leslie Jones) and their navigation from obscurity to validation and recognition through battling a toxic geek named Rowan (Neil Casey), *Ghostbusters: Answer the Call* engages and responds to the (environ)mental toxicity women endure in their professional lives and uses humour to navigate it. This humour displaces men from the role of 'hero' to that of 'villain', or in the case of Kevin, the handsome but unintelligent secretary played by *Thor*'s Chris Hemsworth, from the actual role of 'hero' in other franchises to playing 'the stupid, pretty, useless blonde sex object that women have been forced to play in roughly every male-driven comedy ever' (Doyle 2016). This essay seeks to examine the ways in which the Ghostbusters engaged with the (environ)mental toxicity that surrounded the film, in contrast with the 1984 version (*Ghostbusters*) and its 1989 sequel (*Ghostbusters II*).

For the purposes of this essay, '(environ)mental' is stylised as such to represent both the physical and mental environment of the protagonists of these films – that is, the internal and external hostilities women experience when they transgress spaces coded as male-only. The terms 'toxicity' and 'waste' are used both literally and figuratively: as actual polluting substances and metaphors to describe the negative attitudes and rhetoric manifesting as misogyny and racism. They function as both noun and adjective.

'Safety Lights are for Dudes': (Environ)mental Pollution and Ruined Childhoods

Answer the Call launched with infuriated social media pushback from fans angry at '"their" franchise being "rewritten"' (Frankel 2019: 48). The film, which was made with the full blessing and participation of the surviving cast of the original, endured unmitigated racism and misogyny from the *Ghostbusters* fandom. 'Internet outrage over the reboot has been at a fever pitch ever since the female-fronted project was greenlit back in August 2014,' Zack Sharf (2016) wrote on *IndieWire* a week before the film's release, 'and every part of Sony's release strategy (from trailers to soundtrack updates and even press screenings) has only seemed to encourage more mean-spirited attacks from fanboys and internet users unhappy with the new film's direction'.

When critics of *Answer the Call* vocalise their discontent, the foremost complaint is that the *Ghostbusters* reimagining 'ruined [their] childhood'. Describing the response as 'a feeble cover for what is basically an enraged anti-feminism backlash, something which is a depressing inevitability when women attempt to do anything, in any context, ever', neuroscientist Dean Burnett argued in *The Guardian*: 'The prominence in our memories of our childhood entertainment may mean they are a disproportionately large aspect of our identity ... any attempt at updating or change could ... be perceived as an attack on our identity' (Burnett 2016). This conflict prompts the question as to what kind of childhood is ruined or rewritten by *Answer the Call*. What is this identity under perceived attack: one in which the pursuit of free market capitalist ghostbusting with no regard for regulation nor environmental impact can continue unimpeded and ghosts represent an 'other' to be conquered and eradicated, or one in which neoliberalism and late capitalism are sidelined in favour of other definitions of progress?

What that 'childhood' contained in terms of the original source material demands interrogation. According to Salter and Blodgett (2017), 'pop culture

Figure 30. Tweet from feminist writer Clementine Ford.

Source: Twitter, @Zachheltzel, 11 July 2016.

holds recurring examples of the geek turned hero, often through redefined masculinity or context', and 'the defense of geek culture might be correlated to expressions of masculinity'. The original *Ghostbusters* present a unique twist on this trope. Harold Ramis (co-writer and actor) said that Dan Aykroyd (also co-writer and actor) gave a one-line version of *Ghostbusters* (1984) as 'ghost janitors in New York' (Matloff 2014): they took on traditionally 'masculine' roles, or jobs largely populated by men. Significantly, Aykroyd contextualised the characters from inception as workers who manage and dispose of waste. While 'garbage man' may not be a likely hero, it is a relatable one, and *Ghostbusters* romanticised the otherwise unglamourous work performed in coveralls with a surname patched on.

The first *Ghostbusters* holds multiple contradictory concerns: the Ghostbusters were simultaneously working-class heroes and fully funded academics that bankrolled their own business with the sale of inherited assets; they were concerned with protecting the city of New York from the pollution of an invasive spectral force, yet regarded Walter Peck (William Atherton), the local representative of the Environmental Protection Agency, as an antagonist worthy of ridicule and emasculation, despite the character being of the same socioeconomic class as the Ghostbusters themselves, who repeatedly quip about the 'unlicensed nuclear accelerators' they wear.

'Ghosts' as a pollutant or waste is furthered in the sequel. Those who criticised *Answer the Call* as having 'ruined childhoods' must have missed the plot of *Ghostbusters II* (1989): the film's antagonist is a 'psychomagnotheric', 'viscous, psychoreactive plasm' running through the city's sewers and tunnels, which 'feeds on bad vibes' and 'responds to human emotional states', and is bested by positive, nurturing, supportive energy in the form of a woman, an animated Statue of Liberty, mobilised by the voice and the sound of a Black person, Jackie Wilson. The *Ghostbusters* fandom, in essence, both made the plot of *Ghostbusters II* a metaphoric reality and became the antagonists in their own canon by attacking every gender of Ghostbuster.

These 'bad vibes', the (environ)mental toxicity that surrounds *Answer the Call*, are embodied in the antagonist Rowan. He refers to people in general as 'walking sewage' and the world itself as 'garbage that needs to be cleaned up', which not only embeds Aykroyd's characterisation that 'calling a Ghostbuster was just like getting rats removed', but also echoes the language of the online

Figure 31. The Ghostbusters (Dan Aykroyd, Ernie Hudson, Bill Murray and Harold Ramis) discuss the 'mood slime' threatening New York.

Source: *Ghostbusters II*; directed by Ivan Reitman (Columbia Pictures, 1989).

rhetoric of Twitter, where the most violent harassment surrounding *Answer the Call* occurred (Matloff 2014). Salter and Blodgett write that 'the narratives within the geek culture become the narratives geeks use to define their own heroism, sometimes with dangerous results for groups marginalised by those very narratives' (Salter and Blodgett 2017: 11), which is evident in the fandom's response to *Answer the Call*. In Rowan, the insecurities and fears of the *Ghostbuster* fandom become realised on-screen as the guy who 'should', be the hero in a *Ghostbusters* film becomes the villain. 'There were nasty comments before there was even a movie. There's nothing for you to watch, nothing has been written, and you're already saying it's the worst movie in the world', according to *Answer the Call* screenwriter Katie Dippold (Day 2016). It is possible to read the final film as though the toxicity seeped into its development to form a foundation and narrative, becoming the fandom's self-fulfilling prophecy of *Ghostbusters II* while providing the film-makers with more material for metacommentary, such as when Abby beckons Erin to read comments online that are 'not all crazies' and the first one Erin sees is: 'Ain't no bitches gonna hunt no ghosts' (see Figure 32).

Figure 32. Abby (Melissa McCarthy) shows Erin (Kristen Wiig) the comments on their website while Jillian (Kate McKinnon) looks on.

Source: *Ghostbusters: Answer the Call*; directed by Paul Feig (Columbia Pictures, 2016).

The intersections of race and gender are touched on in the film when Rowan accuses the Ghostbusters, who include middle-aged women, plus-sized women, and specifically a Black woman, how passed over he has been:

ROWAN: Then you must have been afforded the basic dignity and the respect of a human being, which I have been denied.

ABBY: Not really. People dump on us pretty much all the time.

CUT TO: PATTY, nodding

The worst of the online abuse was targeted at Black actress Leslie Jones, who was, as Doyle reports:

> deluged on Twitter with racist threats and rape threats so vile that I couldn't even look at them without getting sick. There were hundreds. There were cartoons of child porn. There was a picture of Jones Photoshopped so that it looked like semen was on her face. There was someone typing the word 'coon' at her over and over and over again, and there were Photoshopped Tweets of her saying vile things, and there were people calling her a monkey or a gorilla, and there were simply some people calling her the n-word, and this. Went. On. For. *Hours*. (2016, emphasis in the original)

The misogynoir, or when racism compounds misogyny, was not anticipated by the white film maker to the same extent. The film recognises but does not fully interrogate its own white feminism in how it treats Patty, who is repeatedly ignored in her Metropolitan Transport Authority job by commuters and graffiti artists alike and is initially underestimated by her own team ('Patty, try a little bit harder'; *Ghostbusters: Answer the Call*, 2016) despite her extensive knowledge on the history of New York City and her physical and emotional strength. On their first job, Patty shouts: 'Okay, you sweaty freaks. I'm 'bout to save you from this ghost!' (Feig 2016) and jumps into the crowd, only to land on her back as they step away. Later, Patty battles a superstrong ghost possessed Abby while holding onto Jillian as she dangles out the window. The Black woman resilience Patty represents was tested in real life. A few days after the film opened, Jones herself tweeted, 'I feel like I'm in a personal hell. I didn't do anything to deserve this. It's just too much. It shouldn't be like this' (Jones 2016), suggesting that even as a Black woman who worked in entertainment, Jones didn't anticipate this level of racial, sexist abuse, either. And it is not without irony that even with Rowan's 'millions of souls' who are 'seeking revenge' being 'mostly dudes' (Feig 2016), it lacked the dignity and respect in their interactions, even during battle that Black woman, Patty, demonstrated throughout.

'Why Am I So Flattered that Little Sociopath Bought Our Book?' Women at Work

In many respects, *Answer the Call* can be read as an allegory for the (environ) mental toxicity women endure at work, and that toxicity is the foundation of the film's comedic subject. When the audience is introduced to Erin, her conservative skirt suit and heels are met with wardrobe policing from the dean of her department, who also claims her referral from Princeton University is not 'prestigious' enough. When Abby and Jillian take Erin to meet their dean, he responds with 'incredibly immature behaviour' by telling them to 'suck it' and performing a series of middle-finger gestures (Feig 2016). The message sent by both deans, one of which is wearing flip-flops to work, is that no matter what they do, women will never be good enough. Erin and Abby mirror one another: while one is overly scrutinised, the other is told 'I just honestly didn't realise your department still existed' (Feig 2016) by a dean who contests the accusation he is unqualified despite allegedly spelling 'science' with a 'Y'.

Superficially, these are not jokes, but reflections of the expectations working women experience. *Answer the Call*'s comedy is heavily laden with dramatic irony and the pathos of 'punching up' at the institutional and patriarchal systems that subvert and oppress women. When Rowan claims, 'I am a genius. I see things no one else does. And for it, I am rewarded with nothing but scorn and mockery', he is making this pronouncement to the two women, who themselves have received nothing but scorn and mockery for their research, including the book they wrote, which Rowan himself used for his plan – further proof that their research provided 'provable, physical results' (Feig 2016) and a grim reminder of how women can be erased from their own success.

Although Frankel argues that the backlash *Answer the Call* endured was from 'a particular anger at stories that dismiss the men entirely' (2019: 48–9), it is worth noting that *Ghostbusters: Answer the Call* did not 'dismiss men entirely' but instead never considered them necessary for inclusion in the first place. Doyle (2016) writes:

> the movie doesn't really grapple with the fact that the leads are all women. None of them ever starts a consciousness-raising group or suggests that the ghosts could be defeated with a vigorous reading of Audre Lorde. They just tell jokes and bust ghosts. [...] Women aren't treated as a big boundary-breaking historic symbol of progress and equality in this movie. They're treated like *people*. (Emphasis in the original)

Reference to male violence, abuse of women and toxic masculinity is on display from the first scene in *Answer the Call*, and the film takes aim at these repeatedly. The tragic irony of its audience of women laughing at men being the butt of the jokes for maybe the first time ever is perhaps the true source of the fandom's outrage. Or perhaps that men looked to *Answer the Call* and did not see their own wish fulfilment, but someone else's, may go some way to answering the question as to why the film inspired so much toxicity. The humour of *Answer the Call* relies on the audience's recognition of and identification with the situation and the escapist wish fulfilment to see these characters succeed, much like men can at will look on-screen for empowerment found in superheroes and 'geek' culture.

It is a wish fulfilment set specifically in a professional milieu: what the women of *Answer the Call* want is professional recognition and success based on their hard work, and like many women, they take what wins they can, including the limited validation of 'creepy little sociopath' Rowan buying their book. It is a stark contrast to the male Ghostbusters, whose primary concerns within academia were 'money and facilities'. (Reitman 1984) – voiced particularly by Peter Venkman, played by Bill Murray in the first two *Ghostbusters* instalments.

First identified in the opening scene of *Ghostbusters* hitting on a student, Venkman is the smarmy, balding, self-proclaimed fraud in the first two who gets the girl, in *Answer the Call*, Erin pointedly does not get the guy. Whereas Venkman represents the arrested development of the geek hero from the first two films, *Answer the Call* specifically positions itself in opposition to the juvenile. Venkman is the antithesis of the Ghostbusters in *Answer the Call*: he is initially accused of treating science as a 'dodge' or 'hustle'. With this in mind, Murray's role in *Answer the Call* takes on additional weight as he plays cynical ghost debunker Martin Heiss, who taunts, goads and belittles the team to the point that Erin releases their captured ghost to 'prove herself', which results in Heiss being blasted out the window to his death. It is a moment that complements Venkman's first ghost encounter, in which the ghost woman responds with 'Sssh!' when he attempts to engage her with a pickup line. As both Venkman and Heiss, Murray plays bullies. While the former is cheered, the latter is just one more example of the (environ)mental toxicity the women Ghostbusters endure in trying to pursue their field of study and have their research be both acknowledged in general and recognised for the groundbreaking advancement it is.

It is interesting to note fan and critic response to the fourth instalment of the *Ghostbusters franchise*, Ghostbusters: Afterlife (Reitman, 2021), which had delayed release due to the COVID-19 pandemic, but comments from Murray suggest an undercurrent of toxic elements were present. In an April 2021 interview, Murray said *Afterlife* is 'a Ghostbusters movie that really brings [the franchise] back to life. It really has the feel of the first one, more than the second one or the girls' one. It has a different feel than two out of four' (qtd in Lavin 2021).

Murray capitalises on the inherent toxicity of the franchise as economic model by placing the films in competition with one another and equating 'quality' with financial performance. His comments give fans and critics a narrative that prioritises profit over performance, craft or story – the aspects of the films for which he may be culpable. Evaluating the worth or authenticity of films based only on fan response and ensuing financial performance is not a reliable, impenetrable metric, which the deliberate tanking of *Answer the Call* should have proved. Further, part of Murray's rationale for the quality of *Afterlife* is based on the fact the shoot 'was hard. It was really hard. That's why I think it's gonna be good' (qtd in Lavin 2021).

It is indicative of the toxicity discussed in this essay that Murray's struggle with the physical aspects of filming *Afterlife* are in his view an indication of 'quality'. He said: 'Usually, when something has a very high misery quotient, something comes of that and some quality is produced that, if you can capture it and project it, comes on the screen and affects you' (qtd in Lavin 2021). However, the emotional abuse endured by the cast of *Answer the Call* did not, in fact, "affect' an audience of viewers who wrote at length at how affected they were by the film, its message and its representation.

Conclusion

Margaret Atwood said men are afraid women will laugh at them, and in the case of *Answer the Call*, women laugh at them. If this is the childhood they claim the film destroys, then their response – to tank the film at all costs – fulfils the second half of Atwood's axiom, which is that women are afraid men will kill them.

In the first *Ghostbusters*, the male characters redefine themselves by embracing the masculine roles of 'being your own bosses' and taking on working-class jobs – roles previously identified as being only performed by men through the socioeconomic constructs feminism seeks to dismantle. The presence of women Ghostbusters therefore confirms that in some spaces, success has been achieved. The pushback *Answer the Call* endured towards a *fictional* representation of women's success is indicative of the levels of toxicity women currently endure, much like the pink slime permeating *Ghostbusters II*. As Maris Kreizman (2016) puts it: 'It's only on later reflection [...] that a silly movie like *Ghostbusters* would feel revolutionary. The hope that girl power can be harnessed to great effect cannot die. That we can wear a Ghostbuster suit or a pantsuit and we can hold power in our hands and use it.' Unfortunately, a national monument in the shape of a woman is unlikely to positively charge the (environ)mental toxicity of the slime-ridden hearts and minds who attacked *Answer the Call*, even if she did reappear.

Debaditya Mukhopadhyay

Kabir Singh, Sandeep Reddy Vanga (2019)

Though the presence of blatant misogyny in commercially successful films has been met with a significant number of critical responses, the safeguarding of its presence within the world of film reviews for popular platforms has received little attention. In this chapter, one such attempt will be made by focusing on the fracas ensuing from the polarising reviews of Bollywood's hit film *Kabir Singh* (2019), which is an official remake of the Tamil hit film *Arjun Reddy* (2017) by the same director. While Bollywood, like many other commercial film industries, has recurrently witnessed disagreements between makers and reviewers of films, in the case of *Kabir Singh* this conflict reveals more than just a difference of opinion. Rather, it highlights how Bollywood strives to suppress dissent against its trend of rehashing love stories featuring toxic males as heroes by way of its review system, and its coercion of media that host non-positive reviewers, signalling a larger problem of enabling certain toxic behaviour within Bollywood.

The film *Kabir Singh* and the brouhaha over its negative reviews provide significant scope for tracing an emergent network of normalising toxic behaviour. Taking note of this scope, the essay will explore both the initiation of this normalising process by Vanga's film and the review system's way of carrying on the process by remaining silent about the deliberate downplaying of toxic elements in the film and silencing negative reviewers. Keeping this aim in mind, this discussion will at first analyse the politics of representing toxic masculinity within the film in question, to trace the first phase of this network of safeguarding. Thereafter, the analysis will be developed further by a category-wise close reading of written and YouTube reviews of the film and analysis of the politics underlying the trolling by the film's director, Sandeep

Reddy Vanga, of the negative reviews of the film. In other words, a quick description of the important scenes within *Kabir Singh* will be followed by a summary of the toxic elements involved in the entire process of reviewing the film (such as the defence of many characteristics of toxic masculinity and the abuse of reviewers who critique the film's valorisation of these traits). These overviews will be collated to show how despite the clear presence of what one might call a rhetoric of downplaying toxic masculinity in the film as well as in the majority of its reviews, the director (and, by extension, the Bollywood industry itself) desperately tried to troll the few and far between negative reviews.

The Film and Its Downplaying of Toxic Masculinity

Being a widely popular film with lengthy Wikipedia and IMDb entries on its plot, the film *Kabir Singh* hardly requires a plot summary per se, but the various elements of the film that collectively make a hero out of a thoroughly abusive and toxic personality certainly need to be mentioned. Rather than making ample room for its viewers to form their own opinions about Kabir, the film starts by carefully crafting a heroic as well as poetic image of him. At the start, the film shows Kabir (Shahid Kapoor) lying in bed with absolute serenity, embracing his beloved Preeti (Kiara Advani), with the sounds of sea waves and Kabir reciting lines written by Amir Khusrau (see Figure 33).

The recited lines describe love as an ocean in which one must drown in order to conquer it, and add that whoever finds the waves of this ocean of love to be chaotic *has never really loved at all*. Such lines, the sound of sea waves (that become metaphorical when conjoined with Khusrau's lines) and the dominance of the colour white (symbolic of peace) call on the viewers to henceforth see this couple and their love story as an ideal one. In other words, the serene opening sequence is intended as a defence of the numerous scenes that follow showing Preeti being mishandled by Kabir. Seen in the light of Khusrau's lines, that basically set the tone for the rest of the film, the problematic moments of the film where Kabir abuses, manhandles and even slaps

Kabir Singh, Sandeep Reddy Vanga (2019)

Figure 33. Kabir and Preeti in the opening scene.
Source: *Kabir Singh*; directed by Sandeep Reddy Vanga (AA Films, 2019).

Preeti become those chaotic waves of the ocean of love in which one must find serenity in order to fall in love genuinely.

Aside from the opening scene, the film's story is adorned with a large array of components that glorify Kabir. We often see in the film that Kabir is named after a renowned Indian mystic poet. Subsequently, on several occasions in the film, he recites poetry to illustrate his deep and spiritual nature, as when consoling his father after the death of Kabir's grandmother – in fact, Kabir has a very strained relationship with his father, as he is the only person who openly criticises his son for his behaviour. However, this is purposeful misdirection, as these traits have very little consistency within the narrative.

This kind of purposeful misdirection is shown in three ways throughout the film. First, the screenplay's non-linear narrative, by rearranging the development of Kabir's character, impedes the viewers ability to notice his growing toxicity. In reality, Kabir is a haughty and arrogant college student with no respect for female consent and whose toxicity increases alarmingly when he takes to drugs after Preeti is forced to marry a man chosen by her father. Viewers, however, get very little scope to notice this growing toxicity of Kabir's character, as the non-linear narration disrupts the story flow and is even detoxified to some extent by the constant use of melodious songs in the background. An example of this is seen at the start of the film when we see Kabir as an aggressive alcoholic, but this is tempered by the song 'Bekhayali' playing in the background; the song decries those that behave nonchalantly when defeated in love, consequently showing Kabir's excessive behaviour as a sign of genuine love.

Second, the screenplay's overall structure is such that the audience is constantly encouraged to view Kabir's toxic behaviour as a tragic love story. But, as pointed out by the controversial film reviewer Kamaal R. Khan (2019), the entire second half of the film is about Kabir and his drinking. In this way, the film's story becomes a notable instance of manipulative narration: on the one hand, the larger portion of the total runtime displays toxic behaviour such as drug abuse and violence towards women, while, on the other, melodic songs played throughout the movie keep reminding the audience to view it as a tragic love story. Third, the plot ensures that Kabir always appears fair, as those he abuses are shown to be deserving in some way – comical (as in the case of Preeti's brother), villainous (as with a student of a rival college, who reportedly molests Preeti) or regretful of their initial reactions to Kabir's behaviour (his own father, the college dean and Preeti's father).

The Film Reviews: Downplaying Continued

Instead of drawing attention to the above-mentioned strategies of the film that downplay Kabir's toxic behaviour, the majority of the film's reviewers seem to further downplay Kabir's behaviour. To see how this works, a close reading of a select number of reviews of *Kabir Singh* will follow. Reviews that represent positive, negative and supposedly neutral takes on the film have been chosen purposefully. Typically, positive reviews of the film were released even before it had its official release on 21 June 2019. In one such review (published on 19 June), Nitya Prakash, simply ignoring the film's endorsing of toxic masculinity, called the film 'a must watch' and hailed its director as 'a man with guts' for coming up with a film that, in Prakash's opinion, exists in 'a space' which Bollywood hardly dared to enter before. Kabir's actions, in his opinion 'show his recklessness and free-spirited attitude', and he also adds that it is Kabir's 'madness' and

Kabir Singh, Sandeep Reddy Vanga (2019)

'unwillingness to change' that makes Preeti accept him so gladly at the end (Prakash 2019). Among the reviewers publishing their write-ups in popular platforms before the film's screen release, only Ronak Kotecha (20 June 2019) mentions the presence of what he calls 'brash male toxicity' in the film. Interestingly, in terms of a recommendation to the audience, he calls the film 'a welcome change from stereotypical love stories' and ends his review by saying that the director has presented Kabir's character with such perfection that one can 'love him or hate him' but one can never 'ignore him' (Kotecha 2019).

Rajeev Masand's review (21 June 2019) takes a different view, calling the movie an 'unmistakably misogynistic film' and 'an unapologetic celebration of toxic masculinity'. More importantly, Masand (2019) reminds the reader that the problem lies with the fact that the film simply refuses to answer why men like Kabir exhibit 'such proprietary behavior' and instead 'peddle' these acts as signs of 'intense love'. Concurrently, Shubhra Gupta's review (21 June 2019) manages to detect the film's issues in terms of its amplification of toxic masculinity, pointing out how Kabir as a character does not really capture the 'vulnerability' of Arjun Reddy and ends up being 'all flourish, mostly surface'. Further, he points out that Kabir Singh's display of toxic behaviour is even more problematic because Arjun Reddy comes from the provinces while Kabir undertakes his antics in the urban (and, therefore, progressive) backdrop of megacities like Delhi or Mumbai. Among the negative reviewers, only Raja Sen (21 June 2019) goes the extent of making an indirect appeal to avoid the film, calling it 'injurious to health'.

Significantly, written reviews of *Kabir Singh* by women are very few in number. The only female critic, Priyanka Sinha Jha (21 June 2019), who reviews films for popular online domains, adopts a strategy similar to that of Nitya Prakash and does not mention anything specific about Kabir's toxic traits and how they are shown in the movie. Instead, she focuses mostly on the positive aspects of the film, like the lead actor's performance, popular music, cinematography, etc. Though she does identify Kabir to be 'a problematic character reprised and modelled along the film heroes of yore, the kind who would persist and refused to take no for an answer', she does not dwell further on how problematic it is for Bollywood to rehash such a character for present-day audiences, thereby showing a near neutral stance (Jha 2019).

It is also to be noted that Priyanka reviews the film for the same platform (News 18) that hosted Masand's negative review. Arriving about eight hours after Masand's review, Priyanka's write-up looks more like damage control than a regular review.

The female reviewers using YouTube to share their responses show more directness, however. Sucharita Tyagi (21 June 2019), in a scene-by-scene review of the film, admits frankly that she had never previously felt uncomfortable watching a film in a theatre, but she was uncomfortable viewing *Kabir Singh*. This was because the scenes of Preeti meekly letting Kabir do anything he wanted to her – which in themselves made Tyagi, as a woman, uncomfortable – elicited joyous approval from the larger audience (Tyagi 2019). Similarly, Stutee Ghosh (2019) explains how the film is a scene-by-scene rehash of the original Tamil film and adds that it is problematic because it 'reinforces very problematic notions about love'. None of these reviewers, however, make an appeal to the audience to boycott the film. Instead, Tyagi begins her review with a 'heads up', stating clearly that her review is meant only for those who *do not* intend to watch the film; those interested in viewing *Kabir Singh* are requested to just skip her video. The proportion of 'likes' and 'dislikes' for each of these videos shows that instead of being influenced by the videos, the public expressed their solidarity with the film and its director. Within twenty-four hours of uploading and posting the first batch of reviews – which, as has been shown, either recommended that the audience watch the film or explained the content of the film without any call to avoid it – Sandipan Sharma (22 June 2019) took to the website of *The Federal* to offer a defence of making films like *Kabir Singh*, reminding the reader that critics did not bother to respond to problematic female characters in recent Bollywood films and that society has many characters like Kabir Singh. Significantly, this particular review by Sharma was reposted on *First Post* (28 June 2019) within a week of its initial appearance. Such reiteration clearly shows that a certain section of the industry were eager to protect the film from negative reviews.

Kabir Singh, Sandeep Reddy Vanga (2019)

The Director's Trolling of Negative Reviewers

Surprisingly, despite having his film garlanded with praise by reviewers even before its release and defended by others afterwards the fact, the director Sandeep Reddy Vanga, in his YouTube interviews, accused the negative reviewers of damaging his film's revenues. In the first of his two interviews for the popular YouTube channel Film Companion, Vanga attacked the negative reviewers (particularly Sucharita Tyagi and Rajeev Masand), calling them a threat bigger than piracy and adding that they are parasites living off the films they criticise (Vanga 2019a). Taking his abuse a notch higher, in the second interview with Bollywood Hungama, Vanga dared the negative reviewers to wait at least a week before posting their reviews and accused them of creating serious commercial damage to his film and Bollywood in general (Vanga 2019b).

Beginning of a New Problematic Trend?

The series of events outlined in this essay represent the emergence of a problematic tendency in Bollywood. It shows Bollywood's perennial fascination for rehashing narratives of self-destructive love and the problematic turn that sees the toxic male as self-destructive hero. More importantly, this problematic turn is aided by reviewers and the trend of calling out dissenters. As pointed out by Masand (2019), Kabir's character has striking similarities to that of Devdas (Shah Rukh Khan) from the eponymous film (Bhansali, 2002), who is 'patron saint of self-destructive romantics'. Exploring this connection further, Viswamohan and Chaudhuri describe Devdas as the source of the recent Bollywood films they collectively refer to as 'angromance', a term reflective of these films' portrayal of the 'angst-ridden hero' who asserts his 'passion, sexuality, and masculinity' through 'anger' (2020: 154).

Interestingly, before *Kabir Singh*'s release, the angromantic hero had remained absent for more than fifteen years in Bollywood, but with the release

Figure 34. Devdas, played by Shah Rukh Khan.
Source: *Devdas*; directed by Sanjay Leela Bhansali (Red Chillies Entertainment, 2002).

of Vanga's film, this figure returned in an even more toxic avatar at a time when Bollywood was witnessing the emergence of 'women-centric movies' (Viswamohan and Chaudhuri 2020: 148). Kabir's character, repeatedly shown to be unsophisticated and physically aggressive, is more aggressive than that of Devdas, who, in the words of Ashis Nandy (in the earliest *Devdas* films), appears 'effeminate' and 'maudlin' (qtd. in Sarkar 2016: 30). Figures 34 and 35 clearly bring out the similarity between these two characters (using Shah Rukh Khan's *Devdas*, the last traditional Bollywood adaptation of the character, as a reference) while also marking an amplification of aggressiveness in *Kabir Singh*.

Additionally, as a film, *Kabir Singh* is more problematic than Satish Kaushik's *Tere Naam* (2003), which, according to Viswamohan and Chaudhuri, is *Kabir Singh*'s immediate predecessor as an angromance. While *Tere Naam* ended punishingly by showing its toxic hero lose everything, in Vanga's film, Kabir wins back Preeti and his social life. More importantly, neither the *Devdas* films nor *Tere Naam* were defended to the extent of attempts to silence negative reviews.

Kabir Singh, Sandeep Reddy Vanga (2019)

Figure 35. Kabir Singh.
Source: *Kabir Singh*; directed by Sandeep Reddy Vanga (AA Films, 2019).

Kabir Singh, thus, in many ways marks a new development in Bollywood's review culture in which reviewers who refuse to accept Bollywood films' representation of problematic behaviour as heroic are actively silenced. In this way, all those shown to contribute to the affirmation of such depictions of toxic masculinity, such as the reviewers defending the film and its director, are no less than willing enablers of continued violence against women.

Bethan Jones

Star Wars Episodes VII–IX, Various (2015–2019)

The Fandom Menace[1]

Much scholarly work has been produced on the ways in which fans and fan communities have protested injustice, raised money for various causes and improved the lives of individual fans through the development of these close-knit communities. But fandom has also been plagued since its beginnings with 'shipping' wars,[2] disagreements with producers and the gatekeeping of certain practices. And that is to say nothing of the racism and homophobia which has existed alongside the squee but has largely been overlooked in scholarly circles (see Pande 2018). Since 2003, work has been done on the less savoury sides of fandom: Jonathan Gray coined the term 'anti-fandom' to describe 'those who strongly dislike a given text or genre, considering it inane, stupid, morally bankrupt and/or aesthetic drivel' (2003: 70), and scores of scholars have subsequently adopted, adapted and built on Gray's work. But as Melissa Click notes, 'while this work, and the necessity of studying anti-fandom generally, has been enthusiastically received, anti-fan scholarship has progressed only slightly in the last few years' (2019: 2).

---

1   The Fandom Menace is also the name of a right-leaning *Star Wars* fan group created by former Comicsgate supporter Ethan Van Sciver and formed in response to *Star Wars: The Last Jedi* (Johnson, 2017).
2   Shipping is the fannish practice of imagining or investing in a relationship between two characters. To ship Rey and Kylo, for example, is to hope for a canonical relationship to develop between the two. However, shipping is not limited to fictional characters, and fans can and do ship 'real life' celebrities. It is an often-contentious practice.

Digital communication tools have made it easier for people to express their feelings towards a variety of subjects. From hate-watching reality TV shows on Twitter to criticising the move to the right in global politics, social media platforms have 'facilitated the growth and visibility of public expressions of dislike and hatred as well as the growth and visibility of anti-fans themselves' (Click 2019: 7). The emergence of Gamergate in 2014 was perhaps one of the most visible instances of anti-fandom, when game developer Zoe Quinn was accused by her ex-boyfriend of sleeping with a games journalist in order to secure a good review for her recently released game *Depression Quest*. Although on the surface Gamergate was about ethics in video games, it soon led to attacks on Quinn and other women in gaming, like Anita Sarkeesian and Brianna Wu. These attacks include rape and death threats, doxing and hundreds of racist and misogynistic comments. Matt Hills (2018) suggests that Gamergate forced toxic online practices into the mainstream, and indeed fan studies has begun to interrogate these toxic practices and what they mean for fandom and its academic analysis. But what do I mean by toxic fandom? Think about hemlock, or deadly nightshade. Fast-acting poisonous plants which can cause death if not treated quickly enough, and which can also cause serious damage in small doses, affecting the respiratory, nervous and cardiovascular systems. These plants become dangerous when interacted with – deadly nightshade in your garden is unlikely to do any harm, but once ingested its toxins seep through the body, affecting every part. Toxic fandom operates – literally and figuratively, as Conway notes in this collection – in much the same way. Fans can, and do, hold opinions which are homophobic, racist and sexist, and those become harmful when shared. Toxic behaviours and practices may start small, but their effects can quickly spread through a fandom. Much like poisonous plants, these practices can affect multiple groups and even spread into other fandoms. Too many toxins and fandoms fracture and collapse, and even a small dose means that fandom may take a long time to recover.

In this chapter, I am interested in fan responses to the *Star Wars* sequels *The Force Awakens* (Abrams, 2015), *The Last Jedi* (Johnson, 2017) and *The Rise of Skywalker* (Abrams, 2019). In particular, I focus on the fans who ship Rey (Daisy Ridley) and Kylo Ren (Adam Driver), how they have been received by fans who are opposed to that pairing, and their interactions with John Boyega, who plays former stormtrooper Finn in the films. As already noted, shipping wars are not new in fandom. Victoria M. Gonzalez notes that shipping 'can be a highly contentious fan activity that leads to disputes within fandoms as shippers attempt to regulate ships and the ways in which fans go about shipping them' (2016: 1.1), and Leora Hadas (2013) identifies shippers as one of the two types of fans who suffer the most open condemnation on fan forums. These forms of gatekeeping can be seen in reactions to Reylo shippers, but rather than being cowed or deterred, Reylos have clapped back, drawing actor John Boyega into the middle of the shipping war and perpetuating forms of toxic, racist fandom.

'Two that Are One': Shipping and Subcultural Superiority

When *The Force Awakens* was first released, many fans were rooting for a relationship between Finn and Poe (Oscar Isaac), but by the end of *The Rise of Skywalker*, Rey and Kylo had emerged as one of the main, and most controversial, ships from the sequels. Reylos – the term a portmanteau of the characters' names – are a predominantly female subgroup of fans dedicated to the ship. Rey and Kylo, like many heroes and villains, are inextricably linked. Kylo describes them as 'a dryad in the force' and a Force-bond exists between them that allows them to communicate across light years and eventually fight together as one against the Elite Praetorian Guard. The Force-bond allows Rey and Kylo to connect on an intimate level, a fact that contributes to Reylos' beliefs that the two belong together. Indeed, *The Rise of Skywalker* focuses on the relationship and Kylo's redemption arc, and ultimately canonised the ship with a kiss between Rey and Kylo before he – now Ben Solo, having returned to the light side of the Force – died. Many of the criticisms aimed at *Twilight* (Hardwicke, 2008) and *Fifty Shades of Grey* (Taylor-Johnson, 2015) are used against the Reylo ship, chief among them that it promotes an abusive relationship, but much like *Twilight* and *Fifty Shades*, the toxic nature of these posts targets women who find pleasure in a specific ship.

The use of slurs, the statements that Reylo shippers should die and the mocking of Reylo shippers' intelligence are not new practices in shipping wars.

Figure 36. Some of the tweets posted about Reylo shippers.
Source: collected by K. M. McCort.

When *GQ* magazine published an interview with boy band One Direction, fans took umbrage at its portrayal of Harry Styles and flooded the *GQ* Twitter account with tweets which included threats to bomb their headquarters, chop their heads off and other similar exhortations. In this case, fans were targeting an organisation that had no involvement in the fandom, but the type of language used reflects that of anti-Reylo shippers who target other *Star Wars* fans. The goal is the same – to express outrage at specific practices and to ideally make that behaviour stop. Within fandom, this forms what Kristina Busse (2013) describes as 'border policing'. She argues that 'what underlies much of this border policing is a clear sense of protecting one's own sense of fan community and ascribing positive values to it while trying to exclude others' (2013: 75). Those fans criticising Reylo shippers thus position themselves on the side of good fan practice (not supporting a ship which presents as abusive in the source material) and attempt to elevate that position within the fandom and its discourse. As I have noted in relation to One Direction fans' responses to the shipping of Harry Styles and Louis Tomlinson, tweets posted by fans 'function as a form of embodied subcultural capital, and the meaning decoded by fans is either one of subcultural superiority (for Larry haters) or subcultural inferiority (for Larry shippers)' (Jones 2016: 62). Anti-Reylos (or 'antis' as they are referred to in the fandom) thus position themselves as subculturally superior to Reylos.

Of course, as Rebecca Harrison writes:

> there are multiple viewing positions available to viewers of the films, and it's not a straightforward case of saying Kylo is or isn't abusive given the complex nature of his and Rey's relationship with each other and with senior male figures including Snoke, Palpatine and Luke [...] *no one deserves hatred on the basis of shipping two age-appropriate adult characters*. (2020, emphasis mine)

However, K. M. McCort (2020), a data analyst and fan, published an essay in which she suggests two additional reasons why Reylos are harassed in fandom: they are sexist because they 'write sexually explicit fanfiction between the "pure" heroine and the "bad guy"'; and they are racist 'because they support a romantic pairing between two white characters' (see Figure 36). I do not have scope in this essay to examine the first assertion, though sexually explicit fan fiction between the hero/heroine and the bad guy is certainly not limited to *Star Wars* fandom. However, the second assertion is the subject of the next section, which examines in more detail the allegations of racism levelled at Reylos and the racism which emerges within toxic fandom more broadly.

Reylos, Racism and John Boyega

As already mentioned, one of the more popular ships that came out of *The Force Awakens* was that of former stormtrooper Finn and resistance pilot Poe Dameron, or Finnpoe. Both men of colour (Boyega is British Nigerian and Isaac, born in Guatemala, has a Guatemalan mother and a Cuban father), they developed a deep bond during their escape from the Star Destroyer, and moments like Poe giving Finn his jacket led to fans shipping the pair. By the end of *Rise of Skywalker*, however, the ship had been overtaken by Reylo. A search on Archive of Our Own (n.d.), one of the largest fan fiction sites on the internet, shows 638 results for Finnpoe and 23,307 for Reylo at the time of writing. Fans may, of course, ship Reylo for a variety of reasons not linked to race, but for Reylo to have thirty-six times the fan fiction results as Finn/Poe suggests that there are broader issues at play. Harrison (2020) notes that

> the shipping of white relationships over interracial relationships as part of a broad pattern among multiple fandoms *is* evidence of racism. A Reylo might not ship these characters for racist reasons in particular, but the Reylo fandom in general contributes to a wider, racist behaviour of shipping that overlooks or ignores characters of colour (Finn; Poe) in favour of white ones (Kylo). (2020, emphasis in the original)

Even beyond the fan fiction itself, however, Reylos have been engaging in toxic, racist fan practices online.

On 31 December 2019, John Boyega shared a post on Instagram of himself dancing. One fan responded with 'My boy after realizing Kylo died so he can date Rey', to which Boyega replied: 'It's not about who she kisses but who eventually lays the pipe. You are a genius' (the post has since been deleted). Further replies criticised Boyega for being misogynistic, yet it seemed to be Boyega's phrasing (the slang term 'laying pipe' is common African-American Vernacular English phrase for having sex) which sparked outrage. Many comments also referred to the Reylo ship, suggesting that Boyega was jealous of Adam Driver or was salty that Finn did not end up in a relationship with Rey. Following this backlash, Boyega tweeted a series of photos taken from the *Star Wars* sequels showing Rey and Kylo in a variety of antagonistic positions, accompanied by the text 'Star Wars romance' and a series of emojis, which seemed to suggest his opinion of the ship (see Figure 37).

Lynn Zubernis and Kathy Larsen suggest that '[f]ans who bring certain fan activities to the attention of actors, writers and showrunners are sanctioned within fandom' (2012: 144), yet the relationship between Reylos and antis seems far more fraught. Rather than Reylos being sanctioned, they have fought back, at times employing tactics used by the far right to do so. Scholars Stitch and Rukmini Pande have written extensively about the racism underpinning Reylo, and both have been on the receiving end of hate as a result, being accused of bullying and of being fake scholars and racists.[3] A post by

---

3   Stitch and Pande are among the scores of BIPOC (black, Indigenous, and people of colour) who have been calling out racism within the fandom long before white fan studies scholars began to take notice. I am indebted to them and their work.

Star Wars Episodes VII–IX, Various (2015–2019)

Figure 37: Tweet from John Boyega apparently mocking the romance between Rey and Kylo Ren.
Source: @JohnBoyega, 31 December 2019.

Holly Quinn on the 'Diverse High Fantasy' Tumblr blog shows that this pattern was followed wherever fans tried to point out the anti-blackness inherent in *Star Wars* fandom:

> Speaking up about racist patterns in the fandom was a high crime. Posts pointing it out were dealt with aggressively to the point of harassment [...] Finn fans, especially Black women, started either leaving the fandom or leaving Tumblr altogether.
>
> If you didn't leave [...] it would get nastier and nastier. It would get personal (we were fair game; talking about observed racist patterns was deemed a personal attack on all Reylos). There were smear campaigns. If you defended yourself, they'd sneer that they couldn't wait for you to delete your blog. This went on for months, in my case. The

strategy was to project the bad behavior of a total stranger who was apparently an 'anti' [...] on me. (Quinn 2020)

It is these practices which evidence the toxic nature of *Star Wars* fandom. There are not simple disagreements about which characters are the most moral or the best pairing; rather, there are poisonous practices whose sole purpose is to remove some (critical, non-white) fans from the fandom altogether. Individuals are attacked personally, in their offline lives as well as on social media platforms. It is important to note that not all Reylos are white or women, but a large number do appear to be white women who, as Stitch (2020) notes, portray fans of colour as aggressive interlopers when they simply 'talk about fandom as critical fans who literally just want fandom to be better for everyone'.

Conclusion

This chapter has only briefly skimmed the toxic behaviours and practices evident in *Star Wars* fandom. Boyega has been on the receiving end of racism since the trailer for *The Force Awakens* aired in 2014: comments on YouTube used racial slurs, and trolls took to Twitter with the hashtag #BoycottStarWarsVII and argued that the inclusion of a black stormtrooper was 'political correctness' (Callahan 2014). But this is not new: Kelly Marie Tran, who plays Rose Tico, was also faced with racist and misogynistic abuse and deactivated her social media accounts as a result, and Jar Jar Binks actor Ahmed Best contemplated suicide because of the hate he received.[4] It is not just trolls who attack actors and fans; fans themselves turn on members of their own fandom, hurling abuse, spreading rumours and encouraging large-scale action to try and force

---

4   This treatment of actors of colour is not, of course, limited to *Star Wars*. As Conway notes in this collection, Leslie Jones was subject to online abuse following the release of *Ghostbusters* in 2016.

them out of the space. While toxic online practices may only have come to mainstream attention in 2014, it is clear that they have already been co-opted by fans and fandoms to silence those they disagree with and shift attention elsewhere.

Part IV

Society

Melody Blackmore

Paradise Hills, Alice Waddington (2019)

Toxic Positivity

> Everything worthwhile in life is won through surmounting the associated negative experience. Any attempt to escape the negative, to avoid it or quash it or silence it, only backfires. The avoidance of suffering is a form of suffering. The avoidance of struggle is a struggle. The denial of failure is a failure. Hiding what is shameful is itself a form of shame. (Manson 2016: 11)

Paradise Hills (2019) is an American/Spanish fantasy horror film starring Emma Roberts as Uma and Mila Jovovich as the Duchess of Paradise. The story tells of a superior girl, Uma, who, having fallen in love with a lower worker, Markus (Jeremy Irvine), is sent away to be reformed into a more obedient, positive young woman so that she will finally accept an unwanted marriage proposal from a superior and wealthy man, Son (Arnaud Valois). The island, however, is not as blissful as it first appears, and a deep sinister secret is uncovered by Uma and her new island friends. The film does not just highlight marginalised class systems; for the purpose of this chapter, it is the film's focus on how positivity can be dangerous when it comes to the true self and one's own authenticity that will be explored and discussed. At first, the island, with its beautiful gardens, appears to offer a form of Utopian reform, but realistically it uses positivity to hide its true intention – to replace the true self with the more obedient false self that both parents and society want. The island's leader, the Duchess, is very much a maternal figure who appears simply to want to nurture the girls and help them transition; yet she is ultimately a dangerous and devouring mother, and plays a fundamental role in the destruction of the true self. This essay will review toxic positivity and true/false self as concepts within the film, using psychoanalytic theories to highlight the importance of the true self and that positivity can easily become toxic to someone's authenticity. Beginning with toxic positivity and what it means, the themes of beauty, medical pathology, happiness and ungratefulness will be discussed. Next, Winnicott's (1965) theory of true/false self will be considered along with themes of the mother, authenticity and that survival of the true self, despite toxic positivity, can be achieved.

Toxic Positivity

> Toxic positivity is a recipe for creating a thick, dense shadow, that harbours all the undesirable traits that you're not supposed to have. Because you must wear the mask of happiness all the time, all your sadness and grief and anger, and other emotions that you can't show because you're forced to be 'positive,' are kicked down into the darkness of the unconscious; rotting and festering, creating a monster that will come to the surface when you least expect it. (Einzelganger 2019)

A general definition for toxic positivity from The Psychology Group (2019) has it as a 'happy optimistic state that results in denial, minimisation and invalidation of the authentic human'. In our modern society, positivity is believed to be the key to happiness, but there is a dark and quite sinister side to this mindset – a refusal to see the negative also signifies a rejection of reality itself. According to Lomaia (n.d.), in 'Toxic Positivity in the Context of Lacanian Psychoanalysis', the toxic effects of positivity are the prohibiting of bad feelings such as, anxiety, sadness and anger. There is a toxic emphasis on happiness and well-being that can only result in being unable to achieve all these positive ideals, and as a result, our upbeat society deems any negative feelings to be a failure. Therefore, we constantly feel we are failing at happiness and, thus, cultural life itself.

Paradise Hills (2019) shows an island overflowing with positivity, the implication being that happiness comes from self-positivity with no room for negative emotions. This means that the island embodies toxic positivity – the pushing of happiness and well-being in order to create obedience and compliance, what civilisation deems necessary in our modern world. The film begins with Uma's wedding, where she is told that her new husband awaits her arrival in the bedroom – she dutifully goes to him. We next see Uma being pinned to the bed and her husband, Son, stating: 'You could be so difficult before, but now it's as if that girl never existed.' This line foreshadows the film's central theme of the true/false self. The film next takes viewers back two months – to the Paradise Hills Island. Obedience here is enforced from the very beginning, and it is clear that the island's use of positivity is to achieve compliance through deeper and more malevolent motivations. The island girls must comply with the rules, eat all their meals and drink all their 'milk' (a sleeping drug). In a scene where we see Uma's first therapy session, on a carousel horse, she is repeatedly shown a 'positive' promotional video of her suitor, Son. This is showing toxic positivity through repeated persuasion, pushing the positive and misleading media onto the person in order to change the individual's mindset.

When it comes to toxic positivity, the medical and beauty industry are both equally guilty of enforcing harmful images and views onto society. Negativity has been pathologised and has become something to be 'got rid of' through cognitive behavioural therapy, mindfulness or antidepressants. In *Paradise Hills* (2019), we see pure white clothing, clinical orderlies with medical trolleys, surgical procedures and the Duchess' holistic and therapeutic talks. Uma is told that the island is a 'centre for emotional healing' and a place where she must address her anger issues in order to reconsider Son's marriage proposal. The medical overuse of positivity is clearly emphasised in this film. Individuals are robbed of the right to experience negativity in a toxic positive culture, and so anything negative is pathologised – but what if it is not pathological but perfectly normal to feel negative? Uma is forced to change because her lack of enthusiasm to marrying Son is seen as negative and, so, pathological. Her anger is perfectly acceptable given the circumstances that she finds herself in, and yet because it is a negative emotion, she is shunned by family and island staff and made to feel that her anger must be curbed immediately. Lomaia (n.d.) mentions that often we are told that we have a chemical imbalance in order to reduce stigma or shame of one's environment. However, this is effectively telling the individual that 'it is in their head' – their thoughts, and not their surroundings or environment – which then leads to seeking answers only from within the mind; in other words, people are encouraged to internalise rather than look towards outside circumstances. At Paradise Hills, the girls must drink the milk each evening so that they sleep through the night and so that the sinister procedures that they undergo during the night can be secretly performed. This represents that the pathologising of issues comes not from the girls, but from others, particularly parents and society. The girls are happy with their negativity – Uma does not want to marry Son; Chloe (Danielle Macdonald) does not mind not being beauty pageant material; and Yu (Awkwafina) would rather be herself than be forced to fit into a culture that she does not understand. At the beginning of their stay, Uma and her new friends, Chloe, Yu and Amarna (Eiza González), are taken to the beauty room and encouraged to undergo treatments and get new hair and make-up in order to achieve a better self-image. This form of toxic positivity is a well-known part of the beauty industry – body image and self-confidence are over-positivised through television, literature and social media. New hair, more make-up and being 'body positive' are meant to help us achieve happiness and mental well-being. The island of Paradise Hills reflects contemporary culture and the use of positivity in order to enforce compliance and reject negativity.

At the centre of the notion of toxic positivity is the notion of happiness. Freud (1930) believes that happiness is not simply about an individual's internal responsibility for well-being. In his essay 'Civilisation and its Discontents', Freud ([1929] 2011) writes that society functions by the suppression of self so as to achieve 'civilisation'. We all experience internal conflict between individual desires and societal demand to repress these desires.

> What we call happiness [...] comes from the [...] satisfaction of needs which have been damned up to a high degree and it is from its nature only possible as an episodic phenomenon. [...] Thus our possibilities of happiness are already restricted by our constitution. (Freud [1929] 2011: 4475)

According to Lomaia, there is a definitive link between unhappiness and ungratefulness. This is because ungratefulness can be seen as causing depression in our modern, positive society.

> A most shocking manifestation of science poisoned by ideology was when I heard a very respected psychiatrist giving a lecture, where she mentioned that 'today, the opinion of many psychiatrists became similar to the religious view, that ungratefulness causes depression, i.e. unhappiness' [...] it does not matter if you possess a lot or a little, it does not matter if you are grateful for the piece of bread and roof over your head or if you own all

the luxuries in the world, the bottom line is: if you can be grateful for what you have, you will be happy. Or at least you will not be unhappy and depressed. (Lomaia n.d.: 12–13)

In the film, Uma and her new friends have been sent to the island because they were each ungrateful: Uma should have gratefully accepted a marriage proposal from a rich man; Amarna should be thankful for her singing career, regardless of whether she can sing what she wants; Chloe and Yu should be grateful their parents want them to fit in. The parents see their children as ungrateful and in need of positive reformation in order to conform to what they are expected to want rather than what the girls really desire.

True/False Self

In Donald Winnicott's 'The Maturational Processes and the Facilitating Environment' (1965) he developed the concept of the true and false self in contemporary object relations. Winnicott saw that the false self is often developed in order to protect the inner and more vulnerable true self. If we are denied the opportunity to be our true self (in this case, through toxic positivity), we construct the false self as a defence and to comply with society – but at the expense of authenticity of self. Toxic positivity brings shame from the feelings of denial and an attempt to hide real emotions. According to Lomaia (n.d.), suppression of emotions is unnatural, and when we do not show emotions, we create a fake persona. By denying our true self in this way, we live inauthentically.

An important part of achieving self-authenticity lies with the mother, and in *Paradise Hills* (2019) this is represented by the Duchess – the maternal figure who helps shape the self. Winnicott (1965) introduced the term 'good enough mothering', referring to the maternal role in adequately meeting the infant's needs. If the mother is successful in this, a true self begins, but if she fails, a false self emerges in order to counter the mother's inability to attend to the needs of the infant. The Duchess of Paradise Hills not only oversees the running of the centre but also attends to the girls' needs, at first in an apparently caring manner. There is a scene in which Uma meets with the Duchess to talk about herself, and she is asked by the Duchess about her own mother: Does her mother look after her? What is the one thing her mother gave her? The Duchess here is determining 'good enough mothering'. In a further scene where a boat approaches and breaches the security line, causing the alarm to go off, the Duchess finally reveals her darker side and herself as 'bad mother'. Melanie Klein (1946) wrote on the infant splitting the mother into 'good mother' and 'bad mother' prior to the development of the ego. The splitting that takes place will see the maternal representing both good nurturing object and bad destructive object. Until the child takes a more realistic view of self and understands integration, this good/bad, safe/threat binary will remain. The Duchess in *Paradise Hills* (2019) takes the role of both good nurturing mother and bad threatening mother. Additionally, the film, also sees the Duchess represent another kind of mother – the 'devouring mother'. Lacan ([1956] 1991) wrote of the concept of the devouring mother, which describes cannibalistic fantasies of being devoured by the mother. Linking to Klein's concept of splitting, the infant will perceive the bad mother as a threat during this phase and when there is interruption of the symbiotic relationship with the mother. Towards the end of the film, Chloe and Uma have escaped to an underground cave. Chloe suddenly disappears and Uma discovers dead island girls that had been supposedly released back home, including her beloved Amarna. Uma then finds Chloe being 'devoured' by the Duchess.

Uma's escape and the films ending also embody a central concept of *Paradise Hills* (2019) – the authenticity of the true self. In a memorable scene, as Uma and friends attempt to escape, they come across the 'replicant room' and discover lower-class substitutes ready to replace the girls. They have been undergoing surgeries and training not only to look like the originals, but also to sound like, act like and become them. The replicants are the false selves. Uma and friends are escaping as a refusal to change or ultimately be replaced by their false selves – they are fighting for their authenticity. As the girls talk with the replicants, Uma makes a fundamental point as she hands over her memory locket of her deceased father – that suffering cannot be replicated. The substitutes can copy their looks, their expressions and even their lives, but they can never copy pain, heartache and human suffering. Nevertheless, it is Uma's false self, Ana, that saves Uma and performs what the false self does in certain circumstances – it protects. As Winnicott (1965) mentions, the false self can develop in order to protect the inner true self and serve as a defence. Uma is captured by the Duchess and is about to be 'devoured', but Ana appears, and she and Uma manage to confuse the Duchess long enough (as to who the 'real' Uma is) for the Duchess to be killed. With the film's ending, Ana performs a protective duty as the false self. Uma and Ana escape the island and return home with a plan. The film then takes viewers back to the wedding that we saw at the beginning. Yet we now see that 'Uma' is actually Ana and that the real Uma waits for Son upstairs to kill him. Because Ana is downstairs at the wedding, there is no suspicion on Uma for killing Son. Uma is finally free to leave and follow her own path and pursue her own version of happiness. As Winnicott (1965) notes, the false self is there to comply and be obedient at the expense of its own authenticity. Uma was protected and saved, and finally set free, by Ana, who stays to be the false self that society and her parents want.

Ken Monteith

'Sadfishing' (2019–Present)

On 1 October 2019, parents in the United Kingdom woke to headlines warning of 'the latest toxic social media trend': sadfishing (Blakeman 2019). Headlines such as ' "Sadfishing": New Toxic Online Trend Threatens Mental Health of Vulnerable Children' (Sky News 2019) and 'Social Media "Sadfishing" Trend Found to Be Harming Mental Health of Children, But What Is It?' (Dorking 2019) were attached to reports on a study commissioned by The Headmasters' and Headmistresses' Conference (HMC), released in late September 2019. The study itself, outsourced to and conducted by Digital Awareness UK (DAUK), claimed to have interviewed more than 50,000 British young people. It found, among other things, that troubled teens reaching out for emotional or mental support were either sadfishing or being accused of sadfishing. While people may allude to emotional or mental issues in social media posts, sadfishing is the intentional posting of apparent or fictitious emotional or mental difficulties in order to gain empathy and accrue sympathetic responses. Media reporting on sadfishing frames the practice as toxic since it intentionally misleads the reader into providing unwarranted support and empathy; in other words, the reader is tricked into believing a false narrative. Additionally, sadfishing critiques suggest young people post their vulnerabilities online to gain attention, and naively do so only because they have been influenced by a media landscape that has warped or misinformed their sense of responsibility and understanding of authenticity. Beyond invoking a call to emotion through clickbait headlines – what about the children! – the branding of sadfishing as toxic highlights an inherent toxicity within social media: a social media post serves as both a text and a testimonial, but it can never be an embodied message. There is an unspoken social contract that those who give voice to impairment or pain are morally obligated to support that voice through physical evidence. When the nature of that pain or impairment is invisible or unrepresentable, this unspoken obligation does not hold, casting doubt on the speaker and reshaping that voice as morally toxic.

A reader expects a post to be authentic and to directly represent the person who posts it—A testimonial. More than an avatar, the post is like a diary entry or confessional. We expect the post to come from an authentic place and therefore place it in our world view as 'real'. And yet the post, the text itself, has a life beyond the act of posting, living in its own media space, subject to interpretation, and in turn calling into question how authentic or 'real' it may be. In other words, what we regard as testimony becomes tested. Social media posts concerning illness or emotional suffering invoke expectations of an imagined social contract where the person who is suffering must show evidence of suffering in order to be granted a voice. The reader wants the surety of a suffering body in a medium where the only body to examine is the body of the text. As a hybrid of text and testimony, social media is not well-suited to share pain experienced without physical markers or Instagrammable evidence. How do you prove your condition is authentic and communicate your pain when there are no physical markers giving authority to that pain? In reporting the sadfishing story instigated by the DAUK report, media raise the alarm that vulnerable children with real emotional and illegible illnesses are being dismissed as 'faking it' for attention and are being prevented from finding the help they sought out. If you cannot post physical evidence of your pain, then how can a listener or social media reader be expected to give your story credence? Above and beyond giving the opportunity for splashy headlines warning of a threat to our children, calling sadfishing toxic highlights the inherent difficulty of social media to convey, and seek out support for, health issues that have few physical markers.

On their website, the HMC describes sadfishing as a 'social media phenomenon' attributed to 'celebrities, such as American media personality Kendall Jenner', who post vague comments or unfounded statements about their emotional and mental states in the hope of attracting followers and gaining sympathy (Petre 2019). When young people seek to copy their social media heroes, the argument goes, they open themselves up not only to social criticism and rejection, but also to 'becoming more vulnerable to sexual "grooming" online' (Petre 2019). The reporting of the DAUK study was quick to pick up on the suggestion that social media influencers and celebrities are one of the toxic influences that might cause young people to misrepresent themselves online for attention, as well as the toxic reason legitimate posts seeking attention and help for a problem might be dismissed as inauthentic. The suggestion that sadfishing could lead to sexual grooming of vulnerable teens gave many media outlets the opportunity to invoke an emotional appeal – won't someone please think about the children?

Media Reaction: Toxic Sensationalism

News sources covering this story portray social media as a toxic brownfield upon which Britain's youth play unsupervised. The reporting itself could be called toxic, since it seeks to raise the alarm that children are vulnerable, invoking cultural taboos of childhood innocence while at the same time blaming, and then forgiving, parents for what this same reporting frames as something beyond the parents' control. In short, the media is reporting on something most parents, having grown up in the world, already know: there are bullies and unscrupulous people out there, and now they are on the internet. While several news items portray sadfishing as overtly toxic, others take a more nuanced stance. Sky News, for example, leads with the headline '"Sadfishing": New Toxic Online Trend Threatens Mental Health of Vulnerable Children'. Calling it the 'latest toxic media trend', Sky News presupposes a long line of precedents to prove the point, but gives no details or elaboration. Reporting little about the DAUK study itself, Sky News ends its piece with the example of 'one school pupil in Year 7', who 'told researchers he was having problems at home and shared his feelings on Instagram when he was feeling down' (Sky News 2019). There is no elaboration as to whether this particular Year 7 student was bullied because of his Instagram use or if he was accused of sadfishing. Repeating the Sky News headline almost word for word, social media platform BBN Times report in their piece 'Sadfishing – the Latest Toxic Media Trend' (Blakeman 2019) that young people are being bullied as a result of posts concerning their mental well-being. 'If you don't know what sadfishing is', the piece begins, talking down to its reader, 'then the simple explanation' is broken down for the every-parent blissfully unaware of what happens online (Brogunier 2019). BBN Times – 'A unique platform for Influencers and Content Creators', which claims to 'publish refreshing views outside of the mainstream rhetoric' (BBN Times n.d.) – ends its piece by referencing a previous study of 250,000 teachers from forty-eight countries that concludes Britain has the 'highest incidents of problems with online behaviour' (Blakeman 2019). The message in short: British parents, what are you going to do about it?

Other media outlets used the release of the DAUK report as an occasion to delve into the issue of online safety and conduct their own research: *The Wall Street Journal* published a piece – 'Sadfishing, Predators, and Bullies: The Hazards of Being "Real" on Social Media' (Jargon 2019) – encouraging parents to become involved in their children's social media use, emphasising vigilance as the answer. *The Guardian* (Weale 2019) and MSN (Dorking 2019) quote more directly from materials released by the DAUK report, without critique or analysis of those materials. Both relate the study's finding that one parent thought her daughter was actually talking online to an adult, rather than another teen, concerning her mental health issues. Both also relate DAUK report materials that put the focus on parents, but also let parents off the hook, framing social media as 'an inescapable aspect of the landscape' of children's lives, which children themselves are becoming savvier and more capable of dealing with, suggesting that even if parents do nothing, most kids will be alright (Jargon 2019). 'But despite the concerning findings', MSN tells the reader, 'the report notes that youngsters are becoming more tech-savvy and are more likely to manage their own use of technology responsibly' (Dorking 2019). In relating the DAUK report's concern that changing technologies have 'left many parents feeling overwhelmed by how best to empower their children to navigate the online world safely' (Dorking 2019) but then also explaining that most children are going to be fine without any intervention, media appeals to the inadequacies inherent in parenting in the modern era while at the same time exonerating the parent for not doing enough. Unless your child is an outlier, vulnerable and has mental health issues, and you have not done enough to empower your child, you as a parent will probably be fine.

The Report Itself: Parents are the Solution, the Audience and ... the Problem?

Before moving on to discuss how social media embodies its own form of toxicity, I want to first examine the DAUK sadfishing report itself. The reporting on the DAUK study does not question some of the claims made by DAUK/HMC – to begin with, their statement that this was a study of 50,000 face-to-face interviews. According to materials appearing on their website, DAUK appears to be an organisation consisting of two people. How was the study conducted? By what process did DAUK interview, face to face, 50,000 students? And what was the time frame? The report was commissioned by the HMC, but it does not appear to be available to the public either as a published document or online resource. The DAUK report is not included on the HMC website, referred to instead in online press release by the HMC.[1] Did reporters assigned the sadfishing story have access to the full report or actually get to read the report for themselves? In the reporting, all quotations regarding sadfishing seem to be taken from the HMC press office statement.

Diagnosing Toxicity

When diagnosing what makes social media 'so toxic', media itself lays the blame on money, notoriety and the rise of social media influencers. Being given attention on social media translates into being paid, period. More engagement leads to posts being featured more prominently and more widely on social media platforms, 'accustomizing social media users', to a sensational toxic environment where users compete for attention (Brogunier

---

[1] In response to my own inquiries and interest in viewing the report, the HMC press office referred me to the DAUK for details concerning the report. The DAUK did not respond to email.

2019). While it might be inspirational for teens to see social media personalities share struggles and emotional health issues, these influencers are often looking to gain followers and, in turn, corporate sponsorship. 'Influencers see an increase of 7 to 10 times the level of engagement', *The Wall Street Journal* comments, 'when posting about mental-health issues than they do with more mundane posts' (Jargon 2019). 'When influencers share personal struggles, it tends to result in more followers, likes and comments, which results in more brand sponsorships' (Jargon 2019). When children emulate social media influencers, they may not be aware that the influencers themselves do not have pure intentions.

Calling sadfishing toxic exposes the oxymoron that is social media, illustrating how the authorial presence of social interaction is often at odds with a textual reading demanding the author be absent. At its heart, social media is a forum built upon testimony, but a testimony where individual stories are granted authority based on the act of posting itself. A social media post is a hybrid, at once an actual text existing independent of its author, subject to interpretation, and a signature authorised by and embodying the individual it represents. The reader must gauge how believable or authentic a post may be, but that believability is tied to what can be gleaned from the text itself. In a medium populated by posts showing a curated or an ideal life, a post showing vulnerability appears more authentic or real. Julie Jargon (2019) suggests that vulnerability as authenticity is a generational trait: 'With millennials, everything on social media was about curation, showing the perfect life [...] Gen Z is an inclusive, open-minded generation, and vulnerability is social currency now.' To show vulnerability on social media may be a way to react against behaviours that have come before; however, I would argue that competing definitions of what it means to be authentic play out when sadfishing accusations are made. On the one hand, a post on social media may be using vulnerability to show a sense of 'realness' or personal integrity, while, on the other hand, the post's reader may be expecting an authenticity based on an unspoken social contract wherein stories of illness and testimony rely on proof of pain to make the story valid.

Telling stories of illness is intrinsically linked with embodiment and testimony – the audience of an embodied story insists on proof of authenticity so that they can share in that experience. As Arthur Frank attests in *The Wounded*

Storyteller: 'Storytelling is *for* an other just as much as it is for oneself. In the reciprocity that is storytelling, the teller offers herself as guide to the other's self-formation' (Frank 2013: 17–18; emphasis in the original). In listening to someone else's testimony, the listener expects to be able to take on the teller's experience and grow from that experience. Frank continues: 'the other's receipt of that guidance not only recognizes but *values* the teller' (2013: 18; emphasis in the original). The power of storytelling, then, relies on an exchange of validations and personal assessments. But in taking on the teller's story and valuing the teller, the listener expects that story to come from an authentic place. In 'Authenticity and Social Media', Wang and Skovia explain authenticity's expected requirements:

> As an authentic self is not to live *for* and *by* oneself, but to, ideally, *forget* oneself and to *be present* in the situation, of interacting with others, the environment, and nature, an authentic self should respect and associate, and cause no harm to others, the environment, and nature. (2017: 3; emphasis in the original)

And here lies the contradiction, how is one to testify to a lived experience while forgetting the self that authorises that experience? How does one instruct the listener in their experience, but cause no harm, especially when the testimony being conveyed involves the personal suffering, pain and/or vulnerability of the teller? As Frank suggests: 'Illness stories require an interplay of mutual presences: the listener must be present as a potentially suffering body to receive the testimony that is the suffering body of the teller' (2013: 144). And this is why, I would argue, a social media post, especially one concerning one's health experience, stands as both text and signature – the author of an illness story is always present within that story. 'This presupposition of embodied presence', Frank continues, 'could not be further from the practice of literary deconstruction, with its negation of the author's presence and treatment of the story as "text"' (2013: 144). The social part of social media expects reader and author to engage in a conversation of presences, while the media component of social media expects text to stand alone and be subject to analysis.

Seeking support on social media becomes all the more difficult when an ailment is largely invisible or unseeable, or as Mack Hagood explains, illegible. Hagood writes that even 'disability scholars often engage media texts by assuming a certain kind of visibility in disability, in which an already-recognizable (or *legible*) impairment is shaped into a disability through cultural discourse' (2017: 315, emphasis in the original). Mental, emotional and even physical disabilities do not all have legible markers which can be Instragrammed or photographed and shared. '[I]llegibility', writes Hagood, 'is a problem faced by many others with non-apparent and contested impairments, from lupus to poorly understood mental disorders' (2017: 316). And without legible or, I would argue, textual proof, the authenticity of a social media post, and the poster behind it, becomes a subject of scrutiny. 'Those with illegible impairments or invisible disabilities', Hagood comments, 'are often perceived as moral failures rather than disabled people' (2017: 321). In the social interplay of stories suggested by Frank, the tellers of illegible illness stories are seen to be breaking the contract between teller and listener, suggesting that the teller is attempting to cause pain rather than share and give the listener the opportunity to understand and learn in their own self-formation.

If posting a fabricated illness story about one's pain to gain sympathy is toxic – sadfishing – then accusing a posted illness story of sadfishing when that pain cannot be legibly expressed represents the other side of that toxic coin. As Elaine Scarry explains:

> for the person in pain, so incontestably and unnegotiably present is it [that pain] that 'having pain' may come to be thought of as the most vibrant example of what it is to 'have certainty,' while for the other person it is so elusive that 'hearing about pain' may exist as the primary model of what it is 'to have doubt.' (1987: 4–5)

In other words, to experience your own pain is all the proof you need to believe it is real, but to hear of another's pain is 'to have doubt' since testimony of experience does not transfer the experienced pain to the listener. Scarry continues, 'thus pain comes unsharably into our midst as at once that which cannot be denied and that which cannot be confirmed' (1987: 5). Experiencing one's own pain is to experience oneself as intrinsically, intimately, present, but to hear and acknowledge another's pain, as Scarry suggests, is to have some doubt since the other's pain does not have that same physical presence.

Conclusion

Skovira and Wang argue that social media's burden of authenticity lies squarely with the poster, who is expected to create a persona within certain social media norms: 'Being authentic also means being free [...] but that freedom is not without constraints. The constraints are of "cause no harm," ethical behaviours, and morality. Within these bounds, one can be freely expressive of one's spontaneities' (2017: 5). As Scarry, Hagood, and Frank explain, trying to share or seek help for an experience that does not have legible evidence crosses the line of 'cause no harm' for the listener, rescinding any authority or authenticity or validation the author of the post may have gained in being heard. Traditional media has a series of authenticity checks: editors, interviewers, broadcast managers serving as a filter or controller of reported information – social media does not have these filters, claim Skovira and Wang: 'There are no such professional equivalents in social media' (2017: 5).

Jay Daniel Thompson

Troll Hunting, Ginger Gorman (2019)

Australian journalist Ginger Gorman's book, *Troll Hunting,* is an important contribution to studies of online toxicity. The text investigates the profound psychological toll that trolling takes on its victims. Gorman's book also features interviews with a number of self-identified trolls. In undertaking these interviews, Gorman demonstrates what she terms 'radical empathy', the ability to understand an individual, recognise them as human, despite their harmful behaviour.

This chapter suggests journalists have an ethical imperative to demonstrate the kind of radical empathy modelled throughout *Troll Hunting* when they report on trolls and trolling. This empathy could, the chapter suggests, play a role in stemming online toxicity. Journalists have been chosen as a focal point because of the important roles they play in enabling public sphere discourse about social issues. Specifically, journalism is one important means through which public understandings of trolling are constructed. In advancing this argument, the chapter acknowledges some challenges associated with showing empathy towards those who perpetrate online abusiveness.

Trolling in the Digital Public Sphere

The term 'trolling' refers to the posting of material online with the aim of generating heightened and usually adverse responses from targets. The best-known strand is that which seeks to insult, offend and degrade its targets. This is the strand that *Troll Hunting* investigates. As Gorman puts it, trolling does not simply lead to 'hurt feelings', as some of its proponents might claim; it can cause profound psychological and physical injury, and even death (2019: 18). The trolling that Gorman discusses exists in a continuum with other toxic online behaviours such as revenge porn, cyberstalking and doxing (sharing an individual's personal details – such as home address, contact details, photos of loved ones – without their consent). Trolling can silence victims, sometimes permanently (e.g. through suicide), and can precede or accompany offline brutality; for example, Brenton Tarrant was involved in trolling activity prior to killing fifty Muslim worshippers in Christchurch, New Zealand, in 2019 (Boseley 2019). Trolls can ruin jobs and create unsafe workplace environments (Gorman 2019: 18; Jane 2018). Trolling can also reinforce existing inequalities pertaining to gender, race, sexuality and religion. For instance, Gorman describes the anti-Semitic and misogynist trolling that she has been subject to (2019: 6–11).

My own research has understood trolling as being a major impediment to democracy. This research situates trolling within the 'digital public sphere'. That term conceptualises the internet as a sphere, or a number of networked spheres, whereby individuals can work, socialise and deliberate on the issues of the day (Parnes 2016; see also Castells 2010). The digital public sphere represents a digitised and globalised version of the 'public sphere', that has been theorised by scholars such as Jurgen Habermas (1989). The publicness of the digital public sphere stems from the fact that it can be accessed by potentially anybody in the world, albeit with a number of provisos, the most significant being access to an internet connection.

The key word in the paragraph above is 'deliberate', which refers to 'the process of exchanging and listening to each other's views, weighing evidence, and reflecting on preferences' (Curato 2020). Deliberation has been crucial to the functioning of healthy democracies. As Lincoln Dahlberg puts it, a democratic society should 'not only recognise the empirical and necessary [...] existence of differences, divisions, and disagreements, but accommodate and indeed actively encourage their surfacing and expression' (2018: 37). Trolling has been shown to reduce a victim's willingness and ability to participate in this sphere in any meaningful way (Lumsden and Morgan 2017: 928). Reduced participation in that sphere is particularly difficult in an era in which so much of our lives are lived online (the 'pivot online' during the COVID-19 pandemic is evidence of this). The silencing effect of trolling is in addition to the threats that trolling poses to one's health and safety. For these reasons, trolling is antithetical to democracy.

Troll Hunting's aim is to catalogue the harms that trolling causes. There are interviews with victims of trolling and researchers on online toxicity. Gorman also seeks to hear the voices of those who frequently go unheard in media coverage: the trolls themselves. As she puts it: 'It's time to reach our hands back across the cold water not just to predator-trolling victims, but to the perpetrators themselves. Because we all live in the society that made them' (2019: 264). This call for empathy towards trolls is what makes Gorman's book a significant contribution to studies of trolling and a useful case study for this chapter.

Specifically, and drawing on Gorman's insights, this chapter argues that it is imperative for journalists to demonstrate radical empathy towards trolls. This is because of the responsibilities that journalists have towards those individuals they interview and/or write about. Media scholar Denis Muller elaborates on that point when he states:

> If we present ourselves as people who are seeking information for the purposes of journalism, we are making some implicit promises to our subjects, too. These are promises about truth-telling, portraying them fairly, treating them decently, being respectful of them as human beings, and keeping any secrets they confide to us. We are also implicitly promising to use the access we gain to them for the purposes we say we have obtained it – the purposes of journalism – and not for anything else. (2014: 18)

These responsibilities would also include a commitment to mitigating harm, both to subjects and audiences. I write 'mitigating' because 'journalism sometimes entails doing harm – causing pain, hurt, embarrassment, and loss of livelihood or reputation – in pursuit of the public interest, or in placing the public interest ahead of someone's private interest' (Muller 2014: 20). There is no space here to determine what might count as being within the 'public interest'. This term would not apply to information that dehumanises others (including those who perpetrate online abuse) or that distorts public understandings of online toxicity.

Troll Hunting and Radical Empathy

Gorman uses the term 'radical empathy' to describe the approach she took towards the trolls she interviewed for her book. In a 2020 essay, the author quotes the writer and podcast host Cheryl Strayed as saying:

> Having radical empathy is not about letting people off the hook for their misdeeds and mistakes, but rather holding them – and ourselves – to a higher standard. It's about saying, I believe we are capable of doing better, of being kinder, braver, more honest, and more generous – even after we have failed to do so. In action, it means willingness to contemplate the decisions and actions of others with consideration rather than condemnation, with compassion rather than scorn. (Strayed, qtd in Gorman 2020: 9)

The above passage is consistent with the definition of radical empathy provided by other commentators. For example, in a study of archival research, Michelle Caswell and Marika Cifor write that 'empathy is radical if we allow it to define archival interactions even when our own visceral affective responses are steeped in fear, disgust, or anger' (2016: 25). Thus, the 'radical' in radical empathy stems from the ability to understand others, to view them as human and to avoid simply condemning their actions, even when these actions are objectively despicable. This is what distinguishes radical empathy from empathy, the latter of which describes 'our capacity to grasp and understand the mental and emotional lives of others' (Susan Lanzoni, qtd in Joseph 2020: 3). The term 'empathy' does not take into account the emotional labour required to understand and humanise those who subject others to life-threatening harassment.

Importantly, Gorman's radical empathy towards trolls takes the form of a journalistic enquiry. I write 'importantly' because of the role that journalists have played in offering up information and topics for public deliberation. Journalists belong to the 'communications media', which is 'central' to the cultivation of 'spaces' in which members of the public can deliberate on ideas (Dahlberg 2018: 37). Journalists help construct public understandings of what constitutes trolling. Karen Lumsden and Heather Morgan make this point in a study of how trolling has been represented in media reportage. They argue that this reportage threatens to add insult to the injuries caused by trolls.

> It is important to examine how trolling is discussed within the media to understand how it might frame public opinion, debate, and action, and implicitly victim blame via 'silencing strategies' [...] 'Silencing strategies' are reflected in the ways in which the media report on trolling, including: the reconstruction of the trolling event (such as rape threats, death threats, and body shaming); the representation of the (female) victim; and the advice given to victims on how they should respond to online abuse. (2017: 927–8)

Gorman is cognisant of journalists' power to construct popular understandings of trolling. She refers to a number of media commentaries in which the term 'trolling' is used unthinkingly to describe 'a deliberate type of needling' (2019: 15). For example, one reporter is quoted as writing about a popular reality TV programme: 'Now in its fifth season, it's just trolling' (Gorman 2019: 14). This kind of use is more than just sloppy; it obscures what trolling really is and the harm that it can cause.

In examining how Gorman's text cultivates radical empathy, this chapter focuses on two aspects. The first is the rejection of popular stereotypes about trolls. These include the stereotype of the troll 'as a loner in his mum's basement, harassing others online' (Gorman 2019: 24). For example, many trolls operate in syndicates. Of one interviewee, Gorman writes that 'if you happened to pass him on the street or in the supermarket, nothing would grab your attention. [...] Outwardly, there was nothing to suggest he was a highly organised, and dangerous, troll' (2019: 20). Elsewhere, she states that 'trolls aren't usually who you expect. They don't necessarily think or feel what you expect. They are often better educated than you expect' (2019: 19). These clarifications are necessary, I suggest, insomuch as they humanise the so-called 'trolls'. Far from being 'others' who exist in some parallel universe, these individuals live in the same society as 'we' do; they have been shaped by the same society that we inhabit. 'We' are 'them', and vice versa. As such, 'we' have a moral responsibility to treat these trolls as one of 'us', even as we may abhor their behaviour.

The second aspect in *Troll Hunting*'s cultivation of radical empathy is the book's emphasis on listening to the trolls being interviewed. This may seem obvious and unremarkable; after all, listening to interviewees is surely a routine aspect of a journalist's professional life. In fact, listening can be highly political, as Tanja Dreher suggests when she writes that

> listening requires the listener to quiet their inner voice and to listen is to leave oneself open to persuasion. Listening thus entails an incompleteness, an openness to the other.

> It is also challenging in that it opens up possibilities – for learning and connection, but also for challenge, conflict, dissonance and persuasion. (2010: 100)

Gorman's aim is not to let her interviewees persuade her about the merits (or otherwise) of trolling. The author does appear to quieten her 'inner voice' and avoid casting judgment on the trolls when she allows them to talk about their trolling and how it makes them feel. Gorman does indeed form a 'connection' with some interviewees, maintaining contact throughout the writing process. Through these interactions, the author further emphasises their humanity; these interviewees are represented as being fellow citizens, with feelings and voices, albeit voices that can profoundly damage lives.

Further, listening is a crucial aspect of deliberation. The idea of engaging trolls in democratic deliberation might seem perverse; after all, such a respect-based dialogue seems antithetical to the interviewees' modus operandi. This deliberation also runs counter to the popular wisdom 'don't feed the trolls' (Lumsden and Morgan 2017: 927). Nonetheless, listening to her interviewees does enable Gorman to ascertain some of the reasons for their actions. These reasons include 'boredom' and 'lulz' (internet-speak for 'laughs'; Gorman 2019: 26). The racism and misogyny of certain interviewees reflects the power imbalances and injustices that have long existed in the 'offline' world and that can now (thanks to web affordances) reach a larger audience than might previously have been possible. Broad-ranging structural and attitudinal changes are required before this behaviour can be eradicated.

Through dialoguing with trolls, Gorman also makes make them aware of the damage that their actions cause. This is quite different to casting judgment on the interviewees as people, and it signals to the reader that the text is not implicitly condoning the actions being described. Nor is the author hiding behind journalistic objectivity, the latter of which she has elsewhere criticised as being disingenuous: 'Humans are subjective and the public knows it' (Gorman 2020: 11). For example, Gorman asks one troll: 'Do you understand why the things that you're doing make people so upset and so angry?' (2019: 25). That interviewee replies: 'I have a really good understanding of it. That's why I do it so well' (qtd in Gorman 2019: 25). Most other interviewees also appear unmoved to change their ways. One interviewee does, however, remark that his interview with Gorman 'made me think about what I was doing and why I was doing it ... I realised I couldn't justify trolling' (qtd in

Gorman 2019: 26). This quote suggests that there is at least some hope that trolls can change their ways.

Of course, the very act of listening to trolls is ethically fraught; it can pose a grave psychological threat to those who partake in this activity. That is acknowledged by the author when she discloses that '[w]riting *Troll Hunting* left me with PTSD and depression' (Gorman 2020: 12). There is growing research into the ways in which trauma impacts on journalists and how journalism students might be best equipped to deal with traumatic events and phenomena that they report on (see Amend, Kay and Reilly 2012 and Dworznik and Garvey 2019). This kind of training could assist current and prospective journalists to protect their mental health when reporting on online toxicity. That training could also help journalists to avoid (re)traumatising their subjects. As Dworznik and Garvey (2019: 379) point out, a lack of trauma training can 'increase the possibility of a reporter causing harm to a victim if they cannot recognize or do not understand the impact a traumatic event can have on those involved'.

Also ethically fraught is the act of giving trolls a(nother) platform on which to make themselves heard. The damage that these internet users cause is surely evidence enough that their voices are being heard in the digital public sphere. Gorman concedes that she has been criticised for providing that platform, and she has responded to such criticisms by asking whether 'we want to understand why this is happening, so we've got a shot at stopping it' (2020: 12). Determining why individuals troll others will not in itself end trolling, or even encourage the trolls to rethink their actions. Nor will demonstrating radical empathy towards those individuals. Nonetheless, the measures elucidated in Gorman's text – for example, increased social media regulation (2019: 259) – along with others, can at least help to create less toxic online spaces.

Conclusion

This chapter has argued that *Troll Hunting* is significant since it provides journalists (as enablers of public sphere discourses) with an insight into how they can demonstrate radical empathy in their reportage on trolling and other forms of online toxicity. That demonstration of empathy is, the chapter has argued, an ethical imperative for journalists, albeit one that can be challenging to fulfil. Gorman achieves her aim firstly by rejecting stereotypes of the troll as a monstrous 'other'. These 'trolls' are humans, socialised in the same society as 'we' are, though capable of devastating hostility. The author also cultivates radical empathy by listening to (though not condoning the actions of) her interviewees. This listening enables Gorman not only to ascertain the factors that compel an individual to troll others, but also to remind them of the harmfulness of their actions. Her text should not be read as the last word in reportage on online toxicity; rather, for reasons elucidated throughout this chapter, it is a notable contribution to ongoing work on this phenomenon.

Madeline Muntersbjorn

'The Denialist Playbook', Sean Carroll (2020)

On 11 June 2020, @JennyENicholson tweeted: 'We're gonna have to retire the expression "avoid it like the plague" because it turns out humans do not do that.' Some time on, her wry viral post still resonates. Despite a rapidly rising death toll, angry humans took to the streets to demand entry to a closed bar in December of the same year, as Jon Skolnik and John Annese reported on 2 December in '*"The People Have Rights! Open The Door, I'm Thirsty!"* Hundreds Rally for Defiant Staten Island Bar Shut Down After Violating Coronavirus Rules'. On 26 May, historian Jon Meacham appeared on MSNBC News and criticised Trump's lack of leadership, saying, 'he has managed to weaponize the deaths of 100,000 people' and 'God help us if this becomes a partisan pandemic' (MSNBC News 2020). Alas, so it has come to pass. On 4 December, in 'The U.S. Has Passed the Hospital Breaking Point', Robinson Meyer and Alexis C. Madrigal reported that '[t]he pandemic nightmare scenario – the buckling of hospital and healthcare systems nationwide – has arrived'. And to make matters worse, as Sarah Krouse reported on 3 December, 'Covid-19 Disbelief Saddles Health-Care Workers with Another Challenge', namely community scepticism about the rampant spread of the virus. Pandemic denial is a pernicious problem with well-established roots in extant varieties of denialism. By using what Sean Carroll (2020) calls 'The Denialist Playbook' as a lens, we see how this recent strain of denialism resembles others from the past. However, this most recent strain of denialism is particularly toxic insofar as it severely underplays the scope of the present health crisis and, thereby, leads people to either take actions, like hosting large events, or avoid actions, like wearing masks, both of which spread disease and endanger these actors' lives and the lives of those who come into contact with them. This virulent partisan denialism also has an extraordinary reach thanks to a temperamental president in the digital age.

Several authors published books denouncing government overreach in response to the pandemic on partisan grounds. In July 2020, science writer John Iovine published *Scamdemic: The COVID-19 Agenda: The Liberal's Plot To Win The White House* wherein he argues the pandemic has been blown out of proportion specifically to defeat Trump. He incorrectly predicted that 'COVID-19 hysteria will likely end after the November 2020 election' (2020). Nutritionist Bruce Fife's *Plandemic: Exposing the Greed, Corruption, and Fraud Behind the COVID-19 Pandemic* was published in August 2020. Fife calls the pandemic a 'manufactured' health crisis and echoes other books' claims that Dr Fauci and philanthropist Bill Gates, in tandem with the pharmaceutical industry, deliberately planned the viral outbreak (2020: 57 ff.). Pamela A. Popper and Shane D. Prier's *COVID Operation: What Happened, Why It Happened, and What's Next* was published in October 2020. They argue, without irony, that US citizens are easy prey for overblown hype because our literacy skills are lacking: 'It is easier to "sell" a false story to a population of people if a significant percentage of them cannot read or comprehend or think critically' (2020: 3). Indeed. The details in similar volumes vary depending on whether the materials are presented by cranks, who believe what they say, or grifters, who wittingly promote nonsense for cash. Cranks cite dozens of sources and sketch complex theories as to why expert consensus is mistaken, while grifters write more proofread prose, distilling dissent into memorable catchphrases and rhetorical questions, unburdened by too much math. Iovine released *Scamdemic* for free online, replete with links, because, for him, getting 'the truth' out there, before the presidential election, was more important than personal profit. For each such book there are even more blogs, vlogs, podcasts and posts that collectively decry an implausible international plot to use pandemic panic to manipulate people for power and profit.

In 'Why False Claims About COVID-19 Refuse to Die', Cailin O'Connor and James Weatherall note not only that a pandemic of misinformation about COVID-19 is spreading on social media sites but also that some misinformation has taken on a life of its own:

> In recent months, claims with some scientific legitimacy have spread so far, so fast, that even if it later becomes clear they are false or unfounded, they cannot be laid to rest. Instead, they become *information zombies*, continuing to shamble on long after they should be dead. (O'Connor and Weatherall 2020, emphasis in original)

They observe how the relatively slow pace of peer-reviewed science, compared to the wildfire pace of editorial hyperbole, has created a 'perfect storm for information zombies'. For example, one of the most contentious variables is the fatality rate of this disease. Consensus among experts and denialists alike is that the case fatality rate (CFR) is lower than early estimates from the World Health Organization (WHO), of 3.4 per cent; how much lower is unclear. Iovine (2020) states that the 'actual morality rate as estimated by our CDC [is] less than 0.3 percent' and cites a USA Today fact check report (Richardson 2020) that rates this claim as 'PARTLY FALSE'. The title of Ian Richardson's article has two parts: 'CDC Estimates COVID-19 Death Rate Around 0.26 %, Doesn't Confirm It'. Even lower estimates may be found in *The European Journal of Clinical Investigation* by John Ioannidis (2020), a Stanford epidemiologist who wrote in his widely cited essay 'Coronavirus Disease 2019: The Harms of Exaggerated Information and Non-Evidence-Based Measures' that Germany's CFR in early March was only 0.2 per cent. However, as O'Connor and Weatherall (2020) note, 'by mid-April [Germany's CFR] had climbed to 2.45 percent, far closer to the original WHO estimate' and, further, 'Ioannidis has not updated the editorial to reflect the changing numbers'. Unsurprisingly, Ioannidis is the focus of Iovine's second source, a link to another news article with a two-part title, 'Stanford Researcher Says Coronavirus Isn't as Fatal as We Thought; Critics Say He's Missing the Point', by Lisa M. Krieger (2020). To support the second part of her title, Krieger quotes Andrew Noymer, a flu expert and public health professor: 'We shouldn't fetishize a number when we can look out the window at an epidemic and see the real situation,' he said. 'We have seen more COVID-19 deaths in the U.S. in three months – with a lockdown – than in the six-month flu season, without a lockdown.' Both Richardson and Krieger report the welcome news that the COVID-19 CFR is lower than once feared; both reports embed these lower numbers in a larger context that *Scamdemic* glosses over. The lower CFR is due to more widespread testing and the fact that this virus inhabits a larger number of asymptomatic carriers than previously thought. After testing asymptomatic people for COVID became more common, these positive cases were included in the 'people with COVID who did not die' total, making those who did die a smaller percentage of 'COVID positive people'. What is the prior probability you will die given that you have tested positive for COVID? It varies depending on who and where you are. On 19 November 2020, in their article 'How Many Americans Are About to Die?', Alexis C. Madrigal and Whet Moser reported 'the virus has, with ruthless regularity, killed at least 1.5 percent of all Americans diagnosed with COVID-19 over the past four months'. However, this relative frequency is not necessarily a reliable guide to the future; experts agree that definitive answers to questions about fatality rates are elusive, as odds of survival depend on several contextual factors, including access to quality medical care, which is now both in short supply and hampered by disbelief that COVID is a dangerous disease.

On the one hand, COVID denial is akin to other disease denials in recent memory. Bruce Mirken, in 'COVID Denial is a Grim Rerun of AIDS Denialism', observes that debunking AIDS deniers was not difficult so much as a matter of checking their own footnotes, since popular authors 'regularly made "factual" assertions that were easily contradicted by reviewing the scientific literature – often by the very references they claimed as "proof"' (Mirken 2020). Mirken draws parallels between AIDS and COVID denialists, namely 'the dismissal of facts, the venomous denunciations of anything trying to tell the truth as either bought off or part of the Evil Conspiracy: same cult, same rhetoric, different disease'. As Pascal Diethelm and Martin McKee noted more than a decade ago in 'Denialism: What Is It and How Should Scientists Respond?', when confronting denial 'it is necessary to shift the debate from the subject under consideration, instead exposing to public scrutiny the tactics they employ and identifying them publicly for what they are' (2009: 4). Inspired by this strategy, in 'The Denialist Playbook', Sean Carroll (2020) draws parallels between COVID denial and polio vaccine denial by American chiropractors. According to Carroll, denialists of all kinds – from anti-vaxxers to anti-evolutionists – use similar tactics to 'give the appearance of legitimate debate when there is none'. Each of the six 'principal plays' Carroll discusses are readily found in contemporary COVID denialist media:

'The Denialist Playbook', Sean Carroll (2020)

1. Doubt the Science
2. Question Scientists' Motives and Integrity
3. Magnify Disagreements among Scientists and Cite Gadflies as Authorities
4. Exaggerate Potential Harm
5. Appeal to Personal Freedom
6. Reject Whatever Would Repudiate A Key Philosophy (Carroll 2020)

On the other hand, contemporary COVID denial differs from previous instances of denialism in significant socially mediated and politically motivated ways. As Mirken (2020) notes, COVID denial has a novel means of propagation that AIDS denial did not have, including, but not limited to, 'social media, instantly amplifying its nonsense to hundreds of millions via Facebook' and 'the president of the United States, who has turned COVID denial into a badge of MAGA honor'.

President Trump's COVID denial has fuelled widespread disregard for public health. Just before the election, Christian Paz (2020) published 'All the President's Lies about the Coronavirus', remarking that it was necessarily '[a]n unfinished compendium of Trump's overwhelming dishonesty during a national emergency'. For example, in a news briefing in April, Trump called a group of anti-lockdown protesters 'very responsible people' (Smith 2020) and claimed they were adhering to social distancing guidelines despite the fact that photos show densely packed, unmasked crowds holding signs we can sort into kinds based on Carroll's playbook: 'Shutdown is based on Lies!!' (1); 'Fauci is Corrupt!' (2); 'Tyrant Communist Cooper Destroying NC Lives!' (4); 'Freedom Not Tyranny' (5); 'Enough is Enough' (6). Admittedly, (3) – 'Magnify Disagreements among Scientists and Cite Gadflies as Authorities' – is difficult to do in a poster. Even so, Carroll's playbook helps us to see that when it comes to COVID denial in the United States, a dishonest president has become the gadfly often cited as an authority on the severity of the pandemic.

In April in 'Leave Politics Out Of Pandemic', Elaine Ruth Fletcher and Grace Ren (2020) quoted WHO Director General Dr Ghebreyesus: 'Don't use this virus as an opportunity to fight against each other or score political points. It's dangerous. [...] This is a devil that everybody should fight, and for that we need global solidarity, cemented in national unity.' Since then, no national unity has emerged in the United States. In May, Cary Funk and Alec Tyson (2020), in 'Partisan Differences over the Pandemic Response Are Growing', noted that according to the Pew Research Centre, 'Trust in Medical Scientists Has Grown in U.S., but Mainly Among Democrats'. In September, Trump held an event in Nevada that was in violation of large gathering rules, 'brazenly' disregarding state restrictions and safety guidelines, as Charlotte Klein (2020) reported the next day in 'Trump's COVID Denialism Reaches New Heights With Packed Indoor Rally'. Susan B. Glasser (2020) wrote 'Donald Trump's 2020 Superspreader Campaign: A Diary' wherein she documents an astonishing week of pandemic-denying tweets, from 26 October to 1 November. For example, on Wednesday 28 October, President Trump tweeted:

> COVID, COVID, COVID is the unified chant of the Fake News Lamestream Media. They will talk about nothing else until November 4, when the Election will be (hopefully!) over. Then the talk will be how low the death rate is, plenty of hospital rooms, & many tests of young people. (qtd in Glasser 2020)

As Glasser observes, '[n]othing has come to represent the Trump era more than his late-night and early-morning Twitter rants'. She sees his tweet storms as 'signs not only of his fragile, undisciplined ego but also of the hold he has managed to maintain over our collective consciousness'. Since the election, the rate at which the president has preached COVID denial via Twitter has dropped precipitously. As of this writing, the president's 'denialist playbook' tweets are directed towards denying the outcome of the recent presidential election. Whether Biden's decisive victory is enough to free our collective consciousness remains to be seen.

Economists Andrea Robbett and Peter Hans Matthews, in their essay 'The Partisan Pandemic: Do We Now Live in Alternative Realities?' (2020), report on their research into the differences between how people answer questions as individuals versus how they answer questions as members of a group. Their 2018 research into topics such as immigration and climate change showed that when individuals were rewarded according to whether their own answers were correct, 'people answering as individuals were much less partisan than people voting as part of a group' (Robbett and Matthews 2020). However, when the reward was tied to how well members of their group did, the researchers found that 'despite the financial rewards for correct responses, a partisan gap did indeed emerge among voters' when people answered questions as part of a group, 'tending to give answers more favourable to their own party's position' (Robbett and Matthews 2020). This gap between individual belief and partisan alignment did not re-emerge when Robbett and Matthews conducted their survey in March 2020 on the topic of COVID-19. Again they asked respondents to answer questions either as individuals or as members of a group. Again they found that 'voter responses varied with their political affiliation' when people answered questions as members of a group (Robbett and Matthews 2020). However:

> The surprise was that these percentages did not change much, if at all, for individuals, who were rewarded when their own answer was correct. One in 3 Republicans (33.7%) still chose the incorrect options that were most favorable to President Trump, while the number of Democrats who did likewise fell a little, from 14.2% to 12.6%. Thus, unlike the patterns we observed for non-COVID-19-related questions, we found that little of the difference can be attributed to partisan expression. (Robbett and Matthews 2020)

In other words, COVID-denial is not simply something folks do as part of their expression of partisan affiliation, but also reflects individuals' beliefs about the severity of the present crisis.

When people die needlessly from toxic misinformation that promotes reckless behaviour, it is no wonder tempers flare. Pundit Bob Cesca has written scathing essays decrying the dangers of President Trump's lack of a sound pandemic policy, from 'Trump's Gruesome New Pandemic Pivot Would Be Ludicrous – if His Followers Weren't So Ready to Swallow the Poison' (Cesca 2020b) to 'Our Politics Isn't about Left Vs. Right Anymore – It's about Reality Vs. Dreadful Fantasy' (Cesca 2020a). Philosopher Peter McLaren pulls no punches in his essay 'Religious Nationalism and the Coronavirus Pandemic: Soul-Sucking Evangelicals and Branch Covidians Make America Sick Again', writing that 'the pathological logic and demonic invective of right-wing broadcasters like Rush Limbaugh could be a contributing factor to the madness that surrounds us'. Probably so, but are any pandemic-denying individuals going to be swayed by either Cesca's or McLaren's pointed prose? Probably not.

How best to respond to toxic denial remains an open question. Would that a simple 'no' would be enough to dispel Robert Turner's (2020) query,

'Is Your Covid Test Being Used to Covertly Harvest Your DNA?' Even the more fulsome message that '[t]here is no evidence that this test is ever used to identify an individual person's DNA' – as Patrick Worrall (2020) observes in 'Conspiracy Theory about DNA from Covid Tests Makes no Sense' – hardly seems up to the task. Consultant Prudy Gourguechon, in 'What No COVID Risk? No Climate Change? How to Overcome Toxic Denial', urges that to overcome denial we must understand its origins as a defence mechanism:

> Understand that logic and information will never defeat denial. [...] Messaging needs to be emotional, personal, vivid, direct. Remember that denial operates because it protects against painful emotion so it can only be attacked by dealing with painful emotion in an emotionally vivid way. (Gourguechon 2020)

If Gourguechon is correct, intercessors must be prepared to engage with the negative emotions that arise from accepting the reality of a dreadful contagion that does not care about anyone's politics and is not (yet) under anyone's control in the United States.

Further, cognitive science research shows that small nudges – like asking 'is this true?' – before hitting the 'share' button can make a big difference in how people think. Research by Gordon Pennycook and others 'found that a simple accuracy reminder at the beginning of the study [...] nearly tripled the level of truth discernment in participants' subsequent sharing intentions' (2020: 770). According to Under-Secretary-General for Global Communications Melissa Fleming, 'pausing before we share' is but one way 'every one of us can help break the chain' (United Nations 2020). In this press release from October 2020, she and others from the United Nations enjoined the public to think before sharing posts, to help stop the spread of misinformation. While systemic changes in education to promote equity and scientific literacy are undoubtedly overdue, #PledgeToPause is a cheap and reasonable first step towards combatting the partisan pandemic given that it spreads so quickly on the internet.

Deborah G. Christie

'Title X Gag Rule' (2019–Present)

Toxic is usually best understood as a negative influence or outcome, something harmful and to be avoided. It has gained quite a bit of traction as a ubiquitous adjective signifying both tangible harm and the potential harm of antiquated or outmoded ideology. Toxic mould is not something we want growing in our basements, but toxic hostility and prejudice is just as unwelcome. With an understanding that the word 'toxic' can be slippery to define at times, it seems prudent to lay out a framework for how toxicity applies in my examination of the global gag rule and the more recent Trump-sponsored Title X gag rule expansion. By mandating silence as a condition of humanitarian aid, the United States contributes to an increasingly toxic situation that threatens the health of women and children worldwide.

About fifty-six million abortions are done annually, and almost half (twenty-five million) are unsafe; of the latter number, 97 per cent occur in developing countries (Ganatra et al. 2017). An estimated 8 per cent of all maternal deaths are due to abortion (Say et al. 2020), leaving a massive unmet global need for access to safe abortion services. Despite this situation, the United States, the world's largest global health donor, takes a hard-line stance, both at home and abroad, against abortion. It really was not until the invention of birth control that family planning became a science issue, though it seems it has always been a religious and political one. Suzanne Petroni argues that family planning first became an issue of policy concern for the United States in the 1960s, part of larger bipartisan concerns at the time:

> The initial aims of these early policies were, admittedly, not entirely altruistic. Eugenics and a desire to stem immigration played a role. But US support was also focused on humanitarianism concerns such as alleviating food crises and extreme poverty, and bolstering environmental and national security [...]. Within just a few years, the U.S. became the

world's most significant sponsor of voluntary family planning, both at home and abroad. Today, according to USAID, it supplies 35 to 40 percent of donor-provided contraceptives to the developing world. (2008)

But in a backlash to the 1973 *Roe* v. *Wade* decision, both domestic and international family planning assistance became politicised by right-wing forces. The Helms amendment, passed in 1973, prohibited U.S. foreign assistance from being used for abortion services. Three years later, the Hyde amendment cut off Medicaid funds from being used for abortion in the United States (Petroni 2008). In 1984, the global gag rule, officially known as the Mexico City Policy, was announced by President Ronald Reagan at the 2nd International Conference on Population, which was held in Mexico City, Mexico, on 6–14 August 1984 (Kaiser Family Foundation 2021).

According to Planned Parenthood Global, the global gag rule is 'driven by ideology instead of evidence' and prevents foreign organisations receiving US global health assistance from providing information, referrals, or services for legal abortion or advocating to access to abortion services in their country – even with their own money (Planned Parenthood Global n.d.-a: 24). International healthcare providers must choose between 'the ability to counsel and provide clients with an accurate and full range of safe and legal reproductive health options' (Planned Parenthood Global n.d.-b) and access to desperately needed funds. According to Amanda Klasing, Interim Co-Director of the Women's Rights Division at Human Rights Watch, the United States is one of the largest core donors for the United Nations Population Fund, and withholding those funds will cripple the agency's ability to provide the poorest women in over 150 countries with family planning, maternal and child health services, HIV prevention assistance and campaigns against child marriage and female genital mutilation:

> UN Population Fund is an agency that goes where few others do – into war zones and countries wracked by natural disasters – to try to make sure that pregnant women and girls get health care, can deliver babies safely, and are protected from gender-based violence even as the world falls apart around them. There is more need than they can address, and without US funding even more women will fall through the cracks. (Klasing n.d.)

Despite the uncontested necessity of humanitarian aid, the United States places unreasonable and prohibitive restrictions on accessing that aid for political expediency, ignoring the fact that abortion is, in fact, legal in most of the countries receiving aid – as it is in the United States. The logical cartwheels get even more demonstrative in the specific admonition that foreign health organisations cannot even use *their own money* for abortion-related services, even if not one penny of US aid is spent in that area. The end result of the global gag rule is ideological coercion and an absolute stranglehold on treatment options and the reproductive autonomy of the world's poorest and most vulnerable. And the ramifications do not end simply with abortion; according to Vicki Saporta, president and CEO of the National Abortion Federation:

> Since many clinics offer comprehensive healthcare services in addition to family planning, the loss of funding under the Global Gag Rule has meant that children have not been immunized, couples have not been able to receive HIV testing and treatment, and families have not been able to access malaria services. (Qtd in Germanos 2017)

Since its inception in 1984, the global gag rule has subsequently been revoked and reinstated by Democratic and Republican presidents, respectively, but on 23 January 2017, President Donald Trump signed an executive order that reinstated and expanded the global gag rule to include not just family planning, but most other forms of US global health assistance. In a press release from May of 2017, The Center for Reproductive Rights reported that the expanded plan, Protecting Life in Global Health Assistance, would expand

> the Global Gag Rule restrictions to virtually all global health assistance provided by the federal government, including from the Department of State, the USAID, and the Department of Defense – restricting $8.8 billion dollars in financial support for global health programs ... the Trump Global Gag Rule affects a pool of funding nearly 15 times as large as the George W. Bush-era Global Gag Rule.

In their determination to enforce conservative policy worldwide, supporters of Trump's expanded Global Gag Rule place serious and often insurmountable barriers to global health efforts to spread comprehensive sexuality education (CSE; Center for Reproductive Rights 2018).

A 2015 study published by UNESCO, in consultation with the United Nations Population Fund and the UNAIDS Secretariat, *Emerging Evidence, Lessons and Practice on Comprehensive Sexuality Education*, defines CSE as 'an "age-appropriate, culturally relevant approach to teaching about sexuality and relationships by providing scientifically accurate, realistic, non-judgmental information"' (UNESCO 2015: 12). UNESCO makes it clear that CSE

> leads to improved sexual and reproductive health, resulting in the reduction of sexually transmitted infections (STIs), HIV, and unintended pregnancy. It not only promotes gender equality and equitable social norms, but has a positive impact on safer sexual behaviors, delaying sexual debut and increasing condom use. (UNESCO n.d.)

Senior Programme Specialist in Health Education at UNESCO, Joanna Herat states:

> Young people are consequently often denied even the most basic information about their sexual and reproductive health and rights. [...] Thankfully, a global movement has galvanized around ensuring universal access to CSE, with youth-led movements calling for stronger responses, and sustained commitment. This has played a major role in the scaling up of sexuality education and sexual and reproductive health services globally. (UNESCO n.d.)

These efforts are multilayered and unilaterally designed to increase the quality of healthcare and life for women and children around the world, but they depend on funds provided in great part by the United States, and because conservatives in the United States are offended by abortion, all funding becomes contingent on erasing it as word, deed, even concept. It is not even an option to reserve other US funds for healthcare or to channel funds from other countries into areas that conflict with those conservative policies. Even in countries that allow abortion, conservative US policy states that NO funds can be spent in any area that involves or even mentions abortion. US aid can be withheld from any group that does not silence itself entirely on the topic of abortion. That silence endangers women and children everywhere, but failure to abide by the global gag rule can endanger them even more.

According to the International Planned Parenthood Federation (IPPF):

> At the time of the reinstatement of the Global Gag Rule (GGR) in January 2017, IPPF had 53 projects operating in 32 countries in Latin America and the Caribbean, Sub-Saharan Africa, and South Asia. These projects were managed by our Member Associations (MAs) and provided essential and life-saving healthcare to underserved and marginalized

communities. In some MAs, service delivery decreased by up to 42% from 2016 to 2017 – part of this loss in services is attributable to the GGR. (IPPF n.d.)

Since the global gag rule was reintroduced by Donald Trump, funds have been denied to organisations like Family Health Options Kenya if they 'use any money to provide abortion services, counselling or referrals. This means that critical funding is blocked for other sexual and reproductive services like contraception, maternal health, and HIV prevention and treatment' (IPPF 2019). Health workers with Family Health Options Kenya say they have seen a definite 'rise in sexually transmitted infections, especially syphilis, as well as an increase in unsafe abortions'. The IPPF keeps data on lost funds globally: India lost over two million in funds designated for maternal and child health efforts; Guatemala and Honduras (among others) lost nearly a million in funds to help fight the spread of the Zika virus; Senegal lost a million and a half in funds earmarked for maternal and child health, nutrition initiatives, and prevention and treatment of HIV and STIs. It is the height of arrogance to enforce a first-world, religiously based preference as a condition on humanitarian aid to the rest of the world, and in this case silence can kill.

According to the World Health Organization (2019) '94% of all maternal deaths occur in low- and lower-middle-income countries', where economic inequalities determine the level and quality of maternal care available. Access to healthcare is essential, but when funding is compromised – as it has been by the global gag rule – clinics are forced to reduce staff, hours, and even close entirely. Women cannot receive prenatal care or education, pregnancy check-ups or safe obstetric care during and post delivery. Infants already at risk because of the mother's compromised healthcare fail to receive proper nutrition, immunisation and medical support during the critical early months. In heart-breaking irony, the cessation of funding puts far more lives at risk than the gag rule believes it protects, and abortion is ultimately not prevented at all – simply made more dangerous. Ganatra et al. (2017) observe that 'despite scientific advances that enable the provision of safe abortion at the primary care level, unsafe abortions persist and result in a high burden of complications; maternal death; and substantial costs to women, families, and health systems'. The International Women's Health Coalition shows what can happen when providers are forced to forego US funding or stop abortion-related activities:

> 118 interviews with health service providers, civil society organizations, government agencies, and anti-abortion groups in Kenya, Nepal, Nigeria, and South Africa revealed that access to services for abortion and post-abortion care has been reduced, along with contraceptive services, antenatal care, HIV testing and treatment, and screening for cervical, breast, and prostate cancer. They also report a shrinking of civil society spaces, with some stakeholders concerned that the policy will exacerbate divisions between the HIV/AIDS and sexual and reproductive health and rights communities. Indeed, the spirit of the global gag rule is inherently anti-democratic, insofar as it blocks local organizations that receive US global health funding from advocating for law reform in their own countries. (The Lancet 2019)

As noted in *The Lancet* (2019):

> Abortion is the rallying cry that unites conservative attempts to control and coerce women. By targeting funding for abortion, the global gag rule weaponizes US global health funding against sexual and reproductive health and rights more broadly, with the most severe consequences affecting the most vulnerable.

Louis D. Brandeis once famously suggested that sunlight made the best disinfectant, and there is something intuitive in the thought that making something *visible* inherently makes it better, though in this instance we are dealing with a different sense. Toxic silence is not just about the absence of sound or voice; it is about the ability to share information, what information is *allowed* to be shared, and the right of an individual to self-advocate for themselves and to ask the kinds of questions that will lead to better health. The US Supreme Court deliberated over the question of whether access to safe abortion was a constitutionally protected right. The 1973 decision in *Roe* v *Wade* preserved a woman's right to have all options open to her, to have access to whatever data or medical advisement would help her make an informed choice. *Roe* v *Wade* spoke loud and clear, and despite forty-eight years of conservative protest and repeated attempts to undermine the Supreme Court of the US decision, current popular feeling is overwhelmingly in favour of keeping *Roe* v *Wade* intact (73 per cent according to PerryUndem, 2019). It is the ultimate hypocrisy to hold the world's most vulnerable accountable for partisan policy unrest in the United States, especially while abortion remains legal in the United States and in most of the countries receiving the conditional humanitarian aid. Per historical precedent, there is every likelihood that the incoming administration in 2021 will scale back the global gag rule and restore the vital funding necessary to continue world health initiatives in healthcare and disease management. What we should really hope for, rather what we should demand, is for the abortion clause to be permanently removed as condition for desperately needed humanitarian aid globally.

Part V

Humanity

Martyn Colebrook

The City & the City, China Miéville (2009)

A toxin is defined not by any inherent properties, but by the effect it has on living organisms – it is, so to speak, a conditional poison. In a more literary sense, the term can act as a linguistic link between the chemical and the organism. Toxicity also can be highly specific to the circumstances in which it exists. For Illing, toxicity can be seen as 'ill-health and environmental degradation' (2001: 5). Toxins, and especially industrial chemicals, occupy a boundary between bodies and environments, resisting tidy distinctions between the two categories: they are remnants of an industrial society, yet operate within the realm of natural processes as fundamental as cellular metabolism and the water cycle.

Refuse and dirt held a paradoxical place in nineteenth-century society as matter that was economically valuable yet had the capacity to contaminate. From this, visions of strange, contaminated environments offered novel versions of the 'natural' order, which in turn allowed them to depict alternative social orders that emphasised stewardship and care while challenging the logic of industrial capitalism. As McQuiston argues:

> An SF-inflected toxic discourse also appears in late twentieth and early twenty-first century 'mainstream' fiction. Across this wide body of literature, three themes appear consistently: a fascination with the permeability of bodies, the dramatization of mundane and/or invisible threats (especially through gender and reproductive failure), and a deeply ambivalent attitude toward technology and the scientists who wield it. (2014: ii)

Further exemplifying this development through the genre of urban fantasy, Miéville (like other authors mentioned by Neilsen) moves 'beyond the nineteenth century desire for the containment of filth to inscribe otherwise monstrous spaces with possibility' (Nielsen 2018: 24). He directly engages not only with technology but with the social, psychological and aesthetic aspects of the use of technology, often in such powerful ways that the resulting genre tropes and conventions cross genre boundaries and enter the general cultural awareness.

In this respect, *The City & the City* lends itself well to understanding the increasingly complex and culturally pervasive toxic narrative. The depiction indicates a 'culturally practicable alternative to the ideal of a pristine, un-touched nature; the toxic narrative represents a serious effort to reconcile the global with the microscopic, the natural with the unnatural, and the body with its environment' (McQuiston 2014: ii). With fiction that is often characterised by the 'complex infiltration of the boundaries of fictionalisation and genre' this metaphor can be extended to the city of this narrative, where the atmosphere and activities 'echo the infiltration of toxins across the boundaries of body' (Neilsen: 8). This chapter suggests 'toxic discourse' (Buell 1998: 639–40) can offer an insight into *The City & The City*, where Miéville draws on images of abnormality and disruption, fractured communities and compromised bodies.

Drawing on multiple genres, Miéville throws the reader into the worlds of Besźel and Ul Qoma, partitioned geographically and seemingly located in a European setting redolent with the ravages of Berlin, Istanbul, the Soviet Union and the last vestiges of decaying Eastern European metropolises. Using the focus of the toxic city as a lens through which to investigate the expression of genres in Miéville's fiction, this chapter seeks to identify the ways in which the author is able 'to map the imaginative and material reordering of space' (Hefner 2015: 192) and the ways in which the architectural and urban geographies of the city come to represent this state of being.

The premise of *The City & The City* is three-pronged. First, a student from overseas, Mahalia Geary, who was living in Ul Qoma, has been found dead in a Besźel street with a disfiguration to her face. Inspector Borlú and his sidekick, Corwi, are assigned to investigate. Second, the second city of Ul Qoma, which occupies much of the same geographical space as Besźel, is dominated by political structures that mean the inhabitants of each city must 'unsee' one another (i.e. consciously erase the image and knowledge of one another from their minds) lest they commit the act of 'breaching', punished by the entity known as the Breach, an authoritarian enforcement group that acts as a cohort of secret police hidden within the 'deep state'. The third prong of the plot is the rumoured existence of a third city, Orciny, which is said to exist between the spaces between Besźel and Ul Qoma.

The novel commences as Inspector Borlú attends the discovered body of Mahalia Geary, and the reader is immediately pitched into the post-industrial urban Gothic landscape:

> We could not see the street or much of the estate. We were enclosed by dirt-coloured blocks, from windows out of which leaned vested men and women with morning hair and mugs of drink. This open ground between the buildings had once been sculpted. It pitched like a golf course – a child's mimicking of geography. (3)

Miéville establishes a clear sense of enclosure – that they cannot 'see the street or much of the estate' highlights the twofold points of escape: a street where seemingly other members of the population would live or work and the rest of the estate which may offer other avenues for refuge. The 'dirt-coloured blocks' suggest dereliction and decay, and infer imprisonment or close, cramped living quarters redolent of the military. Those who 'lean' out of the window have the air of those unprepared to leave the house and engage with society, leering and gazing, an unspoken air of threat and potential violence. Miéville's depiction intensifies with the 'open ground [...] [that had] once been sculpted', which implies that the landscape was crafted and artistically created, artifice from a regeneration project that has now been rendered as a 'child's mimicking of geography'. Here the caricature and self-conscious language renders the men and women of the estate as having descended into childlike behaviour. Unable to appreciate or maintain the high-quality status of their landscape, it becomes a dumping ground, infantilised and ignored. The interrelation of the Gothic and the noir creates the opportunity for depictions of cityscapes and townscapes which appear to exist as living entities alongside the inhabitants of these environments. It is as though there is a tension between the question of whether the inhabitants shape the toxic characteristics of the urban or the urban environment shapes the toxic tendencies of its inhabitants.

The significance of the toxic in relation to 'post-industrial space' is suggested by Linda Dryden, who observes: 'The city itself is figured as monstrous in its geographical and social divisions. The duality that some of its citizens exhibit is also manifest in the oppositions of light and dark, atmospheres of airiness and stifling oppression' (2003: 188–9). The inherent sense of enclosure, entrapment and stifling atmospheres which come to inhabit these environments contribute to the monstrosity, as well as the aberrancies of behaviour and societal breakdown which are witnessed among the population. These urban 'topolgangers' (Miéville 2009: 159) embody the doubling underpinning the cityscape, and the urban environment comes to be depicted as a 'massively ramified ecosystem that comprises humans, other species, and objects, and is also embedded in larger systems like capitalism and environmental catastrophe' (Prystash 2017: 275). The Gothic places emphasis on a conviction that the protagonists will suffer or endure the consequences of actions and that they are unavoidable, hence the atavism or sense of inheritance which is present. Dryden further suggests: 'Issues of duality – split personalities, physical transformations, mistaken identities, doppelgängers – [are] found to be manifested in the social, geographical and architectural schisms of the modern city' (Dryden 2003: 19). The duality and doubling operate on multiple levels within *The City & The City* and the idea that they are 'manifested [...] in the modern city' further embellishes the idea that the city and its populace will ultimately become fused and embody one another. This is why 'the city becomes 'corrupt, diseased' (Dryden 2003: 188), a site of anxiety and decay, and the inhabitants all too often become 'preoccupied with systems from which life seems unable to escape' (Crawford 1992: 7). To escape is to transgress or to commit a 'breach'.

Beginning with a dead body, the narrative is driven by a 'gothic causality' (Skenazy 1995: 114) and the 'hauntings that structure most crime narratives' (Scaggs 2005: 16). If this concept is broken down and replicated in *The City & The City*, then there are two hauntings at work – the unexplained death of Melania Geary and, as the reader discovers, the death of Borlú's wife on GunterStrasz, which is a recurring trauma. The secrets from the past are Geary's reasons for crossing from Ul Qoma and for her death, and the reasons for the death of Borlú's wife. In a cityscape and political structure such as this, two transgressive acts threaten to disrupt the social order – their existence posits a challenge to the authority of Breach and the infrastructure of 'unseeing', on which the polis' lack of rebellion is founded. Developing the concept further by noting and then transgressing one of the central conventions of the detective genre, John G. Cawelti states that 'the criminal act rips apart the social fabric and the detective must use his unique investigative skills to sew it back together again' (2004: 300). By demonstrating that the principle of unseeing can be questioned and challenged, that the borders between the cities are liminal and potentially porous for future transgressions, the murderer threatens to explode the fundaments upon which the bipartite structure of the cityscapes is built. It is interesting that Borlú takes on the status of the individual who must 'sew it back together again', because, at times, a specific type or version of honour is possible in such crime narratives, despite it being challenging and an uncommon achievement. More broadly, in such narratives, 'human beings are assumed to be driven mainly by simple material greed' (Freedman 2015: 16).

This further suggests another example of toxicity – this time between prosperity and deprivation – which underpins the geography of *The City & The City*. The markers of past self-sufficiency and industry (as a noun and as a verb) are now rendered as the scrawled-upon subject of frustrations articulated by the local population, a space now perpetually in economic crisis where fear of robbery and illicit, temporary respite from everyday life represent the only possible routes of escape. The language used to describe the attire of people in Besźel is telling: 'Poverty deshaped the already staid, drab cuts and colours that enduringly characterise Besź clothes – what has been called the city's fashionless fashion' (Miéville 2009: 21). 'Deshaped' as opposed to 'reshaped' emphasises the hopelessness of the area, where shape is removed rather than reformed – there is no opportunity for change or transformation, for 'fashion' to be recontextualised. The irredeemable atmosphere is of a downward spiral seemingly without end.

The fantastic and discursive space is emphasised when encountering the Besźel ghetto, which 'was only architecture now, not formal political boundary, tumbledown old houses with newly gentrified chic, clustered between very different foreign alter spaces' (26). The new urban Gothic and Miéville's relentless interrogation of capitalism's architectural space functions to identify and depict how the actions of individuals within the urban space affect and have an impact upon their environment and how the process of writing the cityscape is an ongoing artistic dialogue. In such instances, the reader is forced to '*think the cities*' (Baker 2016: 13; italics in the original). Mahalia Geary's training as an archaeologist informs the continued explorations between the architecture of the cities and the new urban Gothic. As the detective reads Mahalia's work, there is a knowing underpinning sense of how this archaeology is a creative process of working with history in a framework of censure and oppression: 'I read Mahalia's annotations. I could discern phrases of annotation, though not in any page-wise chronology – all the notes were layered, a palimpsest of evolving interpretation. I did archaeology' (Miéville 2009: 308). The 'palimpsest' identified is an archaeology in itself, a sequence of historical fragments which must be put together in order to deduce a particular conclusion. Much like the fragmentary nature of the city itself, which is composed of multiple historical layers, archaeology becomes the ideal mechanism by which Miéville is able to interrogate the cityscape as a product of capital.

As Borlú and Corwi pass through Besźel, it is apparent that the unsettling and pervasive sense of fear which inhabits the cityscape manifests itself in the geography. They are aware that Breach is there, 'organising, cauterising, restoring' (66). Rather than Borlú and Corwi feeling paranoid, the behaviour of the Breach and the atmosphere make it apparent that their fear is justifiable as opposed to an overactive response to a space which has the trappings of hostility. As Borlú comments: 'Of course there would be paranoia, for a visitor to this city, where the locals would stare and stare furtively, where I would be watched by Breach, of which snatched glances would not feel like anything I had experienced' (211). At this point, Borlú is in Ul Qoma, and it is demonstrated that the feelings of surveillance, worry and political fear are embedded in the other city and its populace. This is a novel where power and identity 'perpetually emerge, molten, during times of crisis' (Prystash 2017: 279). For Miéville, cities are zones within a larger 'threatening geography' (2009: 18). The intensity of the 'snatched glances' suggests an atmosphere where 'seeing' and 'unseeing' can easily be misinterpreted, where the foreign are observed with an assumed suspicion and are, essentially, guilty until their actions allow them to leave and remain not guilty. Death between the cities can constitute breach since the individual is effectively stateless and could, potentially, symbolise the presence of an interstitial or liminal space between them. When Breach act, they are swift, decisive and ghostlike in their arrival and departure. When transgression occurs, the depiction is of individuals who had been present but not seen – a panoramic surveillance:

> In seconds, the Breach came. Shapes, figures, some of whom perhaps had been there but who nonetheless seemed to coalesce from spaces between smoke from the accident,

moving with authority and power so absolute that within seconds they had controlled, contained, the area of intrusion. (Miéville 2009: 81)

The figures have a spectral composition, capable of moving, forming and reforming without being observed. The analogy would be of a necessary liquid which moves within the cities' circulation system and then rapidly congeals and clots to heal an injured body – in this instance, the body politic of the two cities.

Among the many elements of paranoia which underpin the daily lives of citizens living in Besźel and Ul Qoma, there are dangerous and potentially deadly confessions imparted to Borlú which relate to the existence of Orciny, the third city, responsible for Geary's murder. Its description is the language of pure conspiracy thriller: 'Orciny's the third city. It's between the other two. [...] Orciny's the secret city. It runs things' (Miéville 2009: 61). Later a more provocative statement – 'I think Orciny is the name Breach calls itself' (254) – will emerge to further embellish the legendary status of the city between cities. The hidden city, the possibility of an invisible agency holding sway over the other named and (partly) visible cities tempers the radical potential and possibility of liminal spaces between the cities, transgression of societal suppressions and the process of 'not seeing', a transgressive act in itself since it suggests a rejection of the authorities and their use of the cityscape as a tool for controlling the inhabitants.

After learning and witnessing how the cities' inner operations are able to work, Borlú is not permitted to be free, but becomes enmeshed in the machinations of the cities. Enlisted by Breach, he is now an enforcer, policing and continuing to ensure the unbreachable, invisible border. The conclusion of the investigation leads to a transgression whose conclusion 'closes any prospective porosity in the cities' protective membrane' (Prystash 2017: 279). This ending indicates that 'transgressions, presupposing the laws or norms or taboos against which they function, thereby end up precisely reconfirming such laws' (Jameson 2015: 68). In this respect, the city seals the membrane to prevent further cross-contamination and infection, maintaining the integrity of its own toxicity and the architecture and 'citizens' it has created – a body politic reliant upon its acquisition of those who infect it and conversion of them to an antigen of sorts, a method by which it preserves its toxic health, but at the expense of its citizens.

Phil Fitzsimmons and Edie Lanphar

Brimstone, Martin Koolhoven (2016)

This essay focuses on the current state of American education as microscopically and telescopically viewed through the lens of the movie *Brimstone*. The theoretical mechanism by which this movie came into specific critical focus is the principles found in trauma research and, in particular, the related concept of 'multidirectional memory' (Rothberg 2009: 1). This is a collective cultural memory that arises from deep traumatic wounds often created in a culture's colonial past and which recursively appear. These social memories are 'unstable, aporetic and often very frightening indeed' (Blake 2008: 3). Collective cultural wounds are more often than not repressed and smoothed over by false myths of coherence and positivity. However, unless dealt with, they repeatedly surface 'in the fabric of culture and history that bleed through conventional confines of time and space' (Lowenstein 2005: 1). Notwithstanding the complexity of trauma and its association with cinema as a whole, and the compression of narrative that cinema naturally employs, it is through horror films and the mis-en-abîme process that often occurs within them that trauma in cultural memory may be revisited and it may be possible to begin a cultural shift to 'a mode of healing' (Blake 2008: 115). In discussing the concept of narrative conflation, Rotherberg (2009: 173) notes that it is often a 'difficult task [to break] out of taken-for-granted frameworks of historical and cultural understanding'. However, this is one of the key functionalities of horror film in that its compression of traumatic cultural foundations heightens the false terrain on which a social imagination or cultural narrative is based. Horror compels reflection on how the inevitable mimetic narrative outbreaks related to historical trauma 'in the ruins and traumas of modernity force readers to confront the legacies of violence that persist beyond the places and times of textbook history and television documentary'. Set in the early decades of the American frontier, *Brimstone* is an example of how historical traumatic events in the beginning of American settlement have left memories just as real as those imprinted in the people in the original setting.

Described as a deeply troubling horror movie, *Brimstone* moves elegantly through the interplay of an overall anachronic elliptical narrative divided into four 'jump-cut' storied pathways. This takes the viewer through the brutal lived experience and introspective life journey of the main character, Liz (Dakota Fanning). Through the back and forth time shifts of the four narratives, the film unpacks the intersecting paths of Liz, from a young girl into womanhood, and an unnamed psychotic pastor.

However, there is a second elliptical and parallel cinematic orbit, which encompasses the story of Liz's young daughter, Sam (Ivy George). The movie begins and ends with a focus on Liz's death, with comments and visuals provided by Sam. In the initial scenes, we see what we later learn is Liz's suicide by drowning, and at the end point, she is shown sinking out of sight while being shot at by a sheriff seeking to arrest her. Threads and streams of sunlight follow her down through the water. While these two scenes intertextually echo the symbolism of the 'black river of the underworld or the Waters of Death' (Deardorff 2004: 168), they also form an inverted linkage to the religious perspective of the Pilgrim Fathers and their concept of Christian baptism by immersion. Rather than a cleansing in parallel with Christ's baptism in the Jordan, and a representation of rising to new life, these mise-en-scène connectors highlight the eternal and ultimate death of the abyss experience. It is this cosmological site of eternal damnation, pain and annihilation that The Reverend (Guy Pearce) fears and believes is his fate. Through this deformed existential perspective, he sees his only chance of salvation arise only through the sacrificial killing of Liz. Her death by drowning represents not only her 'simultaneous release from every context of the world above, where darkness no longer is an absence of light but an experienced force' (Campbell 1960: 66) but also his deranged act of revenge. Her willing slippage into the crushing depths indicates this was Liz's only means of escaping the final clutches of the Old Testament perspectives of the pastor that had haunted her earthly life and that of her daughter. Thus, these characters and the entire cultural setting are framed overall as an emotional and psychosocial space of sacrificial liminality, a place of 'terrible incompleteness' (Mitchell 1989: 111).

The sense of lack of incompleteness in this film is carried forwards and backwards through a web of metonymic facets. Not the least of these elements are the notions of discipline, time and muteness. Set in an undisclosed time period and in an indeterminate season, the narrative time frame is somewhere in between the firm establishment of the staunch religious ideologies of Calvinistic settlements in the early 1600s, which took root soon after the arrival of the Pilgrim Fathers, and the establishment of American settlements.

As is typically the case with any narrative modality that deals with 'in-betweeness', *Brimstone* is also riddled and ringed with the corollaries of silence and submission. It is these two underlying narrative threads that form the analytic construct of this chapter, and their direct relationship to the ongoing toxicity of American education is examined.

Core Threads of Toxicity

Issues that beset this early period of American settlement and expansion were grounded in religiosity rather than religion. Fleeing Europe and seeking to create a place of religious freedom, the Calvinists also brought with them a primary focus of strict religious adherence and service. They saw education as the means 'to instruct children in Biblical interpretation' (Lambert 2003: 112), to achieve these ends. Also, education was intended to be the bulwark against change, which they understood threatened the conservative and traditional moral values of the age. With its other emphases of hard work, simplicity, following the directives of a religious leader and self-sufficiency, the shaping of a future republic, if not a future capitalist society, was formed. As McCallum states, the underlying principal of 'pulling yourself up by your bootstraps, that originated with those early years in education, where religion and piousness undergirded the pursuit of education, are still in effect today' (2018: 106). Also embedded in this educational ideology were the supposed biblical principles of 'spare the rod and spoil the child' and 'children should be seen not heard'.

However, as is the case with all colonisers, and in particular European colonisers, the narrative related that the 'powerful sense of divine mission into the wilderness' (Crow 2017: 100) shifted when confronted with physical, social and emotional boundaries that became unstable. As indicated in *Brimstone*, with the inevitable deadly clashes with the native inhabitants and the initial clearing of the dark, unknown and unforgiving forest of trees they could not name, that gradually gave way to pastureland, a new dominant cultural narrative arose. Arising out of the need for sheer survival and to keep alive their religious narrative of dominance, these inward-looking religious spaces gave way to an ever-increasing dominance of a violent frontier masculine myth. 'The violent spirit of the warrior hero, and the violent means by which he gained his wisdom, are inseparable from the regenerative spirit which he initiated' (Slotkin 1998: 374–5). This newly developing cultural narrative of aggression simply reinforced the previous ideals of punishment and silence.

Frontier Myth Contrasted with Authentic Learning

Following on from the paratextual opening scenes of Liz sinking slowly to death in unknown catchment, *Brimstone* then shifts the first segment of this four-part narrative, under the subheading of 'Revelation'. This first cycle of narrative focuses on her family in an unknown and unnamed farm in a remote and unnamed state. From the outset of this section, it is clear that she is mute. While she and her husband, her stepson and their daughter are able to communicate via sign language, her immediate sphere of the small Calvinistic world cannot. With her daughter by her side helping with chores, the narrative then encompasses her stepson being taught to shoot by his father. This introduces an educative counterpoint that weaves through this this movie. Under the silent guidance of this father, Matthew (Jack Hollington) picks up the rifle and attempts to shoot at a tree. Clearly distressed, Liz attempts to dissuade her husband from allowing his son to use this gun, but his reply is simply that he would prefer Matthew shoot a gun in his care, and this is the way it is. The ideal of the frontiersmen and the need for guns, and the use of guns to settle disputes, runs the entire length of this movie. In contrast to this, Sam is an indispensable link in Liz's role as a midwife. Unable to speak and give instructions, Sam acts as her mother's voice and is the conveyor of instructions and mediator between both male and female parents. Although only 11 or 12 years of age, it would appear that she has been doing this for some time and clearly understands many of the aspects of childbirth.

Another silence in this cinematic narrative is the absence of a centralised school in the community. Scenes of the community building a church show a collective group that is large enough to also have a specific educational focus. As indicated already, education was a primary element of these communities, and although isolated, the community here would certainly have had, at the very least, a rudimentary schoolhouse. Thus, this absence or silence focuses the reader-viewer on the learning processes that Michael and Sam undertake in their daily lives.

While, due to the gendered role division and the social pressure of masculinity, Matthew is becoming immersed in the way of the frontier, Sam is undertaking what would now be called apprenticeship learning. Currently recognised as being authentic, apprenticeship learning is underpinned by a key ideological element, which is the ideal of the learner being included in a practical sense in a real-world experience as an expert when, clearly, they are not. This provides a positive psychosocial space in which the mind and language space is decreased so there is no power struggle, but rather a deep relational and communicative bond is formed.

As Sam's experience clearly indicates, looking over her mother's shoulder facilitates her learning. However, she is not treated as a novice midwife, but as an essential partner and expert in her mother's work. Indeed, in the initial scenes, she is treated as such by the community as well. As an intermediary between her mother's knowledge and signing, it would appear that initially even the men in this loosely clustered male religious enclave gave her respect.

Essentially, Liz had initiated an apprenticeship model that viewed her child as a doer, a knower, a thinker and as knowledgeable. However, when the pastor enters this community for the first time and preaches his first sermon, it is clear that the religious perspective clashes with the constructivist world of this community. While on the narrative surface it is clear this new minister terrifies Liz – in ensuing narrative segments we learn that he is the one who had previously attempted to sexually assault her and that, in order to escape, she cut out her tongue to take on another woman's identity – it is also clear the religious dogma of hell and punishment is diametrically opposed to the learning model developed by Liz.

Punishment Contrasted with Authentic Care

Although there are multiple threats in the subtext that are related to religion and early colonial American society, the concept of punishment is one of the more dominant themes. Although the myth of the wild frontier became embedded very early on in the national psyche, religious settlements such as that portrayed in *Brimstone* were still offshoots from the older cultures in Europe and retained much of the latter's national tendencies and beliefs. A component of these was the trauma of persecution they had suffered in their homelands, which arrived on the American continent as 'an archive of both visible and invisible ghosts of traumatic memory' (Elaca 2016: 2). However, the web of trauma ran far deeper in these early colonial settlers with the biblical and mythic association 'of sacrificial massacres and last stands' deeply embedded in their psyche (Slotkin 1998: 27). This Old Testament view of the world also encompassed retribution and punishment. The title of this movie implies there was a clear carry-over of this belief system into communities of this brief period in the development of early America.

In contrast to this apparent biblical dictum, the small cultural group of isolated believers in this movie appear to have operated as a relatively stable and content cultural group for some time. It is only the appearance of The Reverend and his first fire and brimstone sermon that completely disrupts the social harmony of this group. The cornerstone of his sermon is that there are members of the congregation who have strayed, and if they continue on this path they are deserving of hellfire: 'Retribution is coming'. It is from this point on that this movie takes a radical turn towards the belief that punishment sets miscreants on the right pathway.

In later segments of the film, we learn that this pastor has been in pursuit of Liz for some considerable time, meaning to kill her to atone for his psychosis and sexual deviance. As a contrast to this, as soon as his sermon is over, one of the congregation goes into labour in the threshold of the church. Liz and Sam take over under the damning glance of The Reverend. However, the birth goes horribly wrong, and Liz must make the choice of saving the mother or saving the baby. She chooses the former, and in doing so earns the wrath of The Reverend for not allowing God to choose who should live and who should die. He then turns the congregation on a path of retribution and punishment aimed at Liz and her family.

This simple scene then sets the tenor for the entire movie, eventually leading to Liz's death. Thus, this movie's unending metonymic thread, bound up with theological perceptions of religious dominance, and the frontier motif is indicative of the continuation of these toxic elements in the actual context of American education.

Conclusion: A Continuation of Toxicity

Brimstone clearly deals with one of the greatest issues embedded in American culture: the toxicity created when colonial thinking, religion and education merge. 'The ghost of colonialism continues to precipitate conflict and also influence how we interpret people and events' (Demos and Texler 2013: 10).

This triple helix of malevolence has seeped relatively unabated into the overall American social network and belief structures as a whole. It is only through movies such *Brimstone* that allow the process of *Trauerarbeit* – 'the work of mourning; exploring trauma by remembering it and repeating it in the form of diagetically mediated symbolisations of loss' (Blake 2008: 2) – to occur.

Blake I. Collier

Martyrs, Pascal Laugier (2008)

Conspiracy theories are just one of many forms of human speculation about a world that does not always make sense. They are an attempt at tying together the outlying evidence that does not quite fit neatly within the official narrative. At best, these practices can be beneficial to developing critical thinking; however, at their worst, most toxic forms, they can endeavour to upend reality and embrace forms of power and totalitarian governance which instigate violence and the silencing of those who have the least power and voice in society. In this essay, I will explore the rise of QAnon, specifically in American society under Donald Trump's presidency, and how it is becoming its own religious cult with tendrils reaching into mainstream Christian churches, and then I will turn to a prescient connection between QAnon's cult and the philosophical cult of the 2008 New French Extremity film *Martyrs*, and how seeking to pierce the veil of human 'knowledge' can lead to its own unique form of toxic culture.

    The work of spinning conspiracy theories requires use of the imagination, which has been, to some extent, de-emphasised in a culture that values science and empirical data above all else. It is not hard to see connections to the work of journalism in terms of seeing counterfactuals to the official narrative which require the tracking down of sources and following of paper trails to see if there is an actual story going on behind the scenes. When we think of the Watergate Scandal in the United States during the 1970s, there is an overarching conspiratorial cloud to the proceedings around Nixon's administration. If it had not been for the 'conspiracy theory' of Bernstein and Woodward, it is possible that Nixon would have achieved his goals under the guise of 'the official account'. However, the key terms associated with journalistic accounts are 'counterfactuals' and 'paper trails', elements that require evidence which can be confirmed and are not *just* taken on faith.

Conspiracy theories can help us be mindful that the official account is not always the most truthful or accurate account – it is often created from the mouths of the powerful. However, conspiracy theories have taken on a more sinister tinge in the twenty-first century, particularly from 2017 with the arrival of 'Q' and his/her/their information dumps, which conveniently demonise Democrats and Progressives. Under the Trump administration – which has been incorporated into the Q web of conspiracies – and the Republican Party's control of the Senate under Mitch McConnell, it seems that QAnon – the self-styled cult title for Q and his/her/their followers – has become informally entangled in a parasitic relationship with the political party in power. Trump and McConnell's Senate are too coy to give official credence to the conspiracy movement's presence; however, Trump's base seems increasingly overtaken by those who affiliate themselves with QAnon, and Trump is smart enough to know where the source of his power comes from and that it must be wielded in order to maintain loyalty.

If we look at the demographic make-up of Trump's base, we can ascertain common traits. According to statistical data for 2018 from Data for Progress (supported by a Pew Research Center study from the same year), the typical Trump supporter fits into one or more of the following categories: white men; white Evangelicals; whites over 50; whites who make over $50,000; rural whites; and working-class, non-college whites (McElwee 2018). While there is much to draw from each of these characteristics, I want to focus on the demarcation of white Evangelicals. There is a long, complicated history behind the creation of the Evangelical movement out of fundamentalist Christianity in the 1950s. The two are not diametrically opposed and probably share more in common than not. The central disagreement is in the level of engagement they have within society. Evangelicals are less isolationist in their political and cultural tendencies. Margaret Bendroth (2017) writes:

> It is best to say that fundamentalism persists in a lingering set of attitudes, articulated in a rhetoric of persecution and alienation that has persisted despite the rising cultural power and economic stature of most evangelical believers. […] It has been a powerful political tool, mobilizing evangelicals in defense of 'family values' and other conservative causes. Fundamentalism is, in other words, far from an aberration in an American narrative of

tolerance and progress. It is a story essential to understanding some important disagreements and divisions in the past, which though invisible remain potent in the controversies of the present – and promise to remain so for decades to come.

Seeing how the threads of Christian Fundamentalism weave through the fabric of modern-day Evangelical Christianity, it is easy to see a general political allegiance to the party that will remain the most apt to conserve majority – white, Christian, male – social values and fend off any form of progressive or liberal policy or ethics. In the eyes of American Christianity, this has been, at least since the 1950s, the Republican Party. The persecution narrative continues even to this day. Any attack against Christianity or Republican political values is rhetorically seen as an attack on the Christian God and His people and law. The Evangelical movement, unlike Fundamentalist Christians, became activists instead of being isolationist, aligning themselves with the party that, at the very least, gave lip service to their political ends.

However, one can also see how the threads of QAnon can just as easily find their way into this white, Evangelical Christian narrative, especially when Q includes Christian elements in his/her/their information dumps. Whoever this Q may be, they claim to have high security clearance, which has allowed him/her/them to reveal a supposed Democratic sex trafficking and paedophilia ring and that Donald Trump is working to uncover the plot along with the help of Robert Mueller – the Mueller Report having been ordered by Trump to secretly investigate the sex ring. QAnon uses the threat to children (i.e. the threat to the nuclear family) to bring Evangelicals into the cult.

Even in the ways that Q frames 'Q Drops' feels somewhat messianic in their obscuration of clarity, somewhat like the parables that Jesus of Nazareth spoke in.

> The [original Q] post contains a cryptic series of questions, clues and predictions – a format Q has consistently used when posting information online. 'Q crumbs' – also sometimes called 'Q drops' or 'Q clues' – are little more than a series of clues that often come in the form of letter or number riddles. Q's followers are meant to research and decipher these clues on their own. This is the most important thing I could do. If I do the research and decipher the clues, I'll be prepared for the proof. (Cheney 2020)

By conservative estimates, white Evangelicals make up only 7 per cent of QAnon, and just over 2 per cent of white Evangelicals know about or believe in all of the core conspiratorial beliefs of the cult (Schaffer n.d.; see also Edelman 2020). Yet it shows no signs of disappearing any time real soon. If it becomes more engrained in the banality of everyday ritual for Evangelical Christianity, then it is possible it could spread simply by way of interpersonal relationships within normal church socialising and right-leaning political groups. Yet there is an element of QAnon that breeds a specific form of toxicity within society. Some mass shootings have been tied to the QAnon cult, as has the general spread of disinformation that can stunt healthy election cycles and increasingly polarise an already divided American politik. Unlike Bernstein and Woodward's discovery of Nixon's conspiracy, QAnon is driven by the accumulation of power rather than seeking truth and justice.

It is within this current atmosphere that we look back on the 2008 film *Martyrs*, directed by Pascal Laugier – one of the proponents of the New French Extremity movement – and find it strangely prescient in its exploration of the world of toxicity and violence which cults that trade in gnostic thought – that is, groups which rely on systems of esoteric knowledge as means of salvation or enlightenment – practices perpetuate. At the beginning of the film, we are thrown into the escape of a young girl, who we come to know as Lucie Jurin (Mylène Jampanoï). Who she is escaping from, we do not know, but we can tell it has taken a toll on her physically and psychologically as she runs down the industrial roads away from her captors.

Lucie is placed in an orphanage and befriends another girl, Anna Assaoui (Morjana Alaoui). From that point on, Anna becomes the comforter to Lucie, who is plagued by visions and nightmares of an emaciated woman. They become bonded, and the film jumps ahead in time by over a decade. We are then introduced to a seemingly normal French family who are going about their morning in what appears to be the traditional ideal of the nuclear family unit. Lucie shows up at their door and proceeds to dispatch each of the family members, including the kids, with a shotgun, believing them to be responsible for her captivity and trauma. Lucie tells Anna what she has done, and Anna comes to the home to find the mother still barely alive; Anna attempts to help the woman escape Lucie's massacre. But Lucie catches her and bludgeons her to death.

This final manifestation of the emaciated woman causes Lucie to take her own life due to the belief that she will never be sane again. Anna remains in

Figure 38. Sarah (Isabelle Chasse) blinded.
Source: *Martyrs*; directed by Pascal Laugier (Wild Bunch, 2008).

the home and ends up hearing noises in an underground chamber, where she finds a tortured young woman named Sarah (Isabelle Chasse; see Figure 38). Lucie had been right about the family. A group of strangers arrives, dispatches Sarah, and imprisons and tortures Anna. The leader of this cult, this gnostic philosophical society, is an elderly lady who goes by the name of Mademoiselle (Catherine Bégin). The cult seeks knowledge of the afterlife through the creation of martyrs, who all seem to be women. According to the cult's beliefs, the martyrs' progressive suffering will lead to transcendental connection with the other side of the veil.

Anna goes through an ever more violent system of torture and ends up going further than any other girl before her. In the final phase of torture, she is completely flayed alive. In this state, skinless, she finds transcendence and receives a message that we, the audience, never find out the substance of (see Figure 39); yet the content causes Mademoiselle to tell her assistant to 'keep doubting', before she kills herself with a handgun. The substance of Anna's message was either one of nihilism or divine judgment on the acts of the group. Whatever the content, it bred an utter hopelessness in Mademoiselle.

The philosophical cult in *Martyrs* is strikingly reminiscent of modern-day conspiracy cults like QAnon in terms of their attempt to pierce the veil of the

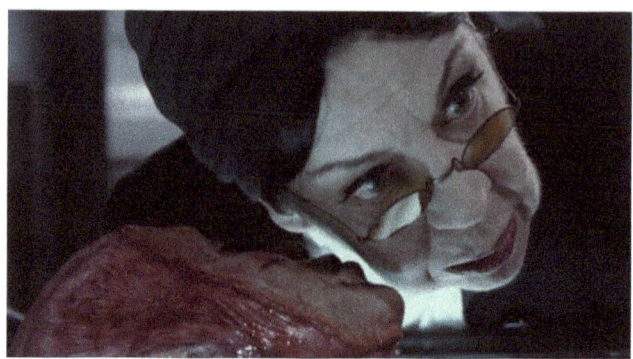

Figure 39. Mademoiselle listening.
Source: *Martyrs*; directed by Pascal Laugier (Wild Bunch, 2008).

unknown and, in doing so, exert themselves on the world and on the voiceless to gain power and control. Secret knowledge delineates them as superior to others. When QAnon activists make connections between child sex trafficking rings and Wayfair cabinet sales, due to each cabinet being given a girl's name, they are manipulating a real event and the trauma associated with those who actually suffer in trafficking rings for the sake of their gnostic religio-political narrative. The power to be gained is in the defeat or distrust accorded to the Democratic Party in favour of Republican politics. This is how QAnon has gained a foothold in the Evangelical imagination. In a 2020 interview with Ari Shapiro on NPR, reporter for Religion News Service Katelyn Beaty spoke about how their spiritual imagination has been utilised by QAnon:

> They are picking up on the overt spiritual language that Q, whoever that is, is using in his messages on the Internet, and they see that as connecting directly to the Bible, to the God of Christianity and to God's hand at work in the world. So they see the QAnon messages as revealing truth in the world and that they are supposed to take up a spiritual battle to reveal truth. (Beaty and Shapiro, 2020)

Mademoiselle's language plays with a specifically Christian image when she speaks to a tortured Anna about her 'privilege' of place in their grand scheme. 'Martyrs are exceptional people. They survive pain; they survive total deprivation. They bear all the sins of the earth. They give themselves up. They transcend themselves ... they are transfigured' (Laugier 2008).

In the context of the film, this speech appears to be no more than a locker-room monologue. Mademoiselle is utilising a notoriously weak and often skewed link in Christian theology (martyrdom) to justify the torture done to many women. What Mademoiselle gets wrong about the proper understanding of being a martyr is the *willingness* unto death for one's faith. None of these women give consent to die for this cult's search for gnostic information; nor do they share the same faith in the first place. Anna comes to *acceptance* of her plight, but acceptance is far from *willingness* (see Figure 40). And, yet, one reading of the ending could see Anna being given a word of judgment from whatever god, or perhaps indifferent being, is on the other side of the veil. That judgment might have been too much for Mademoiselle to bear.

This *willingness* to suffer torture and multiple deprivations of being is illuminated so clearly by the historical Jeanne d'Arc, the French peasant girl who received a call from God to lead the French to victory against the British during the Battle of Orléans in the Hundred Years War. In many ways, *Martyrs* becomes a distorted reflection of a story that would end in sainthood.

Figure 40. Anna (Morjana Alaoui) chained.
Source: *Martyrs*; directed by Pascal Laugier (Wild Bunch, 2008).

Jeanne d'Arc was captured nearly a year after her victory and killed by the English for being a heretic – this was with the help of French collaborators, including the inaction of King Charles VII. Jean was a woman of low class and means prophesying the destruction of a great power which threatened to torture, rape and ultimately burn her at the stake at the age of 19 years. Yet she refused to denounce the truth of her visions and her Catholic faith. And by all seeming accounts, she did so willingly. She understood that she was not only good, but chosen by God, in *flesh* and *spirit*, and even she was not willing to spare her good embodiment to compromise that which she saw as truth.

Likewise, Anna's acceptance of her fate comes from recognising that truth and justice, especially from the mouth of those without power, is worth death. Yet, regardless of the substance of the message, Mademoiselle's final words to her assistant are 'keep doubting'. Mademoiselle has found her transcendent martyr and the seeming message of truth delivered *is not what she hoped or wanted*, so she tells her group to keep doubting the official narrative. This is how QAnon continues to thrive even when pushed up against evidence to the contrary. This is because they do not want to believe anything else. They have become invested in QAnon's beliefs and attached their identity to them, and whatever it takes to arrive at those specific beliefs is fair game.

It is within that turbulent mixture of gnostic prophecy, human pride and the promise of power and superiority that we find both the philosophical cult and QAnon. The disconcerting element of this whole discussion is that *Martyrs*' philosophical cult and their torture of numerous women is fictional, whereas QAnon is very much real. While QAnon's most devoted believers remain a significant minority of people in America, their growth is steady, and the more voice they are given in society, the more their means to deliver their presupposed results will be lined with toxicity. They are already willing to trade on the actual trauma and pain of those actually affected by child trafficking and use it as a political weapon against the opposing party. To think that their actions of manipulation and control will not come forth from the realms of abstraction into the physical would be short-sighted and naive on our parts.

Martyrs becomes, then, a dire warning for our society right now. If we allow QAnon and other cults like it to grow and exert themselves on this world, the line between the fictional accounts of *Martyrs* and reality will begin to fray. Humanity will do whatever it pleases to pierce the veil of knowledge, power and control. Add in a dose of religious zealotry and we have a potentially deadly and toxic cocktail.

Tom Ue and Alexander Wills

Parasite, Bong Joon Ho (2019)

Bong Joon Ho's *Parasite* tells the stories of three families: the impoverished Kims; the scarcely better-off Moon Gwang (Lee Jeong-eun) and her spouse Geun Se (Park Myeong-hoon); and the wealthy Parks.[1] Ki Woo (Choi Woo-sik), the son of the Kim family, has the opportunity to tutor Da Hye (Ji-so Jung), the Parks' daughter, after lying about and forging his university credentials. After Ki Woo gets the job, the rest of the Kim family follow and acquire other positions in the Parks' household by sabotaging and then replacing the current workers. What follows is a series of chaotic events that ultimately culminates in the downfall of all three families. The film made history as the first foreign-language film to be awarded Best Picture at the Oscars; and it has strong claims as one of the best of all time. At the time of writing, it ranks thirty in the Most Popular Movies meter on IMDb (n.d.), and it has a score of 98 per cent on Rotten Tomatoes (n.d.). Critics have quite rightly singled out its political resonance. The review aggregation website describes the film thus: 'An urgent, brilliantly layered look at timely social themes, *Parasite* finds writer-director Bong Joon Ho in near-total command of his craft.'

In this essay, we explore how *Parasite* addresses the toxicity that arises in late-stage capitalism, of which the film can be seen as a kind of allegory. By juxtaposing the lived experiences of the rich and poor, the film alludes

[1] We thank Simon Bacon, Selmin Kara and the staff of the Dalhousie University Libraries and the University of Toronto Libraries. This article was completed with the support of an Insight Development Grant from the Social Sciences and Humanities Research Council of Canada, and we gratefully acknowledge this organisation. Tom Ue would like to single out his 'Writing for the Arts' classes, in fall 2020, with whom he discussed *Parasite*. All references are taken from *Parasite: A Graphic Novel in Storyboards* (Hachette 2020).

to some of the consequences of extreme income inequality, outcomes that manifest well beyond economic concerns. Class antagonism is personified by the three families. Wallowing in hedonistic self-interest, the Parks are the privileged elite. They have an unconscious disregard for the inequality around them even as they aspire to replicate the American way: they warmly embrace Ki Jung (So-dam Park) because she allegedly studied applied arts at Illinois State University; and they presume, for example, that the tent they had purchased for their son (Hyun-jun Jung) is waterproof just because they ordered it from the United States. Meanwhile, the Kims, Moon Gwang and Geun Se are the labouring masses, egalitarian to a degree, and surviving by any means necessary. The film neither glorifies nor villainises either class. Rather, it demonstrates how the individual can become locked in a predetermined role as a necessity of the economic order.[2]

The opening sequence reveals both the material and post-material needs of the Kims, as they try to steal a Wi-Fi signal while the inside of their home is fumigated, and the outside urinated on (see Figure 41). It follows that they would aspire to the living standards of the socially and economically privileged Parks. Much later in the film, they will help themselves to the Parks' food and whisky while the family is away on a camping trip (see Figure 42), and Chung Sook (Jang Hye-jin) will say, 'Hell, if I had all this money, I'd be nice, too! Even nicer!' (94). Chung Sook is not the first to make such claims. What is distinctive about the sense of modernity represented here is that no one *can* be in a state of sufficiency. All three families hope to progress economically, but what is striking about the Kims is the extent to which they

---

2 See, for comparison, Bong's *Snowpiercer* (2013) and Josh Friedman and Graeme Manson's television series (2020–present) wherein characters are put, literally and figuratively, in classes. Both works foreground the injustice behind this categorisation and the mistreatment of those in the lower classes. Where the film shows the demise of the class system, the series illustrates the challenges inherent in radically shaking it up. At best, the first season of Friedman and Mason's series entertains the idea of representative democracy. See Nam Lee's (2020) insightful comparison of *Parasite* with Bong's earlier films in the conclusion of *The Films on Bong Joon Ho*. According to Lee, 'The tail-enders in *Snowpiercer* unite under the leadership of Curtis and proceed forward to the front section; however, the poor in *Parasite* fight against each other and eventually devolve. This difference is visualized and contrasted through the horizontal space of the train in *Snowpiercer* and the vertical stairs in *Parasite*' (140).

have normalised their aspirations to emulate the wealthy.[3] Ki Taek (Kang-ho Song) agrees with his spouse: 'That's true. Your mom's right. Rich people are naïve. No resentments. No creases on them' (95). Chung Sook concludes: 'It all gets ironed out. Money is an iron. Those creases all get smoothed out' (95). This exchange economically reveals how our needs and wants are not confined to essentials such as food and shelter: if clothes can always be smoother, then the family, by inference, can always live better. Thus, *Parasite* alludes to the socially constructed values people hold, how capitalism shapes them and how it prevents some from ever realising them. It observes the divisions between classes but does not essentialize class conflict as traditionally defined by the struggle between rich and poor. That the Kims help themselves to food in the drivers' cafeteria – food that is not for them – is one of the film's many suggestions that there is a discordance among the working class. It anticipates, for instance, the Kims' distrust and hostility when they discover that Geun Se is hiding in the house's basement. The tension between them indicates the need to outcompete one another, to fight over the breadcrumbs without challenging the idea of the loaf or disturbing its proprietors. Similarly, when Ki Taek expresses concern over the fate of the driver he replaced, Ki Jung rebukes him aggressively: 'We're the ones who need help. Worry about us, okay?' (95).

The Parks remain blissfully unaware of their servants' struggles. The father, Dong Ik (Sun-kyun Lee), directs Ki Taek on how to play a stereotypical Native American at his son's birthday party: 'You're getting paid extra. [...] Think of this as part of your work, okay?' (186). Surely, cosplay is not among Ki Taek's responsibilities; but his job, however well he performs his duties, would be jeopardised if he refuses to comply with his employer's whims. Dong Ik recognizes Ki Taek's discomfort. His casual disregard here is in keeping with an earlier

---

3   In *Discourse on Inequality* (1755), Jean-Jacques Rousseau distinguishes between natural inequality, seen as the differences in genetically endowed mental and physical ability, and socially constructed inequality, attributed to the advent of property. The formation of society and the property rights therein compel the individual to assess his or her conditions and compare them with others. We are never content with what we have, and what we desire is often dictated by what we notice and/or what has been marketed to us. Accordingly, there is more to being rich and having money. The motivations of *Parasite*'s families reflect Rousseau's sentiments by demonstrating how relative deprivation can lead to scorn and extreme behaviours.

Figure 41. During the opening sequence, Ki Woo and Ki Jung attempt to connect to a neighbour's Wi-Fi signal.

Source: *Parasite*; directed by Bong Joon Ho (CJ Entertainment, 2019).

Figure 42. The Kims capitalize on the Parks' absence by consuming their food and their alcohol.

Source: *Parasite*; directed by Bong Joon Ho (CJ Entertainment, 2019).

scene where the Park couple discusses the particular smell of those who ride the subway. This callousness arises out of indifference rather than malice or ill intent. Ki Taek's position is mimetically that of his role as the Parks' driver. Ostensibly in control, he cannot, in fact, decide how quickly (and how slowly) the vehicle moves and/or where it is headed. The Parks are not portrayed malevolently: their neglect of – and almost innocence to – the outcomes of their actions and attitudes on others encourage our sympathy. Nor are the Kims, Moon Gwang and Geun Se portrayed as valiant strugglers: their opportunism destroys lives, both literally and figuratively. The three families are creatures of necessity instilled by the socioeconomic structures within which they exist. The place of the Kims, Moon Gwang and Geun Se in the social order and their dire needs command more of our sympathy because their actions are motivated by material deprivation and encouraged by the inequality the poor observe and experience.

There is a sense of cohesion in the Kim family, but their plans almost always arise spontaneously. After stealing from the Parks and narrowly escaping detection when the family unexpectedly returns from the camping trip, Ki Taek proclaims: 'I've got my own plan' (163). Yet their goal has always been to survive. For his part, Ki Woo entertains and preserves a vision of social mobility. With his sister dead and his father a fugitive in hiding at the end of the film, Ki Woo says that he too has made a plan, or what he thinks of as one. 'I'm going to earn money. A lot of it', he says. 'University, a career, marriage, those are all fine, but first I'll earn money' (234). He is not prioritising things in the right order, since money (we hope) would follow university and a career. He does not realise that he has no tools with which to make the kind of money he needs. In fact, few people can make enough to have substantial savings. Despite what happened to him, there is no proletarian epiphany. The metaphor for false consciousness persists: the system cannot be changed, and the only option is to acquire power if Maslow's hierarchy of needs is to be satisfied. Under capitalism, money is obligatory at every level. To achieve esteem and self-actualisation, all material needs must be met through the market. Therein lies the ultimate paradox: how can a system be transformed if those who exist inside it have neither the interest nor the means to do so? If the relations of production define purpose and produce inescapable hierarchies, then freedom of choice is an illusion, and this toxifies an economic system that promises its subscribers that they have equal access to the American dream. The Kims decide on a very risky endeavour and are not satisfied until every family member has infiltrated the Parks' home. There is rarely time for

Figure 43. The Kims luxuriate while the Parks are away.
Source: *Parasite*; directed by Bong Joon Ho (CJ Entertainment, 2019).

contemplation or reflection. You either grow or die under capitalism, and for the poor, growth often means exploitative work or unethical activity. The Kims' wages – however (in)substantial – do not halt more grandiose aspirations, much like how high quarterly profits do not prevent the shareholder from yearning for more. There is no ceiling, so there is no end to the pursuit of happiness. Transcending class, the individual, whom capitalism so proudly defends, spends his or her life like a heroin addict chasing the metaphorical dragon, but never able to catch it.

Moon Gwang re-enters the film at a crucial stage: the Kims are celebrating their success at the Parks while the family is away. Just before the former housekeeper's return, Chung Sook likens Ki Taek to a cockroach:

> Sure, but suppose Park walked through that door now. What about your dad? He'd run and hide like a cockroach. Kids, you know at our house, when you turn on the light, and the cockroaches scatter? You know what I mean? (96)

Thus far, we have seen the family working as a team. That Ki Taek mutters that he's 'getting fucking tired of this' (96), however, suggests a lengthier history wherein he is singled out and ridiculed, whether by his spouse, by his children or by his employers. Modern political economy helps explain how patriarchy subsidises the capitalist mode of production and how socially constructed gender roles reinforce the system.[4] If Ki Taek has internalised traditional and patriarchal responsibilities, then the pressure that is exerted on him offers partial explanation for his psychotic break. In essence, the capitalist mode of production has toxic effects on post-material identities – in this case, reinforcing oppressive gender roles. The Kims' improved financial circumstances do not compensate or protect Ki Taek against the deprivation that he has internalised and that he is regularly made to feel, and Geun Se operates as his foil. Moon Gwang reveals how she had concealed her spouse in the house's basement:

> Four years ago when Mr. Namgoong moved to Paris, in the time before Mr. Park's family moved in, I brought my husband down here. Many rich houses have secret bunkers where you can hide in case North Korea attacks, or if creditors break in. But it seems Mr. Namgoong was a bit embarrassed about this, because he never mentioned it to Mr. Park's family. [...] So only I know about it. (108–9)

Moon Gwang pleads to Chung Sook: 'We've no house, no money, <u>only debts</u>! [...] Even after 4 years of hiding, those debt collectors won't give up. They're still searching for him, threatening to stab him' (110; original emphasis). If Ki Taek had worked in numerous environments, from valeting Mercedes-Benzes to working at a chicken place, and from a Taiwan cake shop to being a driver, so too had Geun Se, and he was finally brought down by the demise of a cake shop, perhaps even Ki Taek's: 'The Taiwan cake shop. My Taiwanese Wangshui castella shop went bust. I was overwhelmed by debt' (111). The irony is not lost on Ki Taek, who, as a reaction shot makes clear, is listening in attentively. 'The difference between the two', the film scholar Nam Lee reasons,

> is the use of private loans. Kun-Sae, who took out private loans, has to hide in the basement to avoid being hunted down by his creditors, while Ki-Tek could scrape by in the semibasement house folding pizza boxes because he stayed away from the loan sharks. (2020: 142)

---

4   See also Frank J. B. Stilwell's (2012) discussion of women's uncompensated roles in the reproduction of labour power, the production of surplus value and the realisation of surplus value.

Notwithstanding the two families' commonalities, there is no sympathy between them. Chung Sook threatens to call the police when she learns of Moon Gwang's plight. Meanwhile, Moon Gwang is but a click away from sending her former employers a video of the Kims when she learns their secret. Geun Se tells his wife: 'Honey, this "send" button is like a missile launcher. [...] If we threaten to push it, those people can't do anything. It's like a North Korean rocket. A North Korean missile button!' (117). In variously exploiting their newly gained leverages, the two trigger-happy families are firmly rooted in the present, and they make no plans to redistribute their powers. Indeed, neither family realises the irony that the revelation of the Kims' identities would provoke them to reveal Geun Se's hiding place, much as his would theirs. They are on equal footing. The film's doubling of Ki Taek and Geun Se is instantiated when, at the end, Ki Taek displaces him and takes his position in the basement. Ki Woo writes his father, describing his plans to make lots of money, to purchase the house and to release him from his prison. What is striking about this letter is not that it can never be delivered – while Ki Taek can communicate with his son by means of the codes that he signals through the lights, Ki Woo cannot reach his father downstairs – but how Ki Woo's plans are contingent upon his success with capitalism. The only plan he has is to become a Park. Whether Ki Woo is successful in becoming the model breadwinner or consigned to replicating his father's or Geun Se's example, the film's conceit rests in the tenacity of this system to present itself as the only viable model, however much the plight of the less fortunate – the Kims' flooded home, the smells of the subway and Geun Se's experience with loan sharks – is exposed.

Rebecca Booth

The Last Winter, Larry Fessenden (2006)

> The Wendigo is hungry, always hungry. And its hunger is never satisfied. The more it eats, the bigger it gets. And the bigger it gets, the hungrier it gets. It can grow as tall as the trees, and still it aches with hunger. And we are hopeless in the face of it. We are devoured. (Fessenden 2006)

Though Larry Fessenden's *The Last Winter* does not refer to the wendigo, a malevolent creature from Native American mythology, as overtly as in his titular 2001 film *Wendigo*, it returns to and utilises this folkloric construct as a metaphor in order to examine cultural and environmental toxicity. Using the biological definition of toxicity, this chapter examines *The Last Winter* as a discourse on the ethics of Western territorial expansion, specifically crude oil extraction in the Arctic National Wildlife Refuge in Alaska, and how it contributes to climate change and cultural erasure via the deconstruction of the mythical wendigo as a manifestation of Western greed and guilt.

The medical or scientific definition of toxicity is 'the quality, state, or relative degree of being poisonous' (Merriam-Webster.com n.d.) or 'the degree to which a chemical substance or a particular mixture of substances can damage an organism' (Harris 2019: 12). Exposure to the toxic entity, which can be biological, chemical, physical or radiation, can be acute or chronic: acute exposure is singular or occurs for a short duration of time and can cause serious harm or death; chronic exposure describes the detrimental and often irreversible effects of repeated or sustained subjection to the toxic substance (Harris 2019). A more general application of the term refers to 'an extremely harsh, malicious, or harmful quality' (Merriam-Webster.com n.d.).

In its exploration of the relationship between all of the above definitions, *The Last Winter* is a commentary on cultural toxicity framed around the figure of the wendigo. A mythological entity from First Nation Algonquin communities in Canada and the north-eastern United States, the wendigo (or windigo) is generally believed to have once been human, irreversibly transformed after succumbing to cannibalistic urges or committing a terrible crime. Inconsistencies across references to this elusive creature have contributed to a multifarious discourse, and descriptions include an emaciated skeletal creature, an ice giant, a yeti, a ghost and a spirit on the wind. This storied history has led to myriad portrayals of the wendigo across non-Indigenous literature (as a forest demon in *The Wendigo*; Blackwood [1910] 2019), cinema (as a metaphor for American colonisation in *Ravenous*; Bird, 1999), television (as a psychotic manifestation in *Hannibal*; Fuller, 2013–15) and comic books (as a monster afflicted by a cannibalistic curse in 'The Spawn of the Flesh-Eater!', *The Incredible Hulk*, 1973).

In addition to writing and directing *Wendigo*, Fessenden has focused on the creature explicitly in the anthology episode 'Skin and Bones' from the NBC series *Fear Itself* (2008), as director and co-writer, and in the video game *Until Dawn* (2015), which he co-wrote. His fascination with the lore and its sociocultural history resulted in the publication of *Sudden Storm: A Wendigo Reader* (Fessenden 2016). Here, Fessenden curates a series of essays on the subject, including mythology, cryptozoology and metaphorical readings, which are subsequently applied to representations of the wendigo across popular culture. A central theme in the book is the insatiable hunger of the anthropophagus creature, which Fessenden employs metaphorically throughout his works featuring wendigo mythology and most explicitly in its commentary on climate change in *The Last Winter*. Using the term 'American exceptionalism' to describe the hierarchical ideology behind American expansionism, in terms of the colonisation of both land and people, Fessenden notes that 'wendigo mythology has great resonance, whether it is a cannibal story, or a much broader comment on Western culture destroying native people, and the environment. Which is where we are now. Global warming is the final frontier of wendigoism!' (qtd in Abrams 2016).

The Last Winter blends fact with fiction by centring its story around a real test well located in the Arctic National Wildlife Refuge in Alaska, jointly commissioned in 1986 by American petroleum companies and Native American corporations Arctic Slope Regional Corporation and Kaktovik Inupiat Corporation (KIC). In 1968, crude oil was discovered in Prudhoe

The Last Winter, Larry Fessenden (2006)

Bay, a census-designated area in the North Slope Borough of Alaska. Multiple and overlapping landownership claims from the native population, contended before the state of Alaska was established in 1959, reached conclusion in 1971 when the Alaska Native Claims Settlement Act secured 44 million acres of land (the state of Alaska owns 101 million acres) and $962 million for Alaska's native population, divided regionally (PBS n.d.).[1] Despite continued environmental and legal challenges to extraction in the area, the 1973 oil crisis ensured legislation was passed and the Trans-Alaska Pipeline was installed between 1975 and 1977. The results from the Arctic National Wildlife Refuge KIC test well have never been released, despite the petroleum industry's exponential growth in the United States in the years since, with 190,000 miles of liquid pipeline delivering oil from reserves to corporate and domestic consumers (American Petroleum Institute n.d.).

A single, mysterious post marks the KIC well, and this is the focal point on which Fessenden fixes his cinematic lens – depicted within the film as a mysterious white box. A marketing video, produced by the fictional oil company North Industries, outlines their route to energy independence via the previously untapped source. As global demand for petroleum-based energy continues to increase, the narrator informs us that this 'land of black gold' will yield its treasure via pipelines installed within the decade. A small camp of North Industries employees, led by the abrasive Ed Pollack (Ron Perlman), is forced to work with independent environmentalists James Hoffman (James Le Gros) and Elliot Jenkins (Jamie Harrold) in order to prepare ice roads for the rigs to reach the drilling site. Having left the base for a few weeks, the returning Pollack's professional disdain for Hoffman and his procedural red tape is soured by the fact that his former lover Abby Sellers (Connie Britton) is now sleeping with Hoffman. With the film's action largely contained within the camp and surrounding whiteout (the claustrophobic weather condition that renders features in the frozen landscape indistinguishable), the supporting cast fuel the central conflict between the two characters in what is essentially a two-man chamber play. Pollack and Hoffman act as the mouthpieces for

---

[1] 'Landownership' is a term used politically and legally to describe the act of and debate surrounding colonisation and private property claims from non-Indigenous parties. Historically, the Native American relationship to property and space is built upon a communal concept of ownership.

their respective roles: the expansionist and the environmentalist. Hoffman's refusal to approve the next stage of the project around unprecedented temperatures and consistent fluctuations in readings, leaving the terrain unable to safely support the weight of the equipment, is a serious threat to the project, which the corporate-minded Pollack insists must be completed within the allocated 'drilling season'.

The increasingly strange behaviour of the camp members, culminating in Elliot suffering a fatal aneurysm and Maxwell McKinder (Zach Gilford) walking naked into the night, leads Hoffman to believe that the melting permafrost is releasing sour gas – natural gas containing high levels of poisonous hydrogen sulphide. Chronic exposure to this toxic substance causes serious neurological damage and is a potential explanation for the supernatural entities witnessed by the characters.

In *The Last Winter*, the wendigo are depicted as wraithlike ghosts and often signalled by the sound of a fierce wind. They are named by one of the Native American members of the camp, cook Dawn Russell (Joanne Shenandoah), as the Chenoo, a cannibalistic ice giant based in the frozen forests of North America and associated with the Micmac, Maliseet and Passamaquoddy Algonquin tribes. The youngest team member, Maxwell, is the first to witness the phenomenon. After disappearing for hours, feared dead by the team, he returns to the camp in a distressed state and reveals he visited the KIC well. Maxwell stares obsessively into the whiteout and articulates Hoffman's fears that the KIC well is 'haunted', as the drilling site has released 'ghosts' from the ground: 'what is oil anyway, but fossils … plants and animals from whatever millions of years ago? […] We shouldn't be here. We're grave robbers.' This loaded acknowledgement refers not only to conservation concerns around the project and global environmental issues, but contestation surrounding Indigenous land rights within the United States.

Maxwell's wording alludes to a trope used at length in American horror films of the 1970s and 1980s in which an 'Indian burial ground' is revealed to be the source of supernatural activity. This 'hypervisual' representation of Native American culture reaffirms Euro-American identity (Raheja 2011: xii; Smith 2014) and, as such, is part of a wider mainstream narrative propagated in Hollywood, that Raheja terms 'the violence of invisibility', in which Euro-Americans 'desired a highly controlled, mass-mediated, and virtual Native presence at the same time that Indigenous peoples were deemed threatening, excessive, savage, and less-than-human' (Raheja 2011: xii). This theme, inherently bound to the adverse possession of Indigenous land, is part of the ontological effect of toxic contamination on Indigenous communities, termed 'cultural wounding' by Kearney (2017: 33).

> When place and its elemental parts are wounded, this in and out of itself is cause for concern, not only because of the eventual threat it may pose to human life or the security of the ethnic group, but because place matters. The elemental changes that come from poisoning, toxicity and contamination, enacted by invading others or those without care or concern for kinship in place, can only occur if place is stripped of its axiological merit and importance. (Kearney 2017: 160)

Etic ethnographic studies refer to the now factually contested term 'windigo psychosis', a psychological condition culturally specific to northern Algonquin tribes, founded upon an established belief in wendigo mythology and historically manifested as a result of the depletion of resources and resulting famine, causing sufferers to act upon cannibalistic urges (Brightman 1988). While it can be argued that the syndrome has been historically weaponised by Euro-Americans in order to demonise Native American communities, reinforcing colonial claims to an agenda of territorial expansion via violent control and cultural erosion, Brightman (1988) purports that cannibalistic ideation and behaviour can be historically determined via a correlative psychological condition bound to Algonquin dreaming beliefs. As Kearney (2017: 162) states, 'the Dreaming and ancestral beings that are place itself might mutate or change as a result of chemical mess and disorder'.

The creatures in *The Last Winter* can be interpreted as ancestral beings or nature spirits manifested by a hallucinatory or lucid dream state caused by the toxic sour gas. These tensions are internalised by Hoffman as he vacillates between his scientific training and a reverence for such spiritual or supernatural possibilities. His field notes are erratic, jumping from recorded fluctuations in measurements to his fear that 'something is being unleashed from the softening permafrost' that is 'beyond science'. His philosophical musings on humanity's irreverence for the environment end with a shrewd acknowledgement that this will be our demise. Likening humanity to a virus, he notes that the biological response from any infected organism would be to fight back: 'What if the very thing we're here to pull out of the ground were to rise willingly and confront us?' The wendigo, much like the physical post indicating the location of the drilling site, is a metaphorical marker onto which the film's many thematic elements are carved. Though the significance of the creature can be read spiritually, as the literal ghosts of the Earth rising to reclaim it from the virus of humanity, Fessenden centres the film from a humanist position, rendering the wendigo as a manifestation of our own projections:

> you can see the creatures at the end of the film as some sort of nature spirit. A lot of people tended to see that as nature's revenge, but I think of it differently: nature simply is. It's the people's sense of dread that overcomes them, and it is almost like a parable about guilt. When the world falls out of balance as it has, there is hell to pay. The wendigo is a way to discuss that. It's manifested in different ways. (Qtd in Abrams 2016)

The fragility of this balance is revealed in the film's climax: with several members of the team dead or injured, and their only means of communication destroyed after a bush plane crashes into the base, Pollack and Hoffman venture into the whiteout to seek aid. They have taken the last snowmobile and ironically run out of fuel, leaving them no option but to travel on foot to the nearest town. Alone and dependent on each other, they are forced to address their opposing issues and the film's central message: 'the wendigo is a fundamentally cautionary tale about not eating your fellow traveler in times of extreme duress, like if you were stuck in a winter storm. And extrapolating from that, the wendigo is a caution against overreach, and rapaciousness' (Fessenden, qtd in Abrams 2016). Though Hoffman risks his life to pull Pollack free when he falls through the ice, and Pollack concedes to Hoffman in their vying for Abby, restitution is futile: they are confronted and consumed by the creatures, which can be read as vengeful nature spirits or as a humanist manifestation of self-destruction – the corporate avarice Pollack represents and the conscience Hoffman embodies.

The sole survivor, after the rest of her colleagues have succumbed to the phenomenon at the camp, Abby wakes to find she has been rescued and is recovering in a nearby hospital. The building is in disarray, and she discovers an employee hanging in one of the rooms as a televised news programme relays images of natural disasters around the world. The familiar howling din grows louder as Abby steps outside into chaos. Western society's insatiable hunger is the true capitalist monster, destroying natural resources and erasing Indigenous culture. The manifestation of the wendigo, whether read scientifically, spiritually or metaphorically, positions the film as a commentary on the effects of this chronic contamination, and its final message is direct and poetic: as Hoffman is carried away by one of the creatures, he becomes a ghost on the wind. His dying mind returns to a childhood memory in which his mother calls him from the family home, echoing Hoffman's earlier words: 'The world we grew up in is changed forever. There is no way home.'

Elana Gomel

Bird Box, Josh Malerman (2014)

Toxic spaces define our perception of the post-industrial landscape. Pollution, contamination and radiation generate sites of stealthy danger where the body is exposed to imperceptible poisoning: 'toxic spaces have become increasingly interwoven into the economic structures and fabric of everyday life' (Sarathy et al. 2018: 2). But what about toxic time? Can temporality, rather than spatiality, become the source of contamination? And how does the idea of toxic time fit in with the overall articulation of toxicity in contemporary speculative fiction? In this essay, I will analyse the representation of (post) apocalypse in Josh Malerman's novel *Bird Box* as part of the cultural tendency to perceive the future not merely as dangerous or apocalyptic but as attenuated, impoverished, poisoned – in other words, toxic.

The most salient feature of toxicity is invisibility. Environmental toxins are undetectable by sight. Even when toxic sites are marked, the danger itself is as stealthy as the radiation in Chernobyl or the mysterious chemicals causing 're-productive damage' on the obligatory warning labels in California. With the pandemic of the coronavirus, invisibility has become *the* defining feature of the cultural perception of corporeal danger and vulnerability. While viruses are generally not included in studies of toxicity that focus on inorganic poisons or radiation, they blend into the overall picture of the world as permeated by unseen violence towards the human body. A book about the Flint water crisis that has become a symbol of the toxic damage inflicted by corporations upon marginal and vulnerable populations is entitled *What the Eyes Don't See* (Hanna-Attisha 2018).

This could be an alternative title for *Bird Box*.[1] The premise of the novel is that the Earth is overrun by creatures so horrible that a mere glance at them

---

1   This is the novel that was later made into the movie of the same title, directed by Susanne Bier and released in 2018.

poisons the mind and causes the viewer to go insane and commit suicide. The novel follows the story of Malorie, who, with her two children, undertakes a perilous journey down the river to find refuge with a small community of blind people. Malorie and the kids are the only survivors of another community, that was decimated by a madman who tore away the window curtains and exposed his housemates to the unbearable sight.

In the critical responses to the novel, it was described as an apocalyptic thriller. But that is a misnomer. Both in its articulation of temporality and its engagement with the rhetoric of blindness/insight, the novel is radically different from its genetic predecessors. While the traditional apocalypse represents the future as radically different from the present, *Bird Box* sees history as a process of decay and diminution. The future is the slow, insidious poisoning of society and individual, stripping us of communal ties. And the future toxicity is seeping into the present like the poisons that are seeping from dumps and nuclear sites into the environment. Both toxic space and toxic time are contaminating. And while the traditional apocalypse glorifies (in)sight, *Bird Box* abjures both physical and metaphorical vision. The only salvation lies in deliberate blindness.

The difference between *Bird Box* and the traditional (post-)apocalyptic genre can be gauged by comparing it to John Wyndham's classic *The Day of the Triffids* (1951), with which it shares thematic and structural elements. In Wyndham's novel, blindness *causes* the apocalypse, as a meteor shower blinds most of the world's population. They are then attacked by predatory perambulating plants. The protagonist of Wyndham's novel is heroic by virtue of retaining his sight, both literally and metaphorically, as he strives to forge a new community by disseminating knowledge and skills. The future, adumbrated in the novel's last chapters, is almost utopian: having passed through the crucible of blindness, the new humanity is stronger, more cooperative and equitable than the old pre-triffid civilisation. By temporarily losing its sight, humanity acquires insight.

The Day of the Triffids follows the traditional apocalyptic plot, in which a global catastrophe is only a prelude to a utopian/millenarian future. The plot, analysed in such classics as Norman Cohn's *The Pursuit of the Millennium* (1957), follows the trajectory of the Christian meta-historical narrative. Whether in its religious form or in the secularised versions of progress and utopia, the past is destroyed in order to make room for the future; and the catastrophe is a necessary cleansing of the old before creating 'a new heaven and a new earth'.

No such profound transformation occurs in *Bird Box*. The ending of the novel offers only a modest qualified hope, limited to Malorie and her kids: they are not even safe now; they are '*safer*' (Malerman 2014: 294, italics in the original). But even more significant is the novel's rejection of both sight and knowledge.

The word 'apocalypse' itself means 'unveiling'; and the most famous apocalyptic text of all, *The Revelation of St John the Divine*, contains numerous references to vision in the repetitive refrain of its narrator: 'And I saw'. But *Bird Box* is about closing your eyes; turning away; refusing to see. Malorie only succeeds because from the moment the kids are born, she schools them in not looking, wearing a blindfold, navigating the world by touch and hearing alone. During their odyssey down the river, she threatens, cajoles and physically forces them to never open their eyes. And since 'to *see*' also means 'to *know*', Malorie's deliberate blindness is also the refusal of knowledge. Salvation lies not in revealed knowledge but in self-imposed ignorance.

Brandon LaBelle describes 'the regime of visibility' that governs post-industrial space and time as 'visualization becomes a deep logic, shaping how we think and comprehend the world' (2019: 188). This regime of visibility ultimately derives from the apocalyptic tradition of secret knowledge unveiled and made visible: 'But blessed are your eyes, for they see; and blessed are your ears, for they hear' (Matthew 13:16, King James version). In *Bird Box*, however, both knowledge and vision are deadly pathogens.

At the very beginning of the novel, there are two theories explaining the epidemic of suicides. In the house where pregnant Malorie first finds shelter, two men are trying to understand what is going on. George, the initial owner of the house who is forging a self-supporting community of strangers, believes that the epidemic is caused by an alien invasion of sorts and that the deadly sight of the creatures can be mitigated if refracted through technology, such as a video recording or some form of computer filtering.

> George said he got an idea from an old book, *Possible Impossibilities*. It talked about irreconcilable life-forms. Two worlds whose components were entirely foreign might cause damage to one another if they were to cross paths. And if this other life-form

were somehow able to get here … well, that's what George was saying had happened. (Malerman 2014: 76)

George tries to check his hypothesis by placing a video camera outside and then viewing the footage alone, tied to a chair. He ends up killing himself anyway.

The other hypothesis comes from Don, who prefers the eyes of the mind to the eyes of the flesh, believing that the epidemic is a product of an invisible but potentially comprehensible toxic agent.

> I loved it [George's hypothesis]. But Don didn't. He was online a lot back then, researching chemicals, gamma waves, anything unseen that might cause harm if you looked at it because you would not know what you were looking at. (2014: 77)

Both George and Don fall victims to the Medusa-like creatures, because in their hubris to see, they expose themselves to the toxin of the coming future. It is the future that punishes not merely a technological civilisation but any attempt to know and understand our environment. George, in particular, is represented as a product of the scientific regime of visibility: 'he was progressive too, a big *thinker*' (2014: 77). His gory suicide is the end of human history in which the future was knowable by those with 'eyes to see'.

Malorie's heroism, on the other hand, lies precisely in her refusal not just of scientific knowledge but of simple curiosity. Alone, of all the characters in the novel, she almost never wonders about the nature of the creatures. When, in the climax of her journey, one is so near her that it pulls off her blindfold, she keeps her eyes resolutely shut, refusing to imagine or speculate. She is motivated by the simplest of biological imperatives: survival of herself and her children, who are not even given proper names: they are just the Boy and the Girl. The ones who wonder, who are curious, who want to *see* are the villains of the novel. It turns out that some people, while driven mad by the sight of the creatures, survive the exposure and become dangerous psychopaths, doing the creatures' bidding. Malorie's first housemates are killed by Gary who tells her: 'Maybe I am immune, Malorie. Or maybe I'm simply *aware*' (2014: 262). But the same awareness that made Wyndham's sighted characters the saviours of others, makes him their destroyer.

The reader of the novel is thrust into the same position as Malorie: she does not know what the creatures are, and neither do we. No explanation is offered, which is highly unusual for sci-fi and even horror apocalyptic texts. The creatures are unseen not just by the physical eyes but also by the eye of the mind. They are just as unknowable and toxic as the future they represent.

In this withholding of vision and knowledge, we are confronted with the symbolic economy of invisibility. Invisibility is 'that which is present as a negative' (LaBelle 2019: 191). And what is present in the radical impoverishment of Malorie's world is a future without hope and without change.

Malerman's novel exemplifies a mini trend in horror fiction in which sensory deprivation or deliberate abandonment of some human faculty becomes a prerequisite for biological survival. Among other texts in this category are Tim Lebbon's novel *The Silence* (2015), also made into a movie, and the movie *A Quiet Place* (Krasinski, 2018). While in both these texts it is speech rather than sight that becomes a dangerous luxury, they also represent the toxic future that strikes at what makes us human. The survival they offer is purely biological, limited to oneself and one's immediate family, especially children. While traditional apocalypses emphasise the restoration (or improvement) of community and society, these texts limit themselves to the bare-bones biological mechanisms that human beings share with other non-human animals.

Bird Box is set in a future very close to the present. But more importantly, it is the future that *bleeds* into the present. In the duration of impoverished survival, the 'days begin to mush together [...] time doesn't mean a thing anymore' (Malerman 2014: 52). When time is no longer a countdown to either heaven or hell, but the infinite drag of slow poisoning, we are in the temporality of the Anthropocene.

Climate change is radically different from other agents of the apocalypse, such as the nuclear war, sudden technological collapse (the Y2K bug) or even a swift plague. Climate change and the ongoing sixth extinction are slow-moving processes, impossible to visualise on a human scale and yet very much present in our daily lives. The time of the Anthropocene is not the explosive temporality of a radical catastrophe, but rather a gradual accumulation of minute deleterious changes which come together to create a toxic future that is already present in the multiple sites of plastic trash in the oceans, contaminated infrastructure, spreading dumps and polluted cities. The future is leaking into the present, quietly poisoning it.

This intrusion of the slow geological time of natural processes into the much more rapid timeline of human history is theorised by Timothy Morton as an encounter with the non-human:

> we are no longer able to think history as exclusively human, for the very reason that we are in the Anthropocene. A strange name indeed, since in this period nonhuman make decisive contact with humans, even the ones busy shoring up differences between humans and the rest. (2014: 172)

The creatures of *Bird Box* are simultaneously the 'nonhuman' making 'decisive contact with humans', and the embodiment of the toxicity humans have released into the environment, poisoning not just the ecosphere but time itself. 'The end of the world has already occurred' (Morton 2014: 202). We are living in a time without chronology, when all that is left is duration.

The ecological catastrophe of climate change 'has politicized deep time' (Davies 2016: 20). But it has also paradoxically fostered the attitude of despair and paralysis, since deep geological time is impossible to visualise or comprehend on a human scale. The only way the creatures of *Bird Box* are described is as 'infinity'. In the last scenes of the novel when Malorie and the kids are trapped on the river with giant flocks of birds going insane above them (birds react to the creatures, hence the title), she is trying – and failing – to grapple with what is happening:

> What is it? What is it? *What* is it?
> Infinity.
> Where did it come from? Where did it come from? *Where* did it come from?
> Infinity. (Malerman 2014: 241; italics in the original)

In this helpless repetition of the same futile questions, 'infinity' becomes a shorthand for the poisoned and poisonous future that is not the familiar shape of the Tribulations, but rather the slow, inexorable creep of extinction that has no interest in, or regard for, the finite and hurried temporality of human history. This scene ends with the rain of dead birds pelting Malorie and the kids, who are crouching, helpless, in the boat, the blindfolds their only defence against the intolerable vision of extinction: 'The sky is falling, the sky is dying, the sky is dead' (2014: 243).

Poisoned birds, a depleted world without vision, a lost civilisation, a broken community reduced to the bare biological imperatives of survival and procreation: this is Malerman's metaphor for the toxic future that awaits humanity in the age of the Anthropocene. Perhaps the only consolation we can find in this bleak depiction is that we may have a little time before the poison reaches us all.

Helen Gavin

Epilogue
Toxicity and Positivity

Toxic Psychology and the Positivity Tidal Wave

> Leaders who don't listen will eventually be surrounded by people who have nothing to say. (Andy Stanley 2011)

Psychology is one of the helping professions. From clinical and health psychology, focused on the study and treatment of psychological problems, to counselling and psychotherapy as a person-centred paradigm, psychology is designed to aid the human condition. Even forensic psychology, the hitherto darling of TV and literature, is used to investigate and prevent crime, and be the helpmate of justice. How can psychology be toxic? Surely that is an accusation born of misunderstanding and the dismissiveness of the medical profession? Psychology is a powerful set of tools that can be used for good, but weaponising these tools is far too easy, and often people do not know that they are being used against them, or even that they are using them themselves. This is the situation in which relationships, corporations and even nations can suffer from cultural toxicity.

Cultural toxicity refers to an environment where the members of a community become increasingly unhappy and fearful, and devoid of power to do anything about it, and individual or group efficacy falls to a dangerous point. Individual toxicity can be apportioned some blame; a leader whose behaviour poisons the whole organisation is not unknown. Alternatively, there is simply so much poison in the well of a culture that it becomes a toxic entity in its entirety. Throughout history, large organisations have proved to be toxic to those both inside and outside them. Ruling classes, religious groups, the military, education, big business, all appear to be characterised by one form of toxicity or another. This toxicity is not a physical poisoning, but the dysfunction inherent in destructive behaviours such as bullying, intolerance, harassment, and narcissism (or worse) that those within organisations experience, and the effects on those who need to deal with them. Padilla et al. (2007: 179) suggest that we can take into account a working system in which a toxic triangle is at play: leaders who act in destructive ways, followers who are unable or unwilling to resist them, and an environment that allows this situation to exist and persist. Followers are susceptible due to unmet needs; those countries in which the greatest part of the population are in poverty have engendered the most toxic leadership (Hitler being the most obvious example) and continue to do so in the twenty-first century. This impoverishment can also be psychological, explaining the rise of the more devastating and fatal cults of the twentieth century, which seemed to provide followers with a sense of belonging that was missing elsewhere. Alienation such that a cult or a radical political movement is attractive can stem from many sources, but Padilla et al. (2007) suggest that when this occurs in the microcosm of a workplace, there are serious ramifications. All it takes is an unstable environment, for example, one in which people do not know whether or not they will keep their jobs and in which some people rise by taking assertive and rapid decisions. The greater the perceived threat, the more likely people are to follow someone, anyone, who can provide leadership, even a proven misogynist philanderer or profligate wastrel. Once this has happened, the leader is in place and very difficult to dislodge, and the actions of a toxic leader cannot be overruled, because this resistance is met with more toxicity. The toxic workplace that ensues is characterised by dysfunction, with demoralised employees who either leave, confront the leader or develop defence mechanisms. The defence mechanism, or ego-defence mechanism, was first described in Freudian and neo-Freudian psychoanalysis. It is a strategy that a person unconsciously applies to protect themselves from anxiety or other negative emotions due to unacceptable thoughts. Main examples include denial, repression, projection, displacement, and sublimation. These mechanisms sound negative in themselves, but in moderation are natural ways in which we navigate our world and are protective of the self. However, during periods of high stress, particularly in prolonged periods, defence mechanisms can grow into high nervous states, such as hypervigilance, or even obsessions and phobias. Someone who is bullied at work may become hypervigilant to the presence of the bully and withdraw from interaction in defence. Questioning everything one does or thinks becomes second nature, because that is what the bully does. Distress of this nature, akin to post-traumatic stress disorder, will make the individual experience difficulty with social and professional situations, bringing all the problems that entails, coupled with personal problems such as overthinking and sleep disorders (APA 2013: Exhibit 1.3-4).

That psychological mistreatment is more insidiously destructive than physical assault has been known for some time. In 1890, American philosopher William James wrote that the memory of an insult is more damning to the present than a physical affront. His differentiation between physical pain and social pain was clear cut – if an individual is constantly in a state of non-existence in the eyes of others, if no one listened to anything they said, or answered, then that person would prefer a bodily inflicted pain. Remembering being beaten and the fear, humiliation and anger this produced is infinitely easier than reproducing the physical pain. Being sexually abused is a physically painful experience, but the removal of trust due to the attack being perpetrated by a person in a position of care is longer lasting. Furthermore, Chen et al. (2008: 790) discovered that social pain is remembered longer than physical pain and has far-reaching consequences, a distinction similar to that between pain-event and pain-memory, even though they are neurologically shackled (Eisenberger 2012: 423). The toxic environment of organisations that engenders psychological mistreatment is entirely incompatible with effective existence, be that organisation a globally powerful nation, an international corporation, or a nuclear family. For example, Jones et al. (2020) show that being excluded from information loops, first, was deemed a form of mistreatment and, second, had major impact on work experience and efficacy. This toxicity is evident outside the work environment too. Gavin (2011: 520), in a multi-method study exploring childhood experience and adult well-being, found that, concomitant to physical or sexual abuse, experiencing emotional abuse as a child had major consequences for future mental health outcomes and family cohesion. A toxic environment is psychologically fatal and emotionally vampiric (Bernstein 2012: 52), poisoning or consuming civilisations, workplaces, and families alike. An emotional vampire is someone who saps all of one's energy by being aggressive, histrionic, narcissistic, etc. These exhausting people can appear in any walk of life, from the boss who bullies you into completing projects and then takes credit for all your work, to the manipulative and controlling spouse who hides the house keys.

The good news is that cultural toxicity can be combated and positive outcomes achieved. In *Dark Psychology and Manipulation*, Chris Wheatley (2020) outlines multiple ways in which some individuals undermine the workplace or their families by underperforming, making impulsive decisions, requiring constant attention and validation, and even behaving illegally. Using dark psychology is the way in which people manipulate and coerce to get what they want, be that an undeserved pay rise or sexual favours. Recognition that this is happening to you, or even that you are the person doing this, is the first step to combatting toxicity. That observation can be extended to interpersonal relationships, with attention-seeking, emotional blackmailing, and other abusive behaviours mentally draining those involved with vampiric and toxic individuals. The list of behaviours is difficult to read, especially if one acknowledges their existence in one's life. Some of the tactics Wheatley describes include emotional manipulation (which manifests as using excessive artificial positive or negative reinforcement), denial or rationalisation of wrongdoing, and shaming or blaming. Other strategies employed by toxic individuals are emotional blackmail (i.e. playing on natural sympathy or holding something over another person in order to gain rewards) and manipulation and dark empathy, used by those who understand emotions well enough to use them against another person. In the worst cases of toxicity, people have been brainwashed, intimidated, gaslighted, and no longer understand the world in which they find themselves. Wheatley suggests that there are two approaches when faced with someone using these dark psychological strategies against you, providing of course that that person is not you. His first approach is to use the dark psychological strategies against themselves. By mirroring the behaviour of another, we build rapport, strengthening relationships and minimising the likelihood and effect of the behaviour directed towards us. This appears to be a risky strategy, using dark psychology to combat itself – like a Jedi Knight transforming into Darth Vader, with the probability of building a toxic persona worse than the first.

The second, and probably more successful, strategy is to ensure that people involved in toxic situations also manage to have time and space to understand themselves and spend time with non-toxic people. This assumes a certain level of self-awareness and understanding of the psychology of people around you. This is not always easy, even for those with extensive work and relationship experience. The most revealing thing to happen to me in the last few years came as part of a senior management course my employer required me to complete. Grumbling at the perceived waste of time, and behaving like a reluctant teenager, I nevertheless enjoyed the programme. I also achieved a crumb of self-awareness, hitherto unexplored. I realised that I was never going to be the charismatic, transformational leader that I aspired to be, but being a transactional and pragmatic leader was much more effective, and less exhausting to maintain as it fitted my own personality. Another example some years previously came from observing the effect of a new manager on an existing team. She wished to treat all team members fairly. To her, this meant equitably, and some staff moved into a position where their work was now valued and rewarded, unlike before her appointment. However, staff who had previously experienced higher positive regard, in some opinions unjustly, now felt undermined and undervalued, even though they were being treated exactly the same as everyone else. The staff who were being treated better felt empowered, but this meant they were able to develop to a point where they could seek promotion in a different organisation. They left an environment that remained institutionally toxic, despite the best intentions of the manager. She was left with a set of disgruntled staff and the need to recruit replacements for departing staff who were now becoming valuable employees somewhere else.

Wheatley, and other experts in dark psychology, suggest that attempting to counter individual and cultural toxicity runs the risk of tipping the balance too far, catapulting people into toxic positivity. In this latter state, negative feelings are suppressed, minimised, invalidated, and masked by falsely positive thoughts or utterances, such as 'Always look on the bright side of life' (Idle 1989). Monty Python's cynicism aside, the effect of failing to acknowledge negative feelings or outcomes is to undermine well-being in the individual in relation to their relationships (Girme et al. 2020) and the workplace (Quintero and Long 2019). 'Toxic leaders', a term attributed to Whicker (1996), are those who abuse the leader–follower relationship in various ways, effectively subverting both themselves and the organisation. Such behaviour is linked to a range of personality issues, potentially disorders, particularly in high office. The 'Dark Triad' is a term in applied psychology that describes the distinct traits of Machiavellianism, narcissism, and psychopathy appearing in one person. There is considerable debate about whether these are distinct, as there is considerable overlap. A toxic leader will not only manipulate and blackmail and seduce their way to power, but they will also counter with the very tools used to combat them, and true denial of a negative emotion is to rebut it with positivity. However they manifest, Dark Triadic leaders are definitely toxic to those they encounter, and most of us need support to deal with them. Here, we can be failed by those attempting to help. In his book, Wheatley equips us with useful tools to defend against the positively toxic, but what he fails to address is the toxically positive, and how a tidal wave of positivity can be set to drown the unaware. This is the Dark Triad at work indeed.

There are several ways that psychiatry can turn poisonous even as it seeks to fight toxicity. Notwithstanding the early treatments for mental illness (e.g. trephination, purging, hypoglycaemic coma therapy, electroconvulsive therapy, induced seizures, and even irreversible lobotomy), modern psychiatry has effective and safe treatments available. This often means a referral to a psychologist or psychotherapist to undertake a 'talking cure' (Freud [1896] 1962: 274). Newnes (2011: 220) suggests this is a problem, since the therapy is offered as being as efficacious for mental illness as antibiotics are for bacterial infections. When the patient does not feel better as soon as expected, this is viewed as being the failure of the patient to present evidence of the original diagnosis, rather than seeing the theory of treatment for that diagnosis as woefully inadequate. Such a toxic assumption means that psychology becomes a weapon to beat down the vulnerable, and even not so vulnerable, such as those in search of a direction and a purpose. Nowhere is this more evident than in professional malpractice suits or, more insidious, the life coach psychobabble that the twenty-first century has encouraged.

Life coaching can be a good thing. Weight loss, job seeking, self-discovery, relationships, just about any life goal can be improved by the intervention of a life coach. But no life coach has a perfect life, in the same way as a sports coach is not an Olympic gold medallist or a singing teacher does not earn her living by being a world-famous opera star. But Usain Bolt still needed Glen Mills to get to that incredible speed, and Luciano Pavarotti still met with Arrigo Pola to hone his virtuosity. A life coach is *supposed* to help you focus on your goals and realise your potential to reach them. The coach is not supposed to make you more hopeless than before you met them, so without focus that your mind needs spectacles and so lost that you wonder how you manage to find your way home. But some coaches do this, so upbeat and optimistic you feel ashamed of not following the conga line to psychological paradise. And sometimes, it is not even a coach who is doing this to you; and the only positive thing to say about non-professionals in this role is that they are not also taking your money, £30 a visit or £299 for a course of ten. This, then, is the curse of toxic positivity.

Toxic positivity occurs if people are constantly encouraged to see things from the good side without considering the adversity they are experiencing or allowing for a period of often-needed negative emotion, such as grief or anger. Lukin (2019) suggests that repressing negative emotions that are correctly associated with adverse experiences simply magnifies them, and risks the loss of the opportunity to learn coping mechanisms. It may also be that the person exhorting a positive outlook in the face of negative experiences lacks empathy. Now there is a thought, that those on whom one relies for an opportunity to recover from negative experiences are the very ones perpetuating them, because they do not care enough to provide the emotional space. There can be nothing worse than a person swimming against the tide, striving to reach a distant shore and tiring so much that there is a risk of drowning when, finally, a boat approaches, but instead of helping the drowning person into the boat, the rower leans over and says: 'I believe in you, you can do this, just put your mind to saving yourself and you will.' Then the boat disappears back to the shore, the occupant not sparing a glance at the drowning person slipping under the waves for the last time. Translate this to emotional drowning. All we do when we exhort someone to 'be positive!', to 'try harder!', to 'forget about other people', or to see that 'there are plenty more fish in the sea!' is ask our friend/child/sibling to stop feeling, either because we cannot face our own emotions or because we really do not care about theirs. And there is the rub, the social psychopathic tendency that seems to be the worst we can be now – uncaring. In the second decade of the twenty-first century, when beloved icons died, the world faced a global pandemic, and a buffoon almost failed to leave the White House, one beacon seemed to shine – we all cared a little bit more. Approaching the end of 2020, the World Health Organization (2020) reported that it had almost achieved its financial target (US$1.7 billion) to combat the pandemic in countries where it was most needed, due to the solidarity of donors, from individual to nations. And in a little corner of England, an old soldier decided to do 100 laps of his garden with his walking frame before his 100th birthday, hoping to raise £1,000 for the NHS who had cared for him and his family. By the time the fund closed on his centenary, it stood at over £32 million, from over 1.5 million donors (The Captain Tom Foundation n.d.). It is not just charitable behaviour that has changed. Moreno et al. (2020) observe that the COVID-19 pandemic has exacerbated and even created adverse mental health effects, magnifying psychosocial stress and financial worry into fear of negative outcomes. It also threw inadequacies in mental health provision into sharp relief. Adaptations of physical health systems to cope with responses were shared as good practice, and Moreno et al. go on to say that while our very interconnectedness may have made breathing into a toxic behaviour, it made adapting to psychiatric needs by systems and individuals a necessity and an absolute rule. Toxicity may either break or make this world, but it will not win if human spirit continues to shine.

Bibliography

10 Things I Hate about You, dir. Gil Junger (Burbank: Buena Vista Pictures, 1999).
13th, dir. Ava DuVernay (Los Gatos, CA: Netflix, 2015).
A Quiet Place, dir. John Krasinski (Burbank, CA: Buena Vista Pictures, 2018).
A Serbian Film, dir. Srdjan Spasojevic (Belgrade: Contra Film, 2010).
Abrams, Simon, 'Hell to Pay: Indie Horror Icon Larry Fessenden on Wendigos and Ugly Americans', RogerEbert.com (16 February 2016) <https://www.rogerebert.com/interviews/hell-to-pay-indie-horror-icon-larry-fessenden-on-wendigos-and-ugly-americans>, accessed 31 August 2020.
Acar, Feride, and Gulbanu Altunok, 'The "Politics of Intimate" at the Intersection of Neo-liberalism and Neo-conservatism in Contemporary Turkey', *Women's Studies International Forum*, 41 (2013), 1–10.
AccessHollywood.com Editorial Staff, 'Britney Spears Breaks 5 Million Followers Barrier on Twitter', NBC Philadelphia (29 May 2010) <https://www.nbcphiladelphia.com/news/national-international/britney_spears_breaks_5_million_followers_barrier_on_twitter__-_article/1875376/>, accessed 25 October 2020.
Acocella, Joan, 'Murder by Poison: The Rise and Fall of Arsenic', The New Yorker (7 October 2013) <https://www.newyorker.com/magazine/2013/10/14/murder-by-poison>, accessed 9 September 2020.
ACOG, 'The Importance of Preserving Access to Care through the Federal Title X Program' (June 2018) <https://www.acog.org/clinical-information/policy-and-position-statements/statements-of-policy/2018/the-importance-of-preserving-access-to-care-through-the-federal-title-x-program>, accessed 28 October 2021.
Aldag, Ramon J., 'Toxic Waste', Britannica (7 February 2014) <https://www.britannica.com/science/toxic-waste>, accessed 3 October 2020.
Alexievich, Svetlana, *Chernobyl Prayer: A Chronicle of the Future*, trans. Anna Gunin and Arch Tait (London: Penguin Classics, 2016).
Alien, dir. Ridley Scott (Los Angeles: 20th Century Fox, 1979).
'Always Look on the Bright Side of Life', sung by Eric Idle, *Monty Python Sings* (London: Virgin, 1989).
Amend, Elyse, Linda Kay and Rosemary C. Reilly, 'Journalism on the Spot: Ethical Dilemmas When Covering Trauma and the Implications for Journalism Education', *Journal of Mass Media Ethics*, 27, 4 (2012), 235–47.

American Petroleum Institute, 'Pipelines' (n.d.) <https://www.api.org/oil-and-natural-gas/wells-to-consumer/transporting-oil-natural-gas/pipeline?page=1&pageSize=10>, accessed 31 August 2020.

American Psychiatric Association (APA), *Diagnostic and Statistical Manual of Mental Disorders (DSM–5)* (Washington, DC: APA, 2013).

Andrejevic, Mark, *Reality TV: The Work of Being Watched* (Lanham, MD: Rowman & Littlefield Publishers, 2004).

'Andy Stanley' (n.d.) <https://andystanley.com/>, accessed 10 December 2020.

Anonymous, 'I'm an NHS Doctor – and I've Had Enough of People Clapping for Me', The Guardian (21 May 2020) <https://www.theguardian.com/society/2020/may/21/nhs-doctor-enough-people-clapping>, accessed 28 October 2021.

Ante-Contreras, Daniel, 'BioShock's Paranoid States: The Gamer within a History of White Male Victimization', in Felan Parker and Jessica Aldred, eds, *Beyond the Sea: Navigating BioShock* (Montreal: McGill-Queen's University Press, 2018), 172–202.

Archive of Our Own [online database], <https://archiveofourown.org>, accessed 1 February 2022.

Arjun Reddy, dir. Sandeep Reddy Vanga (Hyderabad: Bhadrakali Pictures, 2017).

Asbury, Kathryn, and Lisa Kim (2020) '"Lazy, Lazy Teachers": Teachers' Perceptions of how their Profession is Valued by Society, Policymakers, and the Media during COVID-19', *SocArXiv Papers* (20 July 2020). doi: 10.31234/osf.io/65k8q

Asher-Perrin, Emmet, '30 Years Later, Real Genius is Still the Geek Solidarity Film that Nerd Culture Deserves', Tor (21 May 2015) <https://www.tor.com/2015/05/21/30-years-later-real-genius-is-still-the-geek-solidarity-film-that-nerd-culture-deserves/>, accessed 1 November 2020.

Associated Press, 'White Supremacists see Hope in Obama Win', CBS News (8 August 2008) <https://www.cbsnews.com/news/white-supremacists-see-hope-in-obama-win/>, accessed 20 November 2020.

———, 'Britney Spears "Will Not Perform Again" if Father Controls Career', Billboard (11 November 2020) <https://www.billboard.com/articles/news/9481872/britney-spears-quit-music-father-controls-career/>, accessed 11 November 2020.

Aubrey, J. S., D. M. Rhea, L. N. Olson and M. Fine (2013) 'Conflict and Control: Examining the Association between Exposure to Television Portraying Interpersonal Conflict and the Use of Controlling Behaviours in Romantic Relationships', *Communication Studies*, 64, 106–24.

Avatar [video game], dir. Bruce Maggs, Andrew Shapira and David Sides (Urbana and Champaign: University of Illinois, 1979).

Babul, Elif, 'The Paradox of Protection: Human Rights, the Masculinist State, and the Moral Economy of Gratitude in Turkey', *American Ethnologist*, 42, 1 (2015), 116–39.

Bachechi, Kimberly, 'Our Icons: Ourselves. Britney Spears, Justin Timberlake, Kevin Federline, and the Construction of Whiteness in a Post-race America', *Celebrity Studies*, 6, 2 (2015), 164–77.

Bacigalupi, Paolo, *Ship Breaker* (London: Little, Brown, 2010).

Baker, Daniel, 'Between Worlds: Portal Fantasy as Dialogic in Gaiman and Miéville', *The Refereed Proceedings of the 19th Conference of the Australasian Association of Writing Programs*, Wellington, New Zealand (2014), 1–18 <https://aawp.org.au/wp-content/uploads/2015/05/Baker_D._Words_Between_Worlds_.pdf>, accessed 26 February 2022.

Baker-Sperry, Lori, and Liz Grauerholz, 'The Pervasiveness and Persistence of the Feminine Beauty Ideal in Children's Fairy Tales', *Gender and Society*, 17, 5 (2003), 711–26.

Bayman, Louis, 'The Horror of Knowing: Catastrophe and Meaning in HBO's Chernobyl' We Are the Mutants (30 July 2019) <https://wearethemutants.com/2019/07/30/the-horror-of-knowing-catastrophe-and-meaning-in-hbos-chernobyl/>, accessed 30 November 2020.

BBC News, 'Coronavirus: Boris Johnson Sets Out Plan for "Significant Normality" by Christmas' (17 July 2020) <https://www.bbc.co.uk/news/uk-53441912>, accessed 1 February 2022.

BBN Times, 'About Us' (n.d.) <https://www.bbntimes.com/support/about-us>, accessed 1 February 2022.

Beaty, Katelyn, and Ari Shapiro, 'How QAnon Conspiracy Is Spreading in Christian Communities Across the U.S.', NPR (21 August 2020) <https://www.npr.org/2020/08/21/904798097/how-qanon-conspiracy-is-spreading-in-christian-communities-across-the-u-s>, accessed 15 November 2020.

'Bekhayali' [song], composed by Sachet-Parampara, lyrics by Irshad Kamil, sung by Sachet Tandon (Mumbai: T-Series, 2019).

Bell, Betty Louise, 'Indians With Voices: Revisiting Savagism and Civilization', in William Blazek and Michael Glenday, eds, *American Mythologies: Essays on Contemporary Literature* (Liverpool: Liverpool University Press, 2005), 15–28.

Bendroth, Margaret, 'Christian Fundamentalism in America', Oxford Research Encyclopedia (27 February 2017) <https://oxfordre.com/religion/view/10.1093/acrefore/9780199340378.001.0001/acrefore-9780199340378-e-419>, accessed 7 November 2020.

Benjamin, Walter, 'The Storyteller', in Dorothy J. Hale, ed., *The Novel: An Anthology of Criticism and Theory 1900–2000* [1936] (Malden: Blackwell Publishing, 2006), 361–78.

Berger, Stefan with Christoph Conrad, *The Past as History: National Identity and Historical Consciousness in Modern Europe* (Houndmills: Palgrave MacMillan, 2015).

Bernstein, Albert J., *Emotional Vampires: Dealing with People Who Drain You Dry* (New York: McGraw-Hill, 2012).
Best, Wallace, 'The Fear of Black Bodies in Motion', Huffington Post (4 December 2014) <https://www.huffpost.com/entry/the-fear-of-black-bodies-in-motion>, accessed 7 November 2020.
Bettelheim, Bruno, *The Uses of Enchantment: The Meaning and Importance of Fairy Tales* (New York: Vintage Books, 1975).
Bignell, Jonathan, *Big Brother: Reality TV in the Twenty-first Century* (Houndmills: Palgrave, 2005).
BioShock [video game], dir. Ken Levine (Novato, CA: 2K Games, 2007).
BioShock 2 [video game], dir. Jordan Thomas (Novato, CA: 2K Games, 2010).
BioShock Infinite [video game], dir. Ken Levine (Novato, CA: 2K Games, 2013).
Bird Box, dir. Susanne Bier (Los Gatos, CA: Netflix, 2018).
Biri Bizi Gözetliyor [Big Brother], created by Mischa Zickler (Istanbul: Senkron TV, 2001–2003).
Blackwood, Algernon, 'The Wendigo' [2010], in Xavier Aldana Reyes ed., *Roarings from Further Out: Four Weird Novellas by Algernon Blackwood* (London: British Library Publishing, 2019), 139–99.
Blake, Linnie, *The Wounds of Nations: Horror Cinema, Historical Trauma and National Identity* (Manchester: Manchester University Press, 2008).
Blakeman, Steve, 'Sadfishing – the Latest Toxic Social Media Trend', BBN Times, 12 November (2019) <https://www.bbntimes.com/companies/sadfishing-the-latest-toxic-social-media-trend>, accessed 7 September 2019.
Blandford, James R., *Britney* (London: Music Sales Group, 2002).
Bloodstained: Ritual of the Night [video game], dir. Shutaro Iida (Milan: 505 Games, 2019).
Boise, Sam de, 'Editorial: Is Masculinity Toxic?', *NORMA*, 14, 3 (2019), 147–51.
Bong, Joon Ho, *Parasite: A Graphic Novel in Storyboards* (Paris: Hachette, 2020).
Boseley, Matlida, 'Inside the "Shitposting" Subculture the Alleged Christchurch Shooter Belonged to', The Sunday Morning Herald (17 March 2019) <https://www.smh.com.au/national/inside-the-shit-posting-subculture-the-christchurch-shooter-belonged-to-20190317-p514xt.html>, accessed 9 December 2020.
Boswell, John, 'Toxic Narratives in the Deliberative System: How the Ghost of Nanny Stalks the Obesity Debate', *Policy Studies*, 36, 3 (2015), 314–28.
Bozell, L. Brent, 'For Toxic TV, Tune in During "Family Hour"', *Human Events*, 55, 35 (1999), 22.
Brach, Tara, 'Healing Racialized Trauma: A Conversation with Resmaa Menakem and Tara Brach' (21 October 2020) <https://www.tarabrach.com/healing-trauma-resmaa-menakem/>, accessed on 5 October 2020.
Bracken, Patrick, *Trauma: Culture, Meaning and Philosophy* (London: Wiley, 2002).

Bradley, William, 'Reconsidering Revenge: How Revenge of the Nerds' Misogyny Is Evident in Current Nerd Culture', The Mary Sue (3 April 2015) <https://www.themarysue.com/reconsidering-revenge/>, accessed 1 November 2020.

Brightman, Robert A., 'The Windigo in the Material World', *Ethnohistory*, 35, 4 (1988), 337–79.

Brimstone, dir. Martin Koolhoven (Amsterdam: N279 Entertainment, 2016).

Brogunier, Tobin, '4 Reasons Why Social Media Has Become So Toxic and What to Look for Next', Entrepreneur (22 February 2019) <https://entrepreneur.com/article328749>, accessed 29 August 2019.

Brolley, Brittany, 'The Untold Truth of Shirley Temple', The List (26 July 2018) <https://www.thelist.com/129652/the-untold-truth-of-shirley-temple/>, accessed 25 October 2018.

Bryant, Nick, 'Barack Obama Legacy: Did He Improve US Race Relations?' BBC News (10 January 2017) <https://www.bbc.com/news/world-us-canada-38536668>, accessed 3 November 2020.

Buell, Lawrence, 'Toxic Discourse', *Critical Inquiry*, 24, 3 (1998), 639–65.

Buffy the Vampire Slayer, created by Joss Whedon (Los Angeles: Mutant Enemy, 1997–2003).

———, 'Welcome to the Hellmouth', Season 1, Episode 1, dir. Charles Martin Smith (Los Angeles: Mutant Enemy, 1997).

———, 'Inca Mummy Girl', Season 2, Episode 4, dir. Ellen S. Pressman (Los Angeles: Mutant Enemy, 1997).

———, 'The Wish', Season 3, Episode 9, dir. David Greenwalt (Los Angeles: Mutant Enemy, 1998).

———, 'Earshot', Season 3, Episode 18, dir. Regis Kimble (Los Angeles: Mutant Enemy, 1997–1999).

———, 'Superstar', Season 4, Episode 17, dir. David Grossman (Los Angeles: Mutant Enemy, 2000).

———, 'Fool For Love', Season 5, Episode 7, dir. Nick Marck (Los Angeles: Mutant Enemy, 2000).

———, 'I Was Made to Love You', Season 5, Episode 15, dir. James A. Contner (Los Angeles: Mutant Enemy, 2001).

———, 'Flooded', Season 6, Episode 4, dir. Douglas Petrie (Los Angeles: Mutant Enemy, 2001).

———, 'Life Serial', Season 6, Episode 5, dir. Nick Marck (Los Angeles: Mutant Enemy, 2001).

———, 'All the Way', Season 6, Episode 6, dir. David Solomon (Los Angeles: Mutant Enemy, 2001).

———, 'Tabula Rasa', Season 6, Episode 8, dir. David Grossman (Los Angeles: Mutant Enemy, 2001).

———, 'Smashed', Season 6, Episode 9, dir. Drew Z. Greenburg (Los Angeles: Mutant Enemy, 2001).

———, 'Gone', Season 6, Episode 11, dir. David Fury (Los Angeles: Mutant Enemy, 2002).

———, 'Dead Things', Season 6, Episode 13, dir. James A. Contner (Los Angeles: Mutant Enemy, 2002).

———, 'Seeing Red', Season 6, Episode 19, dir. Michael Gershman (Los Angeles: Mutant Enemy, 2002).

———, 'Villains', Season 6, Episode 20, dir. David Solomon (Los Angeles: Mutant Enemy, 2002).

———, 'Two to Go', Season 6, Episode 21, dir. Bill L. Norton (Los Angeles: Mutant Enemy, 2002).

Bulwer-Lytton, Edward, *The Last Days of Pompeii* [1834] (New York: Quill Pen Classics, 2008).

Burnett, Dean, '"Your Film Has Ruined My Childhood!" Why Nostalgia Trumps Logic on Remakes', The Guardian (1 June 2016) <https://www.theguardian.com/science/brain-flapping/2016/jun/01/your-film-has-ruined-my-childhood-why-nostalgia-trumps-logic-on-remakes?fbclid=IwAR3Gg5xbWweFObgvF69CZ9aDWDmMFVZDRbkfhfXoogYXfFMDMm2C4CSifw>, accessed 26 August 2020.

Burul, Yesim, and Eslen-Ziya, Hande, 'Understanding "New Turkey" Through Women's Eyes: Gender Politics in Turkish Daytime Talk Shows', *Middle East Critique*, 27, 2 (2018), 179–92.

Busse, Kristina, 'Geek Hierarchies, Boundary Policing, and the Gendering of the Good Fan', *Participations: Journal of Audience and Reception Studies*, 10, 1 (2013), 73–91.

Callahan, Yesha, 'Dear Racist Star Wars Fans: There Are Black Stormtroopers, So Get Over It', The Root (12 January 2014) <https://thegrapevine.theroot.com/dear-racist-star-wars-fans-there-are-black-stormtroope-1790885934201 4>, accessed 12 November 2020.

Campbell, Joseph, *The Masks of God Volume 1 – Primitive Mythology* (London: Secker and Warburg, 1960).

The Captain Tom Foundation (n.d.) <https://captaintom.org>, accessed 18 November 2020.

Carlyle, Thomas, *On Heroes, Hero-Worship and the Heroic in History* [1840], Project Gutenberg (2008) <http://gutenberg.org/files/1091/1091-h/1091-h.htm>, accessed 30 November 2020.

Carroll, Noël, 'The Nature of Horror', *The Journal of Aesthetics and Art Criticism*, 46, 1 (1987), 51–9.

Bibliography

Carroll, Sean, 'The Denialist Playbook', *The Scientific American* (8 November 2020) <https://www.scientificamerican.com/article/the-denialist-playbook/>, accessed 6 December 2020.

Castells, Manuel, *The Rise of the Network Society*, 2nd edition (West Sussex: Blackwell Publishing Ltd, 2010).

Caswell, Michelle, and Marika Cifor, 'From Human Rights to Feminist Ethics: Radical Empathy in the Archives', *Archivaria*, 81 (2016), 23–43.

Cavdar, Ceren, 'Gunduz Kusagi Kadin Programlarinda Toplumsal Cinsiyet Esitsizligi ve Kadin Temsili' [Gender Inequality and Women's Representation in Daytime Shows for Women], *Selcuk Iletisim*, 12, 1 (2019), 368–83.

Cawelti, John G., *Mystery, Violence and Popular Culture* (Madison, WI: The Popular Press, 2004).

Center for Reproductive Rights, 'Trump Administration Expands Global Gag Rule', 16 May (2017) <https://reproductiverights.org/trump-administration-expands-global-gag-rule/>, accessed 1 February 2022.

——, 'Center for Reproductive Rights Comment on Proposed Title X Regulations', 31 July (2018) <https://reproductiverights.org/center-for-reproductive-rights-comment-on-proposed-title-x-regulations/>, accessed 28 October 2021.

Cesca, Bob, 'Our Politics Isn't about Left vs. Right Anymore – It's about Reality vs. Dreadful Fantasy', Salon (17 November 2020a) <https://www.salon.com/2020/11/17/our-politics-isnt-about-left-vs-right-anymore--its-about-reality-vs-dreadful-fantasy/>, accessed 6 December 2020.

——, 'Trump's Gruesome New Pandemic Pivot Would Be Ludicrous – if His Followers Weren't So Ready to Swallow the Poison', Raw Story (31 March 2020b) <https://www.rawstory.com/2020/03/trumps-gruesome-new-pandemic-pivot-would-be-ludicrous-if-his-followers-werent-so-ready-to-swallow-the-poison/>, accessed 6 December 2020.

Chen, Zhansheng, Kipling D. Williams, Julie Fitness and Nicola C. Newton, 'When Hurt Will Not Heal: Exploring the Capacity to Relive Social and Physical Pain', *Psychological Science*, 19, 8 (2008), 789–95.

Cheney, Jillian, 'An Evangelical's Guide to QAnon: Inside One of the Most Talked About Internet Groups', Religion Unplugged (13 October 2020) <https://religionunplugged.com/news/2020/10/13/an-evangelicals-guide-to-qanon>, accessed 7 November 2020.

Chernobyl, created by Craig Mazin (New York: HBO, 2019).

——, 'Open Wide, O Earth', Season 1, Episode 3, dir. Johan Renck (New York: HBO, 2019).

Chidley, Joe, 'Toxic TV', *Maclean's: Toronto*, 109, 25 (1996), 36–41.

Chiesi, Roberto, 'Salò: The Present as Hell', Criterion.Com (4 October 2011) <https://www.criterion.com/current/posts/513-sal-the-present-as-hell>, accessed 28 October 2021.
Cigman, Ruth, 'The Gifted Child: A Conceptual Enquiry', *Oxford Review of Education*, 32, 2 (2006), 197–212.
Cinderella, dir. Kenneth Branagh (Los Angeles: Disney, 2015).
Cinderella, dir. Wilfred Jackson, Hamilton Luske and Clyde Geronimi (Los Angeles: Disney, 1950).
Cindoglu, Dilek, and Didem Unal, 'Gender and Sexuality in the Authoritarian Discursive Strategies of "New Turkey"', *European Journal of Women's Studies*, 24, 1 (2017), 39–54.
Clark, Robin E., Judith Freeman Clark and Christine Adamec, *Encyclopedia of Child Abuse*, 3rd edition (New York: Facts On File, 2007).
Clarke, Rachel, 'NHS Doctor: Forget Medals and Flypasts – what We Want is Proper Pay and PPE', The Guardian (2 May 2020) <https://www.theguardian.com/society/2020/may/02/nhs-doctor-forget-medals-and-flypasts-what-we-want-is-proper-pay-and-ppe>, accessed 28 October 2021.
Click, Melissa, *Anti-Fandom Dislike and Hate in the Digital Age* (New York: New York University Press, 2019).
Clover, Carol J., 'Her Body, Himself: Gender in the Slasher Film', *Representations*, 20 (1987), 187–228.
——, *Men, Women, and Chain Saws: Gender in the Modern Horror Film* (Princeton, NJ: Princeton University Press, 1992).
——, 'Preface', in Carol J. Clover, *Men, Women, and Chain Saws: Gender in the Modern Horror Film* (Princeton, NJ: Princeton University Press, 2015), ix–xiv.
Coates, Ta-Nehisi, *Between the World and Me* (New York: Random House, 2015).
Cohen, Jeffrey Jerome, 'Monster Culture (Seven Theses)', in Jeffrey Jerome Cohen, ed., *Monster Theory: Reading Culture* (Minneapolis: University of Minnesota Press, 1996), 3–25.
Cohn, Norman, *The Pursuit of the Millennium* (London: Secker and Warburg, 1957).
Combahee River Collective, 'The Combahee River Collective Statement' [1977], BlackPast.org, 16 November (2012) <https://www.blackpast.org/african-american-history/combahee-river-collective-statement-1977/>, accessed 28 October 2021.
Community, created by Dan Harmon (Culver City, CA: Sony Pictures Television, 2009–2015).
Couldry, Nick, 'Reality TV, or the Secret Theatre of Neoliberalism', *Review of Education, Pedagogy and Cultural Studies*, 30, 3 (2008), 3–13.
Courcier, Nicolas, Mehdi El Kanafi and Raphaël Lucas, *BioShock: From Rapture to Columbia* (Toulouse: Third Éditions, 2017).

Cowie, Elizabeth, 'Fantasia', *m/f*, 9 (1984), 71–104.
Crawford, Robert, *Devolving English Literature* (Oxford: Clarendon Press, 1992).
Crazy Ex-Girlfriend, created by Rachel Bloom and Aline Brosh McKenna (Los Angeles: CBS Television Studios, 2015–2019).
———, 'Josh Just Happens to Live Here', Season 1, Episode 1, dir. Marc Webb (Los Angeles: CBS Television Studios, 2015).
———, 'Josh's Girlfriend is Really Cool!' Season 1, Episode 2, dir. Don Scardino (Los Angeles: CBS Television Studios, 2015).
———, 'I'm Going on a Date with Josh's Friend', Season 1, Episode 4, dir. Stuart McDonald (Los Angeles: CBS Television Studios, 2015).
———, 'My First Thanksgiving with Josh', Season 1, Episode 6, dir. Joanna Kerns (Los Angeles: CBS Television Studios, 2015).
———, 'I'm Going to the Beach with Josh and His Friends', Season 1, Episode 9, dir. Kenny Ortega (Los Angeles: CBS Television Studios, 2016).
———, 'Josh and I Go to Los Angeles', Season 1, Episode 13, dir. Michael Patrick Jann (Los Angeles: CBS Television Studios, 2016).
———, 'Paula Needs to Get Over Josh', Season 1, Episode 18, dir. Aline Brosh McKenna (Los Angeles: CBS Television Studios, 2016).
———, 'Where is Josh's Friend?', Season 2, Episode 1, dir. Marc Webb (Los Angeles: CBS Television Studios, 2016).
———, 'All Signs Point to Josh ... or Is It Josh's Friend?', Season 2, Episode 3, dir. Stuart McDonald (Los Angeles: CBS Television Studios, 2016).
———, 'When Will Josh and his Friend Leave Me Alone?', Season 2, Episode 4, dir. Paul Briganti (Los Angeles: CBS Television Studios, 2016).
———, 'Josh Is the Man of My Dreams, Right?', Season 2, Episode 11, Michael Patrick Jann (Los Angeles: CBS Television Studios, 2017).
———, 'Nathaniel Is Irrelevant', Season 3, Episode 13, dir. Aline Brosh McKenna (Los Angeles: CBS Television Studios, 2018).
Creed, Barbara, *The Monstrous-Feminine: Film, Feminism, Psychoanalysis* (London and New York: Routledge, 1993).
Crenshaw, Kimberlé, 'Mapping the Margins: Intersectionality, Identity Politics, and Violence against Women of Color', *Stanford Law Review*, 43, 6 (1991), 1241–99.
Crow, Matthew, 'Atlantic North America: From Contact the Late Nineteenth Century', in Edward Cavanagh and Lorenzo Veracini, eds, *The Routledge Handbook of the History of Settler Colonialism* (New York: Routledge, 2017), 95–108.
Cupach, William R., and Brian H. Spitzberg, *The Dark Side of Relationship Pursuit: From Attraction to Obsession and Stalking* (Mahwah, NJ: Lawrence Erlbaum, 2004).
Curato, Nicole, 'Asserting Disadvantaged Communities' Deliberative Agency in a Media-saturated Society', *Theory and Society*, 50 (2020) 657–77.

Curtis, Ron, 'Narrative Form and Normative Force: Baconian Story-telling in Popular Science', *Social Studies of Science*, 24, 3 (1994), 419–61.

Cvetkovich, Ann, *An Archive of Feelings: Trauma, Sexuality, and Lesbian Public Cultures* (Durham, NC: Duke University Press, 2003).

Dahlberg, Lincoln, 'Visibility and the Public Sphere: A Normative Conceptualisation', *Javnost - The Public*, 25, 1–2 (2018), 35–42.

Dark Souls [video game], dir. Hidetaka Miyazaki (Tokyo: Namco Bandai Games, 2011).

Davies, Jeremy, *The Birth of the Anthropocene* (Oakland: University of California Press, 2016).

Davis, Bradford William, 'Succession – Jesse Armstrong Shares the Inspiration for the Roy Family', HBO (n.d.) <https://www.hbo.com/succession/season-1/6-which-side-are-you-on/Season-1-interview-jesse-armstrong>, accessed 1 December 2020.

Dawson, Ruth, 'Trump Administration's Domestic Gag Rule Has Slashed the Title X Network's Capacity by Half', Guttmacher Institute (5 February 2020) <https://www.guttmacher.org/article/2020/02/trump-administrations-domestic-gag-rule-has-slashed-title-x-networks-capacity-half>, accessed 28 October 2021.

Day, Elizabeth, 'Ghostbusters Writer Katie Dippold: "They Said It Was the Worst Movie Ever Before I'd Written a Word"', The Telegraph (24 June 2016) <https://www.telegraph.co.uk/films/2016/06/24/ghostbusters-writer-katie-dippold-they-said-it-was-the-worst-mov/>, accessed 23 September 2020.

Deardorff, Daniel, *The Other Within: The Genius of Deformity in Myth, Culture and Psyche* (Ashland, OR: White Cloud Press, 2004).

Death Stranding [video game], dir. Hideo Kojima (Tokyo: Sony Interactive Entertainment, 2019).

Deleuze, Gilles, and Felix Guattari, *A Thousand Plateaus*, trans. Brian Massumi (London: Athlone, 1987).

DELIVER, *DELIVER: Final Project Report*, for the US Agency for International Development (Arlington, VA: DELIVER, 2007) <https://pdf.usaid.gov/pdf_docs/Pdacko82.pdf>

Demos, Vasilikie, and Marcia Segal Texler, 'Gendered Perspectives on Conflict and Violence', in Vasilikie Demos and Marcia Segal Texler, eds, *Gendered Perspective on Conflict and Violence* (Bingley: Emerald Publishers, 2013), 1–18.

Depression Quest [video game], dir. Zoë Quinn (The Quinspiracy, 2013).

Devdas, dir. Sanjay Leela Bhansali (Mumbai: Red Chillies Entertainment, 2002).

Diaz de Arce, Laura, *Diamonds and Ash: Class and Social Mobility in Seventeenth Century Cinderella* [master's thesis] (Boca Raton: Florida Atlantic University, 2016) <http://fau.digital.flvc.org/islandora/object/fau%3A33443/datastream/OBJ/view/Diamonds_and_Ash__Class_and_Social_Mobility_in_Seventeenth_Century_Cinderella.pdf>, accessed 28 October 2021.

Diethelm, Pascal, and Martin McKee, 'Denialism: What Is It and How Should Scientists Respond?', *European Journal of Public Health*, 19, 1 (2009), 2–4.

Dignam, Pierce Alexander, and Deana A. Rohlinger, 'Misogynistic Men Online: How the Red Pill Helped Elect Trump', *Signs: Journal of Women in Culture and Society*, 44, 3 (2019), 589–612.

Dizikes, Peter, 'Our Itch to Share Helps Spread Covid-19 Misinformation', in MIT News (9 July 2020) <https://news.mit.edu/2020/share-covid-19-misinformation-0709>, accessed 6 December 2020.

Dnd [video game], dir. Gary Whisenhunt and Ray Wood (Urbana and Champaign: University of Illinois, 1975).

Doane, Mary Ann, *The Desire to Desire: The Woman's Film of the 1940s* (Basingstoke: Palgrave Macmillan, 1987).

Dodson, P. Claire, 'Penn Badgley Reminds Fans His You Character Joe Goldberg Is the Worst', Teen Vogue (9 January 2019) <https://www.teenvogue.com/story/penn-badgley-reminds-fans-his-you-character-joe-goldberg-is-the-worst>, accessed 28 October 2021.

Dominion, dir. Chris Delforce (Sydney: Delforce, 2018).

Dorking, Marie Claire, 'Social Media "Sadfishing" Trend Found to Be Harming Mental Health of Children, but What Is It?', MSN (1 October 2019) <https://www.msn.com/en-gb/health/mindandbody/social-media-sadfishing-trend-found-to-be-harming-mental-health-of-children-but-what-is-it/ar-AAI6Gfu?li=AABCYXu>, accessed 7 September 2020.

Douglas, Mary, *Purity and Danger: An Analysis of the Concepts of Pollution and Taboo* (London: Routledge, 1966).

——, *Natural Symbols* (London: Routledge, 2013).

Douglas, Susan J., 'Young Women Learn Harmful Gender Stereotypes from Reality TV', in Karen F. Balkin, ed., *At Issue: Reality TV* (San Diego: Greenhaven Press, 2004), 61–3.

Doyle, Jude Ellison Sady, 'Ghostbusters Is a Classic Summer Escape Film – but from Misogyny', In These Times (20 July 2016) <http://inthesetimes.com/article/19309/ghostbusters-is-a-classic-summer-escape-filmbut-from-misogyny>, accessed 23 September 2020.

Dreher, Tanja. 'Speaking Up or Being Heard? Community Media Interventions and the Politics of Listening', *Media, Culture & Society*, 32, 1 (2010), 85–103.

Drobnic, Angie Holan, 'In Context: Trump's "Very Fine People on Both Sides" Remarks', Politfact (26 April 2019) <https://www.politifact.com/article/2019/apr/26/context-trumps-very-fine-people-both-sides-remarks/>, accessed 30 November 2020.

Dryden, Linda, *The Modern Gothic and Literary Doubles: Stevenson, Wilde and Wells* (Basingstoke: Macmillan, 2003).

Dutton, Donald, and Susan Painter, 'Emotional Attachments in Abusive Relationships: A Test of Traumatic Bonding Theory', *Violence and Victims*, 8, 2 (1993), 105–20.

Dworznik, Gretchen, and Adrienne Garvey, 'Are We Teaching Trauma? A Survey of Accredited Journalism Schools in the United States', *Journalism Practice*, 13, 3 (2019), 367–82.

Earthlings, dir. Shaun Monson (Malibu, CA: Nation Earth, 2005).

Ebert, Roger, 'Why Movie Audiences Aren't Safe Anymore', *American Film*, 6, 5 (1981) 54–6.

Edelman, Gilad, 'QAnon Supporters Aren't Quite Who You Think They Are', Wired (6 October 2020) <https://www.wired.com/story/qanon-supporters-arent-quite-who-you-think-they-are/> accessed 28 October 2021.

Edwards, Leigh H., *The Triumph of Reality TV: The Revolution in American Television* (Santa Barbara, CA: Praeger, 2013).

Eggermont, Steven, 'Television Viewing, Perceived Similarity, and Adolescents Expectations of a Romantic Partner', *Journal of Broadcasting & Electronic Media*, 48 (2004), 244–65.

Einzelganger, 'The Shadow of Toxic Positivity' (2019) <http:einzelganger.co/the-shadow-of-toxic-positivity>, accessed 24 November 2020.

Eisenberger, Naomi I., 'The Pain of Social Disconnection: Examining the Shared Neural Underpinnings of Physical and Social Pain', *Nature Reviews Neuroscience*, 13, 6 (2012), 421–34.

Elaca, Dijana, *Dislocated Screen Memory: Narrating Trauma in Post-Yugoslav Cinema* (London: Palgrave Macmillan, 2016).

The Elder Scrolls V: Skyrim [video game], dir. Todd Howard (Rockville, MD: Bethesda Softworks, 2011).

Eliscu, Jenny, 'Britney Spears Returns', Rolling Stone (22 March 2011) <https://www.rollingstone.com/music/music-news/britney-spears-ret urns-254594/>, accessed 25 October 2020.

Esra Erol ile Evlen Benimle (Erol, 2013).

Faces of Death, dir. John Alan Schwartz (Englewood, NJ: Aquarius Releasing, 1978).

Faludi, Susan, *Backlash: The Undeclared War against American Women*, 15th anniversary edition [1991] (New York: Three Rivers Press, 2006).

Fatal Attraction, dir. Adrian Lyne (Hollywood: Paramount Pictures, 1987).

Fessenden, Larry, curator, *Sudden Storm: A Wendigo Reader* (Fiddleblack Publishing, 2016).

Fife, Bruce Fife, *Plandemic: Exposing the Greed, Corruption, and Fraud Behind the COVID-19 Pandemic* (Colorado Springs, CO: Piccadilly Books, 2020).

Fifty Shades of Grey, dir. Sam Taylor-Johnson (Universal City: Universal Pictures, 2015).

Fletcher, Elaine Ruth, and Grace Ren, 'Leave Politics Out Of Pandemic', Health Policy Watch (20 April 2020) <https://healthpolicy-watch.news/who-director-general-rebuts-united-states-criticism-regarding-who-role-in-pandemic>, accessed 6 December 2020.

Foucault, Michel, 'Preface', in Gilles Deleuze and Félix Guattari, *Anti-Oedipus: Capitalism and Schizophrenia*, trans. Robert Hurley, Mark Seem and Helen Lane (Minneapolis: University of Minnesota Press, 1983).

Frank, Arthur, *The Wounded Storyteller: Body, Illness, and Ethics* (Chicago: University of Chicago Press, 2013).

Frankel, Valerie Estelle, *Fourth Wave Feminism in Science Fiction and Fantasy Volume 1: Essays on Film Representations, 2012–2019* (Jefferson, NC: McFarland & Co. Inc, 2019).

The Free Dictionary, 'Gag Rule' (n.d.) <https://legal-dictionary.thefreedictionary.com/Gag+Rule>, accessed 28 October 2021.

Freedman, Carl, *Art and Idea in the Novels of China Miéville* (Canterbury: Gylphi Ltd, 2015).

Freeman, Joan, *Gifted Lives: What Happens When Gifted Children Grow Up?* (New York and London: Routledge 2010).

Freud, Sigmund, 'The Aetiology of Hysteria' [1896], in *Standard Edition of the Complete Psychological Works of Sigmund Freud, Volume III (1893–1899): Early Psycho-Analytic Publications* (London: Hogarth Press, 1962), 251–82.

———, 'Civilisation and its Discontents' [1929], in Ivan Smith, ed., *Freud: Complete Works* (eBook: 2011), 4462–532.

Friedan, Betty, *The Feminine Mystique* (New York: W. W. Norton, 1963).

Friedmann, Joachim, *Storytelling* (Stuttgart: UTB, 2019).

Funk, Cary, and Alec Tyson, 'Partisan Differences over the Pandemic Response Are Growing', *Scientific American* (30 May 2020) <https://blogs.scientificamerican.com/observations/partisan-differences-over-the-pandemic-response-are-growing/>, accessed 6 December 2020.

G20, *Women at Work in G20 Countries: Progress and Policy Action* (International Labour Organization, 2019).

Gabe, Jonathan, Michael Bury and Mary Ann Elston, *Key Concepts in Medical Sociology* (London: Sage, 2004).

Ganatra, Bela, Caitlin Gerdts, Clementine Rossier et al., 'Global, Regional, and Subregional Classification of Abortions by Safety, 2010–14 Estimates from a Bayesian Hierarchical Model', *Lancet*, 390, 10110 (2017): 2372–81.

Gas Light [play], by Patrick Hamilton (1938).

Gavin, Helen, 'Sticks and Stones May Break my Bones: The Effects of Emotional Abuse', *Journal of Aggression, Maltreatment & Trauma*, 20, 5 (2011), 503–29.

Gelin Evi [Bride's House], created by Cem Semerčioglu (Istanbul: Show TV, 2015–2019).

Germanos, Andrea, 'Reinstating "Global Gag Rule," Trump Attacks Women Worldwide', Common Dreams (23 January 2017) <https://www.commondreams.org/news/2017/01/23/reinstating-global-gag-rule-trump-attacks-women-worldwide>, accessed 1 February 2022.

Gessen, Masha, 'What HBO's "Chernobyl" Got Right, and What It Got Terribly Wrong' The New Yorker (4 June 2019) <https://www.newyorker.com/news/our-columnists/what-hbos-chernobyl-got-right-and-what-it-got-terribly-wrong>, accessed 30 November 2020.

Get Out, dir. Jordan Peele (Los Angeles: Universal Pictures, 2017).

Ghosh, Stutee, 'Film Review: Kabir Singh Starring Shahid Kapoor and Kiara Advani', YouTube, 21 June (2019) <https://youtu.be/hu2YOzF2I_M>, accessed 14 December 2020.

Ghostbusters, dir. Ivan Reitman (Culver City, CA: Columbia Pictures, 1984).

Ghostbusters II, dir. Ivan Reitman (Culver City, CA: Columbia Pictures, 1989).

Ghostbusters: Afterlife, dir. Jason Reitman (Culver City: Sony Pictures Releasing, 2021).

Ghostbusters: Answer the Call, dir. Paul Feig (Culver City, CA: Columbia Pictures, 2016).

Gilmore, Jane, 'How Toxic Femininity Is Damaging Us', The Sydney Morning Herald (17 May 2018) <https://www.smh.com.au/lifestyle/life-and-relationships/how-toxic-femininity-is-damaging-us-20180517-p4zfvt.html>, accessed 14 September 2020.

Girme, Yuthika U., Brett J. Peters, Levi R. Baker, Nicola C. Overall, G. Fletcher, Harry T. Reis, Jeremy P. Jamieson and Matthew J. Sigal (2020) 'Attachment Anxiety and the Curvilinear Effects of Expressive Suppression on Individuals' and Partners' Outcomes', *Journal of Personality and Social Psychology* (20 August 2020). doi.org/10.1037/pspi0000338

Glasser, Susan B., 'Donald Trump's 2020 Superspreader Campaign: A Diary', The New Yorker (3 November 2020) <https://www.newyorker.com/news/letter-from-trumps-washington/donald-trumps-2020-superspreader-campaign-a-diary>, accessed 6 December 2020.

Gonzalez, Victoria M., 'Swan Queen, Shipping, and Boundary Regulation in Fandom', *Transformative Works and Cultures*, 22 (2016) <http://dx.doi.org/10.3983/twc.2016.0669> accessed 28 October 2021.

Good Bye Lenin! dir. Wolfgang Becker (Berlin: Ex-Filme, 2003).

Gorman, Ginger, *Troll Hunting: Inside the World of Online Hate and Its Human Fallout* (Melbourne: Hardie Grant Books, 2019).

———, 'Breaking the Compassion Drought', *Meanjin* 79, 2 (2020), 9–13.

Goss, Theodora, *The Extraordinary Adventures of the Athena Club* [trilogy] (London: Saga Press, 2017–2019).

Gourguechon, Prudy, 'What No COVID Risk? No Climate Change? How to Overcome Toxic Denial', in Forbes (19 October 2020) <https://www.forbes.com/sites/prudygourguechon/2020/10/19/what-no-covid-risk-no-climate-change-how-to-overcome-toxic-denial/?sh=da285c133d92>, accessed 6 December 2020.

Graves, Allison, 'Politifact – Did Hillary Clinton Call African-American Youth "Superpredators?"', @Politifact (28 August 2016) <https://www.politifact.com/factchecks/2016/aug/28/reince-priebus/did-hillary-clinton-call-african-american-youth-su/>, accessed 28 October 2021.

Gray, Jonathan. 'New Audiences, New Textualities: Anti-fans and Non-fans', *International Journal of Cultural Studies*, 6 (2003), 64–81.

Greenhalgh, Trisha, and Brian Hurwitz B, 'Narrative Based Medicine: Why Study Narrative?', *British Medical Journal*, 318 (1999), 48–50.

GREVIO (Group of Experts on Action against Violence against Women and Domestic Violence), *Baseline Evaluation Report: Turkey* (France: Council of Europe, 2018) <https://rm.coe.int/eng-grevio-report-turquie/16808e5283>, accessed 29 September 2020.

Grossman, Lawrence, 'The Perversity of Intersectionality', American Jewish Community (21 March 2018) <https://www.ajc.org/news/the-perversity-of-intersectionality>, accessed 28 October 2021.

Gupta, Shubhra, 'Kabir Singh Movie Review: In the Mood for Misogyny', The Indian Express (21 June 2019) <https://indianexpress.com/article/entertainment/movie-review/kabir-singh-movie-review-rating-shahid-kapoor-5791976/>, accessed 14 December 2020.

Guterres, António, 'UN Urges People to #PledgetoPause Before Sharing Information', UN News (21 October 2020) <https://news.un.org/en/story/2020/10/1075742>, accessed 6 December 2020.

Habermas, Jurgen, *The Structural Transformation of the Public Sphere: An Inquiry into a Category of Bourgeois Society*, trans. Thomas Burger and Frederick Lawrence (Cambridge: Polity Press,1989).

Hadas, Leora, 'Resisting the Romance: "Shipping" and the Discourse of Genre Uniqueness in Doctor Who Fandom', *European Journal of Cultural Studies*, 16 (2013), 329–43.

Hagood, Mack, 'Disability and Biomediation: Tinnitus as Phantom Disability', in Elizabeth Ellcessor and Bill Kirkpatrick, eds, *Disability Media Studies* (New York: New York University Press, 2017), 311–29.

Halloween, dir. John Carpenter (Los Angeles: Compass International Pictures, 1978).

Halloween, dir. David Gordon Green (Los Angeles: Universal Pictures, 2018).

Hancock, Matt, 'Oral Statement on Coronavirus and the Government's Plans for Winter', Department for Health and Social Care (17 September 2020) <https://www.gov.uk/government/speeches/oral-statement-on-coronavirus-and-the-governments-plans-for-winter>, accessed 28 October 2021.

Hanna-Attisha, Mona, *What the Eyes Don't See: A Story of Crisis, Resistance and Hope in an American City* (New York: Random House, 2018).

Hannibal, created by Bryan Fuller (New York: National Broadcasting Company, 2013–2015).

Hansen, Per Krogh, 'Illness and Heroics: On Counter-narrative and Counter-metaphor in the Discourse on Cancer', *Frontiers of Narrative Studies*, 4, 1 (2018), 213–28.

Harari, Yuval Noah, *The Ultimate Experience: Battlefield Revelations and the Making of Modern War Culture, 1450–2000* (Houndmills: Palgrave MacMillan, 2008).

Harrington, Carol, 'What Is "Toxic Masculinity" and Why Does It Matter?', *Men and Masculinities* (2020) <https://doi.org/10.1177/1097184X20943254>, accessed 1 February 2022.

Harris, Noel, *Green Chemistry* (Waltham Abbey: ED-Tech Press, 2019).

Harrison, Rebecca, 'It's a Trap: Reylos, Racism, and the Whiteness of Data in the Harassment of Women Online', Medium (17 January 2020) <https://medium.com/@beccaeharrison/its-a-trap-reylos-racism-and-the-whiteness-of-data-in-the-harassment-of-women-online-be3a7fed040b>, accessed 12 November 2020.

Hawkins, Stan, and John Richardson, 'Remodeling Britney Spears: Matters of Intoxication and Mediation', *Popular Music and Society*, 30, 5 (2007) 605–29.

Heaf, Jonathan, 'This One Direction Interview Got Us Death Threats', GQ Magazine (23 August 2015) <https://www.gq-magazine.co.uk/article/one-direction-gq-covers-interview> accessed 11 February 2022.

Hefner, Peter J., *Cities of Affluence and Anger: A Literary Geography of Modern Englishness* (Charlottesville: University of Virginia Press, 2015).

Hesse, Monica, 'Ignorance about the Female Body Hurts Us All', The Seattle Times (13 May 2019) <https://www.seattletimes.com/opinion/ignorance-about-the-female-body-hurts-us-all/>, accessed 28 October 2021.

Hills, Matt, 'An Extended Foreword: From Fan Doxa to Toxic Fan Practices?', *Participations: Journal of Audience & Reception Studies*, 15, 1 (2018), 105–26.

Hinton, Devon E., and Byron J. Good, *Culture and PTSD: Trauma in Global and Historical Perspective* (Philadelphia: Pennsylvania State University Press, 2015).

Homeland, created by Alex Ganza and Howard Gordon (Los Angeles: 20th Television, 2011–2020).

How I Met Your Mother, 'Ten Sessions', Season 3, Episode 13, dir. Pamela Fryman (Los Angeles: 20th Television, 2008).

———, 'Everything Must Go', Season 3, Episode 19, dir. Pamela Fryman (Los Angeles: 20th Television, 2008).

Howard, Vickie, 'Recognising Narcissistic Abuse and the Implications for Mental Health Nursing Practice: Issues in Mental Health Nursing', 40, 8 (2019), 644–54.

Hyde, Marina, '"Over by Christmas": Now Where Have We Heard Johnson's New Slogan Before?', The Guardian (17 July 2020) <https://www.theguardian.com/commentisfree/2020/jul/17/christmas-johnson-slogan-prime-minister-pmqs>, accessed 28 October 2021.

Idle, Eric. 'Always look on the bright side of life', on *Monty Python Sings* (London: Virgin, 1989).

Illing, H. Paul A., *Toxicity and Risk: Context, Principles and Practice* (London: CRC Press, 2001).

IMDb, 'Most Popular Movies' (n.d.) <https://www.imdb.com/chart/moviemeter>, accessed 26 February 2022.

International Planned Parenthood Federation (IPPF), 'The Global Gag Rule and Its Impact in Kenya' (23 January 2019) <https://www.ippf.org/blogs/global-gag-rule-and-its-impact-kenya>, accessed 28 October 2021.

———, 'Global Gag Rule' (n.d.) <https://www.ippf.org/global-gag-rule>, accessed 1 February 2022.

Ioannidis, John, 'Coronavirus Disease 2019: The Harms of Exaggerated Information and Non-Evidence-based Measures', *The European Journal of Clinical Investigation* (9 April 2020) <https://www.ncbi.nlm.nih.gov/pmc/articles/PMC7163529/>, accessed 6 December 2020.

Iovine, John, *Scamdemic – The COVID-19 Agenda: The Liberal's Plot to Win the White House* (Staten Island, NY: Images Si Inc, 2020). Kindle edition B08DHMYQNK.

Irréversible, dir. Gaspar Noé (Paris: Studio Canal, 2002).

James, William, *The Principles of Psychology: Vol. 1* [1890] (New York: Dover, 1950).

Jameson, Frederic, *The Political Unconscious: Narrative as a Socially Symbolic Act* (Ithaca, NY: Cornell University Press, 2015).

Jane, Emma A., 'Gendered Cyberhate as Workplace Harassment and Economic Vandalism', *Feminist Media Studies*, 18, 4 (2018), 575–91.

Jardel, Jacob, 'Toxicity in Modern Nerd Culture', *Aggie Central* (20 February 2017) <http://aggiecentral.com/2017/02/toxicity-in-modern-nerd-culture/>, accessed 30 October 2020.

Jargon, Julie, 'Sadfishing, Predators and Bullies: The Hazards of Being "Real" on Social Media', *The Wall Street Journal* (12 November 2019).

Jha, Priyanka Sinha, 'Kabir Singh Movie Review: What a Fantastic Actor Shahid Kapoor has Turned Out to Be', News18 (21 June 2019) <https://www.news18.com/news/movies/kabir-singh-movie-review-what-a-fantastic-actor-shahid-kapoor-has-turned-out-to-be-2197987.html>, accessed 14 December 2020.

Johnson, Boris, 'Prime Minister's Statement on Coronavirus (COVID-19)', The Prime Minister's Office (17 March 2020) <https://www.gov.uk/government/speeches/pm-statement-on-coronavirus-17-march-2020>, accessed 28 October 2021.

Johnson, Kimberley R., and Bjarne M. Holme, 'Contradictory Messages: A Content Analysis of Hollywood-produced Romantic Comedy Feature Films', *Communication Quarterly*, 57, 3 (2009), 352–73.

Jones, Bethan, '"I Will Throw You Off Your Ship and You Will Drown and Die": Death Threats, Intra-fandom Hate, and the Performance of Fangirling', in Lucy Bennett and Paul Booth, eds, *Seeing Fans: Representations of Fandom in Media and Popular Culture* (New York: Bloomsbury, 2016), 53–66.

Jones, Eric E., Alex T. Ramsey, Eric D. Wesselmann, Heather Jaffe Rosenthal and Matthew S. Hesson-McInnis, 'Being Ostracized Versus Out of the Loop: Redundant or Unique Predictors of Variance in Workplace Outcomes?', *Journal of Applied Social Psychology* (20 August 2020). doi.org/10.1111/jasp.12712

Jones, Leslie, @Lesdoggg, 6.44 a.m., Twitter (19 July 2016) <https://twitter.com/Lesdoggg/status/755261962674696192?s=20>, accessed 23 September 2020.

Joseph, Sue, 'Interrogating Empathy in Two Long Form Texts: A Comparative Textual Analysis of Trauma Affect', *Journalism* (8 August 2020) <https://doi.org/10.1177/1464884920949343>, accessed 1 February 2022.

Just, Julie, 'The Parent Problem in Young Adult Lit', The New York Times, Book Review (1 April 2010) <https://www.nytimes.com/2010/04/04/books/review/Just-t.html>, accessed 7 November 2020.

Kabir Singh, dir. Sandeep Reddy Vanga (Mumbai: Cine1 Studios & T-Series, 2019).

Kahan, Dan, 'Protecting or Polluting the Science Communication Environment? The Case of Childhood Vaccines', in Kathleen Hall Jamieson, Dan M. Kahan and Dietram A. Scheufele, eds, *The Oxford Handbook of the Science of Science Communication* (Oxford: Oxford University Press, 2017), 421–32.

Kaiser Family Foundation, 'The Mexico City Policy: An Explainer' (28 January 2021) <https://www.kff.org/global-health-policy/fact-sheet/mexico-city-policy-explainer/>, accessed 28 October 2021.

Kandiyoti, Deniz, 'Locating the Politics of Gender: Patriarchy, Neo-liberal Governance and Violence in Turkey', in *Research and Policy on Turkey*, 1, 2 (2016), 103–18.

Kaplan, Ann E., *Trauma Culture: The Politics of Terror and Loss in Media and Literature* (New Brunswick, NJ: Rutgers University Press, 2005).

Kaufman, Gil, '#FreeBritney: Why the Movement Started and How Its Leading Voices Are Keeping It Going', Billboard (9 October 2020) <https://www.billboard.com/articles/news/9445049/free-britney-spears-movement-started?utm_medium=social&utm_source=twitter>, accessed 25 October 2020.

Kaya, Tebrike, 'Televizyonda Yayinlanan Izdivac Programlarinda Toplumsal Cinsiyetin Temsili' [Gender Representations in Marriage Programmes on Television], *Kadin Arastirmalari Dergisi*, 13 (2013), 81–110.

Kearney, Amanda, *Violence in Place: Cultural and Environmental Wounding* (New York: Routledge, 2017).

Khan, Kamaal R., 'Kabir Singh | Review by KRK', YouTube (20 June 2019) <https://youtu.be/EabeMPX6ftA>, accessed 14 December 2020.

Khazan, Olga, 'Why Do Women Bully Each Other at Work?', The Atlantic (3 August 2017) <https://www.theatlantic.com/magazine/archive/2017/09/the-queen-bee-in-the-corner-office/534213/>, accessed 28 October 2021.

Kilicbay, Baris Bora, *Turkiye'de Gerceklik Televizyonu ve Yeni Televizyon Kulturu* [Reality TV in Turkey and the New TV Culture], PhD Dissertation (2005) <https://dspace.ankara.edu.tr/xmlui/bitstream/handle/20.500.12575/28308/2339.pdf?sequence=1>, accessed 25 August 2020.

King, Deborah K., 'Multiple Jeopardy, Multiple Consciousness: The Context of a Black Feminist Ideology', *Signs*, 14, 1 (1988): 42–72.

Kingsman: The Secret Service, dir. Matthew Vaughn (Century City, CA: 20th Century Fox, 2015).

Klasing, Amanda, 'US Blocks Funds to UN Population Fund – Again' (n.d.) <https://www.hrw.org/node/315887/printable/print>, accessed 1 February 2022.

Klein, Charlotte, 'Trump's COVID Denialism Reaches New Heights With Packed Indoor Rally', Vanity Fair (14 September 2020) <https://www.vanityfair.com/news/2020/09/trumps-covid-denialism-reaches-new-heights-with-packed-indoor-rally>, accessed 6 December 2020.

Klein, Melanie, 'Notes on Some Schizoid Mechanisms', *Journal of Psychoanalysis*, 27 (1946), 99–110.

Knott-Dawson, ShaRhonda, 'The Suffragettes Were Not Allies to Black Women, They Were Racist', Education Post (26 August 2019) <https://educationpost.org/the-suffragettes-were-not-allies-to-black-women-they-were-racist/>, accessed 28 October 2021.

Kohlt, Franziska E., '"Over by Christmas": The Impact of War-metaphors and Other Science-religion Narratives on Science Communication Environments during the Covid-19 Crisis', *SocArXiv Papers* (9 November 2020). doi: 10.31235/osf.io/z5s6a

Korkut, Umut, and Hande Eslen-Ziya, 'The Discursive Governance of Population Politics: The Evolution of a Pro-birth Regime in Turkey', *Social Politics*, 23, 4 (2016), 555–75.

Kotecha, Ronak, 'Kabir Singh Movie Review', Times of India (20 June 2019) <https://timesofindia.indiatimes.com/entertainment/hindi/movie-reviews/kabir-singh/movie-review/69879261.cms>, accessed 14 December 2020.

Kotton, Vikki, 'A Look at a Greatly Misunderstood Mental Illness – Borderline Personality Disorder', *Mental Health Matters*, 4, 2 (2017), 38–40.

Kozol, Wendy, 'White Privilege and the Pink Pussy Hat', Medium (4 March 2017) <https://medium.com/vantage/white-privilege-and-the-pussy-hat-a282f98d9a02>, accessed 28 October 2021.

Kreizman, Maris, 'I Was Rooting for Ghostbusters. I Didn't Think the Trolls Could Win', Esquire (15 December 2016) <https://www.esquire.com/entertainment/movies/a51593/ghostbusters-2016-canon/>, accessed 23 September 2020.

Krieger, Lisa M., 'Stanford Researcher Says Coronavirus Isn't as Fatal as We Thought; Critics Say He's Missing the Point', in The Mercury News (21 May 2020) <https://www.mercurynews.com/2020/05/20/stanford-researcher-says-coronavirus-isnt-as-fatal-as-we-thought-critics-say-hes-missing-the-point>, accessed 6 December 2020.

Kristeva, Julia, *Powers of Horror: An Essay on Abjection*, trans. Leon S. Roudiez (New York: Columbia University Press, 1982).

Krolокke, Charlotte, and Anne Scott Sørensen, *Gender Communication Theories and Analyses: From Silence to Performance* (Thousand Oaks, CA: Sage, 2006).

Krouse, Sarah, 'Covid-19 Disbelief Saddles Health-care Workers with Another Challenge', *The Wall Street Journal* (3 December 2020).

LaBelle, Brandon, 'Invisibilities', in Ruthie Abeliovich and Edwin Seroussi, eds, *Borderlines: Essays on Mapping and the Logic of Place* (Warsaw: Sciendo, 2019), 187–99.

Lacan, Jacques, *Seminar IV: Relation to Object* [1956] (Paris: Seuil, 1991), 118–95.

Lakoff, George, and Mark Johnson, *Metaphors We Live By* [1980] (Chicago: University of Chicago Press, 2003).

Lambert, Frank, *The Founding Fathers and the Place of Religion in America* (Princeton, NJ: Princeton University Press, 2003).

The Lancet, 'The Devastating Impact of Trump's Global Gag Rule', 393, 10189 (2019) <https://www.thelancet.com/journals/lancet/article/PIIS0140-6736(19)31355-8/fulltext>, accessed 28 October 2021.

———, 'The Erosion of Women's Sexual and Reproductive Rights', 396, 10183 (2019) <https://www.thelancet.com/journals/lancet/article/PIIS0140-6736(19)30990-0/fulltext>, accessed 28 October 2021.

The Last Winter, dir. Larry Fessenden (New York: Antidote Films, 2006).

Lavie, Noa, 'Justifying Trash: Regulating Reality TV in Israel', *Television & New Media*, 20, 3 (2019), 219–40.

Lavin, Will, 'Bill Murray Says Filming "Ghostbusters: Afterlife" Was "Physically Painful"', NME (7 April 2021) <https://www.nme.com/news/film/bill-murray-says-filming-ghostbusters-afterlife-was-physically-painful-2914319>, accessed 28 October 2021.

Lay, Genziana, 'Understanding Relational Dysfunction in Borderline, Narcissistic, and Antisocial Personality Disorders: Considerations, Presentation of Three Case Studies, and Implications for Therapeutic Intervention', *Psychology Research*, 9, 8 (2019), 303–18.

Lebbon, Tim, *The Silence* (London: Titan Books, 2015).

Ledder, Simon, 'Evolve Today! Human Enhancement Technologies in the BioShock Universe', in Luke Cuddy, ed., *BioShock and Philosophy: Irrational Game, Rational Book* (Chichester: John Wiley & Sons, 2015), 150–60.
Lee, Nam, *The Films of Bong Joon Ho* (New Brunswick, NJ: Rutgers University Press, 2020).
Limpár, Ildikó, 'Masculinity, Visibility and the Vampire Literary Tradition in What We Do in the Shadows', *Journal for the Fantastic in the Arts*, 29, 2 (2018), 266–88.
Linz, Daniel G., and Edward Donnerstein, 'Sex and Violence in Slasher Films: A Reinterpretation', *Journal of Broadcasting & Electronic Media*, 38, 2 (1994), 243–6.
Lippman, Julia R., 'I Did It because I Never Stopped Loving You: The Effects of Media Portrayals of Persistent Pursuit on Beliefs about Stalking', *Communication Research*, 16 (2015). doi:10.1177/0093650215570653
Lockhart, Eleanor Amaranth, *Nerd/Geek Masculinity: Technocracy, Rationality, and Gender in Nerd Culture's Countermasculine Hegemony* [PhD dissertation] (College Station: Texas A&M University, 2015).
Loeb, Jeph, and Geoff Johns, 'The House of Dracula', *Superman*, 2, 180 (New York: DC Comics, 2002).
Lofgren, Eric T., and Fefferman, Nina H, 'The Untapped Potential of Virtual Game Worlds to Shed Light on Real World Epidemics', *The Lancet: Infectious Diseases*, 7 (2007), 625–9.
Loja, Ema, Maria Emília Costa, Bill Hughes and Isabel Menezes, 'Disability, Embodiment and Ableism: Stories of Resistance', *Disability & Society*, 28, 2 (2013), 190–203.
Lomaia, Natalia, 'Toxic Positivity in the Context of Lacanian Psychoanalysis', Sapereaude Magazine (n.d) <http:saperaudemagazine.com/toxic-positivity-in-the-context-of-lacanian-psychoanalysis>, accessed 24 November 2020.
Lopez, Ricardo, 'Jordan Peele on How He Tackled Systemic Racism as Horror in *Get Out*', Variety (1 November 2017) <https://variety.com/2017/film/news/jordan-peele-get-out-systemic-racism-1202604824/>, accessed 22 October 2020.
Love Actually, dir. Richard Curtis (Universal City, CA: Universal Pictures, 2003).
Lowe, Melanie, 'Colliding Feminisms: Britney Spears, "Tweens," and the Politics of Reception', *Popular Music & Society*, 26, 2 (2003), 123–40.
Lowenstein, Adam, *Shocking Representations: Historical Trauma, National Cinema and Modern Horror Film* (New York: Columbia University Press, 2005).
Lukin, Konatantin, 'Toxic Positivity: Don't Always Look on the Bright Side', Psychology Today (1 August 2019) <https://www.psychologytoday.com/us/blog/the-man-cave/201908/toxic-positivity-dont-always-look-the-bright-side>, accessed 18 November 2020.
Lumsden, Karen, and Heather Morgan, 'Media Framing of Trolling and Online Abuse: Silencing Strategies, Symbolic Violence, and Victim Blaming', *Feminist Media Studies*, 17, 6 (2017), 926–40.

Lutgen-Sandvik, Pamela, Elizabeth A. Dickinson and Karen A. Foss, 'Priming, Painting, Peeling, and Polishing: Constructing the Woman-Bullying-Woman Identity at Work', in Suzy Fox and Terri R. Lituchy, eds, *Gender and the Dysfunctional Workplace* (Northampton: Edward Elgar Publishing, 2012).

MacCammon, Sarah, 'Planned Parenthood Withdraws From Title X Program Over Trump Abortion Rule', NPR (19 August 2019) <https://www.npr.org/2019/08/19/752438119/planned-parenthood-out-of-title-x-over-trump-rule?t=1634971074402>, accessed 28 October 2021.

Madrigal, Alexis C., and Whet Moser, 'How Many Americans Are About to Die?', The Atlantic (19 November 2020) <https://www.theatlantic.com/science/archive/2020/11/coronavirus-death-rate-third-surge/617150/>, accessed 6 December 2020.

Maier, Kodi, 'Princess Brides and Dream Weddings: Investigating the Gendered Narrative of Disney's Fairy Tale Weddings', in Amy M. Davis, ed., *Discussing Disney* (New Barnett: John Libbey Publishing, 2019).

Malerman, Josh, *Bird Box* (London: Harper Collins, 2014).

Manchester, Julia, 'David Duke: Charlottesville Protests about "Fulfilling Promises of Donald Trump"', The Hill (8 August 2017) <https://thehill.com/blogs/blog-briefing-room/news/346326-david-duke-charlottesville-protests-about-fulfilling-promises>, accessed 3 November 2020.

Manson, Mark, *The Subtle Art of Not Giving a F*ck: A Counterintuitive Approach to Living a Good Life* (New York: HarperOne, 2016).

Manzoni, Alessandro, *The Betrothed: A Tale of XVII Century Milan* [1827], trans. Archibald Colquhoun (New York: Alfred A. Knopf, 2013).

Martyrs, dir. Pascal Laugier (Berlin: Wild Bunch, 2008).

Marx, Karl, 'Speech at the Anniversary of the People's Paper' [1856], *Marx/Engels Selected Works Vol. I* (Moscow: Progress Publishers, 1969), 500.

Masand, Rajeev, 'Kabir Singh Movie Review: Arjun Reddy Remake is Unapologetic Celebration of Toxic Masculinity', News18 (21 June 2019) <https://www.news18.com/news/movies/kabir-singh-movie-review-arjun-reddy-remake-is-an-unapologetic-celebration-of-toxic-masculinity-2198859.html>, accessed 14 December 2020.

Matloff, Jason, 'An Oral History of Ghostbusters', Esquire (24 February 2014) <https://www.esquire.com/entertainment/movies/news/a27498/ghostbusters-oral-history/>, accessed 26 August 2020.

McCallum, Corie, 'Exploring Federal Financial Aid Networks: Who Cares and Why', in Joel Spring, John Ferguson, Corie McCallum and Diane Price-Banks, eds, *The Business of Education: Networks of Power and Wealth in America* (New York: Routledge, 2018), 105–7.

McCann, Hannah, 'Is there Anything "Toxic" about Femininity? The Rigid Femininities that Keep Us Locked In', *Psychology & Sexuality* (2020). doi: 10.1080/19419899.2020.1785534

McCort, K. M., 'When Systemic Hatred of Women Online Goes Unnoticed, What Does It Say About Us?', Medium (15 January 2020) <https://medium.com/@KMMcCort/when-systemic-hatred-of-women-online-goes-unnoticed-what-does-it-say-about-us-930cccb683e0>, accessed 12 November 2020.

McElwee, Sean, 'Data for Politics #14: Who is Trump's Base?', Data for Progress (23 August 2018) <https://www.dataforprogress.org/blog/2018/8/21/data-for-politics-14-who-is-trumps-base>, accessed 7 November 2020.

McGuire, Seanan, *Every Heart a Doorway: Wayward Children 1* (New York: Tom Doherty Associates, 2016).

―――, *Down Among the Sticks and Bones: Wayward Children 2* (New York: Tom Doherty Associates, 2017).

―――, *Beneath the Sugar Sky: Wayward Children 3* (New York: Tom Doherty Associates, 2018).

―――, *In an Absent Dream: Wayward Children 4* (New York: Tom Doherty Associates, 2019).

―――, *Come Tumbling Down: Wayward Children 5* (New York: Tom Doherty Associates, 2020).

McIntosh, Jonathan. 'Buffy vs. Edward: Twilight Remixed [original version]', YouTube (20 June 2009) <https://www.youtube.com/watch?v=RZwM3GvaTRM&t=2s>, accessed 1 November 2020.

―――, 'The Adorkable Misogyny of The Big Bang Theory', YouTube (31 August 2017a) <https://www.youtube.com/watch?v=X3-hOigoxHs>, accessed 2 November 2020.

―――, 'The Complicity of Geek Masculinity on the Big Bang Theory', YouTube (29 September 2017b) <https://www.youtube.com/watch?v=7L7NRONADJ4>, accessed 2 November 2020.

McKernan, Bethan, 'Murder in Turkey Sparks Outrage over Rising Violence against Women', The Guardian (23 July 2020) <https://www.theguardian.com/world/2020/jul/23/turkey-outrage-rising-violence-against-women>, accessed 29 September 2020.

McLaren, Peter, 'Religious Nationalism and the Coronavirus Pandemic: Soul-Sucking Evangelicals and Branch Covidians Make America Sick Again', *Postdigital Science and Education* (19 May 2020) <https://www.ncbi.nlm.nih.gov/pmc/articles/PMC7234870/>, accessed 6 December 2020.

McQuiston, Erin Schroyer, *Toxic Gardens: Narratives of Toxicity in Twentieth-century American and British Fiction*, PhD Thesis, University of Illinois at

Urbana-Champaign (2014) <https://www.ideals.illinois.edu/bitstream/handle/2142/72966/Erin_McQuiston.pdf?...1> accessed 26 February 2022.

McSweeney, Leah, and Jacob Siegel, 'Is the Women's March Melting Down?', Tablet Magazine (11 December 2018) <https://www.tabletmag.com/sections/news/articles/is-the-womens-march-melting-down>, accessed 28 October 2021.

Mean Girls, dir. Mark Waters (Hollywood, CA: Paramount Pictures, 2004).

Men Behind the Sun, dir. Tun Fei Mou (Hong Kong: Sil-Metropole Organization, 1988).

Menakem, Resmaa, *My Grandmother's Hands: Racialized Trauma and the Pathway to Mending Our Hearts and Bodies* (Las Vegas: Central Recovery Press, 2017).

Merriam-Webster.com, 'Toxicity' [Def. a and b] (n.d.) <https://www.merriam-webster.com/dictionary/toxicity>, accessed 30 July 2020.

Meyer, Robinson, and Alexis C. Madrigal, 'The U.S. Has Passed the Hospital Breaking Point', The Atlantic (4 December 2020) <https://www.theatlantic.com/health/archive/2020/12/the-worst-case-scenario-is-happening-hospitals-are-overwhelmed/617301/>, accessed 6 December 2020.

Miéville, China, *The City & the City* (London: Pan Books, 2009).

Mirken, Bruce, 'COVID Denial Is a Grim Rerun of AIDS Denialism', 48hills, 17 November (2020) <https://48hills.org/2020/11/covid-denial-is-a-grim-rerun-of-aids-denialism/>, accessed 6 December 2020.

Mitchell, Stephen, *The Selected Poetry of Maria Rainer Rilke* (New York: Knopf Doubleday, 1989).

Moreno, Carmen, Til Wykes, Silvana Galderisi et al., 'How Mental Health Care Should Change as a Consequence of the COVID-19 Pandemic', *The Lancet Psychiatry*, 7, 9 (2020), 813–24.

Morton, Timothy, *Hyperobjects: Philosophy and Ecology After the End of the World* (Minneapolis: University of Minnesota Press, 2014).

Moss, Richard, 'Want to See Gaming's Past and Future? Dive into the "Educational" World of PLATO', Ars Technica (29 October 2016) <https://arstechnica.com/gaming/2016/10/want-to-see-gamings-past-and-future-dive-into-the-educational-world-of-plato/>, accessed 9 September 2020.

Motz, Anna, 'Female Violence and Toxic Couples', *Psychoanalytic Psychotherapy*, 29, 3 (2015), 228–42.

MSNBC, 'Arkansas cases climb TRANSCRIPT', 26 May (2020) <https://www.msnbc.com/transcripts/msnbc-live/2020-05-26-msna1362326>, accessed 6 December 2020.

MSNBC News, 'Meacham: By Politicizing Facemasks, Trump Has "Managed to Weaponize the Deaths of 100,000 People"' (2020) <https://www.msnbc.com/msnbc/watch/meacham-by-politicizing-facemasks-trump-has-managed-to-weaponize-the-deaths-of-100-000-people-83934277756>, accessed 1 February 2022.

Muller, Denis, *Journalism Ethics for the Digital Age* (Melbourne: Scribe Publications, 2014).

Mulvey, Laura, 'Visual Pleasure and Narrative Cinema', *Screen*, 16, 3 (1975), 6–18.

Musial, Jennifer, 'We're Country': Britney Spears, Southern White Femininity, and the American Dream', *Feminist Formations*, 31, 3 (2019), 72–94.

Neilsen, Kate, *Toxic Ecologies: Contamination and Transgression in Victorian Fiction, 1851–1900* [Dissertation] (Boston: Boston University, 2018) <https://www.proquest.com/openview/f2007351c4896c72faab8f6a992d42ba/1.pdf?pq-origsite=gscholar&cbl=18750>, accessed 28 October 2021.

Newnes, Craig, 'Toxic Psychology', in Mark Rapley, Joanna Moncrieff and Jacqui Dillon, eds, *De-medicalizing Misery: Psychiatry, Psychology and the Human Condition* (Basingstoke: Palgrave MacMillan, 2011), 211–25.

Nie, Jing-Bao, Adam Lloyd Gilbertson, Malcom de Roubaix, Ciara Staunton, Anton van Niekerk, Joseph D. Tucker and Stuart Rennie, 'Healing Without Waging War: Beyond Military Metaphors in Medicine and HIV Cure Research', *American Journal for Bioethics*, 10 (2016), 3–11.

North, Anna, 'The Women's March Changed the American Left. Now Anti-Semitism Allegations Threaten the Group's Future', Vox (21 December 2018) <https://www.vox.com/identities/2018/12/21/18145176/feminism-womens-march-2018-2019-farrakhan-intersectionality>, accessed 28 October 2021.

O'Connor, Cailin, and James Weatherall, 'Why False Claims About COVID-19 Refuse to Die', Nautilus (16 April 2020) <http://nautil.us/issue/84/outbreak/why-false-claims-about-covid_19-refuse-to-die>, accessed 6 December 2020.

Okwonga, Musa, 'You Cannot Sing "Rule Britannia" to a Virus', Byline Times (19 March 2020) <https://bylinetimes.com/2020/03/19/you-cannot-sing-rule-britannia-to-a-virus/>, accessed 28 October 2021.

The Originals, created by Julie Plec (Santa Monica, CA: CBS Television Distribution, 2013–2018).

Oxford Languages, 'Word of the Year 2018' (n.d.) <https://languages.oup.com/word-of-the-year/2018/> accessed 1 February 2022.

Padilla, Art, Robert Hogan and Robert B. Kaiser, 'The Toxic Triangle: Destructive Leaders, Susceptible Followers, and Conducive Environments', *The Leadership Quarterly*, 18, 3 (2007), 176–94.

Page, Clarence, 'How White Supremacy Morphed Into White 'Victimization', Daily Advertiser (17 August 2017) <https://www.theadvertiser.com/story/opinion/columnists/2017/08/17/how-white-supremacy-morphed-into-white-victimization/572210001/>, accessed 2 November 2020.

Pande, Rukmini, *Squee from the Margins* (Iowa City: University of Iowa Press, 2018).

———, *Fandom: Now in Color* (Iowa City, University of Iowa Press, 2020).

Paradise Hills, dir. Alice Waddington (Barcelona: Nostromo Pictures, 2019).

Parasite, dir. Bong Joon Ho (Paris: MK2 Films, 2019).
Pardun, Carol J., Kelly Ladin L'Engle and Jane D. Brown, 'Linking Exposure to Outcomes: Early Adolescents' Consumption of Sexual Content in Six Media', *Mass Communication & Society*, 8 (2005), 75–91.
Parnes, Jakub, 'Internet Media as the Digital Public Sphere: Possibilities and Problems', *Central European Journal of Communication*, 9, 16 (2016): 90–103.
Parsons, Linda T, 'Ella Evolving: Cinderella Stories and the Construction of Gender Appropriate Behavior', *Children's Literature in Education*, 35, 2 (2004), 135–54.
Pascal, Blaise, 'Pensée 162', Project Gutenberg (1669) <https://www.gutenberg.org/files/18269/18269-h/18269-h.htm>, accessed 30 November 2020.
Paskvalin, Jadranka, *Order, Chaos, and the City: Space and Urban Forms into the Twenty First Century* [Thesis] (Winnipeg: Manitoba University, 1998).
Paz, Christian, 'All the President's Lies About the Coronavirus', The Atlantic (2 November 2020) <https://www.theatlantic.com/politics/archive/2020/11/trumps-lies-about-coronavirus/608647/>, accessed 6 December 2020.
Paszkiewicz, Katarzyna and Stacy Rusnak, eds, *Final Girls, Feminism and Popular Culture* (Basingstoke: Palgrave Macmillan, 2020).
PBS (Public Service Broadcasting), 'The Impact of the Pipeline on Alaska Natives' (n.d.) <https://www.pbs.org/wgbh/americanexperience/features/pipeline-impact-pipeline-alaska-natives/>, accessed 30 August 2020.
Peck, Tom, 'It'll be Over by Christmas, Says Boris Johnson, As Long As You All Wish Hard Enough', The Independent (17 July 2020) <https://www.independent.co.uk/voices/boris-johnson-coronavirus-infections-deaths-christmas-care-homes-a9624661.html>, accessed 1 February 2022.
Pennycook, Gordon, Jonathon McPhetres, Yunhao Zhang, Jackson G. Lu and David G. Rand, 'Fighting COVID-19 Misinformation on Social Media: Experimental Evidence for a Scalable Accuracy-Nudge Intervention', *Psychological Science*, 31, 7 (2020): 770–80.
Perrault, Charles, 'Cinderella; or, The Little Glass Slipper', *The Blue Fairy Book*, trans. Andrew Lang [1697] (London: Longmans, Green, and Co, 1889), 64–71.
PerryUndem, 'Voters' Views on Abortion Policy: With Emphasis on the New Supreme Court and State-level Access', 16 January (2019) <https://view.publitas.com/perryundem-research-communication/2019-abortion-policy/page/1/>, accessed 28 October 2021.
Peryakoil, Vejayanthi S., 'Using Metaphors in Medicine', *Journal of Palliative Medicine*, 11, 6 (2008), 842–44.
Petre, Johnathan, 'New DAUK/HMC Report Identifies Latest Online Trends', HMC Press Office, 1 October (2019) <https://www.hmc.org.uk/blog/new-daukhmc-report-identifies-latest-online-trends/>, accessed 7 September 2020.

Petroni, S., *Research Proposal: The Politics of US International Family Planning Policy* [Unpublished] (George Washington University, 2008).
Pew Research Center, 'Trends in Party Affiliation among Demographic Groups' (20 March 2018) <https://www.pewresearch.org/politics/2018/03/20/1-trends-in-party-affiliation-among-demographic-groups/>, accessed 11 February 2022.
Phelan, James, 'Rhetoric/Ethics', in David Herman, ed., *Cambridge Companion to Narrative* (Cambridge: Cambridge University Press, 2007), 203–16.
Phillips, Whitney, *This Is Why We Can't Have Nice Things: Mapping the Relationship Between Online Trolling and Mainstream Culture* (London: The MIT Press, 2015).
Pitchfork, 'Top 50 Singles of 2004' (n.d.) <https://pitchfork.com/features/lists-and-guides/5933-top-50-singles-of-2004/?page=5>, accessed 25 October 2020.
Pizarro-Sirera, Margalida, 'Toxic Masculinity in American Politics: Donald Trump's Tweeting Activity in the US Presidential Election (2016)', *European Journal of American Culture*, 39, 2 (2020), 163–81.
Planned Parenthood Global, *Assessing the Global Gag Rule: Harms to Health, Communities, and Advocacy* (n.d.-a) <https://www.plannedparenthood.org/uploads/filer_public/81/9d/819d9000-5350-4ea3-b699-1f12d59ec67f/181231-ggr-d09.pdf>, accessed 1 February 2022.
———, 'What Is the Global Gag Rule?' (n.d.-b) <https://www.plannedparenthoodaction.org/communities/planned-parenthood-global/end-global-gag-rule>, accessed 1 February 2022.
Plohy, Serhii, *Chernobyl: History of a Tragedy* (London: Allen Lane, 2018).
Popper, Pamela A., and Shane D. Prier, *COVID Operation: What Happened, Why It Happened, and What's Next* (Zanesville: Proving Press, 2020).
Pozner, Jennifer, *Reality Bites Back: The Troubling Truth About Guilty Pleasure TV* (Berkeley, CA: Seal Press, 2010).
Prakash, Nitya, ' "Kabir Singh" Review: Visually Compelling, Haunting Performances and Nuanced Writing Make It a Must Watch', Bombay Weekly (19 June 2019) <https://bombayweekly.com/kabir-singh-review-visually-compelling-haunting-performances-and-nuanced-writing-make-it-a-must-watch/>, accessed 14 December 2020.
Projansky, Sarah, *Watching Rape: Film and Television in Postfeminist Culture* (New York: New York University Press, 2001).
Prystash, Justin, ' "The Misplaced Familiar": Aesthetic Crisis in China Miéville's *The City & the City*', *Concentric: Literary and Cultural Studies*, 43, 2 (2017), 275–95.
The Psychology Group, 'Toxic Positivity' (2019) <http:thepsychologygroup.com/toxic-positivity>, accessed 21 November 2020.
Pushkin, Aleksandr, 'The Bronze Horseman' [1833], trans. Yevgeny Bonver (2004–2005), Poetry Lovers' Page <https://www.poetryloverspage.com/poets/pushkin/bronze_horseman.html>, accessed 30 November 2020.

The Pussyhat Project, 'Our Story' (n.d.) <https://www.pussyhatproject.com/our-story>, accessed 28 October 2021.

Quinn, Holly, 'Racism in the Star Wars fandom: The Tumblr Years', Diverse High Fantasy (15 January 2020) <https://diversehighfantasy.tumblr.com/post/190278683781/racism-in-the-star-wars-fandom-the-tumblr-years>, accessed 18 November 2020.

Quintero, Samara, and Jamie Long, 'Toxic Positivity: The Dark Side of Positive Vibe', The Psychology Group for Lauderdale (2019) <https://thepsychologygroup.com/toxic-positivity/>, accessed 28 October 2021.

Raheja, Michelle. H., *Reservation Reelism: Redfacing, Visual Sovereignty, and Representations of Native Americans in Film* (Lincoln: University of Nebraska Press, 2011).

Rai, Kavita, 'Women's March Controversy Illuminates Why We Need Intersectionality', Brown Girl Magazine (22 January 2019) <https://browngirlmagazine.com/2019/01/womens-march-controversy-illuminates-why-we-need-intersectionality/>, accessed 28 October 2021.

Ravenous, dir. Antonia Bird (Los Angeles: 20th Century Fox, 1999).

Real Genius, dir. Martha Coolidge (Los Angeles: Tristar Pictures, 1985).

Redcay, Alex, and Christina Simonetti, 'Criteria for Love and Relationship Addiction: Distinguishing Love Addiction from Other Substance and Behavioral Addictions', *Sexual Addiction & Compulsivity*, 25, 1 (2018), 80–95.

Redden, Guy, 'Is Reality TV Neoliberal?', *Television & New Media*, 19, 5 (2018), 399–414.

Reed, Gail S., ed., *On Freud's Screen Memories* (London: Routledge, 2014).

Reinstein, Mara, 'I Lost Myself', *US Weekly*, 3 December 2008.

Revenge of the Nerds, dir. Jeff Kanew (Los Angeles: Twentieth Century Fox, 1984).

Richardson, Ian, 'Fact Check: CDC Estimates COVID-19 Death Rate Around 0.26%, Doesn't Confirm It', USA Today (5 June 2020) <https://www.usatoday.com/story/news/factcheck/2020/06/05/fact-check-cdc-estimates-covid-19-death-rate-0-26/5269331002/>, accessed 6 December 2020.

Rieser, Klaus, 'Masculinity and Monstrosity: Characterization and Identification in the Slasher Film', *Men and Masculinities*, 3, 4 (2001), 370–92.

Risam, Roopika, 'Toxic Femininity 4.0', First Monday, 20, 4 (2015) <https://firstmonday.org/article/view/5896/4417>, accessed 1 February 2022.

Robbett, Andrea, and Peter Hans Matthews, 'The Partisan Pandemic: Do We Now Live in Alternative Realities?' The Conversation (20 August 2020) <https://theconversation.com/the-partisan-pandemic-do-we-now-live-in-alternative-realities-140290>, accessed 6 December 2020.

Robeznieks, Andis, 'Why the Supreme Court Should Take Up Title X Gag Rule Case', AMA, 1 October (2020) <https://www.ama-assn.org/delivering-care/patient-support-advocacy/why-supreme-court-should-take-title-x-gag-rule-case>, accessed 28 October 2021.

Robinson, Joanna. 'How Buffy the Vampire Slayer's Most Hated Season Became Its Most Important', Vanity Fair (10 March 2017) <https://www.vanityfair.com/hollywood/2017/03/buffy-season-6-anniversary-warren-jonathan-andrew>, accessed 30 October 2020.

Rogers, M. Brooke, and Julia M. Pearce, 'Risk Communication, Risk Perception and Behavior as Foundations of Effective National Security Practices', *Strategic Intelligence Management*, 9 (2013), 66–74.

Rolling Stone, 'The 100 Greatest Debut Singles of All Time' (19 May 2020) <https://www.rollingstone.com/music/music-lists/greatest-debut-songs-singles-990470/the-smiths-hand-in-glove-991045>, accessed 25 October 2020.

Rosenberg, Lizzy, 'Britney Spears Can't Get Remarried for Legal Reasons #FreeBritney', Distractify (31 March 2021) <https://www.distractify.com/p/why-cant-britney-spears-remarry>, accessed 25 October 2021.

Roth, Andrew, 'Russian TV to Air its own Patriotic Retelling of Chernobyl Story', The Guardian (7 June 2019) <https://www.theguardian.com/world/2019/jun/07/chernobyl-hbo-russian-tv-remake>, accessed 30 November 2020.

Rothberg, Michael, *Multidirectional Memory: Remembering the Holocaust in the Age of Decolonization* (Stanford, CA: Stanford University Press, 2009).

Rotten Tomatoes, 'Parasite' (n.d.) <https://www.rottentomatoes.com/m/parasite_2019>, accessed 10 September 2020.

Rowling, J. K., *Harry Potter and the Philosopher's Stone* (London: Bloomsbury, 1997).

Rushdie, Salman, 'Reality TV: A Dearth of Talent and the Death of Morality', The Guardian (9 June 2001) <https://www.theguardian.com/books/2001/jun/09/salmanrushdie/>, accessed 10 September 2020.

Ryan-Bryant, Jennifer, 'The Cinematic Rhetorics of Lynching in Jordan Peele's *Get Out*', *The Journal of Popular Culture*, 53 (2020), 92–110.

Ryrie, Alec, 'Our Sacred Story', BBC Radio 4 (7 November 2020) <https://www.bbc.co.uk/programmes/m000p60n>, accessed 28 October 2021.

Sadeghi, Nakisa B., and Leana S Wen, 'After Title X Regulation Changes: Difficult Questions For Policymakers And Providers', *Health Affairs* (24 September 2019) <https://www.healthaffairs.org/do/10.1377/hblog20190923.813004/full/>, accessed 28 October 2021.

Salò, or the 120 Days of Sodom, dir. Pier Paolo Pasolini (Rome: Produzioni Europee Associati, 1975).

Salter, Anastasia, and Bridgett Blodgett, *Toxic Geek Masculinity in Media: Sexism, Trolling, and Identity Politics* (London: Palgrave, 2017).

Salter, Michael, 'The Problem with a Fight against Toxic Masculinity' The Atlantic (27 February 2019) <https://www.theatlantic.com/health/archive/2019/02/toxic-masculinity-history/583411/>, accessed 27 November 2020.

Sarathy, Brinda, Vivienne Hamilton and Janet Farrell Brodie, *Inevitably Toxic: Historical Perspectives on Contamination, Exposure, and Expertise* (Pittsburgh: University of Pittsburgh Press, 2018).
Sarkar, Abhishek, 'Haider and the Nation-State: Shakespeare, Hollywood, and Kashmir', *South Asian Review*, 37, 2 (2016), 29–46.
Say, Lale, Doris Chou, Alison Gemmill et al., 'Global Causes of Maternal Death: A WHO Systematic Analysis', *Lancet Global Health*, 2, 6 (2014), e323–e333.
Say Anything, dir. Cameron Crowe (Century City, CA: 20th Century Fox, 1989).
Scaggs, John, *Crime Fiction* (Abingdon: Routledge, 2005).
Scarry, Elaine, *The Body in Pain: The Making and Unmaking of the World* [1985] (New York: Oxford University Press, 1987).
Schaffer, Brian, 'QAnon and Conspiracy Beliefs' (n.d.) <https://www.isdglobal.org/wp-content/uploads/2020/10/qanon-and-conspiracy-beliefs.pdf> accessed 28 October 2021.
Schick, Laurie, ' "Hit Me Baby": From Britney Spears to the Socialization of Sexual Objectification of Girls in a Middle School Drama Program', *Sexuality & Culture*, 18 (2014), 39–55.
Science Learning Hub (n.d.) <sciencelearn.org>, accessed 1 February 2022.
Segal, Hanna, *Introduction to the Work of Melanie Klein* (London: Karmac, 1998).
Segal, Judy Z., 'Cancer Experience and its Narration: An Accidental Study', *Literature and Medicine*, 30, 2 (2012), 292–318.
Sen, Raja, 'Kabir Singh Movie Review: This Shahid Kapoor Film is Injurious to Health', The Hindustan Times (21 June 2019) <https://www.hindustantimes.com/bollywood/kabir-singh-movie-review-shahid-kapoor-plays-the-fool-in-this-toxic-troubling-film/story-rBQXfpOZmcFDqRSHIlVrXM.html>, accessed 14 December 2020.
Sexton, Jared Yates, 'Opinion | Donald Trump's Toxic Masculinity', The New York Times (13 October 2016) <https://www.nytimes.com/2016/10/13/opinion/donald-trumps-toxic-masculinity.html>, accessed 28 November 2020.
Sharf, Zack, ' "Ghostbusters" Reboot Tweaked a Scene as Reaction to Internet Backlash', IndieWire (8 July 2016) <https://www.indiewire.com/2016/07/ghostbusters-scene-change-internet-backlash-1201703854/>, accessed 26 August 2020.
Sharma, Sandipan, 'In Defence of Kabir Singh, a Man Flawed Like Many around Us', The Federal (22 June 2019) <https://thefederal.com/opinion/in-defence-of-kabir-singh-a-man-flawed-like-many-around-us/>, accessed 14 December 2020.
Sharma, Sandipan, 'In Defence of Kabir Singh: Filmmakers Should Have the Right to Explore the Mind of a Flawed Person', Firstpost (28 June 2019) <https://www.firstpost.com/entertainment/in-defence-of-kabir-singh-filmmakers-should-have-the-right-to-explore-the-mind-of-a-flawed-person-6897371.html>, accessed 26 February 2022.

Shaw-King, Crystal, 'In Jordan Peele's Horror Film, *Get Out*, Racism is the Real Monster', Ebony (24 February 2017) <https://www.ebony.com/entertainment/get-out-jordan-peele/>, accessed 5 November 2020.

Shkliarov, Vitali, 'In Belarus, Covid-19 Is a Modern-day Chernobyl', CNN (12 April 2020) <https://edition.cnn.com/2020/04/12/opinions/vitali-shkliarov-belarus-covid-19-chernobyl/index.html>, accessed 30 November 2020.

Silverman, Kaja, 'Masochism and Subjectivity', *Framework*, 12 (1980), 2–9.

Skenazy, Paul, 'Behind the Territory Ahead', in David Fine, ed., *Los Angeles in Fiction: A Collection of Essays* (Albuquerque: University of New Mexico Press, 1995), 103–25.

'Skin and Bones', *Fear Itself* [series created by Mick Garris], Episode 8, dir. Larry Fessenden (New York: National Broadcasting Company, 2008).

Skolnik, Jon, and John Annese, '"The People Have Rights! Open the Door, I'm Thirsty!" Hundreds Rally for Defiant Staten Island Bar Shut Down After Violating Coronavirus Rules', The New York Daily News (2 December 2020) <https://www.nydailynews.com/new-york/nyc-crime/ny-staten-island-pub-rally-20201203-e4rcab6375alvorgkvrfahaemu-story.html>, accessed 6 December 2020.

Skovira, Robert, and Wang, Wenli, 'Authenticity and Social Media', Twenty-third American Conference on Information Systems, Boston 2017, 10–12 August (2017).

Sky News, '"Sadfishing": New Toxic Online Trend Threatens Mental Health of Vulnerable Children' (1 October 2019) <https://news.sky.com/story/sadfishing-new-toxic-online-trend-threatens-mental-health-of-vulnerable-children-11824280>, accessed 7 September 2019.

Slotkin, Richard, *The Fatal Environment: The Myth of the Frontier in the Age of Industrialisation: 1800–1890* (Norman: University of Oklahoma Press, 1998).

Smith, Ariel, 'This Essay Was Not Built on an Ancient Indian Burial Ground: Horror Aesthetics within Indigenous Cinema as Pushback against Colonial Violence', Offscreen, 18, 8 (2014) <https://offscreen.com/view/horror-indigenous-cinema#ref-1-a>, accessed 26 August 2020.

Smith, David, 'Trump Calls Protesters against Stay-at-Home Orders "Very Responsible"', The Guardian (18 April 2020) <https://www.theguardian.com/us-news/2020/apr/17/trump-liberate-tweets-coronavirus-stay-at-home-orders>, accessed 1 February 2022.

Smith, Mikey, 'Boris Johnson Declares War on Coronavirus with New Emergence "C-19" Committee', The Mirror (17 March 2020) <https://www.mirror.co.uk/news/politics/boris-johnson-declares-coronavirus-war-21707803>, accessed 28 October 2021.

Snowpiercer, created by Josh Friedman and Graeme Manson (Los Gatos, CA: Netflix, 2020–present).

Snowpiercer, dir. Bong Joon Ho (Toronto: eOne Films, 2013).

Spanos, Brittany, '#FreeBritney: Understanding the Fan-led Britney Spears Movement', *Rolling Stone* (15 July 2020) <https://www.rollingstone.com/feature/freebritney-britney-spears-legal-829246/>, accessed 25 October 2020.

'The Spawn of the Flesh-Eater!', *The Incredible Hulk*, created by Steve Englehart, Vol 1. #162, April (New York: Marvel Comics Group, 1973).

Spears, Britney, '... Baby One More Time' (Jive, 1998).

———, *In the Zone* (Jive, 2003a).

———, 'Me Against the Music' feat. Madonna (Jive, 2003b).

———, 'Outrageous' (Jive, 2004a).

———, 'Toxic' (Jive, 2004b).

———, *Blackout* (Jive, 2007a).

———, 'Gimme More' (Jive, 2007b).

———, 'Break the Ice' (Jive, 2008a).

———, *Circus* (Jive, 2008b).

———, 'Piece of Me' (Jive, 2008c).

———, 'Womanizer' (Jive, 2008d).

———, 'Toxic (Official Video)', YouTube (25 October 2009a) <https://www.youtube.com/watch?v=LOZuxwVk7TU>, accessed 25 October 2020.

———, 'Womanizer (Director's Cut)', YouTube (25 October 2009b) <https://www.youtube.com/watch?v=rMqayQ-U74s>, accessed 25 October 2020.

———, 'Make Me' (Jive, 2016).

Spears, Lynne, and Lorilee Craker, *Through the Storm: A Real Story of Fame and Family in a Tabloid World* (Nashville, TN: Thomas Nelson Inc, 2008).

Spitzberg, Brian, William Cupach and Lea D. L. Ciceraro, 'Sex Differences in Stalking and Obsessive Relational Intrusion: Two Meta-analyses', *Partner Abuse*, 1, 3 (2010), 259–85.

———, Annegret F. Hannawa and John Patrick Crowley, 'A Preliminary Test of a Relational Goal Pursuit Theory of Obsessive Relational Intrusion and Stalking', *Studies in Communication Sciences*, 14 (2014), 29–36.

Stanley, Andy. Twitter account @AndyStanley 17 August 2011.

Star Wars: The Force Awakens, dir. J. J. Abrams (Burbank: Walt Disney Studios, 2015).

Star Wars: The Last Jedi, dir. Rian Johnson (Burbank: Walt Disney Studios, 2017).

Star Wars: The Rise of Skywalker, dir. J. J. Abrams (Burbank: Walt Disney Studios, 2019).

The Stepford Wives, dir. Bryan Forbes (Los Angeles: Columbia Pictures, 1975).

Stevens, Amanda, *Britney Spears: The Illustrated Story* (London: Billboard Books 2001).

Stilwell, Frank J. B., *Political Economy: The Contest of Economic Ideas* (South Melbourne: Oxford University Press, 2012).

Stitch, 'What Fandom Racism Looks Like: Weaponized White Womanhood', Stitch's Media Mix (22 January 2020) <https://stitchmediamix.com/2020/01/22/weaponized-white-womanhood/>, accessed 20 November 2020.

Stobbart, Dawn, *Video Games and Horror: From Amnesia to Zombies, Run!* (Cardiff: University of Wales Press, 2019).
Succession, created by Jesse Armstrong (Burbank, CA: Warner Brothers Television, 2018–present).
———, 'This Is Not for Tears', Season 2, Episode 10, dir. Mark Mylod (Burbank, CA: Warner Brothers Television, 2019).
Tere Naam, dir. Satish Kaushik (Karachi: MD Productions, 2003).
Thomas, Jordan, ed., *Deco Devolution: The Art of BioShock 2* (Novato, CA: 2K Marin, 2010).
TMZ, 'Britney Spears Free Britney Movement's Not a Hoax ... and I Don't Trust My Dad!!!' (3 September 2020) <https://www.tmz.com/2020/09/03/britney-spears-wants-conservatorship-case-open-to-public/>, accessed 25 October 2020.
Tomb Raider [video game], dir. Noah Hughes, Daniel Chayer and Daniel Neuburger (Tokyo: Square Enix, 2013).
Tourjée, Diana, 'Why Nerds Are So Sexist', Vice (13 April 2016) <https://www.vice.com/en/article/wnwvgx/why-nerds-are-so-sexist>, accessed 28 October 2021.
The Toxic Avenger, dir. Michael Herz and Lloyd Kaufman (Long Island, NY: Troma Entertainment, 1984).
Turner, Robert, 'Is Your Covid Test Being Used to Covertly Harvest Your DNA?', Medika (15 October 2020) <https://medika.life/is-your-covid-test-being-used-to-covertly-harvest-your-dna/>, accessed 6 December 2020.
Twilight, dir. Catherine Hardwicke (Santa Monica, CA: Summit Entertainment, 2008).
Tyagi, Sucharita, 'Kabir Singh | Not A Movie Review', YouTube (21 June 2019) <https://youtu.be/C-lRyevxevA>, accessed 14 December 2020.
UNESCO, *Emerging Evidence, Lessons and Practice in Comprehensive Sexuality Education, A Global Review 2015* (Paris: UNESCO, 2015).
———, 'Global Review Finds Comprehensive Sexuality Education Key to Gender Equality and Reproductive Health' (n.d.) <https://www.un.org/youthenvoy/2016/03/comprehensive-sexuality-education/>, accessed 28 October 2021.
UNICEF, 'Maternal Mortality Declined by 38 Per Cent Between 2000 and 2017' (2019) <https://data.unicef.org/topic/maternal-health/maternal-mortality/>, accessed 28 October 2021.
United Nations, 'UN Secretary-General Launches #PledgetoPause to Fight Misinformation', 21 October (2020) , <https://unric.org/en/un-secretary-general-launches-pledgetopause-to-fight-misinformation/>, accessed 1 February 2022.
Until Dawn [video game], dir. Will Byles and Nic Bowen (San Mateo, CA: Sony Computer Entertainment, 2015).
The Vampire Diaries, created by Julie Plec and Kevin Williamson (Los Angeles: CBS Television Distribution, 2009–2017).

Vampire the Masquerade: Bloodlines 2 [video game], dir. Ka'ai Cluney and Alexandre Mandryka (Stockholm: Paradox Interactive, 2021).

Vanga, Sandeep Reddy, 'Kabir Singh | Sandeep Reddy Vanga Interview | FC Postmortem | Anupama Chopra', YouTube (6 July 2019a) <https://youtu.be/MIRL06kpuH>, accessed 14 December 2020.

———, 'Sandeep Reddy Vanga BASHES & TROLLS Film Critics & Their Negative Reviews | Kabir Singh', YouTube (8 July 2019b) <https://youtu.be/D3jDk3Yrx1s>, accessed 14 December 2020.

Vary, Adam B. 'Ray Fisher Accuses Joss Whedon of "Abusive, Unprofessional" Behavior on "Justice League" Set', Variety (1 July 2020) <https://variety.com/2020/film/news/ray-fisher-joss-whedon-justice-league-1234695831/>, accessed 28 October 2021.

———, 'Charisma Carpenter Alleges Joss Whedon "Abused His Power" on "Buffy" and "Angel": "Joss Was the Vampire"', Variety (10 February 2021) <https://variety.com/2021/tv/news/charisma-carpenter-joss-whedon-abuse-of-power-allegations-1234904995/>, accessed 28 October 2021.

———, and Elizabeth Wagmeister, 'Inside Joss Whedon's "Cutting" and "Toxic" World of "Buffy" and "Angel" [EXCLUSIVE]', Variety, 26 February (2021) <https://variety.com/2021/tv/features/joss-whedon-buffy-angel-charisma-carpenter-toxic-workplace-1234915549/>, accessed 28 October 2021.

Viswamohan, Aysha Iqbal, and Sanchari Basu ChaudhurI, 'Bollywood's Angromance: Toxic Masculinity and Male Angst in *Tere Naam* and *Kabir Singh*', *Journal of Asia-Pacific Pop Culture*, 5, 2 (2020), 146–70.

Wald, Christina, 'King Lear and Succession: Returns of the Predecessor', in Christina Wald, ed., *Shakespeare's Serial Returns in Complex TV* (Switzerland: Springer International Publishing, 2020), 83–136.

Walker, Leonore E. A., *The Battered Woman Syndrome*, 3rd edition (New York: Springer Publishing Company, 2009).

Wang, Wenli, and Robert Joseph Skovira, 'Authenticity and Social Media', AMCIS Proceedings 7 (2017) https://aisel.aisnet.org/amcis2017/PhilosophyIS/Presentations/7>, accessed 1 February 2022.

Weale, Sally, 'Young People Who Seek Support Online Being Accused of "Sadfishing"', The Guardian (30 September 2019) <https://www.theguardian.com/society/2019/oct/01/young-people-seeking-support-online-accused-sadfishing-bullying-report>, accessed 7 September 2020.

Weatherby, Taylor, 'Britney Spears Taking Indefinite Hiatus After Her Dad "Almost Died"', Billboard (4 January 2019) <https://www.billboard.com/articles/columns/pop/8492231/britney-spears-vegas-residency-postponed-father-health>, accessed 25 October 2020.

WEF (World Economic Forum), *The Global Gender Gap Report 2020* (Switzerland: World Economic Forum, 2020).

Wendigo, dir. Larry Fessenden (New York: Antidote Films, 2001).

Wessely, Simon, and Jo Daniels, 'Why Reassuring the Public May Not Be the Best Way to End Lockdown', KCL News (9 May 2020) <https://www.kcl.ac.uk/news/why-reassuring-the-public-may-not-be-the-best-way-to-end-lockdown>, accessed 28 October 2021.

Wheatley, Chris, *Dark Psychology and Manipulation* (London: Wheatley, 2020).

Whicker, Marcia L., *Toxic Leaders: When Organizations Go Bad* (New York: Praeger, 1996).

Widdows, Heather, *Perfect Me: Beauty as an Ethical Ideal* (Princeton, NJ: Princeton University Press, 2018).

Williams, Linda, 'When the Woman Looks', in Mary Ann Doane, Patricia Mellencamp and Linda Williams, eds, *Re-vision: Essays in Feminist Film Criticism* (Los Angeles: American Film Institute, 1984), 83–99.

——, 'Film Bodies: Gender, Genre, and Excess', *Film Quarterly*, 44, 4 (1991), 2–13.

Williams, Tony, 'Trying to Survive on the Darker Side: 1980s Family Horror', in Barry Keith Grant, ed., *The Dread of Difference: Gender and the Horror Film*, 2nd edition [1996] (Austin: University of Texas Press, 2015), 192–208.

Wilson, Carl, 'BioShock', in Robert Mejia, Jaimie Banks and Aubrie Adams, eds, *100 Greatest Video Game Franchises* (Lanham, MD: Rowman & Littlefield, 2017), 13–15.

Wilson, Natalie, *Willful Monstrosity: Gender and Race in 21st Century Horror* (Jefferson, NC: McFarland & Company, 2020).

Winnicott, Donald, *The Maturational Processes and the Facilitating Environment: Studies in the Theory of Emotional Development* (New York: International Universities Press Inc, 1965), 140–52.

Wise, Adina, 'The Rhetoric of War Implies a Heedless Approach that Undermines the Practice of Medicine', *Scientific American* (17 April 2020) https://blogs.scientificamerican.com/observations/military-metaphors-distort-the-reality-of-covid-19/ accessed 28 October 2021.

'Women in Danger', dir. Chuck Waggoner, *Sneak Previews* [series created by Roger Ebert and Gene Siskel], Season 5, Episode 4 (Chicago: PBS, 1981).

World Health Organization, 'Maternal Mortality' (19 September 2019) <https://www.who.int/news-room/fact-sheets/detail/maternal-mortality>, accessed 28 October 2021.

World Health Organization, 'Weekly Operational Update on COVID-19', (28 August 2020) <https://www.who.int/docs/default-source/coronaviruse/situation-reports/wou-28-august-approved.pdf?sfvrsn=d9e49c20_2> accessed 11 February 2022.

World of Warcraft [video game], dir. Rob Pardo (Irvine, CA: Blizzard Entertainment, 2004).

Worrall, Patrick, 'Conspiracy Theory about DNA from Covid Tests Makes No Sense' (15 September 2020) <https://www.channel4.com/news/factcheck/factcheck-conspiracy-theory-about-dna-from-covid-tests-makes-no-sense>, accessed 6 December 2020.
Wright, Colin, 'Happiness Studies and Wellbeing: A Lacanian Critique of Contemporary Conceptualisation of the Cure', *Culture Unbound: Journal of Current Cultural Research*, 6 (2014), 791–813.
Wyatt, David, *Fall into Eden: Landscape and Imagination in California* (New York: Cambridge University Press, 1990).
Wyndham, John, *The Day of the Triffids* (Garden City, NY: Doubleday, 1951).
The X Factor, created by Simon Cowell (London: Fremantle, 2011–2013).
Yaroub, Ansam, 'The Theme of Child Abuse in Selected Fairy Tales by Brothers Grimm', *AL-USTATH*, 210, 2 (2014), 33–58.
Yazici, Berna, 'The Return to the Family: Welfare, State, and Politics of the Family in Turkey', *Anthropological Quarterly*, 85, 1 (2012), 103–40.
Yolen, Jane, 'America's Cinderella', in Alan Dundes, ed., *Cinderella: A Casebook* (Madison: University of Wisconsin Press, 1988), 294–308.
You, created by Greg Berlanti and Sara Gamble (Burbank: Warner Brothers Television, 2018–present).
You're the Worst, created by Stephen Falk (Century City: FX Networks, 2014–2019).
Zimmerman, Amy, 'The Persecution of Kelly Marie Tran: How "Star Wars" Fandom Became Overrun with Alt-right Trolls', Daily Beast (5 June 2018) <https://www.thedailybeast.com/the-persecution-of-kelly-marie-tran-how-star-wars-fandom-became-overrun-by-alt-right-trolls>, accessed 28 October 2020.
Zubernis, Lynn, and Kathy Larsen, *Fandom at the Crossroads: Celebration, Shame and Fan/Producer Relationships* (Newcastle: Cambridge University Press, 2012).

Notes on Contributors

PAULA ASHE is a PhD candidate in American studies with an emphasis in sociology and new media at Purdue University, USA. Her scholarly interests are grounded in critical examinations of gender construction, social media, popular culture and social justice movements. She has previously published standalone works on Clive Barker's films *Hellraiser* and *Hellbound: Hellraiser II*, the *American Horror Story* series, and Janelle Monáe's 2018 album, *Dirty Computer*. She is also the author of the dark fiction collection, *We Are Here to Hurt Each Other*, from Nictitating Books available via Amazon.

SIMON BACON is an independent scholar based in Poznań, Poland. He has edited books on various subjects, including *The Gothic: A Reader* (Peter Lang, 2018), *Horror: A Companion* (Peter Lang, 2019), *Monsters: A Companion* (Peter Lang, 2020), *The Transmedia Vampire: Essays on Technological Convergence and the Undead* (2021) and *Nosferatu in the 21st Century: A Critical Study* (2022). He has also published a series of books on vampires in popular culture – *Becoming Vampire: Difference and the Vampire in Popular Culture* (Peter Lang, 2016), *Dracula as Absolute Other: The Troubling and Distracting Specter of Stoker's Vampire on Screen* (2019), *Eco-Vampires: The Undead and the Environment* (2020), *Vampires From Another World: The Cinematic Progeny of H. G. Wells' The War of the Worlds and Bram Stoker's Dracula* (2021) – and is working on the next – *Unhallowed Ground: Emergent Terror and the Specter of the Vampire on Screen*.

LOUIS BAYMAN is Associate Professor in Film Studies at the University of Southampton, UK. He has published essays on political understandings of genre, retro and nostalgia in recent film and television and is currently preparing a monograph on the meanings of time in contemporary narrative cinema. He has also contributed to various publications on the manifestations of horror across film history.

MELODY BLACKMORE is a PhD researcher and part-time lecturer at Leeds Beckett University, UK. Her PhD examines the role of madness and landscape in contemporary British horror films. Specialist research areas include psychoanalysis, Gothic literature, the uncanny, history of insanity, and horror analysis. Melody is the current postgraduate representative for Leeds School of Arts and also the president of the Postgraduate Research Society since 2019. Having presented at many conferences, symposiums and workshops, Melody also writes reviews and publications within her field, including 'Trauma, Madness, and Murder in The Invisible Man (2020)', 'The Phallic Mother in Wonderland and a Fight for Masculinity' and 'Gothic Trauma and Landscapes of the Mind in The Descent (2005)'.

REBECCA BOOTH has a master's degree in film studies from the University of Southampton, UK. In addition to contributing essays to collections such as *Tonight, on a Very Special Episode: When TV Sitcoms Sometimes Got Serious: Volume 2: 1986 -1998* (2020) and *Lost Girls: The Phantasmagorical Cinema of Jean Rollin* (2017), she is the co-editor of *Scared Sacred: Idolatry, Religion and Worship in the Horror Film* (2020) and *Filtered Reality: The Progenitors and Evolution of Found Footage Horror* (2022).

DEBORAH G. CHRISTIE teaches at Old Dominion University, USA, and lives in Virginia with her family, including four cats and one enormous dog. She holds a PhD in modern British and American literature from Fordham University, though most of her research interests run to the scarier side. Co-editor of *Better Off Dead: The Evolution of the Zombie as Post-Human* (2011), Dr Christie has also published on vampires, ghosts, serial killers and a variety of things that go bump in the night. How a culture deals with its monsters – how it creates, maintains and ultimately defeats them – reveals its hidden anxieties and how they evolve over time.

MARTYN COLEBROOK is an independent researcher. He completed his PhD at the University of Hull, UK, in 2012, focusing on the novels of Iain M. Banks. He has written numerous articles and chapters, and co-edited *The Transgressive Iain Banks* (2013). Other subjects of study include Don DeLillo, Gordon Burn, Paul Auster, J. G. Ballard and Kevin Barry.

BLAKE I. COLLIER is a Texas Panhandle-bred freelance writer and critic who has written for various sites including Film Inquiry, Rise Up Daily and Mockingbird. He also puts out a newsletter every two months entitled 'Lost in Osmosis' on Substack. He has an MA in nineteenth- and twentieth-century British imperialism from Texas Tech University, USA. His current day job is as a draftsman for a small architecture firm in the Tulsa, Oklahoma, where he lives with his wife, Melissa.

CATHLEEN ALLYN CONWAY is a poet and PhD student at Goldsmiths, University of London, UK, where she is examining intersections of Sylvia Plath, the vampire and the Gothic in experimental poetics. She has published on Plath in *The Guardian* and elsewhere. She also teaches creative writing and is the author of poetry pamphlet *American Ingénue* (2021), *All the Twists of the Tongue* (2018) and *Static Cling* (2012), as well as academic articles on Dracula, vampirism and race, and feminist cultural studies.

PEMBE GÖZDE ERDOGAN received her BA, MA and PhD from the Department of American Culture and Literature at Hacettepe University in Ankara, Turkey. Her MA was on American theatre and her PhD was on the US television series *Southern Gothic*. Her research areas include popular culture, cultural studies, film studies, television studies, horror and Gothic and American theatre. Erdogan has also worked in the Department of American Culture and Literature. She currently resides in Cardiff, UK, and is an independent scholar.

PHIL FITZSIMMONS is Head of Education at Alphacrucis College, Sydney, Australia. Prior to accepting the position, Phil was an independent researcher and educational consultant, assistant dean of research (Faculty of Education, Business and Science, Avondale University College, Australia) and director of research (San Roque Research Institute, USA). His research interests include all things Gothic and monstrous, and adolescent spirituality.

HELEN GAVIN is a criminal psychologist and research methodologist by training and teaches these areas at undergraduate and postgraduate level at the University of Huddersfield, UK. She writes on deviant sexual expression, homicide and sexualised/gendered violence. In order to find relief from such bleak themes, she indulges a fascination with fairy, folk and supernatural tales. However, she has inevitably discovered this world also has its dark side, and people often regret looking over her shoulder to see what she is reading.

ERIN GIANNINI is an independent scholar. She has served as an editor and contributor at PopMatters, and her recent work has focused on portrayals of and industrial contexts around corporate culture on television, including *Joss Whedon Versus the Corporation* (2017). She has also published and presented work on religion, socioeconomics, production culture and technology in series such as *Supernatural*, *Dollhouse*, *iZombie* and *Angel*, and she is currently co-editing a collection on the novel (and series) *Good Omens*.

ELANA GOMEL is Associate Professor in the Department of English Literature and American Studies at Tel Aviv University, Israel. She has taught and researched at Princeton University, Stanford University, The University of Hong Kong and Venice International University. She is the author of several academic books and articles on subjects such as narrative theory, posthumanism, science fiction, Dickens and Victorian culture. As a fiction writer, she has published more than seventy fantasy and science fiction stories and several novels. Information can be found at <https://www.citiesoflightanddarkness.com/>.

CALLIE GRAHAM, PhD, studies communication in romantic relationships in hopes of educating the public, particularly adolescents and young adults, about toxic romantic relationships. She enjoys analysing romantic relationships as portrayed in pop culture, particularly in television and movies. Beyond her research, Callie considers herself a 'dabbler' in all aspects of life and enjoys a dark sense of humour.

BETHAN JONES is a research associate at the University of York, UK. Her work on anti- fandom, toxicity and hate has been published in *Sexualities*, *Participations: Journal of Audience & Reception Studies* and *New Media & Society*, among others. Bethan is also co- editor of *Crowdfunding the Future: Media Industries, Ethics and Digital Society* (Peter Lang, 2014). She is a board member of the Fan Studies Network, a committee member for the Society for Cinema and Media Studies Fan and Audience Studies Scholarly Interest Group and a member of the editorial boards of *the Journal of Fandom Studies* and *Transformative Works and Cultures*.

CYNTHIA JONES is Visiting Assistant Professor at Weber State University in Ogden, USA. Her main research interests lie in the representation of the monstrous in literature and media, especially within nineteenth-century France and Quebec. She is also interested in folklore, fairy tales, and legends and the role they play in creating personal, cultural and national identities. Other research interests include the representation of evil women in nineteenth-century French literature, French decadent literature, and the occult.

FRANZISKA E. KOHLT is a research associate in the Department of Sociology at the University of York, UK, working on science communication and science and religion narratives. She holds a DPhil from the University of Oxford; her thesis examines the emergence of Victorian psychology and fantastic literature as sister phenomena. She is an expert on Lewis Carroll and has published on Victorian science and literature, especially for children, and she has previously worked for Marvel Comics and as consultant for the Royal Entomological Society.

ILDIKÓ LIMPÁR, Senior Lecturer of English, Pázmány Péter Catholic University, Budapest (Hungary), has a PhD in English, an MA in Egyptology, and a special interest in the monstrous. Her monograph titled *The Truths of Monsters: Coming of Age with Fantastic Media* (McFarland, 2021) focuses on the use of monsters as literary tools addressing life challenges in coming-of-age fantasy and science fiction. She is editor of *Displacing the Anxieties of Our World: Spaces of the Imagination* (Cambridge Scholars Publishing, 2017) and a Hungarian anthology of essays in Monster Studies (Athenaeum, 2021).

EDIE LANPHAR is currently Director of Curriculum and Instruction at the Knox School of Santa Barbara, USA, which teaches gifted students. Edie has had an extensive education-related career, which includes teaching from PK to 12th grade and serving as a curriculum director of a progressive/project-based learning PK–12th grade school. She has also been a university lecturer in Australia, an author and a researcher. Her current research is grounded in adolescent development and school-based professional development.

PATRICIA MACCORMACK is Professor of Continental Philosophy at Anglia Ruskin University, Cambridge, UK. She has published extensively on philosophy, feminism, queer and monster theory, animal abolitionist activism, ethics, art and horror cinema. She is the author of *Cinesexuality* (2008), *Posthuman Ethics: Embodiment and Cultural Theory* (2012), and *The Ahuman Manifesto: Activism for the End of the Anthropocene* (2020). She is also the editor of *The Animal Catalyst: Towards Ahuman Theory* (2014) and joint editor of *Deleuze and the Animal* (2017), *Deleuze and the Schizoanalysis of Cinema* (2008) and *Ecosophical Aesthetics: Art, Ethics and Ecology with Guattari* (2018).

KEN MONTEITH has enjoyed an academic career teaching at universities in the United States, the Netherlands and Armenia. Married to a career diplomat, Ken and family currently are posted to Paramaribo, Suriname, where he works as a political economic assistant at the US Embassy. Among other duties, he manages the Environment, Science, Technology, and Health portfolio. As an independent scholar, his current interest examines how disability studies may inform cultural and literary analysis. He is the parent of an increasingly tech-savvy 4-year-old and 3-year-old twins intent on becoming influencers.

KYLE MOODY is Associate Professor of Communications Media at Fitchburg State University, USA. A former programme director, radio station manager and social media consultant, Dr Moody's research interests include social media and business integration across multiple communities, information design and distribution, production of culture studies, media history, online communities across multiple platforms, social media and new media design. He teaches social media production, information design and media history courses.

DEBADITYA MUKHOPADHYAY is Assistant Professor of English at Manikchak College, affiliated with the University of Gour Banga, India. His areas of interest are popular literature and films, myths, adaptations, and theatre. His research articles have been published in peer-reviewed journals including *Muse India* and *Dibrugarh University Journal of English Studies*. He has recently contributed chapters to the collections *Parenting Through Pop Culture: Essays on Navigating Media with Children* (2020), *Excavating Indiana Jones: Essays on the Films and Francise* (2020), *Critical Insights: Life of Pi* (2020) and *Children and Childhood in the Works of Stephen King* (2020).

MADELINE MUNTERSBJORN is Associate Professor in the Philosophy and Religious Studies department at The University of Toledo, USA, where she teaches logic, philosophy of science and philosophy of science fiction. Her approach to toxic cultures is informed by a quote from Henri Poincaré's preface to his book *Science and Hypothesis*: 'To doubt everything or to believe everything are two equally convenient solutions; both dispense with the necessity of reflection' (1905: xxii).

DANIEL SHEPPARD is a PhD candidate at Birmingham City University, UK. His thesis is titled *Gays, Women, and Chainsaws: Queer Approaches to Characterisation and Identification in Contemporary Slasher Film and Television, 1996–2019*. His research is fully funded by the Arts and Humanities Research Council via the Midlands4Cities Doctoral Training Partnership.

MATEUSZ ŚWIETLICKI is Assistant Professor in the American Literature and Culture department at the Institute of English Studies of the University of Wrocław, Poland. He was a Fulbright scholar at the University of Illinois Chicago in 2018. Świetlicki's expertise is children's and young adult literature and culture, gender and queer studies as well as popular culture and film. He is the author of more than sixty publications, including a book monograph and seven co-edited volumes.

JAY DANIEL THOMPSON is a Lecturer and Program Manager in the Professional Communication program in the School of Media and Communication at RMIT University. His research explores ways of cultivating ethical online communication in an era of digital hostility and networked disinformation. Dr Thompson is co-author of two books published in 2022: *Fake News in Digital Culture* (with Professor Rob Cover and Dr Ashleigh Haw) and *Content Production for Digital Media* (with Associate

Professor John Weldon). His research has also been published in journals such as *Convergence*, *Feminist Media Studies*, *Journalism*, *Media International Australia*, *Continuum* and *Sexualities*.

TOM UE is Assistant Professor in Literature and Science at Dalhousie University, Canada. He is the author of *Gissing, Shakespeare, and the Life of Writing* (forthcoming) and *George Gissing* (forthcoming), and the editor of *George Gissing, The Private Papers of Henry Ryecroft* (forthcoming). Ue has held the prestigious Banting Postdoctoral Fellowship, and he is an honorary research associate at University College London, UK.

ALEXANDER WILLS gained his HBA with High Distinction from the University of Toronto, Canada. He double majored in political science and international development studies, with a particular focus on political economy. Wills is interested in the effects of neoliberalism as well as potential alternatives to current economic paradigms and ownership models. He is the author of 'Dystopia in *The Dark Knight* trilogy: How utopian ideas are warped and corrupted in their application' (2018).

CARL WILSON is a contributing guest writer for the Eisner-nominated comic book publishers Fanbase Press and a former film editor for PopMatters. He has published work in over a dozen titles and has chapters forthcoming in the area of transmedia convergence, including the *Indiana Jones* franchise, the *Uncharted* video game series, the depowering of DC superheroes, the representation of women in Batman games and the digital legacy of Superman. Examples of his work can be found at <www.carl-wilson.com>.

NATALIE WILSON is a professor, writer and cultural critic whose work focuses on gender and racial politics, particularly as it plays out in contemporary television, film and fiction. She is the author of *Willful Monstrosity: Race and Gender in 21st Century Horror* (2020) and *Seduced by Twilight: The Allure and Contradictory Messages of the Popular Saga* (2011). She teaches in the Women's, Gender, and Sexuality Studies department at California State University San Marcos, USA. Follow her on Twitter @DrNatalieWilson.

Index

#MeToo 4, 5, 46A

ableism 121
abortion 137, 217–23
abuse 5, 12–13, 14, 45, 63, 97, 104, 107, 119–20, 141, 154, 155, 156, 158, 162, 164, 167, 178, 203, 205, 279, 281
accusations 95, 97, 104, 133, 154, 156, 157, 167, 172, 176, 191, 193, 196, 198, 277
activism 100, 104, 106, 248
agency 13, 27–8, 34, 85–6, 88–90, 91–2, 96, 144, 146, 147, 152, 218, 234
agenda 2, 13, 58, 137, 210, 265
aggression 3, 12, 15, 20, 30, 46, 67, 81, 87, 88, 145, 146, 163, 168, 177, 178, 238, 255, 279
ahuman 10, 23–4
anger 12, 97, 167, 184–5, 204, 279, 283
Anthropocene 10, 15, 17, 18–20, 21–4, 67, 273–5
anti-Semitism 104–5, 202
anxiety 2, 74, 119, 122, 135, 184, 230, 278
appropriation 73
assault 46, 240, 279
authenticity 138, 158, 183, 184, 187–9, 191–3, 196–9, 239

behaviours 2, 4–5, 7, 8, 12, 19, 46, 68–9, 82, 83, 88–9, 91–7, 107–9, 111–13, 116–18, 132, 133, 136, 137, 141, 146, 155, 161, 163–7, 169, 172, 174, 176, 178, 185, 194, 199, 201, 202, 205, 206, 215, 229, 230, 232, 255, 264, 265, 277, 280–1, 284

belief 8, 56, 92, 111, 173, 210, 215, 240–1, 245–7, 250, 265
belonging 14, 17, 18, 37, 122, 278
black bodies 53–61, 103, 177
Black Lives Matter 5, 11, 55, 61
Black power movement 100, 101
body politic 37, 233
bullying 46, 83, 88–9, 91, 93, 95, 157, 176, 193–4, 278–9

cancel culture 8–9, 23
capitalism 11, 15, 17, 18, 24, 102, 150, 151, 174, 227, 230, 231, 232, 237, 253, 255, 257–8, 260, 267
celebrity 8, 141, 142, 146, 147, 171, 192, 193
cities 14, 165, 231–4, 274
colonialism 1, 2, 59, 102, 235, 240–1, 265
communications 64–5, 66, 67, 102, 172, 173, 192, 204, 239, 260, 266
community 8, 15, 40, 54, 58, 81, 87, 96, 103, 133, 171, 174, 209, 221, 222, 228, 239–40, 262, 265, 270, 271, 275
condemnation 173, 204
confession 113, 192, 232
conservativism 24, 39, 45, 46, 133, 134, 136–7, 139, 219–20, 222, 244–5
conspiracy 8, 146, 212, 216, 233, 243–4, 246–7
consumerism 18, 19, 125, 138–9, 263
contagion 4, 5, 10, 11, 14
contamination 35, 233, 265, 267, 269
control 8, 11, 24, 30, 45, 50, 51, 55, 58, 69, 74, 92, 96, 108, 111, 120, 122, 123,

135, 142, 145–7, 166, 193, 216, 217, 222, 233, 244, 248, 250, 251, 256, 264, 265, 280
COVID-19 pandemic 5, 8, 11, 14, 38, 63, 67–8, 157, 202, 209–16, 284
cult 3, 24, 121, 212, 243–4, 245–7, 249, 250–1
culture wars 9, 95
    Western 2, 33, 34, 35, 53, 66, 71, 81–3, 97, 111, 126, 132–4, 186, 193, 235, 238, 262

damage 7, 29, 36, 37, 45, 46, 53, 54, 64–5, 69, 121, 141, 166, 167, 172, 206, 207, 261, 264, 269, 271
danger 8, 11, 13, 41, 43, 57, 63, 69, 78, 94, 97, 105, 125, 138, 153, 172, 183, 205, 212, 215, 233, 269, 273
dating 115, 117, 118
depression 117, 150, 172, 186, 187, 207
digital 28, 172, 191, 202, 210
disability 146, 196–7
discrimination 1, 6, 8, 15
disease 5, 8, 14, 28, 66, 210, 211–12, 223, 230
disenfranchised 101
domestic 36, 105, 134, 137–9, 218, 263
domination 46, 93, 99, 145
dystopia 15, 89, 119

ecology 2, 8, 15, 20, 23, 264
economy 6, 14, 24, 33, 101, 134, 136, 152, 158, 221, 227, 231, 244, 254–5, 257, 258, 269, 273
entitlement 82, 85, 87, 91, 92, 93, 95, 269
environment 2, 3, 4, 5–9, 14, 15, 67, 120, 123, 125, 149–50, 155, 157, 185, 187, 195, 197, 202, 227–31, 277–9
environmental 15, 41, 67, 132, 141, 152, 217, 227, 262–5, 269, 270, 272, 274
epidemic 211, 261, 262

equality 4, 11, 20, 24, 92, 105, 136, 156, 220
ethnicity 2, 5, 6, 11, 100, 265
Evangelicalism 215, 244–6, 248
exploitation 4, 5, 8, 11, 12, 15, 17, 19, 31 99, 104, 106, 112, 119, 141, 258, 260
extremism 1–2, 5, 9, 14, 18, 45, 113, 126, 255

fact 14, 211–12, 265
    counter 243, 244
fake 8, 176, 187, 214
family 11, 24, 33, 45–9, 51, 53, 56–7, 111, 120, 122, 131, 135, 136–7, 143, 146, 185, 217–19, 221, 238, 241, 244, 245–7, 253, 254, 255, 257–9, 260, 267, 273, 279, 284
fan 13, 92, 94, 97, 112, 117, 145, 150, 157–8, 171–9
    anti 172
    fiction 175, 176
fanboy 20, 150
fandom 13, 92, 95, 149, 152–3, 156, 171–9
fantasy 27, 72, 77, 120, 123, 127, 141, 147, 183, 188, 227, 231
fascism 18, 19, 22
feminine 72–3, 76–8, 81, 82, 84, 86, 87, 88, 90, 122, 132
feminisation 74, 77
feminism 4, 5, 71–3, 76, 77, 90, 97, 99–106, 132–4, 151, 158
    anti 71, 132, 150
    post 71, 132
    second wave 100, 101
    third wave 102
    toxic 12, 99, 106
    white 99, 100, 103, 106, 155
fetish 74, 211
franchise 7, 13, 92, 149, 150, 157, 158
freedom 8, 18, 101, 102, 106, 199, 213, 237, 257
    of speech 2, 7, 9
fundamentalism 14, 244–5

Index

gaming 31, 172
gaslighting 12, 107, 112, 113–15, 280
gay 74, 100
gaze 71–2, 74–7, 121
geek 91–3, 149, 152, 157
  culture 92, 96–7, 152–3
gender 2, 4, 6, 8, 11, 23, 24, 46, 72, 73, 75, 76, 77, 86, 89, 96, 103, 122–3, 125–6, 131–4, 136–7, 152, 154, 202, 218, 220, 227, 239, 259
ghost 151, 153, 232, 240, 241, 262, 264, 266, 267
Ghostbusters (2016 film) 13, 149–59
global 5–8, 10, 14, 64, 102, 103, 136, 172, 213, 217–23, 228, 262, 263, 264, 270, 278, 283
globalism 1, 6, 102, 202
govern 28, 33, 271
government 2, 5, 7, 11, 63, 67, 101, 136–7, 210, 219, 222, 243
grief 2, 184, 283

harassment 46, 92, 136, 153, 175, 177, 204, 205, 278
haunting 230, 236, 264
health 2, 8, 12, 21, 28, 33, 38, 40, 63–9, 81–2, 96, 116, 117, 119, 121–2, 145–7, 165, 191, 192, 194, 196–7, 202, 203, 207, 209–11, 213, 217–21
heteronormativity 6, 12, 20, 74, 75, 77
heterosexual 21, 75, 76
home 3, 12, 57, 100, 120–2, 124, 125, 126, 131, 188, 193, 240, 247, 254, 257, 260, 267, 283
homoeroticism 74, 75
homophobia 6, 7, 46, 104, 171, 172
homosexual 24, 74, 100
humane 15
humanity 15, 17, 126, 206, 251, 265–6, 270, 275

identity 1, 3, 4, 22, 23, 100, 105, 150, 230, 232, 240, 250, 259, 260, 264
ideology 6, 7, 10, 11, 15, 40, 45, 46, 51, 71, 73, 76, 82, 99, 109, 126, 131, 134–7, 139, 186, 217, 218, 219, 237, 239, 262
incel 12, 23, 92
Indigenous 176, 262–5, 267
inequality 2, 136, 202, 221, 254–5, 257
injustice 93, 95, 105, 125, 171, 206, 254
Instagram 104, 176, 192, 193
institutionalisation 7, 13, 63, 86, 99, 105, 122, 136, 156, 181
internet 7, 150, 175, 193, 202, 206, 216, 248
intolerance 58, 108, 245, 275, 277

'jock' 21, 91
justice 8, 40, 95, 97, 105, 136, 246, 250, 277

language 2–3, 11, 13, 19, 20, 48, 63, 65–6, 81, 104, 105, 133, 152, 231, 233, 238, 239, 248, 253
law 60, 101, 102, 104–5, 109, 111, 124, 136, 222, 233, 245
lesbianism 100
liberalism 1, 55, 133, 210, 245
liberation 33, 100, 106
lying 7, 8, 38, 40, 43, 48, 50, 83, 92, 213

manipulation 6, 28, 30, 58, 107, 109, 111–13, 114, 116, 118, 164, 210, 248, 250, 280, 282
masculine 4, 47, 82, 83, 87–8, 81, 96, 97, 137, 152, 158, 238
masculinity 1, 4–6, 11, 20, 21, 45–8, 51, 80, 92, 97, 152, 156, 161–2, 164–5, 167, 169
meaning 1, 11, 18, 19, 35, 66, 73, 74, 81, 106
mental heath 12, 117, 145, 146, 147, 191, 193–4, 207, 279, 284
misleading 6, 66, 185, 191

misogynoir 155
misogyny 12, 13, 45, 46, 48, 72, 74–5, 91, 92, 95, 97, 99, 147, 150, 161, 165, 172, 176, 178, 202, 206, 268
monstrosity 22–3, 61, 94, 123–6, 184, 262, 267
monstrous 12, 15, 124, 125, 126, 208, 229, 230
music 4, 12, 30, 107, 109, 112, 141–4, 147, 165
myth 120, 235, 238, 240, 261–2, 265

narrative 11, 14, 21, 24, 27, 30, 33, 34, 39, 40, 45, 50, 56, 63–9, 71–3, 76, 81–7, 90, 94, 111, 120, 123, 139, 153, 163–4, 167, 191, 228, 230–1, 235–40, 243–5, 248, 250, 263, 264, 270–1
nation 1–4, 7–8, 11, 13, 54, 58, 68–9, 104, 136, 209, 213, 216, 217, 219, 240, 260, 262, 279, 284
nationalism 3, 6, 55, 215
negativity 1, 4, 13, 33, 38, 52, 69, 82, 107, 108, 113, 116, 150, 161–2, 165, 166–7, 183–6, 217, 278, 280, 281, 282–4
neoliberalism 1, 6, 133, 135–9, 142, 151
nerds 12, 22, 91–2, 95
non-binary 6

online 6, 7, 8, 13, 28, 103, 133, 152, 153, 154, 165, 172, 176, 178, 179, 191, 193–5, 201–3, 205, 207–8, 210, 245, 271
oppression 1, 72, 86, 88–9, 99, 106, 120, 156, 230, 232, 259
outrage 133, 135, 150, 156, 174, 176

pandemic 5–6, 7, 8, 11, 12, 14, 63, 67, 68, 69, 157, 202, 209–10, 213–16, 269, 283–4
patriarchal 6, 11, 12, 45, 50, 51, 56, 73, 77, 90, 99, 101, 105, 106, 120, 132, 136, 137, 258, 259

poison 4, 17, 23, 24, 27, 28, 41, 45, 53, 64, 81, 186, 215, 227, 270, 273–5, 277, 279
poisonous 4, 18, 21, 54, 67, 81, 106, 135, 141, 172, 178, 261, 264, 265, 269, 281
political 1, 8, 11, 14, 15, 19, 38, 40, 47, 50, 63, 72, 99, 100–2, 106, 133–5, 137, 178, 205, 213, 215, 217, 219, 228, 230, 231, 232, 244–6, 250, 253, 258, 263, 278
politics 1, 4, 24, 41, 42, 105, 137, 161, 172, 216, 233, 248
pollution 2, 41, 42, 53, 67, 132, 150, 152, 269, 274
popular culture 9, 10, 12, 13, 90, 112, 144, 262
populism 2, 4, 6
positivity 10, 13, 15, 113, 183–7, 235, 281–3
privilege 9, 12, 21, 23, 40, 59, 99, 103, 105, 106, 248, 254
protection 31, 112, 152
psyche 58, 82, 86, 240
psychology 10, 13, 15, 69, 87, 108, 112, 122, 184, 201, 202, 207, 228, 246, 265, 277–82

QAnon 243–8, 250–1
queer 23, 92, 144

racism 5–6, 7, 22, 53–4, 61, 99–102, 103, 105, 106, 141, 150, 155, 171, 176, 178, 206
racist 13, 46, 55, 57, 154, 172, 175, 177
regulator 133
religion 1, 2, 43, 68, 186, 202, 215, 217, 221, 236–41, 243, 251, 270, 277
religiosity 237
reproduction 20, 89, 137, 218–22, 227
republicanism 102, 215, 219, 244, 245, 248
responsibility 35, 82, 104, 117, 124, 136, 186, 194, 203, 213, 233, 255, 259

Index

revenge 39, 91, 95, 96, 155, 202, 236, 266
rules 33, 120, 185, 209, 214

science 7, 8, 30, 35, 40, 63, 66–7, 157, 186, 211, 213, 216, 217, 265
sexism 5, 7, 92, 99, 141, 165, 172, 175
shaming 143, 183, 185, 187, 205, 280, 283
slavery 1, 11, 15, 55, 59, 100, 101
social media 2, 6, 7, 8, 10, 13, 92, 103, 144, 150, 172, 178, 189, 191–9, 207, 210, 213
society 3–5, 6, 7, 9, 10, 12–14, 15, 24, 28, 30, 31, 34, 37–8, 41, 43, 67, 81–2, 86, 90, 104, 105, 121–3, 125, 127, 133, 135, 166, 183–7, 189, 202, 203, 205, 208, 222, 227, 229–30, 233, 237, 240, 243–4, 250, 251, 255, 266, 270, 273
space 14, 20, 56, 66, 71, 92, 93, 106, 114, 120, 127, 136, 150, 159, 164, 179, 192, 202, 204, 207, 222, 227–9, 231–3, 235, 237, 238–9, 254, 263, 269–70, 271, 280, 283
spectrality 33, 152, 233
stalking 12, 107, 109–13, 117, 118, 202
subjectivity 20, 24, 30, 72–5, 77, 121, 142
submissive 85–6, 89, 237
suicide 37, 117, 178, 202, 236, 270, 271, 272

technology 6–7, 24, 35, 108, 194, 227–8, 271, 272, 273
television 2, 3, 9, 10, 11–12, 18, 45, 46, 51, 111, 120, 131–5, 236, 254, 262, 267
TERF 106
therapy 23, 64, 67, 117–18, 185, 210–1, 277
threat 10, 15, 27, 58, 64, 74, 122, 125, 154, 167, 172, 174, 188, 193, 203, 205, 207, 227, 229, 240, 245, 264, 278
threaten 2, 19, 41, 43, 69, 88, 92, 110, 119, 133–4, 153, 191, 192, 204, 217, 230–2, 237, 250, 259, 260, 265, 271

toxic
    environment 4, 5, 8, 11, 12, 15, 120, 149, 195, 279
    feminism 2, 99, 101, 132
    ideology 11, 45, 136
    masculinity 1, 5, 6, 11, 20, 45–7, 51, 156, 161–2, 164–5, 169
    nostalgia 6, 11, 73
    positivity 13, 183, 185–7, 281, 283
    relationships 1, 12, 49, 117–18, 112–13, 116–17
    whiteness 11, 54, 58, 60, 106
toxicity 1–2, 4–15, 17–19, 21–4, 30, 35, 36, 41, 43, 45–51, 53–4, 58, 61, 81–3, 93, 96, 108, 115, 117–18, 132–6, 141–2, 145, 149–50, 152, 153, 155–9, 163, 165, 191, 201, 203, 207–8, 227, 231, 237, 241, 246, 250, 253, 261, 265, 269, 274, 277–82, 284
toxin 23, 53–4, 67, 81, 172, 227–8, 269, 272
traditionalism 1, 4, 6, 7, 46, 54, 71–2, 86, 92, 111, 112, 117, 120, 131, 137, 152, 168, 199, 237, 246, 255, 259, 270, 281, 283
transcendence 24, 67, 96, 106, 247, 249, 250, 258
transgender 78, 122
    anti 8
    phobia 46, 106
    women 103, 106
trauma 2–3, 12, 14, 34, 53–4, 117, 207, 230, 235–6, 240–1, 246, 248, 250, 279
troll 13–14, 92, 161–2, 167, 178, 201–8
Trump, Donald 7, 14, 23, 45–9, 54–5, 61, 102–3, 209, 210, 213–15, 217, 219, 221, 243–5
truth 2, 4, 8, 35, 36, 38, 40–1, 52, 109, 113, 116, 203, 212, 216, 244, 246, 248, 250
Tumblr 177
Twitter 153, 154, 172, 174, 178, 214

urban 5, 143, 165, 227–31
utopia 183, 270–1

vaccination 8, 212
vampire 12, 33, 91–3, 111, 120, 125–6, 279–80
victim 22–3, 55, 58, 59, 71, 74–7, 91–4, 96, 126, 134, 141, 201–3, 205, 207, 272
vigilance 194, 278
violence 2–4, 8, 18, 20, 31, 36, 46, 67, 71, 73–4, 76, 78, 83, 88, 102, 105, 120, 133, 134, 136, 153, 156, 164, 169, 229, 235, 238, 243, 246, 247, 264, 265, 269

vulnerability 105, 165, 187, 191–4, 196–7, 219, 222, 269, 282

waste 4, 19, 20, 22–3, 61, 136, 144, 150, 152, 281
website 154, 166, 192, 195, 253
whiteness 11, 21, 54, 58, 60

xenophobia 6, 27

YouTube 92, 244

zombie 17–18, 27, 58, 211

Genre Fiction and Film Companions

Series Editor: Simon Bacon

The *Genre Fiction and Film Companions* provide accessible introductions to key texts within the most popular genres of our time. Written by leading scholars in the field, brief essays on individual texts offer innovative ways of understanding, interpreting and reading the topics in question. Invaluable for students, teachers and fans alike, these surveys offer new insights into the most important literary works, films, music, events and more within genre fiction and film.

We welcome proposals for edited collections on new genres and topics. Please contact baconetti@googlemail.com or oxford@peterlang.com.

Published Volumes

The Gothic
Edited by Simon Bacon

Cli-Fi
Edited by Axel Goodbody and Adeline Johns-Putra

Horror
Edited by Simon Bacon

Sci-Fi
Edited by Jack Fennell

Monsters
Edited by Simon Bacon

Transmedia Cultures
Edited by Simon Bacon

Shirley Jackson
Edited by Kristopher Woofter

Toxic Cultures
Edited by Simon Bacon

www.ingramcontent.com/pod-product-compliance
Ingram Content Group UK Ltd.
Pitfield, Milton Keynes, MK11 3LW, UK
UKHW021253180426
11947UKWH00010B/764